CRITICAL THEORY, DEMOCRACY, AND THE CHALLENGE OF NEOLIBERALISM

Critical Theory, Democracy, and the Challenge of Neoliberalism

BRIAN CATERINO AND PHILLIP HANSEN

UNIVERSITY OF TORONTO PRESS
Toronto Buffalo London

Library and Archives Canada Cataloguing in Publication

Title: Critical theory, democracy, and the challenge of neoliberalism /
Brian Caterino and Phillip Hansen.
Names: Caterino, Brian, author. | Hansen, Phillip, 1949– author.
Description: Includes bibliographical references and index.
Identifiers: Canadiana 20190096950 | ISBN 9781487505462 (hardcover)
Subjects: LCSH: Democracy – Philosophy. | LCSH: Critical theory. |
LCSH: Neoliberalism. | LCSH: Liberty – Philosophy. |
LCSH: Frankfurt school of sociology.
Classification: LCC JC423 .C38 2019 | DDC 321.8—dc23

This book has been published with the help of a grant from the Federation
for the Humanities and Social Sciences, through the Awards to Scholarly
Publications Program, using funds provided by the Social Sciences and
Humanities Research Council of Canada.

University of Toronto Press acknowledges the financial assistance to its
publishing program of the Canada Council for the Arts and the Ontario
Arts Council, an agency of the Government of Ontario.

Canada Council   Conseil des Arts
for the Arts   du Canada

ONTARIO ARTS COUNCIL
CONSEIL DES ARTS DE L'ONTARIO

an Ontario government agency
un organisme du gouvernement de l'Ontario

Funded by the   Financé par le
Government   gouvernement
of Canada   du Canada

Contents

Acknowledgments

This book is the product of a lengthy conversation over nearly three decades about the requirements and demands of critical social and political theory in the face of contemporary challenges. We hope to contribute to ongoing discussions and debates and welcome any comments our readers might have about our ideas and concerns.

Both of us want to thank the readers for the Press for their helpful comments and criticisms. We are grateful as well to the Awards to Scholarly Publications Program of the Federation for the Humanities and Social Sciences for its financial support.

But we want especially to thank Daniel Quinlan, our editor for the Press, who has been stalwart in his support of this project and who has expertly ensured the smooth passage of our manuscript from submission to publication. Daniel's enthusiasm and overall professionalism epitomize the very best qualities of an outstanding academic editor.

Brian Caterino would like to thank Lori for her support during the writing of this project.

Phillip Hansen would like once more to thank the Bushwakker seminar group – Joe, Fay, and Lorne – for yet again being an anchor of friendship and support. Sadly, Sheila is no longer with us. But she lives on in our memories of times shared and cherished.

But above all, Laureen – for whom, as ever, there are no words enough …

CRITICAL THEORY, DEMOCRACY, AND
THE CHALLENGE OF NEOLIBERALISM

Introduction

Contemporary democratic theory represents a paradox. While academic analysis is a robust enterprise, democratic practice in Western society is increasingly fragile and under siege. There is little shortage of opinion on democratic designs, but very few designs on institutions. To be sure, much has been written about how democracy relates to globalization and the nation-state, to immigration and multiculturalism, to human rights and international and cosmopolitan notions and institutions of justice. Yet contemporary states that claim to be or are considered to be thriving democracies present a far less rosy picture.

This picture is at odds with currently dominant accounts of democracy, which have been powerfully shaped by a triumphant liberalism, in particular its neoliberal form. This development is the culmination of a dynamic that began after the Second World War. Neoliberals like Friedrich Hayek, as well as chastened liberals like Karl Popper and Isaiah Berlin, feared that the values of Western society had come under attack and indeed had been subordinated to "collectivist," socialist commitments. They rejected the social democratic version of liberalism – that of John Dewey stands out here – and reformulated a version of the classical liberal conception of the possessive individual, one who is a maximizer of goods. This line of thought, carried forward and further developed by contemporary neoliberalism, is sceptical of the idea of a general will or a participatory democracy.

Yet these neoliberal models are not simply a recasting of the classical Hobbesian or Lockean perspectives. Combined with theories of social choice, they posit models of social action that have an affinity with a large-scale market economy in which the rationality of consumers is identified with a concatenation of choices. This methodological individualism has a weak link to the moral individualism of classical liberalism and its notion of limited sovereignty. While contemporary neoliberalism calls for the deregulation of economic relationships and the marketization of spheres of society previously regulated normatively, it paradoxically rests on the surveillance and control of individual behaviour designed to ensure that this behaviour conforms to market standards. Neoliberal regimes value fealty to the market over commitment to traditional democratic norms.

The rejection of more radical accounts of democratic possibilities is not restricted to neoliberals of whatever theoretical orientation. The idea of a democracy dedicated to the overthrow of hierarchical power relations throughout the width and breadth of society, and to the subjection of social forces to conscious regulation, has withered. Most theories reject the notion that there is any alternative to a moderate revision of existing institutions. Concerns about social and economic structure are safely consigned to the domain of distributive justice, where the tensions and problems they generate can be successfully addressed and managed. There is little fundamental engagement with the constraints, structural conditions, and historical possibilities associated with contemporary capitalism. In other words, there is little evidence of critical political economy in the outlook and theoretical assumptions of much current thinking about democracy. (And a good deal of what political economy does find its way into this theory is decidedly neoclassical and microeconomic, with an emphasis on individual maximization and rational choice; this is the case even for theories harbouring a critical intent.)

One important basis for this restrictive view can be traced to "third way" conceptions of politics in contemporary democracies. Although primarily associated with Tony Blair and Bill Clinton during their days in office as, respectively, prime minister of the United Kingdom and president of the United States, and hence most prominent during the late 1990s and early 2000s, third way accounts of political possibilities continue to provide an important subtext to contemporary public life in leading liberal democratic polities. According to Anthony Giddens, a key adviser to Blair and an important architect of the position, the third way model lays out a revised social democratic alternative to both free market capitalism and state socialism – but without the "statist" commitments of classical postwar social democracy. The third way rejects market fundamentalism but also dismisses state socialism as an implausible option in the face of the supposedly unchallengeable superiority of markets as coordinators of economic activity. Third way assumptions undergird a limited set of possibilities based on an incremental approach to social justice and inequality.

To be sure, proponents of the third way profess commitment to social cohesion and community. However, they typically call for neoliberal rather than Keynesian economic policies to achieve their goals. This has led in practice to deregulation and marketization that is incompatible with the reduction of inequality. In the United States during the Clinton administration, pursuit of the neoliberal agenda brought forth policies of welfare reform, prison expansion, bank deregulation, and (later) school privatization, often in the name of personal responsibility. Subsequent administrations, both Democrat and Republican, have not deviated significantly from this approach.

Even those who do *not* follow the third way have been subtly influenced by the post- Keynesian change in the political and economic climate. For many citizens, the question of what a good life *means* has decidedly narrowed and the barriers to achieving it have become more imposing. It is now more or less taken for granted that there are significant and intractable limits to socio-economic equality. There has been a noticeable move away from classically socialist and social democratic understandings of economic power and the perceived need to at the very least strongly regulate capitalist market relations. This is the case, we believe, even with accounts of democracy that openly profess critical and even radical aims – that make the critique of social and political conditions their centrepiece.

One currently significant constellation of critically oriented theories and approaches has sought to replace or at least significantly de-emphasize the traditional focus of radical democratic thought on economic class questions and relations by putting front and centre issues of cultural diversity and openness. As important as these issues may be – in no small measure because they were often underplayed in classical socialist thought and practice – the focus on them has tended either to bypass the socio-economic changes of the current neoliberal phase of capitalism or to decouple them from broader questions of social equality. While such theories provide powerful reasons to include more groups and citizens in the discourse of society and to expand the range of concerns that must be addressed with respect to the meaning of equality and appropriate normative expectations, this "cultural" turn in social and democratic theory has been accompanied by an implicit acceptance that the vast majority of the population need to lower their expectations for a good life. Economic insecurity, decreasing social mobility, ecological crisis, and the offloading of social risks onto less well-off individuals have together meant that most people now find it impossible to envision a future that is significantly better than the present. Only recently have such links between social movements for equality and the political-economic situation been re-examined.

Another avowedly critical and radical perspective on political and democratic theory rose to prominence primarily in the wake of the new left of the 1960s and the radical political mobilization and contestation, in Europe and elsewhere, that characterized this era. In various guises it remains influential today. This approach, which draws upon currents of post-structuralism, emphasizes agonistic theories of politics. Theories of this type provide a largely metaphysical or ontological account of politics. Politics is ontologically constituted by conflict. Agonistic theories of the political and especially theories of democracy tend to associate agreement with subject-centred reason. Ontological unity supposedly establishes finality. From this point of view, agreement equals certainty and eliminates the possibility of political contestation. Thus, agreement is consigned to a realm of quasi-scientific understanding that immunizes society against conflict. From this standpoint, theorists of democratic "agonism" argue that power is omnipresent and formative for all types of thought and action. The ontological powers of agreement are thus merely ideological in their operation. In suppressing conflict, they conceal and sustain domination.

In our view, while each of these perspectives raises important questions for critical and radical democratic theory, they miss or insufficiently stress elements that we see as vital for a critical analysis of the present and its challenges. We contend that in response to those theories that stress diversity and the role of social identities – that is, that assume a cultural perspective – a critical and robust democratic theory must revisit and revive the focus on economic class relations of power centred on capitalist market relations and institutions. Such a theory must stress the need to challenge the currently limited – and limiting – sense of what is possible in relation to the basic structures and processes of economic life. That is, it must restore a critical political economy as a key element in the critical appraisal of existing conditions.

With respect to post-structuralist, "agonistic" accounts, we think their position is likewise too narrow. If the problem with culturalist theories is that they tend to focus too strongly on relations of recognition at the expense of redistribution, the problem with agonistic accounts is that they tend to assimilate agreement in all cases to enforced unity or conformity and to celebrate contestation and conflict *per se* as truly political and transgressive. We call instead for a practical everyday understanding in which truth or rightness is never final and certainty is never fixed. Everyday understanding always needs to be renewed. It lacks the ontological characteristics that agonistic theorists attribute to reason. Political action is not a matter of opposing fixed certainties that block understanding and thereby clearing the way for action; rather, it is a practical matter of acting in concert to create conditions that will facilitate deliberation on matters of public concern. Viewed in this way, the workings of power are not omnipresent but exist when processes of understanding are shaped by forms of domination and oppression that limit the ability of participants to act in concert.

Thus, our view is also different from that of thinkers like Jane Mansbridge, who believe that agreement and conflict are not fated always to be at odds, but who nonetheless think that deliberation requires the incorporation of self-interest if enforced conformity of the sort that troubles agonistic thinkers is to be avoided. They look to situations in which deliberation is incomplete or disagreement is intractable. They posit that in such cases, recognizing the centrality of self-interest is a way of incorporating plurality and diversity into deliberation. This argument views the discourse theory of Jürgen Habermas, for example, as based on a conception of the unified common good that suggests a strong notion of social unity and is hence inadequate as a basis for deliberative practices. However, in our view a theory that takes up the consensual element in the work of critical theorists such as Habermas does not require an excessive emphasis on achieved consensus or similar tropes.

In the face of contemporary democratic theory and its challenges, we propose a different alternative: a recovery of a developmental account of individual agency and democracy that can provide the basis for a more critical democratic theory than is typically on offer these days. To be sure, as our brief account of current conceptions of critical and radical democratic thought indicates, many theorists today are committed to enhanced democratization beyond dominant representative forms and bodies. A wide range of theorists – we've already briefly noted the work of Jane Mansbridge – emphasize the need for deliberative mechanisms that would permit and encourage citizens to mutually engage with one another in multiple forums in order to reach just and equitable social decisions. Such thinking obviously must find a place in a critical democratic theory.

However, a developmental account of the sort we propose represents an attempt to go beyond the range of concerns exhibited by most theorists of deliberative democracy. Our understanding of a critical developmental model assumes that actors do more than decide or deliberate; in deciding or deliberating they produce themselves *as* deciders or deliberators by responding to and shaping the conditions and structures within which they necessarily act. They produce themselves as agents of a certain kind: they provide a rational and hence normative content that can be "read" off the decisions taken and the institutions objectified. This content defines them, their relations to one another, and their ties to their common practices. Our argument here requires, as noted above, that we look to the ways of making sense that are embedded in everyday life. These activities involve processes of mutual recognition and mutual accountability through which individuals constitute the meaning of everyday life. While a theory of democracy clearly requires more than this, it has to begin with the standpoint of the participants who act together to create a social world.

To be sure, all theories of democracy, ours included, must contend with the relation between theory and practice (and "realist" accounts are not exempt, even if their categories and concepts tend to mask this element). They need to convey at least some sense of their own conditions of possibility. That there is a gap between the claims and commitments of democratic theory and the realities of (allegedly) democratic practice is itself nothing new. Democracy itself has always been an idea and a value as much as it has been a set of institutions and practices. At least since the emergence of democracy as a universal value and the consequent spread of at least nominally democratic institutions, democratic theories themselves have tended to divide along empirical and normative lines. But the problem that provides the starting point for our analysis is not simply the gulf between democratic theory and democratic practice. Rather, it involves how democratic theories, whether seen as empirical or normative, whether culturalist or agonistic, have been shaped in terms of their conceptual commitments and structures by existing reality. It involves how these theories, in turn, and whatever the intentions of their architects, have justified the prevailing social and political arrangements, even if frequently critical of specific features of them.

The contemporary situation invites comparisons with the Cold War era. The dominant "realist" theories of democracy of that period, liberal and pluralist in their core assumptions, harboured a commitment to the mainstream tenets of empirical social science. They were hostile to "classical" theories of democracy with their supposedly unrealistic views about active citizenship and participation, to say nothing of the supposedly "totalitarian" theories of democracy propounded by Marxists and communists.

On the surface, the current picture seems considerably different. This difference is reflected in those dominant contemporary accounts of democracy and its possibilities that we have attempted briefly to identify and appraise. Unlike the general thrust of Cold War democratic theory, the "realism" of contemporary theory is avowedly normative and at least in principle linked to more positive conceptions of active citizenship. The fear of "excessive" popular engagement threatening political stability – a central element of the Cold War theoretical consensus – is for the most part absent (although this fear has to some extent resurfaced in current concerns about the global rise of "populism").

Yet at the same time, the Cold War fear of popular eruption that would undermine liberal values and political institutions reflected the sense that, however feared or despised, socialism and/or communism was a serious option. The normative "space" available for theories that justified existing democratic values and institutions was limited. Because there is no current realistic alternative to capitalism, dominant theories of democracy can and do range more freely on normative grounds. But this has the ironic consequence of affirming the status quo even more strongly than was the case during the Cold War. Implicitly embedded in the Cold War outlook was a sense of history and a fear for the future of liberal democratic institutions in the face of a plausible, if disagreeable, option. In the wake of the ravages of depression and war, the survival of capitalism, and thus of liberal democracy itself, seemed anything but guaranteed.

Of course, a significant body of contemporary theoretical work has taken shape against the backdrop provided by the collapse of "really existing socialism" and its claim to have ushered in a "people's" democracy, one more authentic than the "bourgeois" form that characterized advanced capitalist states. Inasmuch as this view of democracy was inherently tied to the demand for economic democracy and not just political democracy, its demise is inextricably linked to that disavowal, already noted, of socialism, or at least extensive regulation of capitalist market forces, as a plausible (albeit much less defensible) social option.

No doubt, reservations about classical Marxist political theory and practice are well taken. Along with deliberative models of democracy and of democratic will formation, recent forms of "republican" thinking – with which to be sure our own efforts possess considerable affinity – have been particularly helpful in reminding us of the autonomy of politics in relation to other social forces and practices and hence the significance of political institutions, law, and citizenship more generally.

In this study, however, we call into question what we believe to be the unduly limited focus of much current democratic theory. As noted above, a democratic theory capable of illuminating the descriptive *and* normative dimensions of democracy and their connections to each other requires a critical political economy. A critical political economy is needed in order to provide a comprehensive picture of the current situation; it is also necessary because if political theory or philosophy is to have a meaningful role in fostering the development of appropriate conceptual tools for understanding and appraising contemporary social and political developments, it must both identify deeply embedded alternative possibilities, good and bad, for the development of contemporary societies and *be prepared to argue that profound human ills and misery would ensue should certain possibilities be blocked, or others realized.*

Thus, our commitment to a developmental account of democracy. To be sure, this requires that we address current critical accounts of democracy, including those that stress the power of and need for deliberation. However, as noted, we believe that dominant forms of deliberative democracy are excessively narrow. We wish to counter this narrowing of deliberative approaches, which typically view deliberation as a supplement to and justification for existing liberal democracy, and instead connect deliberation to radical and participatory forms of democratic theory. Such forms, we argue, should highlight the significance of accountability as a core feature of a robust democratic practice. Accountability – specifically, *mutual* accountability – is a basic feature of social life. This accountability involves not just deliberation as an adjunct to formal political institutions. It also requires the extension of participation as far as possible to all forms of social life in which power is generated and exercised. This expanded participation must be the larger goal of any application of deliberative democracy in society.

Our approach suggests the continuing significance of the critical theory of the Frankfurt School for an account and appraisal of democratic realities and possibilities. Contemporary critical theory in the tradition of the original Frankfurt School is paradoxical from our point of view. It has focused on advanced capitalism, and while it has offered important insights into this social form, it has not provided a similarly detailed account of neoliberalism. And while it still contains the seeds for a radical and participatory account of democracy and has devoted considerable attention to questions of universal justice and cosmopolitan and/ or multicultural citizenship, current critical theory has not always been faithful to its heritage of radical democracy. Universal justice requires this commitment to radical and participatory democracy on a concrete level, not just as a philosophical commitment. We also believe in a universalist program, but such a program would have to be built from the bottom up, from practical solidarity rather than from philosophical insight.

We certainly agree that questions of justice and cosmopolitanism must form a significant component of any critical theory of democracy. However, emphasis on these issues has come at the expense of more detailed analysis of the pathologies of neoliberalism and thus the barriers to the achievement of cosmopolitan identities in a capitalist society. Nor does the ideal of cosmopolitan citizenship in itself serve as a basis for a robust emancipatory theory. Thus, the approaches of recent critical theory seem incomplete. They lack analysis of the intensification of inequality and exploitation under neoliberalism and how these might affect a critical democratic theory. In short, they seem to have de-emphasized the diagnostic dimension of critical theory in favour of a normative reconstruction of current democratic practices and institutions. However, such a reconstructive approach is not clearly connected to conditions under which the norms so generated could be brought into existence. We think that this is a requirement for a critical theory of democracy.

The need for an analysis of neoliberalism and its pathologies would seem to be essential for critical theories. It would be dogmatic, however, to see the terms of this analysis as a choice of either/or: either the politics of recognition or an old-fashioned economic determinism. While we accept a good deal of the neo-Marxist – and, more recently, post-Marxist – challenges to Marx's thought, it remains true that economic conflicts play an important role in social theory and that economic power is a crucial factor shaping social and cultural life. The dominance of neoliberalism is generating social pathologies that are significantly undermining current "realistic" claims about existing democratic practices, to say nothing of the viability of those normative possibilities and requirements identified by contemporary theories that claim to embrace a critical stance. We think that capitalism, especially in its latest form, continues to be a barrier to the achievement of a robust democracy worthy of the name. We cannot formulate a critical theory of democracy without some analysis of the barriers to democracy in its current constellation. This proposition undergirds the approach to democracy that we pursue in this work.

In the first chapter we put forward the idea that a critical theory of democracy enriched by a synthesis of the perspectives of Jürgen Habermas and C.B. Macpherson can become the starting point for such a project. Each of these thinkers provides an approach to a critical theory of democracy that incorporates the claims of both self-determination and self-realization, claims that could provide the basis for a critical democratic theory that meets the challenges of neoliberalism. We reject the assumption that potential reforms are constrained by the demise of Soviet-style socialism and must be limited to slight modifications of the liberal capitalist model. We suggest that Macpherson's notion of the net transfer of powers, whereby owners of capital can by virtue of their command of private property in the means of life and labour extract benefit from those they employ, still has value as an approach to the workings of domination.

The second chapter is an attempt to reformulate the terms of critical theory in a post-Marxist environment. In essays such as "On the Problem of Truth," "The Latest Attack on Metaphysics," and "Traditional and Critical Theory," Max Horkheimer, a founder of the original Frankfurt School and a key architect of "first generation" critical theory, sought to clarify the meaning and significance of a critical theory – historical, materialist, and dialectical – in contrast to then dominant positivist and pragmatic currents of thought. Positivism identified truth with value-free, timeless, and pure categories and concepts that successfully captured the objects of inquiry via the generation of testable hypotheses justified both by experience and by the exercise of a deductive logic seen as the science of the necessary structure of human thought. Pragmatism identified truth with what was useful in achieving desired effects within the given constellation of social and natural forces and possibilities. Horkheimer challenged the claims to truth of both approaches, however faithful they might have been to current possibilities as defined by the existing relations of power and domination. He wanted to demonstrate that the claims to reason, realism, and truth made by these theories made sense only in the context of a historical setting characterized by social pathologies that had been generated by the intensifying contradictory developments of the capitalist form of social organization. These developments threatened to undo the real gains in freedom, justice, and the fulfilment of human needs that the emergence of bourgeois society had brought about. The contradiction between the promise of a modern era of enlightenment on the one hand, and the reality of the prospect of a descent into a new barbarism on the other, needed to be taken up by a critical theory not bound by the current demands of "realism." In other words, reality and truth did not coincide: the whole was simultaneously "really existing" and "false." Horkheimer believed that only a critical theory, one that owed a good deal to Marx, could successfully grasp the contradiction between the existing and the true. It assumed that the propositions of a critical theory that could not be immediately justified by the existing state of affairs could nonetheless lay a claim to truth precisely *because* they sought to identify the necessary conditions for the realization of lives of freedom, reason, and happiness for all that had always served as the benchmarks for human thought and practice, including positivism and pragmatism. The power and claims of the given need not be and must not be the last word.

Critical theory today faces a similar set of challenges. It too must confront currently dominant theoretical and philosophical perspectives that are inheritors of the positivist and pragmatist positions that Horkheimer identified and criticized. Our approach in this chapter recalls Horkheimer's position and commitments while attempting to move beyond the limitations of his original position. In retrieving the "spirit" of critical theory, we reconsider the diagnostic and emancipatory dimensions of a critical theory that challenges the permanence and inevitability of the given constellation of social forces, while at the same time avoiding the temptations of metaphysics. As Horkheimer attempted to do, we emphasize participant's understanding as the basis for a critical analysis of society.

In our approach we take up a version of interpretive social theory that employs the insights of hermeneutics, contemporary interpretive sociology, and elements of Habermas's communicative theory in order to grasp more precisely the reflective and critical elements of everyday understanding. In doing so, we hope to challenge the widespread assumption that the understanding of the theorist or analyst is anchored in a position that transcends that of the participant. We attempt, in other words, to reformulate a notion of emancipation that avoids the pitfalls of earlier formulations. If we succeed, we think we can offer critical insights into other contemporary approaches that either deny or limit emancipation.

We also therefore use this analysis to rethink ideas about power and domination. We try to situate our position in relation to the variety of debates over power that have emerged in recent decades, from the issue of non-decisions – that is, the capacity of dominant interests to ensure that questions of wealth and power are marginalized if not excluded altogether from the public realm – to feminist and post-structuralist perspectives. We attempt to reframe the terms of these discussions so that we might incorporate their concerns into our conception of the participant's perspective. Of course, the shadow of Michel Foucault towers over most contemporary discussions of power. In our discussion we provide an extensive critical evaluation of his contribution.

With this account as a backdrop, in the third chapter we offer an analysis of neoliberalism and its pathologies. As we noted earlier, while neoliberalism may *appear* to represent a return to classical liberal principles and a libertarian social philosophy, this perception is not entirely accurate. On the one hand, many neoliberals combine an economic philosophy of deregulation with a social conservatism that is in some respects illiberal; this goes back to Hayek's combination of conservative traditionalism and a free market economy. Neoliberalism requires a dismantling of the public sphere and employs highly concentrated forms of power to establish more traditionalist social norms and ideas. The neoconservative movement, and much of the social support for neoliberalism, rests on a defensive reaction to the challenges and demands of modern sociality. On the other hand, neoliberal political economy requires more than simply a return to a nightwatchman state. It rejects Keynesian economic policies while at the same time requiring large-scale corporate control over not just the means of production but also the means of reproduction and communication. This control is far less indirect. In this respect it is much closer to what Sheldon Wolin had in mind with his notion of inverted totalitarianism than it is to libertarianism.

One limitation of "first generation" critical theory was that it paid little attention to democratic theory, much less to a critical theory of democracy. Critical theorists saw liberalism largely in a negative light, believing that it was inextricably linked to capitalism. They were thus unable to recognize the possibilities for an enriched political and social life that liberal democracy promised, even if it failed by and large to live up to these promises. Jürgen Habermas, the key "second generation" critical theorist, has addressed this lacuna, as had C.B. Macpherson, who was writing more contemporaneously with the first generation. Like Macpherson, Habermas does not reject liberalism out of hand but has sought to integrate liberal rights into a critical theory of democracy. Nonetheless, the developmental requirements of a critical theory of democracy indicate that the realization of democracy is not compatible with the workings of capitalism and must create tensions. We explore why Habermas's theory has not followed up on the insights his work has produced and explore some recent alternatives in critical theory, particularly as laid out by Axel Honneth.

In the fourth chapter we pursue the implications of our critique of Habermas by suggesting revisions to his account, and that of critical theory as a whole, by developing a treatment of key issues for a critical theory of democracy that builds upon the themes of deliberation, self-interest, and solidarity. More specifically, we examine the unique way in which critical theory can combine justice with solidarity. Because of its intersubjective foundation, the theory of communicative action combines individuality with sociability – that is, it allows for people's capacity to form and be formed by society – without at the same time embracing a notion of society as a unified body or as possessing a common ethos. Communicative action links mutual understanding as a binding force with solidarity. We argue that it provides an antidote to the anti-solidaristic tendencies of neoliberal political theory and rational choice approaches. This communicative approach must, however, be distinguished from individualist liberal and even radical theories, which seek to rehabilitate self-interest against what they see as an overly strong notion of agreement. As we noted earlier, a third tendency opposes an agonistic conception of society to consensus-based theory. However, agonistic theories miss the consensual character of social action as an intersubjective web of relations that form the background condition of individual action; as a result, they cannot account for the binding force of social action through both mutual understanding and care.

The fifth chapter takes up the question of democratic theory in Habermas's work. We argue that despite changes to his theoretical framework, Habermas has been consistent in advocating a radical democracy based on popular sovereignty. Unlike his predecessors, particularly Horkheimer and Adorno, Habermas believes that a democratic theory is a crucial feature of any critical theory of advanced capitalist societies. Politics would not disappear with socialism. Rather than a defence of existing liberalism, radical democracy is tied to a version of socialism that does not rely on the productivist paradigm or on notions of society as a singular subject. Popular sovereignty is rooted in the substratum of communicative interaction, which in turn feeds political and legal processes. It requires a widespread democratization of public life. We argue that Habermas's notion of popular sovereignty is important to a democratic theory that opposes the neoliberal constriction of democratic institutions and the consequent diminution of democratic practices. The wide range of institutionally unbound public spheres, as Habermas understands these, would help guarantee that legal and governmental decision-making is open to all. The existence of these spheres could promote a deliberative formation of political will that would enable the critical examination of governmental decisions.

We also focus on the notion of democratic autonomy that combines elements of communicative freedom, self-determination, and self-development. Habermas has argued for the complementarity of private and public freedom, thus combining elements of both liberalism and republicanism. This formulation requires an egalitarian perspective. Habermas's theory suggests the notion of participatory democracy; however, he is sceptical of some forms of participatory democracy, such as workers' control. Also, he does not take account of some of the larger global issues involved in neoliberal threats to popular sovereignty.

In the final chapter, we attempt to bring together the issues we raised in the previous chapters by identifying and exploring what we believe are key elements of a critical theory of democracy. More specifically, taking up the challenges of developmental individualism and communicative rationality and freedom, both of which demand an intersubjective and interactionist approach to democracy and democratic theory, we argue that a critical theory of democracy could build on two themes: participatory democracy and social freedom. Anchoring our account in the seminal work of Carole Pateman, C.B. Macpherson, and Carol Gould, we seek to show in contrast to Habermas that participatory democracy, which as a critical or radical account of democratic possibilities and requirements has in recent times given way to deliberative democracy, can incorporate a strong conception of deliberation as an essential dimension of communicative freedom. So understood, participatory democratic theory can move beyond most models of deliberative democracy by emphasizing the social constitution of individual agents, the developmental potentials they harbour, and the need to extend democratic will formation to all social spheres in which power is structured and exercised. In other words, a critical theory of participatory democracy highlights the need for fundamental social transformation that demands a critical appraisal of existing forms of both liberalism and democracy. Pateman, Macpherson, and Gould all explore various related dimensions of the challenges involved: Pateman, with a critique of the social contract as a basis for liberal democracy; Macpherson, with an account of the contradictions of capitalism and the need for individuals to move beyond their self-consciousness as limitless consumers and appropriators if a participatory democracy is ever to be possible; and Gould, with a distinctive social ontology and an intersubjective theory of human rights.

We go on to argue that what unites these approaches to radical, participatory democracy is social freedom. With its roots in Hegelian thought, social freedom suggests that our freedom as individuals is established and secured in and through our relations *with* others, not *over* and (often) *against* them. Social freedom involves a kind of mutuality of self-determination and self-realization whereby not only are our actions imbricated – our aims, in other words, are intertwined and not simply overlapping – but so also is our constitution as agents. Social freedom, then, might be said to incorporate both positive (developmental) liberty, as in Macpherson, and communicative freedom, as in Habermas. The contemporary critical theorist who has contributed most significantly to the development of the notion of social freedom is Axel Honneth, and we examine his ideas here as a complement to those of Pateman, Macpherson, and Gould.

Honneth in turn connects his conception of social freedom to a rethinking and reinvigoration of socialism as an idea tied to the achievement of a (radical) democratic form of life. The effort to reimagine what socialism can mean today links Honneth's position to both the ideas of the Frankfurt School, particularly those of Horkheimer, Adorno, and Habermas, and to notions of radical, participatory democracy as laid out by Pateman, Macpherson, and Gould. To put it another way, Honneth's work points to the need to restore the link between political economy and normative political philosophy, a link that throughout our study we have argued must be restored in the face of the pathologies of a dominant neoliberal capitalism.

In confronting the challenges posed by neoliberal globalization, the Canadian political philosopher Frank Cunningham has recently revisited C.B. Macpherson's 1960s account of the "real" world of democracy, in which Macpherson compared liberal democratic, communist, and non-communist Third World conceptions of democracy from the vantage point of the need for democracy to address and incorporate the demands and requirements of developmental individualism. For Cunningham, to be a realistic possibility, transnational or cosmopolitan democratic advance requires the pursuit of more robust democracy *within* states. As he sees it, those countries most able and committed to countering the possessive individualism of neoliberal globalization with the values and practices of developmental individualism would be in the best position to foster a robust democracy both within and beyond their borders and so offer the prospect of more successfully containing the frequently pathological consequences of the globalization project. We concur, and hope that our own study will contribute to restoring a critical theory of democracy as a vital response to the challenges of our era.

At the same time, we continue to hold to Max Horkheimer's claim that only the bad in history is enduring and permanent; all else is potentially threatened. What may be objectively necessary may not be objectively possible. So our own analysis as we attempt to lay it out in this study should be seen as tentative, if hopeful. This is not a counsel of despair but a quest for a kind of realism that is not to be identified with a commitment to things as they are. Or, rather, things as they are always and already point beyond themselves to something richer and finer.

Chapter One

Macpherson, Habermas, and the Demands of Democratic Theory

This study seeks to combine elements of a developmental and communicative theory of democracy as the linchpin of a critical theory of society that can counter the challenges – and what we believe are the pathologies – of neoliberalism: its values, practices, and institutions. In a world in which existing forms of both liberal democracy and capitalist markets are presented not only as compatible with each other but also as essential dimensions of a free and fair society, any defence of a developmental alternative undeniably confronts significant demands and hurdles. So at the outset we want to lay out as clearly as possible what we see as the core components of our approach. We aim to combine both developmental and communicative forms of power in order to provide a framework for making sense of the pathologies of neoliberalism and to stake out a viable alternative.

In the first sections of this chapter we focus on the developmental approach through the vehicle of Macpherson's encounter with the early neoliberals of the postwar period: Milton Friedman and, to an extent, Isaiah Berlin. In the second half of the chapter we deal with the communicative approach developed by Habermas and his formulation of democratic theory that stresses the roots of popular sovereignty as an alternative to neoliberal constrictions. The connecting thread between these two formulations can be found in the search for alternative conceptions of freedom that provide a counterpoint to neoliberal thought.

Foundations of Developmental Democracy

What is a developmental account of democracy that could serve as the basis for what we view as a critical theory of democracy? As noted in the Introduction, a developmental democratic theory shares common ground with both participatory and, more particularly, deliberative accounts of democracy. However, as we also noted, what distinguishes developmental democracy from most currents of deliberative democracy is that the developmental alternative assumes that political actors not only decide or deliberate about political options or choices but also, simultaneously, produce themselves *as* deciders or deliberators by responding to and shaping the conditions and structures within which they necessarily act. Hence this developmental quality is empirical and normative at the same time. Through their actions people generate "measurable" outcomes – decisions are made, and institutions are created and re-created. But they also produce *themselves* as agents of a certain kind. They give a rational and hence normative content that can be "read" off the decisions taken and the institutions thereby sustained. These define their relations to one another and their ties to shared, common practices.

At the heart of an account of deliberative democracy is what has often been called positive liberty, but which, following C.B. Macpherson, we prefer to identify as developmental liberty. As Charles Taylor succinctly notes, theories of positive or developmental liberty "are concerned with a view of freedom which involves essentially the exercising of control over one's life. On this view, one is free only to the extent that one has effectively determined oneself and the shape of one's life."[1] This of course includes political life and hence carries with it the idea of a robust, active citizenship and what the American political theorist Benjamin Barber once called "strong democracy." It holds that liberty or freedom does not consist exclusively of freedom *from* politics; rather, to a significant extent, it means freedom *as* politics.

Positive or developmental liberty, and hence a developmental account of democracy, has long been controversial. As noted in the Introduction, during the Cold War some saw in it a prescription for authoritarianism, if not outright totalitarianism. In recent years, critics – especially those of a postmodern persuasion – have claimed that it suffers from the limits of subjective reason. It is held to represent the unfolding of some (completed) inner essence. For others, developmental democracy is inherently linked to outmoded socialist models that represent the demand for a democracy that is economic and social as well as political. But whatever the specific dimensions of such positions, they have in common – whether stated explicitly or not – the claim that a radical and developmental democracy threatens liberalism and its emphasis on the integrity and freedom of the individual. When linked to the current emphasis on the untrammelled virtues, if not inescapability, of "free market" capitalism, these criticisms provide considerable weight to a dominant neoliberalism.

We call into question the claims that a developmental perspective is fatally flawed. We believe that such a perspective can avoid the apparently disabling defects identified by its critics and in so doing provide the basis for a critical theory of democracy. Such a theory must do more than identify the gulf between democratic theory and democratic practice or offer a critique of subject-centred reason. That is, it must not only present a compelling vision of democratic norms but also develop a diagnosis of the problems and pathologies of democratic life and link these to the challenges faced by citizens who have the capacity to reflect upon the development of democracy as a process that has formed them and that might be changed by them to achieve a better future. And since such problems and pathologies invariably relate to the everyday situations confronting social actors, and since these problems and pathologies involve the demands of economic life, in our view such a theory must also provide, beyond the (laudable) concern with distributive justice, a critical political economy: an account of the constraints, structural conditions, and historical possibilities associated with contemporary capitalism.

In this chapter we begin to explore the nature and potential of developmental democracy by focusing on the ideas of two thinkers who in our view have made significant contributions to the task at hand. In the burgeoning contemporary literature on democratic theory, including progressive or radical accounts of the nature of democracy and the conditions required for it to flourish, the ideas of C.B. Macpherson and Jürgen Habermas are rarely discussed together in a systematic way. This is surprising. Macpherson and Habermas stood a generation apart and emerged from distinct theoretical traditions, yet they were familiar with and respected each other's work. And they had similar aims: to "retrieve" (to use Macpherson's term) democratic theory from its limited role as either a largely uncritical description of existing political reality or a narrowly focused exploration of governmental institutions and decision-making mechanisms, and to restore it to its place as an indispensable element of a critical diagnosis of current liberal democratic societies with all their tensions, conflicts, and limitations.

The ideas of Macpherson and Habermas offer powerful and largely untapped resources for such a project.[2] Each of these theorists confronts questions of self-determination and self-realization that are at the heart of a developmental account. And in so doing they challenge both neoliberalism and other proponents of radical democracy by addressing the task that Macpherson so eloquently laid out and identified as his own and that Habermas pursues as well: "to work out a revision of liberal-democratic theory, a revision which clearly owes a good deal to

Marx, in the hope of making that theory more democratic while rescuing that valuable part of the liberal tradition which is submerged when liberalism is identified with capitalist market relations."[3]

More closely in touch with classical Marxism and the critical, reform liberalism of John Stuart Mill and his successors in the British liberal tradition, such as T.H. Green, F.H. Bradley, A.D. Lindsay, Ernest Barker, and, especially Harold Laski,[4] Macpherson emphasized the idea of self-realization as the core of a democracy understood not merely as a mechanism for choosing and authorizing governments, but also as a kind of society that ensures as much as possible the equal, effective right of individuals to live as fully as they may wish. At the heart of his understanding of the requirements of democracy is precisely the idea of positive liberty as this ability to live as fully as one would wish unconstrained by unnecessary internal and external impediments to exercising one's distinctively human capacities – where the key source of such impediments is the institution of capitalist private property. In his view, this form of liberty complemented and enriched the classical liberal emphasis on negative liberty, that is, freedom from interference by others.

Attuned to more contemporary currents, which shy away from notions of self-realization that imply a specific, concrete "fulfilling" form of life (i.e., a "good" life), Habermas stresses a conception of self-determination that revolves around securing the conditions for both private and public autonomy. Private and public autonomy secure the capacity for individuals both to achieve self-direction in carrying out their personal aims as little constrained by others as possible and to participate actively in the collective determination of the laws by which they are governed. One might think of this as Habermas's own version of the relation of positive to negative liberty, one he believes more suited to the realities of modern, pluralistic societies. In light of this position, Habermas has developed a discourse theory of "constitutional democracy" that attempts to synthesize the liberal value of individual freedom with the communal and democratic emphasis on popular sovereignty and collective self-determination through the maintenance of a vibrant civil society within which citizens are able to actively deliberate and so legitimate the laws by which they are governed. Central to both freedom and democracy is a conception of communicative rationality: a type of reason based on mutual understanding. This reason is explicitly social and intersubjective. It anchors a communicative freedom that secures both a *right* to speak and the *ability* to do so. In short, it addresses a concern that is so important for Macpherson: the impediments to the realization of those human capacities which require and make possible both individual freedom and popular sovereignty.

Our attempt to bring Macpherson and Habermas together can provide elements of an alternative account of democracy and its requirements. It can also illuminate core elements and tensions in the theoretical positions of each, and the clarification of these can in turn bring further to the fore what is involved in a developmental model. Macpherson is, with some justification, seen as having always hewed closely to an avowedly Marxist account of democracy and capitalism (at least until his final published work, *The Rise and Fall of Economic Justice*, in which he does address questions of human rights, for example). However, this judgment may be misleading. In elaborating his "non-market" theory of democracy, he lays out concepts that reflect a sensitivity to questions of law and the nature of the state, rights, agency, and the autonomy of the political more generally that belie any simple reductionism – even if he was likely oblivious to these contrapuntal dimensions of his work.

For his part, Habermas moved away from an emphasis early in his career on the need to recast the terms of historical materialism in order to focus on constitutional and legal issues. To that end, he explored the relation of knowledge to "human interests," coupling this with a concern for the decline of the public sphere in the face of the forces of advanced capitalism. Thus he is understood, again with justification, as having largely abandoned a Marxian-influenced perspective. But this too may be an excessively hasty generalization: an examination of some of his later work, notably *Between Facts and Norms*, brings to light important continuities between his older Marxian and critical theory positions and his current preoccupations. Both Macpherson and Habermas, then, in their obvious differences and perhaps not so obvious similarities, in their moving away from and simultaneously towards each other, provide important elements of a robustly critical democratic theory of the present.

To help set the context for our account of developmental democracy, we pursue the question of positive or developmental liberty by revisiting Macpherson's encounter with Isaiah Berlin's famous examination of negative and positive liberty, a treatment that has been enormously influential in shaping the unfavourable treatment that the idea – and ideal – of positive liberty has often received. Based on this encounter, Macpherson produced a striking and powerful reformulation of the problem of liberty or freedom that in our view can play an important role in rethinking developmental liberty and democracy. We then explore Habermas's version of a radical democratic theory, one that combines self-realization with self-determination, private with public autonomy, while suggesting both its strengths and some limitations that could be addressed by incorporating insights from Macpherson. We then examine another largely neglected aspect of Macpherson's work, namely, his treatment of what he calls the "net transfer of powers," and suggest its role in anchoring a critical, developmental account of democracy by representing a point upon which the distinctive but ultimately overlapping positions of Macpherson and Habermas can converge and demonstrate their power in illuminating the circumstances and challenges confronting both theory and practice in the contemporary period.

However, before we treat in greater detail the ideas of Macpherson and Habermas, and the relation of these ideas to developmental liberty and democracy, we want to identify and briefly discuss what we see as the core elements of neoliberalism and the challenges these pose to a developmental account. With this discussion we intend to indicate why the approach to democracy we seek to defend offers a counterpoint to what we believe are the deficiencies of neoliberalism with respect to democracy and its requirements in the current era. Our discussion here serves as a preliminary outline of our more extensive treatment of neoliberalism in chapter 3.

Neoliberalism and Contemporary Democracy

With its celebration of market values, neoliberalism emerged out of the collapse of Soviet-style socialism and the decline and market-driven transformation of the postwar welfare state and its associated theory and practice of democracy.[5] The welfare state varied considerably from country to country, and its numerous deficiencies have been well documented.[6] It purported to reconcile economic freedom and private property with mass democracy – to combine economic growth and efficiency with equality, social justice, solidarity, and meaningful, popular-democratic will formation. With the erosion of the socio-economic conditions that made it possible, the two components of the welfare state "consensus" – economic liberalism and social democracy, or the "free market" and democratic suffrage – split apart. Neoliberalism represents the triumph of the former over the latter, the "economization" of politics as opposed to the (democratic) "politicization" of the economy. In both theory and practice, its impact has been immense.

The links between neoliberalism and counter-democratic tendencies have been treated insightfully by analysts such as Naomi Klein and David Harvey.[7] Klein has identified a new form of crisis capitalism whereby crises are manufactured and manipulated so as to provide opportunities to restructure social and economic relations. This restructuring is presented as inevitable and therefore beyond the bounds of widespread and potentially open-ended public discussion. Contemporary neoliberalism thrives on a permanent state of emergency, which relies on fear rather than deliberation.[8]

David Harvey, too, sees in the neoliberal project a coercive attempt to roll back the social and political achievements of the welfare state. While some critics see neoliberalism as a utopian project doomed to fail, Harvey views it as a by and large successful strategy for restoring the conditions of capital accumulation and hence the power of economic elites. The emphasis on the restoration of order brings out the conservative or even reactionary character of neoliberalism as a central phenomenon to be explained.

For other analysts, neoliberalism has led to a "risk society." Instead of increasing security for all, neoliberal economic expansion has heightened social, economic, and environmental risks and transferred these to individuals and groups least capable of absorbing them. At the same time, states seek the support of those interests – financial, industrial, and electoral, and at times also labour – required for successful governance.[9] As populations become more vulnerable in the face of economic crises, governments appear less willing or able to protect civil rights or to maintain social rights that would permit the vulnerable to develop their own powers as citizens. It is as if the Hobbesian–Lockean social contract covers fewer and fewer people, with ever larger numbers left to fend for themselves in what amounts to a "state of nature."[10]

Yet as noted in the Introduction, neoliberalism and its theoretical justifications do not represent merely a return to classical Hobbesian or Lockean themes. Combined with theories of social choice, neoliberal theories posit models of social action that comport with the behavioural demands of a large-scale market economy, in which the rationality of consumers is expressed and measured by a concatenation of choices. This methodological individualism has at best a weak link to the moral individualism that was also a feature of classical liberalism and its notion of limited sovereignty.[11]

But at the same time, the commitment to methodological individualism makes clear that neoliberalism is not just about the capacity for capitalist institutions and practices to limit democratic possibilities. It also involves its ability to entrench a possessive individualist understanding of human agency whereby individuals are self-interested maximizers who relate instrumentally to others in ways that undermine possibilities for democratic solidarity. This significantly complicates the task confronting critical democratic theory.

This same methodological individualism, with its ties to instrumental market rationality, has had a profound impact on contemporary democratic thinking, even where it eschews the harsher Hobbesian–Lockean elements of the neoliberal mix and assumes a critical perspective.[12] While it devotes considerable attention to the design of democratic institutions and their successful functioning, this sort of theorizing typically has less to say about the pathologies of democracy produced by neoliberalism. It lacks sufficient reflection on the genesis of existing conditions and considers few alternatives beyond reform of the existing order – the idea of a democracy dedicated to the transformation of hierarchical power relations throughout the society appears to have withered, as has the idea of subjecting social forces to conscious regulation. Its conceptual commitments belie its critical intentions.

Thus Ian Shapiro, no fan of neoliberalism, nonetheless argues that while markets are the primary institutions shaping our notion of work, we should not be concerned about the relevance of their genesis for questions of democratic social justice. Such "counterfactual" speculation is "antithetical to the spirit of justice, whose purpose is to find viable ways of democratizing existing social relations."[13] For Shapiro this counsel of "realism" extends more generally to democratic theory as a whole. In his view, "much academic analysis in both the aggregative and deliberative traditions [of democracy] trades on some version of Rousseau's identification of it with the search for a common good that reflects society's general will. Despite their other differences, this way of framing the problem leads theorists in both traditions to harbour rationalist expectations of democracy on which it is impossible to deliver."[14]

In a similar vein, Joseph Heath, who applies game theoretical insights to critical theory, claims that in the wake of the collapse of the state socialist model, no viable alternatives exist to the market. Methodological individualism, rational choice, and a general rejection of the "totalizing" and utopian spirit of the French Revolution are central to his theoretical framework. Only moderate reform involving "mechanical" institutional design seems possible given the unshakeable reality of individual self-regarding self-interest: "Rather than simply trying to legislate desirable social conditions, the goal … is to develop a set of rules that will indirectly constrain the conduct of individuals in such a way that it will be in their interest to promote desirable outcomes."[15]

To be sure, theorists such as John Dryzek and Nancy Fraser are not so bound by market rationality and attempt to connect politics, economics, and democratic theory in a more extensive critical account of the present and the possibilities for radical change. Nonetheless, their efforts have fallen short of the normative critical analysis of social conflict implied and required by their critical intentions. Dryzek, for example, recognizes the incompatibility between further democratization and the limitations imposed by liberal capitalism, but he makes no sustained effort to develop an emancipatory theory. His work treats the questions of liberty that are central to Macpherson and Habermas as secondary and thus fails to provide a clearly articulated theory of the restrictions on developmental freedom that neoliberalism invokes and the possibilities for transformation that would release the potentials that developmental freedom offers for autonomy and self-realization.[16]

Nancy Fraser includes elements of communicative freedom in her well-known dialectic of redistribution and recognition – elements on which Dryzek does not elaborate. At the same time, however, she fails to fully grasp the role of the politics of recognition in the neoliberal constellation. She seems to equate the rise of neoliberalism with the emergence of this politics and the consequent displacement of issues of redistribution. Questions of recognition open new zones of social conflict that are distinct from, but still elaborations of, developmental freedom. But struggles over recognition also intensify rather than displace conflicts over the social lifeworld. The lifeworld is now being impoverished as a result of the neoliberal "marketization" of social relations and the stifling of the potential for democratic participation and social freedom that has emerged in these zones of conflict.[17]

We think that a developmental account of democracy can provide the basis for a more robust critical perspective. This account stresses active citizenship and views democracy as more than a procedure for collective decision-making.

Some Requirements of a Critical Theory of Democracy

A critical theory of democracy should do more than illuminate the inescapable connections between the economic and the political, between the structures of capitalism as a system of social power and formal political institutions – connections that neoliberal discourse strives to sever, deny, or obfuscate. It must also retrieve the normative core of democracy and its links with solidarity among agents bound together in a common situation shaped by and through processes of mutual recognition and mutual understanding. Radically reformed social institutions would arise from the transformative, developmental possibilities that individuals must be assumed to possess if the aspirations associated with alternatives to neoliberal politics are to be plausible.

At the heart of these aspirations, and therefore of a developmental model of democracy, is a conception of freedom in the tradition of positive or developmental liberty. This conception combines self-realization and self-determination – that is, a "classical" understanding of positive liberty associated with the ideas of Macpherson – with communicative freedom; it also informs a robust conception of agency as intersubjective and interactive – a theme central to Habermas's work. Neoliberalism misses this account of freedom, and in our view, its critics do not sufficiently emphasize it. Macpherson's analyses of two important pillars of neoliberalism – Milton Friedman's celebration of the free market and Isaiah Berlin's defence of negative liberty – open the way to the kind of thinking we want to defend.

Macpherson on Friedman

First published in 1968, Macpherson's appraisal of Milton Friedman's influential defence of laissez-faire capitalism in his *Capitalism and Freedom* presciently identified three elements of Friedman's analysis that were to become central to the neoliberal position: "that competitive capitalism can resolve 'the basic problem of social organization,' which is 'how to co-ordinate the economic activities of large numbers of people' ... by voluntary co-operation as opposed to central direction by state coercion ... that competitive capitalism is a system of economic freedom and so an important component of freedom broadly understood ... [and] ... that capitalism is a necessary condition of political freedom (and that socialism is incompatible with political freedom)."[18] Macpherson lucidly examines each one.

Friedman defends the model of a simple market economy that assumes free and equal exchange among individuals and households who control the resources needed to produce goods and services. As a result, they have the choice of either exchanging goods and services or producing their means of subsistence themselves; hence all exchanges are voluntary because individuals and households only enter into them if they benefit. There is social cooperation without coercion.

For Macpherson, the flaws in Friedman's position become clear when he moves to the real-world capitalist market economy. Friedman argues that in a complex economy, cooperation remains voluntary as long as enterprises are private and parties to exchange are individuals and as long as individuals are freely able to enter into or refuse any particular exchange. But as Macpherson sees it, voluntary cooperation requires not simply that individuals can refuse any particular exchange: they must also be free to refuse to engage in exchange at all. In a capitalist market economy, the conditions of the simple model do not hold because the division between those who own productive resources and those whom they employ – that is, between capital and labour – leads to unequal power between the two groups and hence coercion by one over the other because there is "the existence of a labour force without its own sufficient capital and therefore without a choice as to whether to put its labour on the market or not."[19]

Friedman asserts that competitive capitalism provides the only firm guarantee of political freedom. Political freedom entails the ability to openly promote radical social change and requires those civil liberties that protect individuals from state coercion. According to Friedman, a socialist society (i.e., one in which positive or developmental freedom is central) could not provide those liberties because the government would be a monopoly employer and thus could deprive political opponents of their livelihood. Since it would be difficult if not impossible to promote transformation to capitalism, a socialist order could not meet the standard of political freedom.

Macpherson, though, does not focus on this account of socialist economic relations. Instead he offers a subtle and complex response to Friedman's treatment of freedom. And while he accepts that the capitalist economy is a system of power rooted in the relation between capital and labour, he does something equally vital for establishing the key elements of a developmental democratic theory: he takes up Friedman's arguments (and by extension the neoliberal paradigm itself) on their own grounds. So understood, they fail in their own terms. Since Friedman understands freedom as negative liberty but does not recognize coercion where some control the labour of others, the claim that capitalism secures this freedom, and is in fact the only system that can do so, is at the very least questionable.

But there is another element of Macpherson's position, one implied in his claim that the presence or absence of political freedom under socialism is a matter of political will and not an inevitable consequence of socialist economic and political structures, as Friedman argues.[20] As Macpherson sees it, while under capitalism the political and the economic are intimately connected, they need not always be so in every conceivable circumstance. The problem with (neo)liberalism is not just that it emphasizes in theory the separation of the political from the economic, a realm of coercion from a realm of freedom, while contradicting it in practice. In addition, it unwittingly reveals that in fact the political and the economic *should* be separate but under capitalism *cannot* be.

This accounts for the distinctive quality of Macpherson's theory of radical democracy. The issue of will suggests that politics should be, and ideally would be, autonomous; it also therefore means that individual civil and political rights would remain essential even in a radically transformed and more fully democratic social order. On the one hand, in a complex and technically advanced productive system there would still be the need for structures of rational authority, even if such authority would no longer be subordinated to the demands of class power, or what Macpherson would later call extractive power. This is the Marxian or socialist dimension of Macpherson's outlook. But while accountable to the political will of the society, the productive apparatus could not be directly absorbed into it; nor could political authority dissolve into a free association of producers.

Macpherson assumes there would remain the need for organized political authority to reconcile conflicting interests and to provide security for individuals in the face of possible threats from others. However, this power would itself need to be held accountable because there is no guarantee against holders of political authority abusing their positions. This highlights the liberal or individualist dimension of Macpherson's work, one often overlooked or denied by supporters and critics alike. It does not, though, stand alone in opposition to the Marxian dimension, because Macpherson sought to synthesize both.

Macpherson does simply dismiss Friedman's conception of negative freedom. He seeks also to deepen and radicalize it by exploring those conditions under which it would be possible for individuals to escape all save socially necessary coercion. Macpherson did not fully develop this case in his analysis of Friedman's ideas, but he did explicitly do so in his account of Isaiah Berlin's theory of freedom.

The Limits of Negative Freedom: Isaiah Berlin

Isaiah Berlin's famous discussion of positive and negative liberty formulated in *Two Concepts of Liberty* was more than a simple conceptual exercise. It served as a central text in the neoliberal attack on "collectivism." Seen from this angle, Berlin's critique was an implicit diagnosis of the crisis of the times. Liberal individualism needed to be restored – if not exactly in its original form – to stave off the crisis in Western democracy. That crisis had been triggered by the pathologies of collectivism found in socialist and social democratic states, here represented by theories of positive liberty.

As Berlin sees it, positive freedom is a theory of rational self-mastery. This means that as an individual I am "moved by reasons, by conscious purposes which are my own, not by causes which affect me, as it were from the outside … I wish, above all, to be conscious of myself as a thinking, willing, active being, bearing responsibility for my choices and able to explain them by references to my own ideas and purposes. I feel free to the degree that I believe this to be true, and enslaved to the degree that I am made to realize it is not."[21] For Berlin, this last sentence carries the key to understanding the dangers of positive freedom: I may not realize that I am unfree and so must be "made" to realize it by those who can see what I cannot. Charles Taylor believes it is possible to "second guess" an agent by pointing out what Macpherson called internalized impediments to the articulation and pursuit of one's freely and rationally chosen purposes and thereby foster conditions for self-development.[22] For Berlin, this instead becomes a recipe for domination, whereby the allegedly more fully rational can coerce those not (yet) fully rational and thus not aware of what their "real" interests require. It is a formula for forcing people to be free – for Berlin, an evident logical contradiction that has had monstrous historical consequences.

The problem in Berlin's eyes is that notions of positive freedom, which call forth the creation of "great, disciplined authoritarian structures [incorporating] the ideal of 'positive' self-mastery by classes, or peoples, or the whole of mankind,"[23] assume an ultimate harmony of human purposes and one "true" way of life, when in fact human goals are plural and often contentious. Since self-mastery, or self-government, and the ideal of harmonious human purposes can readily connect up with the ideal of popular sovereignty or the general will and thus radical democracy (as they are often seen to do in Rousseau), the key political point to be drawn from the critique of positive freedom is that "there is no necessary connection between individual liberty and democratic rule ... The desire to be governed by myself, or at any rate to participate in the process by which my life is to be controlled, may be as deep a wish as that of a free area for action, and perhaps historically older. But it is not a desire for the same thing."[24]

Much current democratic theory operates in Berlin's shadow. This is the case in two respects. On the one hand, there is unease about assuming the possibility of anything resembling a substantive general will in the face of the evident reality of social pluralism (this is particularly characteristic of the central place now assumed by questions of multiculturalism in political theory in general and democratic theory in particular). On the other hand, Berlin's distinction survives largely intact in the differences characterizing contemporary conceptions of liberal versus republican forms of democracy.[25] Both liberal and republican theories seem to take for granted that indeed there is a gulf between "freedom from" and "freedom to," between what Berlin had called negative and positive liberty. In other words, according to these views there is, just as nineteenth-century critics of democracy claimed, an inherent and ineliminable tension between liberalism *qua* individual rights and freedoms, and democracy *qua* popular or collective sovereignty. With the rise of discourses of human rights and multiculturalism, liberalism so understood has won out, even among theorists who put democracy first.

No doubt Macpherson saw Berlin's theory as a serious challenge to his own developmental theory of democracy – a challenge that would have to be addressed if such a theory were to be viable. With the hindsight of contemporary events, it seems he may have been ahead of his time in recognizing the extent of the neoliberal challenge. His response was interesting in that it combined two distinct dimensions. First, he argued that the apparent power of Berlin's argument rests on its selective and stereotypical characterization of positive liberty. While some of Berlin's points are valid, the power of his diagnosis rests on accepting the circumscribed conception of positive liberty he presents. Second, Macpherson argues that positive and negative forms of liberty are not mutually exclusive. For Macpherson, positive and negative freedom are closely linked because any discussion of freedom should not be restricted to deliberate coercion emerging from interference by the state, invasive behaviour by other individuals, or the pressures of social conformity in the area in which individuals should not be constrained or pushed around. It should also consider those impediments to both free choice and the determination to pursue one's own conscious, rational purposes that result from denial of access to the means of life and labour, that is, from the institution of capitalist private property and the workings of the market mechanism.

Berlin is cognizant of this, and as a supporter of the welfare state sympathetic to efforts to ameliorate the inequalities of capitalism. However, he considers such impediments and their amelioration only conditions of liberty – they cannot define liberty itself. Macpherson thinks this is a mistake. It leads, in his view, to an impoverished and excessively mechanistic conception of freedom, one more appropriate to the world of Thomas Hobbes and Jeremy Bentham than to contemporary political reality and its challenges. At the same time, he acknowledges that some notion of positive freedom can serve and has in the past served to justify authoritarian regimes that deny the reality of freedom under the guise of realizing it. However, the problem lay not in anything necessarily intrinsic to the concept of positive freedom itself, but rather in two other areas: the unduly restricted understanding of its implications on the part of both certain theorists of positive liberty and Berlin himself;

and the political hurdles those committed to egalitarian and developmental goals have historically confronted, specifically the unwillingness of holders of political power in unequal, class-divided societies to concede ground to movements for fundamental democratic change except under the threat or reality of force. Both turn on the failure, inability, or unwillingness to consider impediments to liberty created by capitalist market relations – that is, in capitalist societies, the denial to most people of that access to the means of life and labour required for self-development.

Macpherson sees Berlin as having fused together three different concepts of positive liberty into one, which he then contrasts with negative liberty and which he sees as the basis for authoritarianism in the name of freedom. One form "is individual self-direction or ... self-mastery. It is the ability to live in accordance with one's own self-conscious purposes, to act and decide for oneself rather than to be acted upon and decided for by others." A second, which according to Macpherson is logically distinct from freedom as self-mastery, is participation in the exercise of popular sovereignty or self-government, "the democratic concept of liberty as a share in the controlling authority."

It is a third conception that, as Macpherson sees it, poses the problem and that makes Berlin's position seem plausible. Although it appears to follow naturally from the idea of freedom as self-mastery, and indeed in Berlin's eyes is virtually indistinguishable from it, in practice it is logically distinct historically and practically as well. This is the idea that "liberty is coercion, by the fully rational or by those who have attained self-mastery, of all the rest; coercion by those who say they know the truth, of all those who do not (yet) know it."[26] This is of course a version of Rousseau's dictum that men must be "forced to be free," a dictum here given its least flattering interpretation.

That liberty as self-realization or self-mastery has been transformed, in theory and practice, into the debased form of supposedly rational coercion of the less by the more fully developed has, as noted above, been the product both in theory and practice of the failure to acknowledge or address non-intended but necessary impediments to self-realization thrust up by capitalist market relations. Idealist theories, such as that of T.H. Green, fall down because they attempt to reconcile individual self-development as the full, non-contentious development of human capacities with capitalist private property – or, if you will, cooperative with possessive individualism.[27] Historically, Macpherson sees Stalinism as an example of a putatively radical political movement committed to the egalitarianism needed for self-development embracing supposedly rational coercion, with authoritarian or even totalitarian consequences. This outcome apparently ensues "only after long-continued and intensive refusal of the beneficiaries of unequal institutions, on a world scale, to permit any moves to alter institutions in the direction of more nearly equal powers."[28]

But it is not just radical left political movements that are prone to embrace a debased notion of positive liberty and to govern their actions accordingly. Macpherson also alludes to a conservative form of political movement committed to the goals of positive freedom as self-mastery and moral autonomy. By failing to recognize even to the extent that Idealist philosophers such as Green do, much less radical movements of the left, the impediments to self-realization that emerge from denial of access to the means of life and the means of labour, conservative movements for positive liberty are apt to become disillusioned with the apparently intractable deficiencies of the people with whom they must achieve their goals. Believing that it nonetheless must be possible to realize the ends of positive freedom, such forces "are pushed into the position of holding that it can be done and should be done by an authoritarian elite using whatever coercive means are necessary."[29] In other words, liberty as self-direction becomes liberty as rational coercion.

Macpherson offers no historical examples of conservative authoritarian movements or states committed to some notion of positive freedom that end up exercising coercion on a mass scale supposedly in the interests of realizing this freedom. But it is not too much of a leap to see certain contemporary fundamentalist religious or cultural movements as exhibiting at least some elements of what Macpherson has in mind. (And such movements are not necessarily so far from mainstream liberalism, or ostensibly liberal values, as is usually thought.)

Obviously, Macpherson's claims are contentious, particularly with respect to his reading of history. But we think his key point is to justify the view that negative and positive freedoms are not inherently at odds, as Berlin thinks. Indeed, he goes further: if properly understood, and under the right circumstances, these two forms of freedom are compatible and even mutually reinforcing. The critical elements here are impediments: where access to the means of life and labour is severely restricted, the range of negative freedom, that is, the area within which individuals cannot be interfered with, is likewise narrowed. In other words, inequality limits all freedom; and the deeper the inequality, the greater the limits.

There is no doubt that much contemporary democratic theory does take inequality seriously.[30] But Macpherson's account is more radical and challenging and is crucial to his argument about the close association between negative and positive liberty. For it is not just that inequality *limits* freedom. Rather, inequality *constitutes unfreedom*. If we understand Macpherson's position here, inequality is not just about the distribution of goods, resources, or life chances. Given the realities of contemporary societies and their core patterns of social, economic, and political organization, relations of inequality fundamentally shape how human potentialities are both defined and denied. It is a modality of necessary and possible experience. Inequality does not express an unrelenting and unalterable human competitiveness that issues in a natural hierarchy of those who are more and those who are less successful in the struggle for eminence. Nor does it represent, however, a deviation from the supposedly natural sociability characteristic of a generic humanity. Rather, inequality has emerged in the face of a specific historical situation and predicament: the present and potential future (or more accurately futures) of human powers understood as capacities of a certain sort. For want of a better term, we would call these capacities for rational self-production, or better, self-constitution.

And this is tied to a critical account of the present that takes the form of a wager about the future. The wager is that what people have been driving towards, and could under appropriate conditions more self-consciously and perspicuously articulate, is self-realization understood as the development and exertion of their distinctively human capacities, where this distinctiveness resides in these capacities being at least in principle non-contentious.

Contrary to Berlin, Macpherson holds that there is a difference between the idea of non-contentious human capacities and conscious purposes and the claim that under positive liberty "the ends of all rational beings must of necessity fit into a single universal, harmonious pattern."[31] That is, "a proliferation of many ways and styles of life which could not be prescribed and would not conflict ... is a necessary stipulation if a society of positive liberty is to be worth striving for. But it is not the same as the postulate of a preordained harmonious pattern."[32] This is not a dubious and dangerous utopian leap, but an essential dimension of any truly democratic society that claims to maximize the prospects for the equal development by all of their distinctively human capacities. "For what would be the use of trying to provide that everyone should be able to make the most of himself, which is the idea of a democratic society, if that were bound to lead to more destructive contention?"[33]

And this conception of human capacities and the developmental idea of power as that which makes it possible to exercise them carries with it a specific understanding of individual rights: the rights that are morally justifiable on egalitarian (i.e., democratic) grounds "are only those which allow all others to have equal effective rights; and ... *these are enough* to allow any man to be fully human."[34] The first part of this claim is familiar enough. It is the second that captures in a nutshell the core of Macpherson's critical account, his diagnosis of the present and his hopes for the future. His challenging claim is that a developmental democracy would maximize human powers, understood as those which facilitate the exercise of one's distinctively human capacities, and furthermore, that only those capacities whose exercise does not prevent others from exercising theirs are truly human, genuine, and fulfilling.

It is for this reason that Macpherson sees negative and positive liberty as complementary and even mutually determining, and not antagonistic. The area within which I cannot be interfered with – that is, have benefit from the use of my capacities extracted from me – both requires and facilitates my ability to develop my capacities under my conscious direction, and vice versa. To emphasize this connection, and thus ensure there is no theoretical space within which it would be possible to justify the debased authoritarian view of positive liberty (Berlin's great concern), Macpherson suggests we dispense altogether with the terms negative and positive liberty. We should instead speak and write of *counter-extractive* and *developmental* liberty.[35] What connects them is the role played by those impediments thrown up by the denial of access to the means of life and labour.

Macpherson's reformulation of the two concepts of liberty is challenging and suggestive, even more so because it seems to have had little impact on contemporary accounts of freedom. But notice: there still are *two* notions of liberty. The "classical" liberal idea that people must be protected from invasion on the part of other individuals and political authorities remains central to Macpherson's account. Whether he felt there would always be a need for both concepts – and those who view him as a utopian proponent of total harmony thought he mistakenly believed we could dispense with negative liberty – is not totally clear. He certainly appeared to doubt that the separation between the two was necessarily ontological and permanent rather than historical and, at least potentially, alterable.

Clearly Macpherson believed that the elimination of extractive power, tied to capitalist market institutions and property relations, was both desirable and possible; in any case, as already noted, this needed to be put on the agenda of any tolerably comprehensive theory of democracy committed to the idea that each individual ought to have the fullest right of and opportunity for self-development. In the current historical context, what makes the need for two concepts of liberty important is not just the real existence of or threat of invasion by other individuals and by political authorities – that is, the actuality or threat of coercion from those clearly dedicated to quashing one's liberty. It is also needed because the existence of impediments to the development and exercise of one's distinctively human capacities has seemed to require – where those impediments have not been abolished (i.e., everywhere) – the use of political authority to limit the extractive power of those in a position to deny to others access to the means of life and labour. What Macpherson has in mind here is the twentieth-century welfare state and its efforts to regulate the free play of capitalist market forces, although his theory envisions a much more extensive challenge to capitalist institutions. But whether one is considering the welfare state or something more extensive, the issue involves the need for and role of freedom-enhancing as opposed to freedom-denying coercion.

Macpherson sees this as a real problem and concern from the point of view of achieving a more richly democratic society because in the circumstances it involves limiting the powers of some in order to enhance the powers of others. But he suggests the difficulty is not insuperable if one does not restrict oneself – as Macpherson believes both Berlin and classical liberals do – to that excessively mechanistic, Hobbesian view of freedom, where it is identified with the absence of *all* obstacles, all barriers to the realization of one's desires. But there are obstacles and there are obstacles. In Macpherson's view, establishing social ownership of capital may remove from the sphere of negative liberty those activities associated with "free enterprise." But this might well enhance negative liberty overall "if the gain in liberty by those who had doors closed to them more than offsets the loss of liberty by those (relatively few) who had been in a position to take full advantage of market freedoms."[36]

Departing from the mechanistic view of freedom allows for a richer, more consistent conception and much more realistic grasp of negative liberty, for while liberals typically argue for freedom from all obstruction in principle, they obviously accept obstructions in practice. But departing from the mechanistic view also demonstrates why we still require such a concept and why we need to distinguish it from positive liberty. Macpherson himself accepts this need, even though he is obviously a staunch proponent of positive freedom. Redefining negative liberty as counter-extractive liberty clarifies what is at stake. According to him, Berlin seems aware of what is at stake as well. But Berlin cannot successfully address the issue because he defines freedom too narrowly, consigning to the category of conditions of liberty the removal of those impediments that Macpherson believes must be central to freedom itself.

It appears that the need to argue in terms of gains and losses of freedom – in other words, in terms of obstructions to freedom that work to remove obstructions – reflects for Macpherson the historically situated tension between the dominant market form of liberalism, or economic freedom, and democracy. This is not just a question, either, of the class conflict that capitalism generates and a that Marxian-influenced thinker such as Macpherson understandably enough emphasizes. There are not only empirical political and sociological but also profound normative philosophical matters at play here.[37]

As Macpherson recognizes, in the "real world" of actually existing liberal (capitalist) democracies, those who exercise extractive power have in the circumstances likely been able to transform this power into enriched forms of the very developmental power that democracy is supposed to promote for all. This indicates two themes that are central to Macpherson's position and to post-Marxist political and democratic theory and, beyond this, that are valuable in bringing current mainstream democratic thought into fuller relief: that democracy exists yet remains to be realized; and that much of what democracy is and can be hinges on the claim that one can imagine that human capacities might be non-contentious, and indeed, that fully or genuinely human capacities simply *are* those that are non-contentious. Otherwise put, "it comes down to the postulate that a fully democratic society cannot permit the operation of any extractive power, and that a society without any extractive power is possible. The serious difficulty about a democratic society is not how to run it but how to reach it."[38] Problems that today exercise many theorists of democracy, such as how to rationally aggregate individual preferences to produce logically coherent outcomes, are on this view second-order problems, not primary ones.

As noted above, Macpherson is not generally seen as someone interested in the actual workings of political institutions and practices. Yet, in engaging Berlin's argument around the question of freedom-enhancing obstructions he makes specific reference to the place of law and its dualistic character as state interference that at the same time can increase net aggregate individual liberty.[39] And he is clear that this is at the core of the counter-extractive liberty that makes positive or developmental freedom possible.

A dualistic conception of law, its origins and purposes, is very much at the heart of the work of Jürgen Habermas. And while he does not as explicitly lay it out or identify it, Habermas too engages the demands of positive freedom and the issues posed by developmental conceptions of democracy. To his account of democracy we now turn.

Jürgen Habermas and Political Freedom: For and Against Macpherson

Developed through engagement with a wide variety of currents in contemporary political philosophy, including the ideas of thinkers ranging from John Rawls and Ronald Dworkin to Nancy Fraser and Charles Taylor, Jürgen Habermas's discourse theory of constitutional democracy has attracted considerable attention.[40] With its focus on law, rights, autonomy, constitutionalism, and deliberation, this theory illuminates core issues defining currently influential currents of democratic thought that have sought to develop fresh insights into democratic possibilities beyond classical liberalism and Marxism/socialism. Indeed, Habermas himself has explicitly set this out as his purpose.[41]

Immersed in the continental tradition of political thought, Habermas has always been more methodologically self-conscious than was Macpherson. Habermas dynamically connects method and content in ways that distinguish him from other current theorists, regardless of how much he might otherwise share with them. He is not always explicit about this and thus ironically shares a bit of the reticence that characterized Macpherson and that has contributed to the failure on the part of analysts to see more clearly and fully what he has been trying to do. But at the core of his position is the assumption – similar to Macpherson's – that liberalism and democracy are compatible and that more radical understandings of each are essential if their full potential is to be realized.

Habermas's discourse principle holds that "[j]ust those action norms are valid to which all possibly affected persons could agree as participants in rational discourses."[42] In the form of "the democratic principle," it "states that only those statutes may claim legitimacy that can meet with the assent [*Zustimmung*] of all citizens in a discursive process of legislation that in turn has been legally constituted." This principle strives to articulate the performative meaning of citizenship under the conditions of modern democracy and the constitutional state: citizens engage in self-determination as "legal consociates who recognize one another as free and equal members of an association they have joined voluntarily."[43] These "legal consociates" are such by virtue of their enjoying equally private and public autonomy, human rights and popular sovereignty, "the individual liberties of the members of the modern market society ... [and] ... the rights of democratic citizens to political participation." The "co-originality" and interdependence of private and public autonomy is such that citizens "can make an *appropriate* use of their public autonomy, as guaranteed by political rights, only if they are sufficiently independent in virtue of an equally protected private autonomy in their life conduct. But members of society actually enjoy their private autonomy to an equal extent – that is, equally distributed individual liberties have 'equal value' for them – only if as citizens they can make an appropriate use of their political autonomy."[44]

Under these conditions, citizens can be simultaneously both authors and addressees of the law. As Rousseau and Kant had it, citizens would enjoy self-government because "the legal guarantee to behave as one pleases within the law" permits "autonomy in the sense of *reasonable* will-formation" whereby they "should bind their wills to just those laws they give themselves after achieving a common will through discourse." So understood, self-legislation "engenders an internal relation between will and reason in such a way that the freedom of everyone – that is, *self-*legislation – depends on the *equal* consideration of the individual freedom of each individual to take a yes/no position – that is, self-*legislation*."[45]

Although he does not use the terminology, Habermas provides an account of the relationship between private and public autonomy that has obvious parallels with Macpherson's argument about negative and positive, or counter-extractive and developmental, liberty. It seems, however, that there are two distinct and important differences between the two positions. In the first place, while Habermas clearly intends his account of the interrelation of private and public autonomy to provide a counterfactual perspective on democratic possibilities rather than a purely empirical treatment of actually existing liberal democracies, it is nonetheless still an immanent reconstruction of the logic at work in existing institutions. While less self-conscious methodologically, Macpherson offered a similar reconstructive account. Yet, in Habermas's analysis the gap between critical reconstruction and empirical reality is significantly narrower; correspondingly, the demands of democracy for Habermas are either more fully realized in existing institutions or are (and must be) considerably more modest.

The second point of departure is connected to the first. Habermas shies away from providing an account of genuine human wants, needs, and purposes comparable to that of Macpherson. He does not believe that, properly understood, these wants, needs and purposes are in principle non-contentious. The differences here go to the heart of Habermas's overall approach to the demands of theory generally and of democratic theory in particular.

Communicative Reason in *Between Facts and Norms*

The work of Habermas comes out of an avowedly philosophical background, the critical theory of the Frankfurt School. This perspective emerged in the context of, and was shaped by, the momentous and mostly horrific developments in the twentieth-century world, notably the rise of Stalinism and fascism (as well as the far less authoritarian but nonetheless reifying forms of mass liberal democracy in the "free world"), and therefore with certain practical/historical and theoretical problems of classical Marxism and socialism. In the face of these forces, the first-generation critical theorists, Max Horkheimer and Theodor Adorno in particular, ultimately offered a deeply pessimistic and even despairing account of the triumph of an instrumental rationality tied to the blind drive for raw self-preservation – the "dialectic" of enlightenment – and the consequent emergence of a rationalized Weberian "iron cage" in the form of a "one-dimensional" or "totally administered" society.[46]

Habermas broke with the totalizing and pessimistic thrust of the original critical theory. His theory of communicative action and communicative rationality, which is at the heart of his democratic theory, has been his alternative to what he sees as the one-sided nature of the Frankfurt School's account of the dynamics of modernity, as well as his own early treatment of the decline of the bourgeois public sphere.

Yet Habermas continues to hold fast to the idea of a philosophical politics. He remains vitally concerned with the theory/practice relationship in the context of a critical perspective on the contemporary world. He thus continues to hold to some conception of an emancipated form of life. However, this can only be undertaken in a fundamentally altered context that considers philosophically the need for what he calls post-metaphysical thinking. Such thinking challenges classical metaphysical commitments as these emerged initially in ancient Greek, primarily Platonic, thought and later were reworked under the rubric of the "philosophy of consciousness," or "philosophy of the subject." They included the idea of unity within the philosophy of origins (identity thinking); the equation of thought with being (the doctrine of Ideas); and the redemptive significance of the contemplative life (the strong concept of theory).[47]

For Habermas, undermining the claims of transcendental philosophy (which of course was also, if differently and with different effect, the goal of Marx and the original Frankfurt School) both required and made possible a move beyond classical conceptions of revolutionary social change and hence classical socialist notions of democracy, according to which the proletariat was the ultimate "collective" subject. In this respect, he remains tied to the legacy of the Frankfurt School. For while he saw its account of the triumph of instrumental rationality as one-sided, this account nonetheless not only pointed to a real problem but also made it possible to demonstrate the limits of other critical perspectives on philosophy and social life (such as that of Heidegger) that failed to account for the possibility of intersubjectivity and a common world, that is, the prospects for solidarity as a force for social integration. Habermas's turn to communicative rationality and communicative action – that is, action governed not by the dictates of strategic rationality but by the quest for mutual understanding – is central to his attempt to demonstrate the lived reality of and possibility for solidarity under contemporary conditions.

It is in relation to this project that law as "fact" and as "norm," partaking of both facticity and validity, and the inner tension between them, finds its place. Like Kant, Habermas sees law as combining freedom with coercion. However, this can only come about democratically: "the concept of modern law, which both intensifies and behaviourally operationalizes the tension between facticity and validity, already harbours the *democratic idea* developed by Rousseau and Kant: the claim to legitimacy on the part of a legal order built on rights can be redeemed only through the socially integrative force of the 'concurring and united will of all' free and equal citizens."[48]

In the context of his post-metaphysical framework, Habermas distinguishes himself from both Kant and Rousseau (and *inter alia* Marx and the early Frankfurt School) and the idea each holds of the social contract as expressing this "concurring and united will" of the people in a way that successfully combines individual autonomy with popular sovereignty. A social contract can result neither from the institutionalization of natural, moral rights individuals bring with them from the state of nature, as in Kant; nor from the ethical idea of individuals constituting themselves through the contract as citizens oriented to the common good and so realizing a substantive form of life, as in Rousseau. Rather, in his deliberative reconstruction of popular sovereignty Habermas stresses the central role of democratic procedures that make possible multiple forms of deliberation. These in turn facilitate the maintenance of responsive parliamentary institutions and vigorous forms of political pluralism, including competitive political parties and autonomous public spheres. On this basis,

> [the] institutions of the constitutional state are supposed to secure an effective exercise of the political autonomy of socially autonomous citizens. Specifically, such institutions must accomplish two things. On the one hand, they must enable the communicative power of a rationally formed will to emerge and find binding expression in political and legal programs. On the other hand, they must allow this communicative power to circulate throughout society via the reasonable application and administrative

implementation of legal programs, so that it can foster social integration through the stabilization of expectations and the realization of collective goals. Government by law is designed to spell out the system of rights in terms of a constitutional order in which the legal medium of law can become effective as a power transformer that reinforces the weakly integrating currents of a communicatively structured lifeworld.[49]

The reference here to "weakly integrating currents of a communicatively structured lifeworld" points to the (rather submerged) critical dimension of Habermas's position. For Habermas, successful fulfilment of the principles of the constitutional democratic state and the securing of private and public autonomy depend upon realizing the potential of modern communicative rationality; all hinges on the capacity to successfully transform communicative into administrative power by means of law, which incorporates both coercion and freedom. Popular sovereignty and solidarity – successful social integration – cannot be secured either through (Kantian) morality, which is too motivationally indeterminate, or through a substantial general will or ethical community (à la Rousseau), which is no longer plausible in the face of social pluralism.

Stated somewhat differently, Habermas does not believe that successful social integration can result from the operation of market mechanisms that aggregate and coordinate self-interested individual actions behind the backs of these individuals. Moreover, such mechanisms could never foster the conditions of solidarity – that is, symmetrical relations of mutual recognition that secure individual identity by taking up and transforming the spirit of face-to-face encounters with concrete others – precisely *because* they require people to treat one another instrumentally. Yet at the same time, there can be no "natural" organic community ensuring a frictionless fit between individual aspirations and communal purposes. In short, like Macpherson, Habermas engages the historically situated tension between negative and positive freedom. He, too, seeks a synthesis that both preserves the critical vantage point and indicates the historically informed tasks that must be undertaken in order to realize (private and public) autonomy and (communicative) rationality – that is, the promise of law itself.

Although he does not explicitly say so – and indeed seems at the outset to rule it out – this synthesis is decidedly Hegelian. *Between Facts and Norms* has a structure reminiscent of the *Philosophy of Right*.[50] In place of Hegel's account of abstract right, morality, and ethical life, Habermas offers the triad of the system of rights, the constitutional state, and procedural (deliberative) democracy as a system of public opinion and will-formation. Instead of absolute spirit by which a substantial ethical life is realized as objective spirit, there is communicative reason (the discourse principle), where an inner connection is secured between the system of rights and the constitutional state, the rule of law and popular sovereignty.

And there is as well here a basis for a critique, reminiscent of Marx, of the *Philosophy of Right* and its account of the state. Marx argued that the state as Hegel conceived it represented no concrete ethical community but was subordinated to civil society and its class-based antagonisms. In light of Habermas's account, it could be argued that in contemporary society communicative rationality is all too often subordinated to the demands of instrumental rationality in that what are inherently moral-practical questions are one-sidedly and misleadingly converted into technical ones (to use Habermas's earlier formulations).

If this is so, there is here further evidence that Habermas's ideas serve as a critical diagnosis of the present. What is specifically at issue here is the nature of a viable democracy that retains a connection with the normative/egalitarian impulses of classical democratic theory and classical socialist doctrine, while acknowledging the realities of societal complexity and pluralism with regard to concrete life plans and motives. At one level, the target is the various "realist" or "empirical" or "elitist" theories of democracy that draw their plausibility from the evident asymmetries of power in society and the existence of social complexity, which supposedly renders unrealistic popular discursive will-formation and normative direction of social processes by self-conscious, acting individuals.[51]

A key to Habermas's attempt to distinguish his view of both traditional Marxist and social democratic conceptions of the state, on the one hand, and the neoliberal revival of classical liberal accounts of the relation of the state to (free market) society, on the other, is located in his treatment of three paradigms of modern law as these have emerged historically, in Europe and elsewhere, over the course of the last three centuries: formal liberal; material welfare state; and proceduralist.[52] This account too exhibits an Hegelian structure: Hegel's three "moments" are here recast in terms of the relations among the three paradigms, with the proceduralist paradigm fulfilling the role of a concrete ethical life. It incorporates the claims of communicative freedom in the same way that ethical life embodied those of objective spirit. Of course, communicative freedom is not equivalent to objective spirit with its ties to the philosophy of the subject or consciousness but is linked instead to an account of intersubjectivity *qua* communication and communicative rationality. The proceduralist legal paradigm is the "spirit" of a plural world in which the mutual recognition of subjects guaranteed by Hegel only at the level of the fully realized universal reason of ethical life now takes the form of the legal guarantees of private and public autonomy as a system of rights among equal legal consociates who must order their relations within the framework of this-worldly positive law. This "spirit" of proceduralist law informs and rationalizes the institutions of political opinion and will-formation that are intended to secure a functional separation of powers "which, at a different level of abstraction, governs the availability of various sorts of reasons and how these are dealt with. This logic requires the institutionalization of various discourses and corresponding forms of communication that, *regardless of local context*, open up possibilities of access to the corresponding sorts of reasons."[53] Hence,

> the social substratum for the realization of the system of rights consists neither in spontaneous market forces [i.e., formal liberal law *qua* abstract right] nor in the deliberative measures of the welfare state [i.e., material welfare state law *qua* morality] but in the currents of communication and public opinion that, emerging from civil society and the public sphere, are converted into communicative power through democratic procedures [i.e., proceduralist law *qua* ethical life, here understood as establishing the identity of the modern democratic constitutional state in terms of which there is a necessary inner connection between private and public autonomy, justice and popular sovereignty].[54]

Habermas's conception of the interpenetration of private and public freedom provides a starting point for a critical democratic theory that recalls key themes in Macpherson's account. Its critical quality resides in its ability to link concrete forms of life that are historical and social in nature to the pathologies of late-modern forms of capitalist globalization. As Macpherson and others have pointed out, and as Habermas accepts, the liberal idea of basic rights is both atomistic and easily transformed into possessive individualism. It fails to account for the impediments to public freedom generated by an exclusive reliance on the market model, which produces inequalities of power and money. Unequal power leads to unequal public freedom. The achievement of equal private rights requires equal public freedoms and social rights.

Habermas argues, however, that public freedom involves not just the interventions of the social welfare state, which in isolation can lead to welfare paternalism, but also appropriate cultural conditions. In other words, he advocates a radical egalitarianism. While he does not fully develop this idea in his recent work on human rights, a radical egalitarian solution requires the establishment of an extensive network of public spheres that enable participation and that feed into political action.

Habermas intends this account to express a dynamic process of development that is conceptual *and* historical, indeed conceptual *because* historical, just as Macpherson intended his account of negative and positive freedom to reflect dynamically a specific historical predicament. He wants to point to immanent possibilities in the present – possibilities that are also necessities if the demands of communicative rationality and freedom are to be realized – for the normatively informed direction of social processes that have come to take on the character of inexorable systemic imperatives. "Realist" theories of democracy and society are wrong to assume away the need for and possibility of normative direction. Yet at the same time, there can be no totalizing social agent with the power to "make" society as an immediately ethical community. Existing democratic forms should not be blindly celebrated, resignedly accepted, or simply and one-sidedly condemned.

Towards a Post-Marxist Critical Theory

Habermas offers a post-Marxist critical theory of democracy in order to address the challenge of anchoring communicative and hence normative possibilities for autonomy and self-development in the face of systemic imperatives that threaten these possibilities. The question is: which possibilities and which imperatives? In Macpherson's language, we are now on the terrain of impediments to individual self-realization and the inner connection between the power to exercise one's distinctively human capacities (which Macpherson in one formulation called the ethical concept of power) and the institutions and values of capitalism and its property relations.

Undoubtedly Habermas sees the idea of essential and essentially human capacities – at least as formulated by Macpherson – as too intertwined with the philosophy of the subject, so this approach is closed off to him. But does this compel him to disavow the classical socialist critique of capitalism, suitably brought up to date, which requires that market forces operating in a nature-like way be subjected to conscious social direction by a body politic capable of developing a common interest in ensuring the well-being of all its members?

We contend that in his recent writings on both global cosmopolitanism and the contemporary crisis of the European Union, Habermas does not fully realize the potential inherent in his theoretical outlook. Notwithstanding a few nods in this direction, this recent work lacks a detailed diagnosis of the pathologies of neoliberal globalization, although to be sure Habermas is highly critical of the market fundamentalism that he believes has come to shape the contemporary political economy of Europe – with disastrous results.[55] Nor has he shown he is capable of taking up the complex problems of global development and underdevelopment at any point in his own biography.[56] But if one were to develop the latent threads of this diagnosis in conjunction with Macpherson's intuitions, the result could provide a powerful critique of the barriers that limit the emergence of egalitarian global justice.

As we have noted, the classical socialist critique of capitalism argued that market forces which operated in a nature-like way needed to be subjected to a body politic capable of a common interest whose realization would ensure the well-being of all its members. At least since the publication of *The Theory of Communicative Action*, Habermas has tended to argue that the economic "system" characteristic of advanced industrial society (i.e., capitalism) can no longer, if it ever could, be subjected to this kind of direction; it can only be indirectly steered.[57]

But do the demands of his own theory call for more, as William Scheuerman suggests they do?[58] For Habermas also acknowledges the presence of unaccountable power emanating from the economic, political/administrative, and cultural systems of contemporary society. From the perspective of post-Marxist democratic theory, the key is to acknowledge the limitations of the classical socialist ideal without at the same time bowing to resignation in the face of the apparent inability to imagine alternatives to the existing order – without which any developmental account of democracy, including that of Habermas, falters.

We want to argue that C.B. Macpherson's concept of the net transfer of powers provides insight into the importance of fundamental change and how such change should be conceived if it is to be plausible in the current social context. This concept can play these roles because it creatively combines political economy and political theory and indeed shows them to be inextricably intertwined.

Developmental Power and Extractive Power

The net transfer of powers is at the core of Macpherson's work – not only his democratic theory but also his landmark study of possessive individualism; indeed, it illuminates the essential connection between them. It refers to the fact that in capitalist market societies, including those that are liberal democracies, "which [operate] necessarily by a continual and ubiquitous exchange of individual powers," those who own capital, that is, the means of life and labour, control access to these for those who do not; yet all require such access if they are to achieve their conscious human purposes or to maximize their powers to use and develop their human capacities. Given that liberal democratic societies justify themselves on the grounds that they facilitate individual self-realization, liberal democracy, in theory and practice, is caught up in a fundamental contradiction: "A society in which a man [sic] cannot use his skill and energy without paying others, for the benefit of those others, for access to something to use them on, cannot be said to maximize each man's powers."[59] The net transfer of powers and the problem of impediments at the core of Macpherson's account of freedom entail each other.

Yet as central as the concept is, it has gone largely unanalysed if not unacknowledged. Where it has been noticed, by critics and defenders alike, it has usually been seen as Macpherson's own Marxist equivalent to the theory of exploitation and surplus value – as interesting, perhaps, but not theoretically original.[60]

This isn't exactly wrong; indeed, Macpherson himself was sometimes apt to see it in these terms. But it is misleadingly one-sided. For in fact the concept has dimensions and implications that permit a fresh look at issues in democratic theory, issues that developmental, post-Marxist theories need to consider. It is neither pure classical Marxism nor abstract humanist liberalism.

As we have seen, Macpherson views democracy as more than a form of government. It is a kind of society within which all individuals have the equal ability to use and develop their essentially human capacities. At the heart of his conception of democracy is the maximization of human powers, with power understood as the ability to use and develop those capacities. As Macpherson seems to understand it, this power is both qualitative and quantitative: it can be both judged and measured. Power as the ability to use and develop capacities is a critical concept with practical intent, immanent or implicit in the actions and behaviour of real social agents, who might otherwise be consciously motivated by other purposes.

The core idea here is explicitly Marxian. In a society divided between owners and non-owners of capital – that is, a class-divided society – those who lack access to the means of life and labour transfer "both the ability to work and the ownership of the work itself; and, consequently, the value added by the work." This transfer is structurally determined in that it is "a continuous transfer between non-owners and owners of the means of labour, which starts as soon as, and lasts as long as, there are separate classes of owners and non-owners; not a momentary transfer occurring at the time of that separation." And this is a measurable transfer: "it is the amount of exchange value (whether in money terms or real terms) that can be added by the work to the materials on which it is applied, and be realized in the value of the product."[61]

Acknowledgment of this relationship and of the transfer involved can lead to the recognition that how production is conducted, and how products and labour are exchanged, are potentially worthy social and political issues. Fair treatment in the workplace and fair exchange in the marketplace can become objects of public policy; typically, this has been the case under the welfare state. In other words, this dimension of Macpherson's argument may suggest a theory of justice, which of course is central to dominant currents of contemporary democratic thought. (And it is also why some radical and Marxist critics of Macpherson view him as "too" liberal.)

But Macpherson does not rest there. He goes on to indicate that what is at stake is not just the *transfer* of powers but also the *diminution* of powers. He distinguishes productive from extra-productive powers – that is, the ability to use one's energies and capacities to produce material goods from the ability to engage in activities beyond the production of goods that provide opportunities to exert and enjoy one's human capacities for their own sake. He argues that during the continuous transfer of one's powers, one loses – beyond the value of this transfer – the fulfilment that comes from exerting one's capacities according to one's own conscious purposes, whether this take place within one's productive activities or outside them. The problem is the same: people lose the (positive or developmental) freedom to consciously use their capacities for their own freely determined purposes. Where they lose their ability to direct their productive capacities, in a society in which production is a central fact, they cannot help but suffer impairment of their ability to do so beyond the sphere of production. People are deprived of the opportunity to become what they could be – to exercise their capacities for self-production or self-constitution. The process of identity formation is skewed by the requirements of what Macpherson calls extractive power and therefore, as he indicated in his critique of Berlin, negative liberty. Because Macpherson identifies *both* the transfer *and* diminution of powers and argues they are inextricably intertwined, his account suggests a theory of justice that necessarily also points to an account of the good life.

Nevertheless, while both productive and extra-productive powers, and thus our lives both in and outside the workplace, must be considered together, the transfer and diminution of powers within the sphere of production itself remains central for Macpherson, as they had been for Marx, precisely because with respect to these powers questions of both justice and the good life emerge with particular force:

> [A]lthough the seller [of one's productive capacities] indeed transfers the whole of his labour-power, the whole control of his productive capacities, for the contracted time, he can transfer only part of the value it would have had if it had been able to keep it; the rest of that value is lost and is lost by virtue of the fact that he has to sell. If he were able to keep his labour-power and use it himself, its value would be the satisfaction value *plus* the value which its application added to the materials on which it was applied.[62]

In short, Macpherson addresses his analysis to both exploitation and surplus-value, and to the alienation of labour in its multiple dimensions as Marx had laid it out in his early writings, namely, alienation from, respectively, the products of labour, the activity of labouring, the human essence and from other humans. His ultimate target, in other words, is the pervasive commodification of society characteristic of advanced capitalism. This puts him in closer contact with the Frankfurt School – and thus with Habermas.

What is important again to note is that while in his account of the net transfer of powers Macpherson builds upon fundamentally Marxian themes, he does so *within* a theory of democracy and not *outside* it. Hence his position has several implications that are decisive for a developmental democratic theory. One in particular stands out against the backdrop of contemporary democratic theory and its specific concerns, and the developmental alternative. Macpherson connects his account of the net transfer of powers to the claim that a fully democratic society must work to maximize human developmental power, understood as the equal ability of all to use and develop their distinctively human capacities, and argues that abolishing this transfer would lead to fuller maximization of capacities that are ultimately non-contentious. It is easy to assume that the abolition of the net transfer (and consequent diminution of powers) would *mean* or *just be* the expression of distinctively human capacities, that the elimination of the class relations of capitalist society would mean a non-contentious society – in other words, a concrete general will. But Macpherson does not offer such a concrete picture. What is important is the *transfer* and *diminution* of powers, not the *powers themselves*. Their specific content presupposes appropriate conditions for their formation. This content cannot be spelled out in advance.[63] Presumably, one of the conditions making for this spelling out would be the opportunity to engage with others and deliberate along the lines of Habermas's account.

This in turn suggests another issue. For Macpherson, the justificatory theory of liberal democracy has relied historically upon not just one maximization claim, but two. Along with the claim to maximize human powers, it has also offered the claim to maximize utilities. Macpherson sees these claims as inherently contradictory. This has plagued efforts to develop a defensible theory of liberal democracy that is faithful to democracy's humanist aspirations. But what is interesting here is that it was in the context of this argument that Macpherson set out his two concepts of power, extractive and developmental. In an earlier formulation he had distinguished between a descriptive and an ethical notion of power. What made this latter way of identifying different notions of power significant for Macpherson is that the so-called descriptive concept – essentially Hobbes's view that power was any apparent means to some future apparent good – was unable to even recognize much less quantify the net transfer of powers because it measured the power of individuals *after* such transfer has occurred.

Arguably, even Habermas accepts this notion of power; hence his view that the exercise of communicative freedom can at best hold existing powers accountable. (Insofar as what is left of existing welfare states – for which Habermas provides a qualified defence – do so, they also regulate power that manifests itself after a transfer has occurred.) But what, then, is the communicative freedom that Habermas defends *about* or *for*? What distinguishes it from the cybernetic feedback mechanisms of the various "realistic" systems theories he has criticized, at length and with eloquence? He seems to need something like the net transfer of powers and the conception of human capacities that undergirds the critical account of the social and political conditions within which that transfer emerges and which it sustains. And acknowledging such capacities need not entail a return to the philosophy of consciousness or the subject; they do not necessarily do so in Macpherson's case.

Of course, as indicated earlier, Macpherson is clear that the maximization of democracy requires the abolition of extractive power, and this clearly entails, at the very least, substantial transformation of existing capitalist market institutions. In an era in which global capitalism seems triumphant, this seems impossible – but perhaps for that reason utterly necessary. The idea of abolishing extractive power and the institutions that embody and preserve it may well expand the reach of the democratic imagination, of our sense of the real and its possibilities. It asks us to think more expansively about our models of democracy and how they fit the current circumstances.

Thus any attempt to theorize about democracy (or indeed any political question of consequence) requires a sensitivity to historical location, both one's own and that of one's ideas. The always dynamic and changing relation between democracy as a value and as a form of political practice, and the need to relate these to fundamental and unavoidable conceptions of human purpose, is at play in all accounts of democracy – it is a condition of their intelligibility, the inescapable hermeneutic dimension of their articulation. Failure or unwillingness to attend to this – and often this is the product of a quest for "realism" – unduly limits the sorts of questions that should be posed and may be unrealistic to boot.[64] Ironically, the quest for realism can widen rather than reduce the gap between theory and practice, between democratic models and democratic realities.

In defending his account of developmental, non-market democracy, Macpherson suggests challenging questions that this account will likely elicit: "For example, can the concept of power as ability to use and develop essentially human capacities be made precise enough to be of any use? Can we assume that all men's essentially human capacities can be exercised not at the expense of each others'? Can the ability to exercise these capacities be sufficiently measured to entitle us to make its maximization the criterion of a fully democratic society?" He goes on to note that if the difficulties these questions pose are the result of conceiving democracy as the kind of society that maximizes human developmental powers, we should probably forget the whole idea. However, "the difficulties are inherent in any democratic theory: our formulation simply enables them to be seen more clearly and dealt with more openly."[65]

We need to have greater clarity and openness. Habermas, and especially Macpherson, can show us why and indicate how to proceed. They thus provide an important starting point for our consideration of democratic possibilities in the chapters that follow.

Chapter Two

Reason, Truth, and Power: The Challenges of Contemporary Critical Theory

In this chapter we explore from a broadly post-Marxist perspective what we see as key methodological requirements for a critical social theory that is adequate for a critical or radical theory of democracy. Our account is informed by the spirit of the critical theory of the Frankfurt School, while departing from some of its key arguments. At the same time, while our position has affinities with "post-metaphysical" theories that distance themselves from both traditional Marxist and Frankfurt School perspectives, we part company as well with certain positions and commitments associated with these alternatives. In responding to both "classical" and contemporary positions we lay emphasis on the importance of the participant's perspective as a central element of an adequate critical theory.

There is no doubt that certain key assumptions and claims of what might be called "classical" Frankfurt School critical theory require reformulation in light of changed historical circumstances and possibilities. Nonetheless, its fundamental commitments, ultimately tied to the possibility of an emancipated, rational social order dedicated to the fullest realization by associated individuals of their capacities in an environment of freedom, equality and solidarity, remain crucial for social analysis and democratic theory in the present. The issues of reason, truth, and power that were central to the work of the first generation of critical theorists are as relevant today as they were when the theory was originally formulated in the face of the momentous historical challenges confronting societies in the context of widespread social crises – war, revolution, and depression.

It is especially important to stress these issues precisely because contemporary reformulations of critical theory have been for the most part recast in line with the assumptions of "post-Marxist" democratic theory. Yet the relation of critical to democratic theory is often unclear or as been underdeveloped, both by contemporary critical theorists and by their critics. For some, the postmodern rejection of totalizing "grand narratives" and scepticism about large-scale theories of politics, along with the collapse of actually existing socialism, have together provided grounds for the dismissal of critical theory's Marxian commitments. New zones of conflict, such as those around gender and multicultural-ism, have challenged its more rigid forms.

We contend, however, that a post-Marxist theory requires not a wholesale rejection of this tradition, but rather its critical renewal, one that respects the legacy of the original formulation of critical theory with its focus on questions of reason, truth, and power. At the core of this renewal is a non-dogmatic approach to Marxian categories that rec-ognizes the limitations of traditional Marxism while at the same time seeking to draw on the continuing significance of these categories for illuminating the present.

We believe that a critical theory of democracy that builds on the insights of the tradition of the Frankfurt School and critical theory should have both a developmental historical-diagnostic and a self-reflexive character. While it should analyse the origins and nature of social structures of power and authority in the context of a broad his-torical trajectory, it should also, as a theory committed to the pursuit of enhanced freedom and equality, offer a critical diagnosis of the present, whereby the status of the theory's concepts would depend upon their success in illuminating for potential addressees the realities and pos-sibilities of their situation.

As suggested above, the Frankfurt theorists creatively revised Marxist theory in the face of dramatic changes to capitalism and world politics wrought by revolution, depression, war, and fascism. They identified key elements of a critical approach to social analysis, most notably the need for a dynamic theory with a practical intent to be both historically diagnostic and self-reflexive, and they pointed to the distinctive characteristics such a theory must possess. These were signal and indispensable accomplishments. However, their attempt to formulate more specifically a theory of democracy illustrates the need for a post-Marxist approach, particularly because the status and character of this kind of theory, and even its plausibility, have been called into question in contemporary debates. Hence the demands on contemporary critical theory have a double aspect: critical theory confronts changed historical and social conditions, but in turn it chal-lenges, or should challenge, currently dominant paradigms of thought and especially democratic theory. It should take on board the task of identifying and exploring social pathologies that threaten if not undermine the normative claims advanced by the dominant strains of democratic thinking.

Because we seek to demonstrate the continuing significance of critical theory for a radical theory of democracy, this chapter serves as a prolegomenon to our own efforts in subsequent chapters to suggest and develop elements of a theory of democracy adequate to the present situation. We thus begin with a summary discussion of key themes laid out by the first generation of Frankfurt School critical theory, specifically Max Horkheimer's account of the problem of truth and its relation to the demands of scientific theory and Theodor Adorno's attempt to formulate an "emphatic" conception of truth that at the same time did not fall prey to the flaws of classical (idealist) metaphysics. We attempt to show what we believe remains valuable in these accounts, while also suggesting their limitations.

These limitations are specifically linked to the failure of the original Frankfurt School thinkers to sufficiently develop a conception of intersubjective interaction adequate to their insights into the blind spots of orthodox or classical Marxism. The first generation recognized that these blind spots were a product of the Marxist commitment to an objectivist understanding of social action and historical change and thus a positivist and scientistic understanding of knowledge and truth. But they did not fully or sufficiently follow up on their insights, although they had within their framework resources for doing so. It was left to "second generation" critical theory, and in particular the work of Jürgen Habermas, to take up the task of further exploring and developing the critique of classical Marxism by focusing on the underappreciated and underdeveloped role of communicative reason and communicative action in establishing the conditions and possibilities, normative and structural, for the recognition and realization of a democratic polity and society built on equality, and on social as well as individual freedom. We explore key dimensions of the "communicative turn" and its role in a critical theory of democracy, while also suggesting its own limitations – limitations emerging from a certain normative thrust detached from a thoroughgoing analysis of social structures and social pathologies.

Of course, the Frankfurt School's early analyses as well as its most recent efforts take on the challenge of contemporary philosophy and social science, not just Marxism. Horkheimer, and later Habermas, took up the critique of positivism and an objectivist social science that separated knowledge from the practices of social life.

The final part of this chapter deals with the relation of communicative reason to the nature and role of power. The issue of power poses distinctive challenges to critical theory in general and to a critical theory of democracy in particular. At the same time, critical theory potentially offers unique resources for an exploration of the dynamics of power in contemporary society that we believe other perspectives lack. These include the postmodernist or post-structuralist theories associated with the well-known and influential work of Michel Foucault. Focusing on the relation between communicative and strategic conceptions of power, we suggest ways in which power could be understood, with Hannah Arendt, as the capacity for associated individuals to pursue common purposes through bonds of trust and solidarity – a key issue for any developmental theory of democracy that is committed to the idea and ideal of a society dedicated to the fullest realization by each and all of their distinctively human potentialities and possibilities.

The Idea of a Critical Theory: Max Horkheimer

For Max Horkheimer, knowledge was never a matter of an objective standpoint detached from the understanding of participants. Horkheimer rejected the "Cartesianism" he saw in much contemporary social science, which sought to find unchanging laws of action that had an independent status. The quest for a unified theory, a system of linked propositions, was of minimal value for Horkheimer because it bore little relation to social practice. For him, the aim of social theory was to transform society. The role of theory was to inform individuals about social conditions and possibilities for change.

Horkheimer was critical of many contemporary approaches to knowledge that detached it from its social roots, but he was especially critical of positivism and pragmatism. Positivism figured prominently in his reflections on the relation of knowledge, and theories of knowledge, to the historical processes and the material relations of society. Though in his earlier work he tended to focus on all forms of positivism, he subsequently emphasized that version embodied in the logical empiricism and logical positivism of his time.[1] This form had become one of the dominant philosophies of the 1930s. More than any other theory it challenged the very idea of a critical theory possessing an objectively partisan character that at the same time respected the demands of reason and truth. Positivism reduced inquiry to a form of natural science. Logical positivists in particular claimed to understand human activity only through the lens of sense experience. They rejected the Kantian notion of a synthetic *a priori*, indeed an active subject of whatever kind. They adopted instead Humean scepticism towards "innate ideas." To be sure, logical positivists went beyond earlier versions of positivism in that they saw language or sentences about experience as the subject of study. But they remained dubious about the notion of an independent subject. The objections of logical positivists to idealism and its postulate of a pure mind that was free of the influence of sense data led them to reject any conception of an organized self that is capable of self-reflection. Ernst Mach, whose work offered a precursor to logical positivism, saw the self only as a bundle of sensations with no unity or centre.[2] Denying the ability to reflect critically on social processes and evaluate them, positivism reduced social theory to the acceptance of already established facts.

Logical positivists wanted to place philosophy on the firm ground of science, specifically natural science. The only valid philosophical statements were either propositions – that is, sentences that could be verified by observation – or logical truths. These versions of positivism separated facts from values, as well as philosophy from science. Science was restricted to the establishment and verification of facts. Only the evidence of experience or the analytic truths of formal logic counted as knowledge. Value judgments were viewed as irrational or emotive utterances and as unverifiable. One could not verify a value judgment by observation or logic.

The logical positivist ideal is based on a mathematical version of natural science. Positivists have sought a unified conceptual system in which all knowledge is deduced from the smallest number of axioms. And like physics, the system could be captured and made transparent and thus knowable by means of mathematical laws. This feature in turn is supposed to allow the scientist to explain the probability of any event.[3] The positivist wants to extend this model from the natural to the social sciences. While admitting this is not yet possible, he believes that the human sciences, much like the natural sciences, will eventually be able to predict the course of social events. Positivism will determine what humanity really *is* more definitively than either religion or speculative philosophy can. It takes an objective, neutral, non-normative approach to knowledge in which history and valuations are absent. The laws of society, just like the laws of nature, are permanent and unchanging.

Positivism fails because its extreme empiricism is unable to grasp the way knowledge is shaped by social context. Instead, positivists see knowledge as a set of isolated facts. Horkheimer was not entirely dismissive of empiricism or the empirical, which in his view played a role in a materialist critical theory. But sense perception is not itself basic. It is shaped by history, by material conditions and culture. In one of his earliest essays, Horkheimer noted that "sense experiences are indeed the basis of knowledge, and we are at every point referred back to them, but the origin and conditions of knowledge are not identically the origin and conditions of the world."[4] In his early studies Horkheimer cited the work of the gestalt theorists who influenced his mentor, Hans Cornelius. Gestalt theorists noted that sense perception was not basic but rather was organized holistically. However, Horkheimer went beyond the idea that knowledge has a holistic contextual basis. He thought that holism was related not just to the organization of the mind but also to the practical nexus of knowledge. He rejected the pursuit of a disinterested knowledge. All knowledge is engaged, caught up in the nexus of human interests. Knowledge is both self-reflexive and critical.

In contrast, Horkheimer contended that "the existing order is a product of the life processes of society in which the individual is an active participant."[5] He accepted the premises of German idealism since Kant that our perceptions are not basic or fixed but are themselves a product of our understanding. Anticipating to some extent Habermas's later work, as well as that of Charles Taylor, Horkheimer also accepted a key assumption of interpretive social science: that our perceptions were mediated through language. Recognizing the work of the neo-Kantians, Horkheimer pointed out that "[t]he given is not only expressed by speech but fashioned by it; it is mediated in many ways."[6] However, he went beyond what he saw as the idealistic commitments of neo-Kantians. He saw the relations between self and society, which neo-Kantians hypostatized as fixed, as historically changing relations affected by social conflict.

Nor is science an independent, isolated activity; it too is embedded in social and material life processes. Scientists who think of themselves as reflexive and active when working as scientists, and then view themselves as passive agents acted upon by causal forces, are denying their own agency. Positivism denies not only the conscious will of the scientist who employs knowledge to create theory but also that of the social actor who puts the knowledge of such sciences into practice. Individuals and social groups must plan deliberately to achieve goals. Here Horkheimer saw ordinary social action as largely purposive. Positivists reduce the individual to a mostly passive product of casual forces whose generative force is independent of human will. In contrast, Horkheimer saw power as the ability to use one's abilities to carry out aims and realize goals.

According to Horkheimer, the social functions of science apply to the whole of social life. Humans cooperate with or oppose one another in order to realize aims. They create their material and social worlds by engaging in what Horkheimer calls the material life process. Moreover, as he indicated, individuals hold notions of a decent life and assess their current circumstances in terms of those notions. They experience deprivations and hardships and are often subject to domination by more powerful forces. Those forces are not always experienced as blindly causal, though when faced with the overwhelming power of nature, people may understand them as such. Rather, they may come to be seen as the result of social arrangements. Clearly, then, participants do not experience values as mere individual preferences that are tacked onto action; rather, they see themselves as inhabiting a social world in which norms are central organizing features of social life. The theorist who ignores all of this cannot really understand the social ties and contexts of participants. This is because humans are capable of self-understanding and of having plans and purposes and so can conceive of their own fate and imagine conditions in which their lives would be better. In other words, they have conceptions of a good life. They can imagine and strive for greater freedom and happiness.

For the positivists this is merely a matter of emotion or feeling, which is extra-scientific and has no rational content. We can determine the goals of human action only through a neutral, non-normative investigation. For Horkheimer, however, a normative perspective is central to the type of theory he wants to formulate: a critical theory. Humans, he argues, have a basic need to seek happiness that can never be eliminated. This is not to be sure simply a desire for pleasure or simple material satisfaction. It is found in the hope for a better life.

Horkheimer took a post-metaphysical view of knowledge.[7] He did not think that truth was a matter of timeless or permanent knowledge outside the bounds of time and history. Rather, for him, truth was a historical and social entity. What we see as truth can change as society changes and as we acquire new knowledge of society and history. Facts and theories are socially constructed. They are part of a nexus of understanding whereby we make sense of the world. Science, and for that matter philosophy, is a social product. Yet Horkheimer did *not* argue that the social and historical character of knowledge led to a relativism in which truth-claims were reduced to mere opinion. Truth is fallible but that does not make it relative. Truth-claims represent our best understanding in the moment at hand.

While Horkheimer did not take what would now be called an interpretive perspective, he did take a holistic view of knowledge that was not resolved into a totality. In his version of this position – which he called "dialectical" – there were no isolated facts or forms of understanding, nor was there isolated consciousness. We understand entities in the world only in their relation to other things: "every insight is regarded as true only in connection to the whole body of theory."[8] Understanding rests on an entire set of conditions and background assumptions. As a consequence of understanding, both subject and object are modified. In more contemporary terms, we might say that facts are theory laden: they do not and indeed *cannot* exist as mere stand-alone entities; they only make sense in a theory that interprets them and brings out their tendencies. However, Horkheimer added to this understanding the idea that this holistic context is not closed on itself; furthermore, it is always changing and rife with conflicts and even contradictions. This conflict-laden process is what, for Horkheimer, defined the "dialectical." Concept and object (to use Adorno's terms) do not fit together without remainder or contradiction. The object of knowledge – in this case, other subjects – may exist in a situation that contradicts the terms used to understand those subjects. This is especially true of key social and political notions such as freedom, which therefore can never be understood as transparently clear and self-sustaining facts capable of being subsumed under social causal laws (i.e., "traditional theory"). A critical theory aims to understand human action in relation to its developmental tendencies and possibilities, some of which are not and cannot be realized.

In Horkheimer's view, Hegel's dialectical theory was undercut by its commitment to finality. Hegel's dialectic relativized forms of understanding to take into account their historically limited and one-sided character and incorporated their relative truths into new forms of understanding, but his idealist premises necessarily led him to envisage an end to the dialectic. He sought a point of final knowledge and reconciliation.

Horkheimer rejected the idealist dialectic and its consequences; in particular, he rejected the notion of a final resolution of all contradictions. A materialist theory is one in which, as noted above, concept and object, thought and reality, are never fully reconciled. Hegel's view "has as its presupposition the basic postulate of idealism that concept and being are in truth the same, and therefore that all fulfilment can take place in the pure medium of the spirit ... Materialism on the other hand insists that objective reality is not identical with man's own thought and can never be merged into it."[9]

Thus we should not see dialectic as revolving around a simple logical schema of thesis/antithesis/synthesis. Dialectic, for Horkheimer, was more properly tied to the view that all knowledge is conditioned by history and commitment. The clash of these conditioned perspectives was what generated the dialectical movement. Such a movement was never completed or finished. The open-ended dialectic that Horkheimer proposed meant that history was never finished or ended.

Critical theory, then, rejects the idea that a theory is best understood as a systematically connected set of propositions. It falls into the domain of a social theory that begins in the attempt to make sense of the life processes of a community with all its conflicts and contradictions and to determine its developmental possibilities. It is not an objective theory in the sense that the theorist can stand outside or hover above social commitments. Horkheimer rejected the vision of the scientist who can separate his work from his life – that is, that notion that the social scientist can be impersonal and disinterested in his work life while at the same time an active citizen in his private life. Social scientists are embedded in the social and material life processes that provide the context for all knowledge. Knowledge cannot be uncontaminated by social interest. The inquirer is a participant in society, just like the ordinary individual. She understands society as a participant.

Critical theory, for Horkheimer, does not aim to construct a system. It is "is a human activity which has society itself for its object."[10] It seems, then, that he was seeking to understand society as a conflict-laden reality, one that to date had not been the creation of rational individuals but that could be placed under the conscious control of humans. Human history has largely been filled with oppression and blind conflict. The critical theorist contends that individuals could bring society under conscious and deliberate control and thereby create a good and human life. Horkheimer saw a conflict between the individual ability to act with awareness and purpose and a society organized in such a way that conscious direction by most is precluded. Thus, in Horkheimer's view critical theory did not seek to ameliorate the conditions of a capitalist society but rather to transform them.

The project of a critical theory, then, does not entail simply a change in the nature of inquiry. The subject is not a detached observer but an involved participant. Horkheimer noted: "Its opposition to the traditional concept of theory springs in general from a difference not so much of objects as of subjects. For men of the critical mind, the facts, as they emerge from the work of society, are not extrinsic in the same degree as they are for the savant or for members of other professions who all think like little savants."[11]

Put in slightly different terms, the material of inquiry is not extrinsic to the scientist or to the participant. The ordinary participant and the inquirer share the same social world and are involved in the same social life processes. Thus, social understanding is an intrinsic element of the participant's perspective. The inquirer takes the perspective of an involved participant. The theorist's aim is not to predict events but to serve as an agent in the practical transformation of society. The theorist does not seek to control things but to engage in reflection on the relation between society and its possibilities and on the conditions that keep individuals from acting both individually and in concert to realize these possibilities. The reflexive relationship to the social world is the basis of a critical perspective on this world, that is, an implicit and sometimes explicit evaluation of the conditions of social life that is shared by both theorists and participants. Both try to make sense of the social world and its possibilities. These evaluations are crucial to the extent that they form part of the attempt to bring about social conditions that can create human happiness and flourishing, reduce domination, and bring social processes under rational control. Critical theory "[is] not merely a research hypothesis which shows its value in the ongoing business of men: it is an essential element in the historical effort to create a world which satisfies the needs and powers of men."[12]

In opposition to positivism, then, a critical theory is inescapably normative. It can never eliminate conceptions of freedom, dignity, or happiness. Critical theory is based on the search for better social conditions, and it is impossible to assess the workings of society without some conception of what those conditions should entail. Without some normative assumptions, the positivist is incapable of making any normative assessments or of reflecting on the nature of society. He takes society as it is. In contrast, the critical theorist takes up these normative concerns as a way of analysing the conflicts and contradictions of the society of his time.

Unlike positivism, pragmatism does not make value-free social inquiry and a passive relation to the facts the key elements of a scientific approach to society. Indeed, pragmatism seems to take up the engaged normative and activist commitments that also characterize critical theory. However, as he did with positivism, Horkheimer saw in pragmatism and its core assumptions an essentially affirmative and conformist orientation to a social order that denied or contradicted its rational potential.

Horkheimer's encounter with pragmatism was conditioned in many respects by the time and place of its reception. By the late 1930s the roots of pragmatism in Hegelian thought, particularly in the work of John Dewey and George Herbert Mead, appeared to have withered or been covered over. They were in the process of being replaced by more analytic approaches. Dewey's work too began to take on a more instrumentalist bent. This instrumentalism was at the heart of Horkheimer's approach to pragmatism.

As essentially a form of means–ends rationality, pragmatism, like other philosophies of the time, left out any dimension of what *can* be.

Note that at the time, a transformed social order seemed unattainable. With its emphasis on consequences, pragmatism subordinated reason to efficiency. Once efficiency emerged as the ordinary criterion of reason, it became a tool of domination rather than an element of freedom. It sought to control and dominate nature, both inner and outer. According to Horkheimer, whatever the political propensities of individual pragmatists, pragmatism reflected and represented a change in the social function of philosophy. Philosophy had long been associated with its critical role – that is, it asked us to examine the prevalent forms of understanding and social organization in light of other possibilities. However, if reason was now simply an instrument for adapting to the demands of the existing irrational state of affairs, then the critical element in thought, the ability to think beyond the horizons of the existing social order, was lost. In *Eclipse of Reason* Horkheimer viewed this situation in terms of the transition from the objective reason at the heart of ancient philosophical thought to the subjective reason that characterized the modern understanding. Objective reason always looked to a source of reason and truth that was not confined to individual minds but existed in nature. As such it was concerned with the proper ends of human beings. By contrast, subjective reason was restricted to the coordination of means and ends. If ends were considered at all, this was solely in relation to the demands of self-preservation. Something was good if and only if it preserved and enhanced the self. Of course, Horkheimer did not simply advocate a return to objective reason, or even a complete rejection of subjective reason; rather, he saw the need for something that mediated between the two.

Horkheimer never fully formulated this perspective. But he did draw on the notion of mimesis that Adorno also used. Here mimesis was akin to a process of imitation or adaption that creates similarities. It represented a non-dominating relationship to the Other that in the view of Horkheimer and Adorno had been suppressed by instrumental rationality. It was, according to Horkheimer, a capacity that was always available to humans, even though there were no current (in their view) possibilities for change.

While the notion of a mimetic non-dominating relation to the Other has some promise, it never rose above the level of a theoretical intuition; it was never developed into an explicit theory. Habermas's notion of communicative reason amounts to a well-formulated attempt to redeem this intuition, although it takes a direction that Horkheimer and Adorno might not have followed and is not without its own problems and limitations.

The Limits of the Early Frankfurt School's Notion of Critique

For Horkheimer, as for most critical theorists, the values used to assess contemporary society were not timeless, nor were they to be found in an ideal realm of the kind the neo-Kantians of his time postulated. Rather, critique was immanent: it took the values of society, such as freedom and happiness, and measured them against the social reality in which they were embedded. Horkheimer contrasted the bourgeois idea of inner freedom and self-determination with the reality that most individuals had little freedom to carry out plans and determine their own lives. They lived in misery rather than happiness. Critical theories could use the resources of existing social science in an interdisciplinary fashion to make diagnoses of the conflicts in society.

While Horkheimer developed many of the basic features of critical theory, his version does suffer from the employment of a productivist framework. To be sure, Horkheimer used this framework to lay out a non-dogmatic account that incorporated psychological and sociological elements, and he took a very broad view of materialism. The latter emphasizes the material element of values and culture. Nonetheless he still saw the social whole as largely structured by the mode of production of a society. While we do not reject the importance of economic elements in a critical theory – indeed, a key theme for us is the extent to which the economic element has been insufficiently emphasized in dominant contemporary versions of critical theory – a theory of society cannot rest simply on a productivist basis. It is not possible to deduce the forms of mutual recognition and mutual understanding from a productivist framework alone.

As is well known, Hegel employed a metaphysical notion of truth to fuse theory and practice. Truth was not simply epistemological or equated with certainty or adequate description. The true was what was "really real," the instantiation of the Idea in the world. This notion of truth was inherently normative. Only when freedom and justice were realties could truth come into its own: "The idea is what is true in and for itself, the absolute unity of concept and object."[13]

Hegel's emphatic notion of truth as the "really real" formed the backdrop for later attempts to connect theory and practice. But neither Marx nor, later, the Frankfurt School accepted Hegel's idealist solution, which seemed to require the postulate of a transcendental subjectivity. Yet the Frankfurt School theorists were hesitant to entirely abandon his emphatic concept of reconciliation.

Horkheimer retained the idea that emancipatory social movements – in his case, the workers' movement – could bring about justice and freedom. But these achievements could never be perfect or final. The emphatic notion of truth and Hegel's idealism were true only in a negative way.[14] As noted above, Horkheimer's early work and indeed that of the first generation of critical theorists were strongly influenced by classical Marxism, and especially the work of Georg Lukács.

Among the original members of the Frankfurt School, Adorno was more definitive in challenging this model. But while he rejected the Hegelian conception of the absolute, he nonetheless remained committed to the emphatic notion of truth as that which can never be reconciled: "After everything, the only responsible philosophy is one that no longer imagines it had the Absolute at its command; indeed philosophy must forbid the thought of it in order not to betray that thought, and at the same time must not bargain away anything of the emphatic notion of truth. This contradiction is philosophy's element. It defines philosophy as negative."[15]

Adorno's notion came to the fore when, in the wake of the failure of the workers' movement to achieve social emancipation in the face of fascism, critical theorists became sceptical of emancipatory movements as such. For them, the basis for a rational reconstruction of society had lost its immanent foundations. The radical injustice of a society that was instrumentally regulated could only be criticized from without. In a totally administered society the hopes for freedom, justice, and happiness could be kept alive only from the perspective of reconciliation, however negatively conceived.

Yet this strategy proved difficult to maintain for critical theory. As Albrecht Wellmer argues with respect to Adorno's position, "[i]n a strict sense no merely human practice could ever reduce the unbridgeable gap that separates the historical world from the condition of salvation."[16] In Adorno's work the link between a critical diagnosis of society and social action, between theory and practice, is severed.

Axel Honneth has tried to rescue the intuition supporting the dialectic of enlightenment by rethinking the critical impulse behind the critique of instrumental reason.[17] He contends that Adorno's and Horkheimer's formulations can be reclaimed by way of a world-disclosing critique. *The* dialectic of enlightenment should be read as a proposal to take up a different way of viewing the world in which new possibilities for change are disclosed. Since from the interpretive standpoint we know the world as mediated though language, our sense of the world also structures the way we understand potentials and possibilities. In a manner reminiscent of Ernesto Laclau and Chantal Mouffe, Honneth stresses the power of disclosure to structure reality. This position is clearly tied to his recent attempt to recast reification as the forgetting of an initial, precognitive, affective relation of recognition to the Other.[18]

While Honneth's suggestion is interesting, it suffers from two serious difficulties. In the first place, it is not entirely faithful to the intuitions of Adorno and Horkheimer. The idea that any form of world disclosure could capture an adequate relation between theory and reality does not seem to coincide with the view of the later Adorno that language itself is inadequate to the emphatic idea of truth.

In the second place, his suggestion recapitulates the same problems that plagued the analysis in *Dialectic of Enlightenment*, but now on the level of linguistic disclosure. World disclosure is detached from everyday communication. What would make participants accept or gain insight from the world that the theorist would propose? If the world-understanding of subjects in late capitalism is restricted, then a new world-forming proposal has no basis for actualization or even acceptance. We believe that a more feasible solution would start not from the world-forming power of language but rather from the ordinary understanding of subjects in the lifeworld, one that could give rise to the synthetic power of acting in concert.

Our position here, with its focus on the competences of subjects as participants in their lifeworld and their capacity to develop forms of power tied to acting in concert, suggests that the normative dimension of communicative reason and the possibilities for developmental democracy are – and must be – inherently linked. To this connection, and what it means for both critical and democratic theory, we now turn.

From Developmentalism to Communicative Action

To realize the potential of the developmental account of democratic theory that we elaborated in the first chapter, we have to supplement a developmental approach with a communicative one. Because social reality is constructed intersubjectively and dialogically, we only understand one another through processes of acting in common. To be sure, the developmental account also shares the notion that human nature is essentially social and requires the backdrop of a world shared with others. The developmental theorist rejects the atomism of the liberal theory of Hobbes and others and grasps that the realization of human powers, plans, and purposes requires a shared social world. The idea that an individual can be grasped prior to society, whether logically or ontologically, is an illusion. In contrast, developmental and communicative theorists rely on Aristotelian and Hegelian notions of the social character of human action. More than neo-Aristotelians, however, communicative theorists are more closely connected to the Hegelian notion of the social development of reason.

In this latter respect, developmental theories – at least those that take their bearings from Aristotle and neo-Aristotelian thinking – do not fully articulate a complete version of the dialogical character of human action. For contemporary neo-Aristotelians, reason is not so much a social relation that involves interaction as it is a process that in the first instance takes place behind the backs of individuals. For example, Ronald Beiner in *What's the Matter with Liberalism* views social life as a set of dispensations that issue in an ethos that exists prior to the individual.[19] If we take the use of the term dispensation seriously, social life is subject to basic rules that are revealed to individuals. In religion, of course, this has the broader meaning of laws and promises revealed by a god who relates to humanity in certain way in a certain era. Dispensation here refers to a forming or granting of power from without; the role of individuals in dialogue is subordinated to the disclosing power.

In opposition to the neo-Aristotelian notions of community, in which the communal formulations are prior to the individual, a modernist notion of development that draws its inspiration from Hegel and German idealism sees the individual as a participant in social processes, within which along with others the individual determines her life through acting in common with others. Such a view anticipates notions of intersubjectivity without elaborating all of its aspects. Developmental theorists such as C.B. Macpherson look at the individual as an exerter of powers. Individuals are capable both of self-determination – that is, of forming their own life plans and purposes – and of self-realization whereby these goals are achieved through exercise of their own capacities. In opposition to the world-disclosing force of a dispensation or an ethos that is in some way beyond individual creation, this second modern strain of developmentalism sees human action as a form of social construction, which comes about through the participation of individuals in the social world.[20] As noted above, these capacities are social; they only manifest themselves in the world we share with others. The formation of individuals capable of determining and realizing their own plans can only take place in the social world. Developmental theories are less successful in dealing with the ways in which individuals are linked together in the social world and why their plans are connected. Some formulations have simply assumed that in a non-coercive society the self-realization of individual plans and goals would be relatively unproblematic. To be sure, we need not think there is an automatic harmony (although he was often criticized for this, neither did Macpherson). However, once we shift focus to the medium in which coordination, linkage, and socialization take place we encounter a new set of problems. These involve the normative nature of social action.

Social action takes place in a medium of communicative action in which individuals are linked through mutual understanding. This suggests that we coordinate our actions by means of a dialogical process. Some thinkers, such as John Stuart Mill, posit a dialogical conception of reason in which debate and discussion figure centrally, and combine this with a conception of self-realization without necessarily presenting self-formation as a communicative process. Mill did not extend the dialogical notion, which he used philosophically, into a medium of social action. He agreed with the criticism of the atomism of liberal theories of natural rights (as did Marx), whereas the more Hegelian T.H. Green saw value in rights as social and based on the moral personality. This relation of rights to the moral personality was rooted in the ability of individuals as active subjects to take up the common good and make it their own. Here rights, which were reciprocally recognized by others, were anchored in a practically oriented conception of the powers of humans.[21] With his Hegelian background, John Dewey also came close to finding the link between the two conceptions with his understanding of the communicative basis of everyday life. For Dewey, social life was transactional or interactional. He saw processes of communication and education as central to self-formation and development.[22]

Dewey's instrumentalism, however, was a limiting factor in his understanding of the social interactive perspective he developed. Instrumentalism cannot fully account for how interaction between participants is connected by understanding and thus institutes both reason and social order. Dewey's conception is more like a theory of strategic action oriented to accomplishment than it is of understanding. More to the point is G.H. Mead's theory of the self. Also drawing on a Hegelian background, Mead integrates the perspectives of mutual understanding that are not clarified in Dewey's instrumentalism. For him both action and understanding seem to have a dialogical structure. Not just interchange but the reciprocal constitution of the self and other is understood as coming into being though consensual forms of action. These consensual forms of social action and rationality are the modality of social life.

The idea that society is constituted through the medium of communicative action in which we are bound by forms of mutual accountability and mutual understanding suggests a different approach to the concept of reason. As it was formulated by Jürgen Habermas, communicative reason is closely linked to practical social action. It is less the quest for a truth outside of or beyond human action than for a truth embedded in the social world.

For Habermas, and we agree, the broadest conception of rationality is found in the notion of accountability. When asked, we can give an account of our actions to others. This form of rationality is reflexive. It requires an awareness on the participant's part of her own relation to herself and others. This takes place in a context of a lifeworld shared with others. However, communicative reason refers specifically to those forms of reason that are concerned with the creation and renewal of a common intersubjective horizon of action. It is characterized by the binding force that comes about through agreement. Communicative reason, like communicative action, is evident when we act with someone to reach an understanding about something in the world. This form of rationality is centred not on accomplishing things in the world but on making a common world in which we act together. It is not just agreement about something; rather, it is part of the constitution and renewal of the lifeworld. It forms the horizon within which we act. Seen in this way, communicative rationality is closely connected to self and social formation. We create and renew who we are as individuals, but also the social identity we share with others within this horizon of action. This is the horizon within which actions for which we can be held accountable take place. Here communicative power is the ability that participants acting in common possess to create these forms of common understanding.

It has become commonplace to view Habermas's approach to rationality as essentially Kantian. This interpretation, however, is based mainly on a reading of his tendency to endorse a theory of justice that does in part have its roots in Kant. Critics see this as the rehabilitation of the notion of the transcendental subject who stands outside of social life and makes universal judgments. The idea that there can be universal judgments does not necessarily rest on the assumptions of a disembodied subject, nor does a communicative theory have to assume a transcendental subject. We want to emphasize those elements of communicative theory that are more Hegelian in inspiration. The theory of communicative action that Habermas develops, and his theory of communicative reason, both begin from the participant's perspective. He notes: "There is no pure reason that might don linguistic clothing only in the second place. Reason is by its very nature incarnated in contexts of communicative action and in structures of the lifeworld."[23]

Habermas's communicative approach to reason is an interpretive one. It also draws from Hegel, contemporary hermeneutics, and other sources to create a theory of consensual social action. Our aim here is not so much to provide a complete history of these ideas and their development in Habermas's corpus – this has been done elsewhere – nor is it to provide a theory that is completely faithful to his formulation; rather, it is to use his insights combined with others to outline a conception of communicative reason that is compatible with the project of a renewed democratic theory. In elaborating some elements of this project, we will see, however, that communicative reason is not just a theory of knowledge but a moral/political and normative theory as well.

Interpretation and Critique

Charles Taylor's approach can provide a first link in the connection of the developmental and interpretive approaches. Taylor sees humans as self-interpreting individuals, as language animals who inhabit a linguistic dimension. We make sense of our world and our place in it – who we are and what we want to be.[24] This interpretive element in human activity links Taylor's account to the communicative model. We conduct our social life and carry out our individual aims through the medium of language, that is, through interpretation. We only have access to our world through interpretation. We understand both our own life and the lives of others through our reflexive understanding of self and other. Mental states are not just an individual possession. They are formed in interaction. Taylor, however, also seems concerned with identity because of its role in developmental processes. We can form and realize plans and develop our own identity. This way of looking at the self-interpretation of subjects via communicative action also entails a broader conception of self-determination. We are not simply choosers who decide among alternatives through attempts to satisfy preferences; our plans of action and choices take place against a backdrop defined by the quest for an understanding of who we are and who we want to be. This essentially ethical conception of self-determination suggests that communicative reason in practice requires a practical moral sensibility as the basis of our sense of knowing the world.

Taylor's conception indicates that we look at these processes of interpretation from the participant's perspective. Social actors are situated as engaged participants in the social world. They relate to others and to the natural world through a series of involvements and commitments. We only have access to the world through the perspective of a participant, never from the perspective of an outsider or observer. We only come to understand the world through our involvements in it and our normative orientation towards it.

Critical theories have always recognized this aspect of knowledge. In formulating his now classic distinction between traditional and critical theory, Max Horkheimer followed Marx in his analysis of material life processes. As we have already noted, the knowledge of the theorist is part of the lifeworld of participants and does not presuppose the "Cartesian" position of pure mind or outside observer. Facts are always embedded in these material life processes. Social actors as well as theorists are embedded as participants in these life processes. Thus the reflective knowledge developed by critical theory is meant to be practically effective.

Contemporary critical theory shares the orientation to the standpoint of a participant who has an equal standing with other members of society. Horkheimer argued that while it takes society as its object, critical theory changes the relation of the "subject" to the "object" of inquiry. Critical theory maintains a reflexive relation to the social subjects who are at the same time the objects of the theory. Here Horkheimer is seeking to overcome the dualities of the social sciences of his time that seek an "objective" perspective and that separate the supposedly detached theorist from the citizen. For critical theory the social inquirer is both analyst and member of society. The aim of theory is not to achieve systematic purity but to elucidate the social process in its interconnections and developmental tendencies. Like subjects who engage in practical activity, theory seeks a better life. It is "not just a research hypothesis which shows its value in the ongoing business of men; it is an essential element in the historical effort to create a world which satisfies the needs and powers of men."[25] Thus critical theory is not concerned with the accumulation of knowledge by itself, but seeks to promote freedom from unnecessary restraint and thereby empower individuals to freely pursue self-development.

In order to place Horkheimer's insights in a contemporary context we have to look more carefully at the way communicative action informs the interpretive elements of the participant's perspective discussed above. A critical theory must begin from the participant's perspective. Here social action is in the beginning practical. We can only come to know the world of ourselves and others by participating in it. We cannot know this world objectively, so to speak, from the outside; we can only do so through these involvements and commitments. From the participant's perspective we are always concerned with the world. Individuals interact with one another through processes of mutual understanding and structures of mutual recognition. These are not theoretical accomplishments; they are *practical*. But they are not simply forms of knowing, they are also forms of acting. We constitute ourselves through processes of mutual understanding and at the same time regulate our actions.

Communicative reason, then, does not begin from the permanent structures of an individual mind, as Kant might have said, but builds from the ground up. Our conceptions of the world are sedimented in a series of background understandings upon which we draw to orient our action. These understandings contain not just shared notions of truth or validity but also shared expectations about how we conduct our lives together. There is no hard and fast boundary between theoretical and practical reason; rather, theoretical reason is an element of *practical* reason. Forms of reason, both theoretical and practical, interconnect in the social world. The insights of the social and political sciences become embedded in everyday understanding and shape our practical expectations.

The mundane actions of individuals in the lifeworld demonstrate that our everyday actions are not detached from social solidarities and identifications. We are members of groups to which we have varying degrees of attachment and commitment. We share common sentiments and sensibilities with which we identify with others. It would be a mistake, however, to see these primarily as unreflective forms of what Max Weber called traditional social action. Traditional social action is largely unreflective – we are, for example, a member of a nation or a religion because we have always been so – whereas in modern societies even our identifications have become reflexive. They depend upon reasons and accounts. Modern subjectivity incorporates elements of self-criticism. We cannot simply identify with our country, right or wrong; we can only do so on the condition that our fellow countrymen are doing the right thing. We can become alienated from our families, our social institutions, or our nation while maintaining a certain attachment to them, or we may become so alienated that our attachments are broken and sentiments are no longer shared.

The anchoring of communicative reason in the participant's perspective also has a bearing on the relation between experts and citizens. Experts do not take a position that is above and outside the ordinary understanding of citizens. Rather, their understanding is on the same level as that of the participant. Experts may have more knowledge or a level of skill in a specific area, but their knowledge is not separate from that of the participants. Claims of expertise must be demonstrated through discussion.

The above considerations, then, concern in different ways the question of what a reflexive reconsideration of our beliefs and their legitimacy requires. In one sense, discourse or deliberation is a special form of social action. While there is already a reflexive element to all social action that makes deliberation possible, discourse – be it formal or informal in structure – requires a certain withdrawal from action. To examine our own commitments, we have to step back from them to a certain extent and take a reflexive approach. We may, as Habermas once said, suspend our immediate connection with action. Here, however, we only suspend specific commitments, beliefs, identities, norms, or sentiments and make them thematic, so to speak, in order to engage in a more elaborate form of (social) self-reflection. We do not, however, suspend our role as committed beings who depend on interpretive access to the social world. This is the basic flaw in the first iteration of John Rawls's theory of justice. We can never discover the basic features of human needs or goods from the standpoint of a disinterested observer who stands outside the fray. We can only do so from the standpoint of a reflective participant for whom problematic elements of the social world have become thematic.

For a theory of communicative action, knowledge has a discursive or dialogical character. This component, however, does not need to be interpreted as a purely formal or procedural one, although procedure can play a role. All social action is constituted though mutual accountability. We regulate our actions through being accountable to others and by renewing the expectations that others have of our actions. Of course, accountability entails the ongoing accomplishment of a social order that we constantly reproduce and renew through our actions. However, we do not simply reproduce that social order in a narrow or conforming manner. We renew our social world through interaction, and thus we can change it by challenging our accepted understandings. Dissonant experiences and unsettling accounts are always possible and can cause us collectively or singularly to create new accounts of action and create new norms and expectations for action.

Here the notions of accountability and expectations are linked. When called upon we can give an account of our actions to others, explaining why we took a certain course of action or made a certain judgment. Our implicit understanding can be made explicit. However, sometimes these accounts are not acceptable to us or to others. Our experiences may even contradict our own understandings. Things do not go as we expected, or people fail to act in the ways we anticipated. This can go all the way from someone betraying us in an interaction to a social or political choice we see as risky or wrong-headed. What is important to remember in these processes is that while there can be challenges to the nature of the world, to what things are and how they work in the world we have in common, there can also be challenges to our own identity – who we are and what we believe. In the most extreme cases, dissonant experiences can create a sense of phenomenological rupture akin to a natural or social disaster in which our expectations are shattered and our taken-for-granted reality is thrown into disarray. These crises in mutual accountability could under certain conditions bring about identity crises, for what we reproduce through interaction is not just the outside world but also our sense of ourselves. In these situations, we require processes of learning, repair, and reconstruction. We have to find new norms and beliefs and new kinds of mutual expectations to make sense of the situation we have encountered. Because our lifeworld is structured around these forms of accountability, what we learn or fail to learn in these situations takes a discursive form.

Our proposal here is that the interpretive and communicative approach to social theory developed through the conception of the participant's perspective is the best one for reconstructing the foundations of a critical theory. It links the practical character of action to a reflexive and critical understanding of the world.

As noted earlier, many contemporary critical theorists view Habermas's account of communicative reason as primarily a Kantian project, especially as it relates to ethics and his attempt to link his theory of justice to Kantian themes. Thomas McCarthy, for example, sees Habermas's theory as continuous with Kant's project: "Habermas' idea of a 'discourse ethics' can be viewed as a reconstruction of Kant's idea of practical reason in terms of communicative reason. Roughly speaking, it involves a procedural reformulation of the Categorical Imperative: rather than ascribing to others as valid those maxims I can will to be universal laws, I must submit them to others for purposes of discursively testing their claim to universal validity."[26]

At the same time, McCarthy in an extended comparison of Habermas and Rawls recognizes that in opposition to Rawls, Habermas develops his theory from the standpoint of the participant and not either the transcendental subject or the impersonal observer. In addition, Habermas considers elements of "public reason" to include many informal processes and public spheres that are not in the strict sense formal.

Looked at from the standpoint we develop in this work, these elements of the participant's perspective refer to the ongoing processes of maintaining, renewing, and transforming social life in the process of acting. This conception of the social world seems to us more like that of Hegel and later German idealism, which stressed the historical character of understanding. This way of reading the lifeworld is certainly not alien to Habermas, who at times interprets his own corpus through a Hegelian lens. For example, in his essay "Morality and Ethical Life,"[27] Habermas sees the complementarity of an ethic of care and a Kantian theory of justice; and in a later essay, "From Kant to

Hegel and Back Again,"[28] Habermas stresses the Hegelian elements in his work.

The major problem in approaching Habermas's theory is the status of what he calls the moral point of view. He argues that theories of justice must remain neutral about theories of the good. When we deliberate about these questions, he argues, we must not and cannot consider any particular conception of the good. However, is this strict separation of the good and the right consistent with the other considerations that derive from the participant's perspective?

The essay on morality and ethical life offers one of Habermas's most sustained efforts to find the linkage between the lifeworld and morality. Here he sees participants in the lifeworld as ethically connected through concern and care. Because we are dependent on one another and vulnerable to harm, we are concerned not just about our own life but the lives of others. We only develop as individuals through socialization, yet every act of individuation through socialization makes our own identity more densely interwoven in social networks. A complex identity while strong in one sense is also dependent on a series of social – we might even say developmental – conditions.

While an ethic of care stresses the vulnerability involved in ethical life, Habermas sees the element of morality as based in the protection of individuality. It elevates respect for the integrity of personhood to a central place. Both identity and self-determination need moral consideration and protection.

Habermas believes that Hegel's thought is central here because his notion of *Sittlichkeit* is not simply a return to an Aristotelian position, it is a modernist notion of situated moral actors. In Habermas's view Hegel rejects the one-sidedness of both individualist notions, which issue in an abstract universalism, and what he sees as the concrete particularism of the Aristotelian tradition. The element of care and concern for others is as universal feature of ethical life as the rights and duties that protect the integrity of subjects. Hegel's notion of intersubjectivity as developed in his early writings is rooted not in a particular ethos but in the general characteristics of all social action. For Hegel, then, we cannot neglect either duty or care.

Habermas thinks, however, that some of Hegel's criticisms of Kant's formalism either are misguided or do not apply to a discourse ethic based in the situation of participants in the lifeworld.[29] A communicative theory relies neither on the individual subject engaged in isolated self-reflection nor on Kant's conception of the moral will. The major problem in Habermas's reformulation is the idea that we can separate in a strict sense the right and the good, agent-neutral and agent-relative considerations, in our treatment of moral theory, and that we can therefore be noncommittal with respect to a theory of the good. Can we discount all conceptions of the good life when considering questions of justice while still maintaining our character as situated participants?

Habermas sees the development of knowledge in a post-metaphysical framework as consistent with a reading of Hegel that is largely what he calls "deflationary." When confronted with the conflicting perspectives of participants we are faced not simply with differing interests but also with differing understanding of how things are. What Hegel sees as the "struggle for recognition" in his Jena work and in the master–slave dialectic can be understood as steps in the formation of a wider intersubjectivity and a more comprehensive standpoint. He sees this as the transition from consciousness to self-consciousness – that is, to our place in a world shared by others. Self-consciousness requires that we differentiate our lives from those of others with whom we share a common world and that we find our own identity. When faced with conflicting perspectives we must find a third perspective – a mediation, if you will – in which we can gain a richer understanding of the situation and greater cognitive resources, on pain of falling into violent conflict. Put in more contemporary terms, we seek a higher-level intersubjectivity. There are no objective or final perspectives available to participants, simply better or more comprehensive ones.

We could view Habermas's attempt to formulate a revised moral point of view as an attempt to follow this process and to propose that conflicts over the various forms of the good life can only be resolved within a higher-level moral intersubjectivity. Whether this formulation can fully resolve the problems to which his position gives rise is a question we will take up in later chapters.

Critical Inquiry and the Participant's Perspective

Inquirers and participants, as we noted, are on the same level. The inquirer has access to the social world of others only in her role as a fellow participant in that world. The participant's perspective is also a performative one. We have a mental representation of the world, and moreover, we manifest our understanding through forms of interaction that have binding force. For example, a promise is not just a belief; it is performed in the act of making it. This performance is also reflective. We are knowledgeable agents who know what we do while doing it.

The inquirer is also a participant, one whose own analyses are not detached from contexts of actions. To understand the meanings that others give to their actions, she must be able to evaluate those actions.

This can mean the ability to reconstruct the contexts of actions or the background conditions under which they make sense, as well as the validity of those actions. To understand them the inquirer must be able to evaluate them. This process is similar to the one that characterizes the stance of ordinary participants in interaction. When we interact with others, we assume that we share a common world in which those others are being sincere and telling the truth about their beliefs and norms. When their actions do not make sense, we ask them to account for their actions, to show why they think what they say is true or why their norms are valid. For example, the inquirer cannot understand the participant's judgment that authority is legitimate without ascertaining whether the participant believes this for good reasons or whether she is merely accepting that legitimacy out of habit and conformity – or is adopting an ironic and therefore critical stance toward authority. The participant may also accept something for the wrong reasons or misunderstand some of the practices she is participating in, or perhaps understand them in a non-standard way. Otherwise the inquirer cannot really make sense of the lifeworld he is examining. This capacity is identical to that of the participant, who can judge the validity and sincerity of other participants through interaction and discussion. Understanding others means being able to grasp the stance they take towards the world.

A communicative theory of reason, then, sees reason as an elaboration of the everyday competencies involved in processes of mutual accountability. It thematizes and refines the analysis of the features of reflection that we employ in such accountability. It does not, then, seek a source of reason that transcends our own standpoint. Reason is internal to understanding. Discourses in which we reflect on our own understanding can never be completely detached from our involved and engaged lifeworld activity. We can if we choose participate in an informal dialogue, or even a formal discussion of these beliefs and norms. Embedded in our practical activity are those senses of what is true or right that we use to orient our actions. These are practically oriented evaluations that both make sense of our lives and allow us to carry out our activities in common. However, participants can also criticize and transcend contexts of action and create new norms or forms of understanding.

The formal characteristics of communicative reason are derived in important respects from the features of the modernist notion of self-determination that we have already discussed. We can assume that subjects who take up the world are capable of independent evaluation of standards of truth and validity and can make their own assessments. Of course, these assessments are never unbounded or pure – reason is both pure and impure at the same time – and we can never strip reason of all external impediments. Nor is it possible to remove reason from our interests and commitments, for we only know the world though our involvement in it. This said, the notion of self-determination refers to the capacity of situated actors to take up the world through their own understanding and make it their own, to accept it or transform it, and to forge their own identities and plans within that world. This ethical understanding of reason and discourse can help us understand the more formal elements of communicative rationality.

For a subject to be self-determining, her judgments have to be carried out under conditions that enhance or at least exhibit freedom in the processes of reflection. Deliberations cannot be coerced or subject to undue pressure. These conditions hold for all participants, who must be treated equally and have an equal opportunity to contribute to discussion. The conditions represent formalizations of the intuition that a legitimate agreement should result from a fair process in which the freedom to consent is guaranteed.

Of course, these conditions rarely apply perfectly, although they can be approximated in formal debates. A bigger problem comes into play when we consider the actual abilities of some individuals to engage in discussion. Thus, in addition to the conditions of self-determination, we also need to stipulate conditions of self-realization. There also needs to be consideration of the conditions under which deliberations take place. These might include material conditions, or an educational setting. They are not meant to exclude participants from discussion but to ensure they have the resources to participate equally. This does raise questions concerning the fairness of large-scale deliberations on social and political issues: Would a political decision be fair under conditions of gross inequality, severe educational stratification, or material need?

At times Habermas seems to think that large-scale deliberative processes such as a democratically elected parliament or congress come close to his conception of fair deliberations. In some cases, they may do this. But if we look, for example, at the United States, with its gerrymandered electoral districts, closed parties, voter suppression, and "dark money" financing of political campaigns, it is difficult to see how these bodies reflect communicative freedom. A good deal of fundamental political and social reform would be required to make the United States and similar jurisdictions effective locations for the exercise of popular sovereignty or ideal deliberative processes.

Still, we think the basic intuition behind communicative rationality has force. We can only understand truth and validity as tied to communicative processes in which subjects come to agreement about something in the world.

The social inquirer too must engage in this evaluation in order to understand the groups she is studying. Whether as a member of a society examining a set of practices or a virtual participant in that society, the inquirer who seeks social scientific understanding cannot avoid evaluation. Like the participant, the inquirer can only understand others when she can ask questions about the misunderstanding those individuals have.

Since interpreters are on the same level as participants, inquiry is better seen as a dialogue between the two rather than as a form of objective knowledge. The inquirer must evaluate the practices of members of a society; by the same token, those participants have the capacity to evaluate inquirers. For the critical theorist this yields a notion of mutual critique, which we discuss below.

Social critique grows out of the ordinary capacities of individuals and inquirers. Everyday action is itself reflexive. We are aware of what we are doing in the course of doing it. Because interaction is intersubjective, we can only understand our own actions in the context of our reflexive understanding of self and other. We are reflexively aware of how our meaningful actions and statements are grasped by others. As a result, we carry out these actions with what Anthony Giddens calls forms of reflexive monitoring.

Social scientific theories are themselves practical. They "constitute moral interventions in the social life whose conditions they seek to clarify."[30] This insight takes two different directions. First, since the social researcher is always a participant who takes a performative attitude towards communication, the results of inquiry have a practical dimension that affects not only the knowledge of the researcher but also her understanding of herself and her world. Second, the results of research are taken up into the lifeworlds of participants and become part of their everyday knowledge, thus changing their understanding of themselves. In both cases, participants have a reflexive relation to forms of knowledge. They are aware of what they do while doing it and engage in ongoing evaluation of their plans and projects and the norms they use to evaluate them.

The power of social critique grows out of this reflexive capacity, which is inherent in ordinary interaction. When dissonant experiences upset our normal expectations, we can reflect on these dissonances. We need to make sense of them in order to restore our common sense of what is going on and to regain or even reconsider who we are. Of course, not all situations of dissonance result in social critique. Some may be easily resolved or be attributed to personal failures, natural forces beyond our control, or even simple misunderstanding. Only when we interpret our troubles as social problems do we reflect on whether social processes are the basis of the dissonances we experience personally. This reflection, however, takes place *within* the participant's perspective, not outside of it. To the extent that the critic seeks to make sense of these social problems, she is engaged in a cooperative process with participants who themselves need to make sense of their troubles. For instance, when the critic and the participant seek to understand these problems by examining their history, they attempt to grasp those common understandings and identities that have arisen. Histories are always internal to the understanding of the participants. Participants then formulate diagnoses that may identify structural problems or question institutional norms and practices. But these structural and institutional factors, too, require participants' perspectives. Such perspectives are reflexive, however, in that they require us not just to re-examine our understanding of social issues but to re-evaluate them and seek alternatives. Thus, to the extent that theorists engage in social critique they offer interpretations that participants must accept as valid, and these too are subject to criticism. They have no objective validity separate from these processes of mutual understanding. In fact, most social critique is an ongoing dialogue between the insights and experience of participants and those of inquirers.

Interpretation and Deliberative Democracy

Communicative and interpretive conceptions of reason and action have been important factors in the rise of what has been called deliberative democracy. Many commentators have seen Habermas's theory of communication as the basis for deliberative democratic thinking. Deliberative or discursive democracy stresses the ways in which processes of accountability are central to democratic decision-making. Theories of deliberative democracy vary widely, however, in their purpose and structure as well as in their use of notions of deliberation. Deliberation is often seen as justifying liberal democracy and majority rule. In one frequently cited formulation by Amy Gutman and Dennis Thompson, deliberative democracy is defined as reason-giving, as public and accessible to all, and as aimed at producing a result that is binding on all and that is dynamic – that is, that recognizes that deliberation is an ongoing process. It can succeed or fail in any circumstance and be reopened for future consideration.[31] In their own words, "combining these four characteristics, we can define deliberative democracy as a form of government in which free and equal citizens (and their representatives), justify decisions in a process in which they give one another reasons that are mutually acceptable and generally accessible, with the aim of reaching conclusions that are binding in the present on all citizens but open to challenge in the future."[32]

Seen in this way, deliberative democracy is compatible with notions of the participant's perspective. It draws upon the communicative power of participants to come to an agreement over matters of common concern. But it adds formal constraints to deliberations – constraints that are meant to ensure a fair procedure. We should, however, pay attention as well to the more informal procedures of everyday deliberation.

Some versions of democratic theory are more limited than the one provided by Gutman and Thompson. These tend to focus almost exclusively on outcomes. For example, in a somewhat different concept of deliberation, James Johnson and Jack Knight focus solely on outcomes as a measure of democracy. They view consensus from an external perspective, as a result, not a process.[33] From this primarily instrumentalist position, democracy is largely useful for what it does and not for its formative powers. Deliberative democrats who take this perspective argue that democratic deliberation could produce the best result by motivating participants to change their preferences through discussion and in the process create the most rational outcome.

An internal approach to democratic theory, however, would stress the self-formative power of democracy. In the tradition going back to Aristotle, participation in politics is central to human flourishing. Participation fosters processes of self-formation that are important for the development and exercise of fundamental human capacities. It is a central element of self-determination. It is not just an effect – it is crucial to the kind of person we want to be. To the extent that discourse theory takes up the demands of communicative reason as laid out by Habermas, it must draw largely on this second understanding. This has implications for a theory of deliberative democracy that we will take up in later chapters.

Clearly, Habermas's version is focused less on outcomes than on ideas of popular sovereignty. The political sphere thus cannot be identified with a concatenation of interests or viewed as an instrument for an end that is strategically deployed but is itself a mode of communicative action. This will, as we note in later chapters, distinguish it from the agonistic view of politics as an intractable conflict or contestation.

But differing conceptions of the nature of the political sphere, the character of will-formation, and the role of interests raises the question of power and how it relates to communicative reason and action. In the next section of this chapter, we turn our attention to questions of power.

Rethinking Power: Some Discourse-Theoretical Considerations

Power is a central issue for social and political theory. Critical theorists analyse the conditions of domination, oppression, and disrespect that characterize contemporary society. They see their work as integral to any movements to change present-day society. Power, though, cannot be understood as an objective force that can be analysed independently of participants. Since the social world is one in which authority and influence are integral to social life, the theorist, like the participant, must evaluate these relations not just in terms of their impact, or as an external observer, but also in terms of their normative rightness and justifications. Critical theory seeks to identify those relations in which power limits the possibilities for freedom or can be used to develop greater freedom.

Critical theorists must also look at domination and oppression from the perspective of the social and intra-psychic processes that institute domination and make individuals prone to accept and even consent to it. Critical theories seek to show how domination works and how it maintains its hold over individuals. Most applications of power in advanced societies are subtle and often invisible. Domination is the smooth surface of a well-functioning social order. Because of its sub-tle yet pervasive nature, questions of power and domination are not straightforward. That is why they have become contested terrain in recent theory.

Classical liberal theories drawn from Thomas Hobbes and John Locke often have difficulties with questions of domination. They hold that individual interests and preferences are beyond doubt or challenge. Typically, they argue that critics who claim that we do not know our own (real) interests assume an objective and authoritarian standpoint.[34] However, this argument mistakes both the nature of the claim and the nature of self-understanding. It supposes first that subjects know their own interests and needs transparently and immediately. It implicitly employs a subject-centred notion of understanding in which inner nature is directly known by an individual consciousness. However, even self-understanding is interpretive. We do not understand our needs or interests immediately, but only through language and interaction. Thus, knowing ourselves, and even our innermost nature, requires self-interpretation. Needs require need interpretations. We have no choice but to use vocabulary and communicative resources that are current in our society and in the intersubjective context in which interpretation takes place. Even on a basic level we could, as Charles Taylor pointed out some time ago, misinterpret our own needs. It is possible to "second guess" an agent by pointing out internalized impediments or barriers to the articulation and pursuit of one's freely and rationally chosen purposes, and so foster conditions for self-development.[35] This problem is more complex when relations of power create not just impediments to interpretation but also internal limits to self-interpretive abilities. In the circumstances, processes of mutual accountability are restricted.

One influential interpretation of power views it as fundamentally purposive or strategic. When freedom is viewed in purposive terms as the unimpeded ability to pursue and achieve goals, then power is seen as the capacity to achieve goals or to prevent someone else (or some other group) from achieving *their* goals. Max Weber starts from a purposive view when he defines power (here in the sense of domination) as "the probability that one actor in a social relationship will be in a position to carry out his will despite resistance, regardless of the basis on which this probability rests."[36]

Weber's formulation is explicitly social. Power, for him, required the mutual influence of one person or group over another. This formulation has been applied and modified by others to explain how social power is employed to both facilitate and impede the will of social actors. Weber often saw politics in strategic terms, as the struggle for power and influence on the national or world stage; however, he also saw it as the creation of community through legitimacy. The latter feature was often lost in later discussions.

Viewed in this way, power is largely strategic. Strategic action can be distinguished from communicative action because in contrast to communication, it seeks to bring about an effect, not to bring about understanding. Strategic action can be defined as the notion that people can be influenced to act through various means – means that run the gamut from reward, to suggestion or persuasion, to fear and coercion and threat of punishment. Strategic action is always social action. It is concerned with the actions of others and by nature is not consensual. In strategic action we do not view the other person as a partner in a dialogical or consensual social world, but as one to whom we react. Although it draws on our capacities as meaningful social actors embedded in interaction, strategic action bypasses structures of mutual accountability. It is concerned less with the normative justification of courses of action than with success in achieving desired effects. Strategic power, then, is simply the power to influence the other to act without seeking agreement over the validity of an action.

Weber's notion of power was employed by American pluralists in the 1950s in the service of a behaviouralist methodology that was alien to Weber's interpretive methodological outlook. For Robert Dahl, power

is the capacity to get someone to do something they would not otherwise do.[37] In Dahl's methodological outlook it is an instrument to trigger certain forms of behaviour, and not simply a device for achieving
goals. This behaviouralist conception, which Dahl shares with David
Easton, Nelson Polsby, and others, interprets power using a physicalist
model of force. Power is conceived as a causal relation.[38] For Herbert
Simon the fact that A has power over B means that A's behaviour causes
B's behaviour. Of course, such approaches, which equate human action
with physics, have problems explaining intentionality. The behavioural
theorists viewed power as an empirical property that could be observed
in specific acts. They used behavioural theory ideologically to reinforce
a liberal view of democracy in which power was evenly distributed
throughout a well-functioning democratic system with civil rights and
freedoms for all. Thus, Dahl argued that power in the United States
was polycentric and essentially plural. The social power of groups is
transmitted through political parties and elections into the legislative
and administrative processes. According to pluralists, there were many
social groups that had a roughly equal ability to get their aims carried out despite differences in income and social status. Inequalities in
power were viewed as either non-existent or insignificant.

Methodological and political criticisms were merged in the behavioural critique. Dahl criticized power elite theorists such as C. Wright
Mills and community power theorists such as Floyd Hunter for their
use of subjective methods, such as reputational analysis and social
cohesion. Pluralists attempted to eliminate those elements of power
that involve domination or oppression by reducing power to empiri-
cally observable decisions.

Ironically, pluralist theory suffers from serious empirical and methodological problems of its own. It was hard to sustain the assertion of
a well-functioning pluralist democracy against the elite theorists, given
the apparent inequalities in economic and political power in the United
States.[39] William Domhoff's re-examination of Dahl's work on New
Haven showed flaws in Dahl's approach and yielded a picture closer to
that of the elite model.[40] For the purposes of this discussion, the methodological flaws are more important. The idea that power *over* others
or power *with* others can be grasped from the standpoint of a detached
or outside observer is problematic. Studying decisions already involves
the observer in the assessment of reasons employed in deliberation that
can only understood from a participant's perspective. It is never simply
the observation of an "outcome." Furthermore, the interpretive analyses of power resorted to by community theorists as well as by Mills
illustrates how power has a symbolic dimension. Besides being used

to manipulate others, it establishes unequal access to resources and can shape sensibilities; it also establishes unequal access to positions of authority that can affect decisions. Interpretative theory recognizes that we act with one another in relations of mutual accountability. Thus we must look at the reasons participants use power, or fail to use it, as well as the accounts they give, in order to understand how they interpret power. Power moves along a continuum from obedience to conformity to command to consent, even if such consent is coerced. It cannot simply be a physical motion or physical state.

It is in fact impossible to treat power simply as a physical relation. We only know if A employs power in getting B to carry out an action when we know what A intended and what B meant by her actions. If A wants B to consent to an order of an authority, she may try to convince, influence, persuade, or even coerce B to act. Each of these actions can be grasped only from the perspective of the participant who acts in the world. They cannot be observed in the same way one observes a physical process. If, for example, B conforms to a norm or carries out an action that has the desired result for A, it cannot be considered an example of power in the behaviouralist schema if B carries out the action or conforms to a norm for reasons other than A's influence. Once again, we cannot tell if A exerts power over B unless as participants we have access to the reasons for B's conforming actions. Even in limiting cases of force, whereby A issues a threat to B that B will be subject to sanctions or punishment if B does not obey, B's act will still be intentional.

Critics of behaviouralist theory such as Peter Bacharach and Morton Baratz identified this problem. They introduced a second dimension of power that did not cast it in the mould of observable effects of power. Instead they examined what they called non-decisions.[41] Power is exerted

when A participates in the making of decisions that affect B ... But power is also exercised when A devotes his energies to creating or reinforcing social and political values and institutional practices that limit the scope of the political process to public consideration of only those issues which are comparatively innocuous to A. To the extent that A succeeds in doing this, B is prevented, for all practical purposes, from bringing to the fore any issues that might in their resolution be seriously detrimental to A's set of preferences.[42]

In any decision-making process, not all issues may be raised for discussion. The control of agendas works inconspicuously to exclude topics and may involve rhetorical strategies to limit discussion. Perhaps one does not raise an issue during a deliberation if one knows that that issue will not be considered. Thus, those who hold positions of authority in a political or social organization may be able to set the agenda or block certain groups or ideas from the discussion by preventing questions from being raised so that decisions on some issues are never made. Failing to allow a question is a form of suppression or exclusion. Bacharach and Baratz borrow the term "mobilization of bias" from E.E. Schattschneider to indicate the ways organizations employ prejudgments that permit some issues to be articulated while others are left out.[43]

At times, however, Bachrach and Baratz accept the empiricist notion of "observation" as a suitable criterion for inquiry and simply want to include non-decisions as material for observations and subsequent empirical judgments that can be validated according to the canons of empirical social science. However, within the framework that Bachrach and Baratz adopt, non-decisions can be identified only where there are "observable" grievances that cannot be expressed in deliberation. This framework is unable to accommodate situations in which grievances cannot be articulated at all.[44] However, once we consider decision or deliberation, we are already on the terrain of interpretation. We understand the types of reasons given in deliberation or those elements of a situation where power is at stake that have been excluded from consideration. We are concerned with mutual accounts that can be given or that are not allowed. So to adequately conceptualize the problem we need a model of deliberation or discourse within an interpretive framework rather than the empirical language of observation.

The second face of power conceived as non-decision-making is encountered in works such as Matthew Crenson's *Unpolitics of Air Pollution* (1972)[45] and John Gaventa's *Power and Powerlessness* (1982).[46] Gaventa's work especially raised the question of power as domination: he examined why miners in an Appalachian town acquiesced to authority that seemed so obviously to run counter to their own interests. In Gaventa's view, powerlessness and acquiescence stem from the sense that nothing can be done, as well as from exclusion from public participation. In the latter case, knowledge of political processes is restricted, which generates ineffectiveness and leads to political apathy. The dominated tend to adopt the rationales found in the dominant discourse.

Gaventa comes close to taking an interpretive position when he cites the phenomenological sociology of Peter Berger and Thomas Luckmann as illustrating how meaning is socially produced – although, in his view, they do not take the effects of power into account. Like others, he views power in terms of its directly observable as well as indirectly accessible effects, when he should be looking at discursive accounts and self-formative processes.

We would do better to view formulations of the second dimension of power as positing ways that power works to limit the communicative processes though which we seek mutual understanding. For example, regarding the ability to set the agenda of public discussion, actors employ strategic means to limit access to discursive forms so that certain individuals either cannot participate or have limited opportunities to do so. Power is also exerted when certain kinds of accounts are excluded from discourses. This is the case, for example, when socialism is treated as if it were an unrealistic or morally repugnant alternative independently of any specific rationale. Public discussion can also be characterized by censorship or repression when certain topics or themes are excluded. In other cases, individuals lack access to resources, both material and symbolic, to formulate options or develop capacities.

In each of these cases, influence, persuasion, coercion, or even threats may be applied strategically to shape communicative practices. If powerful interests threaten to pull advertising from a media outlet, or take a stand in favour of global warming and thereby shape discussion, or hire their own researchers to generate fake studies and testimonies, these dampen the possibility of open communicative action. In such cases, those exercising power are more interested in creating an effect than in mounting a reasonable agreement. When the results of such activities become deeply embedded in the lifeworld, they can form the background assumptions of individual actors and thereby define the situations that individuals share, on the basis of which an issue can become a topic for discussion or action. In this way the "common sense" of a society comes to be determined.

Steven Lukes developed a third dimension of power to show how individuals or groups like Gaventa's Appalachian miners could act in opposition to their own interests.[47] Lukes at first saw his position in terms similar to those of Marx. Individuals had a false consciousness of their own interests, and with the proper theory they could come to identify their real interests. His notion of objective interests was rooted in a counterfactual intuition: What would B do under ideal democratic conditions if A did not interfere? When interpreted in its strongest terms, this seems to imply a theory of objective interests accessible to the theorist but not to the participant. Here he comes close to Georg Lukács's idea of an imputed consciousness. Yet these objective possibilities remain observational.

Lukes has subsequently amended this formulation to address structural power. He argues that individuals may be constrained by their institutional roles. Jeffery Isaac takes up this idea to suggest that power is not exerted when A constrains B, but rather when each takes their assigned institutional roles. The institution exerts causal power on the individual. In taking this position he employs Anthony Giddens's notion of structuration. As he notes, however, social institutions and their roles and rules exist only in and through individuals and their relations. They are reproduced though the activity of social subjects. While they may well contain constraints, they are still reproduced by the mutual accountability of participants. Thus, in order to identify these constraints we have to look at the reasons they employ in acting, the ways they interpret their own needs, and the attitude they assume towards the possibilities they find in the world. The problem with any notion of objective needs is not that individuals can misinterpret their own needs; rather, it is the notion that objective needs could be identified by means of a structural analysis alone. We need an interpretive social theory to construct these accounts. More specifically, the problem with the objectivist view that Lukes employs is not that we can be wrong about our needs, but that he operates with a decidedly limited view of our interpretive capacities. The analyst cannot judge needs from a purely external standpoint any more than the behaviouralist can. Thus we need to engage participants' reflexive capacity to understand pathologies as manifested in their own everyday experience. The discourse about needs is a dialogical one. Any need interpretations provided by the theorist must be accepted as valid by participants.

Power inevitably has a symbolic dimension. Pierre Bourdieu has contributed significantly to our understanding of the symbolic aspects of power. He begins from questions of unequal access to linguistic resources. In social settings, he notes, some can speak with more authority than others based on their positions and their mastery of language. He focuses on the symbolic power involved in the right to speak or the right to be recognized as authoritative in a contested field. He criticizes not only Saussurian linguistics but also theories such as those of Noam Chomsky and to some extent Jürgen Habermas, whom he sees as taking an impersonal approach to communicative competence.

Language is more than an instrument of communication or even knowledge. It is also an instrument of power. One seeks not only to be understood but also to be believed, obeyed, respected, distinguished, where the complete definition of competence involves the right to speak – that is, the right to the legitimate language, namely, the language of authority. Competence implies the power to impose recognition.[48]

Bourdieu sees society as a *habitus* or a lifeworld in which action in embedded. A *habitus* is a "system of durable, transposable dispositions, structured structures predisposed to function as structuring structures, that is, as principles which generate and organize practices and representations ... without presupposing a conscious aiming at ends or an express mastery of the operations."[49] The social lifeworld is a symbolic order that is not owned or controlled by anyone. It holds sensibilities and dispositions that are necessary in order to exert power or be subject to power. Power is exerted not just when A gets B to do something but when A can establish her claims as authoritative and B recognizes those claims as authoritative.

Much as with interpretive social theoretical conceptions of the lifeworld, Bourdieu thus sees social action as taking place against a background of shared understandings and practices. In a *habitus*, individuals learn certain dispositions and authority relationships that are the result either of socialization or of institutional structure. Bourdieu, following Aristotelian usage, calls this *doxa*, or common sense.

If you are in an educational setting, Bourdieu argues, you are in an authority relationship in which the teacher is recognized as the authority. Consequently, social institutions can support forms of power through a disposition that leads one to accept forms of authority. The region of the lifeworld that Bourdieu calls a field also requires forms of know-how that allow access and power. To participate in politics effectively, according to this view, one must know how to play the political game. In other cases, knowledge of rules and norms is a condition of being accepted as a legitimate participant.

Here Bourdieu's work bears comparison with Giddens's conception of structuration. Both theorists share a concern with the interdependence of agency and structure. Agents are in part constitutive of structure, which they reproduce through their own actions. Structures for Giddens involve a recursive form of action in which institutions create roles and rules that persist through time and across social space. They shape expectations for interaction that are relatively stable. In one sense these exist *above* individual actions. Even so, they can only be reproduced and renewed through the actions of individuals. We can look at the ways these rules and roles embed asymmetries and inequalities in resources and access, besides fostering forms of deference. More so than Bourdieu, however, Giddens stresses the reflexive quality of action and thus the possibility for transformation.

Bourdieu often views society more in strategic terms. He uses the model of a market exchange as the template for symbolic interaction. Here cultural capital with its overtones of Marxian analysis is meant to convey the way in which such capital functions as a resource that can be employed to establish power through facility with language, familiarity

with art and high culture, and educational credentials that define status. These resources are symbolic. Symbolic capital is a "credit"; it is the
power granted to those who have obtained sufficient recognition and
are in a position to impose recognition on others.[50]

Here symbolic power is the ability to employ meaning to asymmetrically establish a dominant relationship. Power is transformed primarily
from the threat of physical violence and harm to symbolic forms of domination. Inequalities are maintained and enforced though rankings and
hierarchies embedded in symbolic structure. These provide resources
in Bourdieu's terms that can be used to gain influence and authority.
In general, these are ways of establishing distinction and social status.
Symbolic power is primarily concerned with status and prestige.

The problem with Bourdieu's works stems from his separation of
understanding and authority, strategic and communicative power.
Authority becomes more a matter of staging, or a presentation of the
self in Erving Goffman's sense of the term. Authority is simply the
power to be taken seriously: one's claims trump those of others without regard to their truth. In Bourdieu's sense here, authority becomes
more like the power to influence others rather than a quest to reach an
agreement with them.

However, we can make a clear distinction between forms of authority that are legitimate or authorized and those that are illegitimate or
unjust. This is not simply about belief or power; it also has to do with
power's exclusive authority to be recognized. This involves understanding that has binding force for individuals and groups. Power is
exerted through the ways in which understanding can be structured
to limit or shape what can be said, asserted, or justified. Communicative power is relational and situated. It is not so much exercised by one
party over another; rather, it is an element of a relationship in which
there are unequal chances to engage in forms of understanding.

The limitations of Bourdieu's theory point to a broader conception of
what he terms symbolic power. Hannah Arendt suggested a notion of
power that Habermas termed communicative power. Hers provides a
better account of linguistic understanding and power.

Weber's conception of domination contained other elements that
pointed to another dimension of power. When he spoke of legitimate
domination, he was referring to the belief that a certain political order
is legitimate or worthy of acceptance. Weber inserted a meaning-
constituting communicative relationship into the question of power.
Power is often based on the belief in norms of behaviour, where these
norms shape the expectations of individuals. Still, Weber's conception
often remained at the level of *de facto* legitimacy. That is, his account

involved norms that are generally accepted, and it did not employ a full version of the participant's perspective in which individuals are mutually accountable. However, notions of legitimate order are inevitably open to justification.

What these meaning-interpretive theories point towards is the authorizing force of language. Political legitimacy requires an authorizing force understood not simply as the existence of authority but also as the force that generates a form of collective power acting in common. (This also applies to social interaction in public life.) Adapting Arendt's notion of power as distinguished from violence, and defining it as communicative power, Habermas seeks to develop his position on meaning-interpretive foundations. In these terms power exists, as Arendt noted, when humans gather together to act in concert. And it only exists when these publics exist. Communicative power does not belong to anyone. It cannot it be stored or preserved like an instrument. It can only be created and renewed though our acting together. The authorizing force of communicative power derives first from the deliberative character of action. In Arendt's formulation a plurality of subjects come together to deliberate, discuss, and make decisions. Subjects form opinions, which lead to a will to act or, more precisely, provide the motivations for action. In Habermas's formulations, this deliberative element is refined and elaborated into processes of giving and assessing reasons for action. Its authorizing force stems from this ability to generate a will to act for good reasons. However, it would be a mistake to see deliberation in communicative action as merely cognitive – that is, as detached from motivation that aims at deliberating. It is a practical activity that forms a "common will," if not a unified or singular one, and thus attempts to guide action. However, this will is not an ontological entity that exists in a reified form prior to action. It exists only in the interactions of participants. In short, communicative power stems from the communicative freedom of citizens and participants. It provides a basis for the political freedom and autonomy of a group.

Communicative power therefore must be distinguished from strategic power. Communicative power is not the power A has to get B to do something, nor is it A's power to develop her capacities. Rather, it is the power that arises out of the generative capacity that A and B have together to authorize an action. Because strategic action lacks the capacity to generate norms or laws or norm-laden practices, it cannot produce the motivation to act in common. It can only shape or direct it. In Arendt's theory this problem is somewhat difficult to conceptualize. Arendt understands communicative forms of generating power as tied to the capacity to achieve uncoerced agreements.

But she does not have a clear way of deciding when agreements are coerced rather than uncoerced. Habermas's theory provides more resources for that task.

The exercise of strategic power could in fact lead to subtle forms of coercion, which, as we have seen, limit alternatives or shape communicative actions. This form of power can shape action, or it can shape understanding and identity and thereby ensure obedience. Communicative power can explain better than strategic power the workings of non-decisions. Those who are able to exclude issues from consideration that could put into question existing patterns of power and authority can exert control over others through their ability to control the agenda of a discussion and thereby shape the terms under which such discussion can take place, if at all. Thus, communicative power could allow individuals or groups to create and maintain power by labelling some reasons or sensibilities as illegitimate, or by barring topics or even groups from public discussion.

Communicative power affects not only the social rules but also the interpretive capacities of participants, and hence their communicative freedom. As self-interpreting beings we make sense not only of our world but also of our place in it. Our interpretive capacities and the meanings available to us are elements that condition our personal and collective identities. When the scope of our interpretations and our reflexivity are restricted or shaped and directed, our individual and social identities are constrained. For example, in the cases studied, power over non-decisions relies not just on the agenda-setting capacities of individuals or groups but also on the participants' orientation towards their interaction in political or social institutions.

Theories of hegemony draw on the interpretive capacities of individuals in their analyses of power relationships; notions of the lifeworld often figure as well. Such theories are rooted in the taken-for-granted background understandings and commitments of the participants. However, they view the "common sense" that participants share as constituted by relations of domination – relations that nonetheless create consent on the part of the populace. Domination is not simply a matter of one person or group imposing their will on another. It requires some degree of active consent and participation on the part of the dominated. This common sense comes to define the scope of accepted agreement and disagreement; it also declares who establishes the agenda, who provides authoritative definitions of the social world, and who interprets needs.[51] As an example, in a setting dominated by a neoliberal outlook welfare programs come to be looked on as reflecting a pathological dependency.

For the Italian Marxist Antonio Gramsci, with whom the term is often most closely associated, hegemony referred mainly to the class struggle – a view that in this day seems too narrow. Nonetheless, his theory as he originally expressed it did illustrate that the interpretive capacities of subjects that are in play in instances of hegemony are not simply effects of power. Although it can be restricted, we have the power to say "no" or "yes" to claims advanced by those with the capacity to define the situation we share as well as the ability to take an existential position towards those claims. I can exercise resistance by overtly rejecting a claim to authority or, more indirectly, by showing disrespect. The same communicative power that is a required to obtain consent can become the communicative freedom to reject "common sense." We cannot simply do away with or eliminate the communicative capacities of subjects unless social order becomes a function of mere force. This is crucial to critical theories of domination: that we have the capacity to take up interpretations and to be accountable to others means that we can take up the world.

The notion of communicative freedom suggested here also has advantages over Philip Pettit's conception of freedom as non-domination. In this view, the concept of non-domination offers a superior alternative both to notions of positive liberty and to Berlin's purely negative conception of liberty as freedom from observable interference. Here, domination consists in a situation in which (1) someone has the capacity to interfere (2) on an arbitrary basis (3) in certain choices that the other is able to make.[52] However, communicative power is also a generative power. It is not just the capacity to choose but precisely this generative power that is at issue in any conception of domination. In domination or oppression, the generative power of participants acting in common is restricted or shaped in ways that limit the possibility for free agreement.

We hope we have provided here a sufficiently comprehensive account of communicative freedom and power to suggest their central place in a contemporary critical theory of democracy and society. However, we would be remiss if in our consideration of critical theory and power we did not consider the highly influential position of Michel Foucault. Foucault's reflections on power, which offer important insights into the mechanisms by and through which power is generated and exercised, share concerns with the form of critical theory to which we are committed, while departing in some fundamental respects from the analysis we have attempted to offer. In the final section of this chapter we consider Foucault's legacy and its relevance for our position.

Foucault and Power

Some recent attempts by critical theory to develop a conception of power can be of use in an approach to Foucault's work. Martin Saar has identified two strains of thought about power in modernity. One strain, which derives from Benedict Spinoza, involves a reworking of the ancient notion of power as potentiality. The second, which derives from Thomas Hobbes, is more of an instrumental notion of power where one controls another person. The first view, which Saar associates with the work of Arendt, is a constitutive conception. It concerns the power to create and change that is inherent in nature. It is, if you will, ontological. The latter is a kind of action- theoretical notion in that its instrumental or strategic focus entails a conception of constitutive power. This two-sided understanding may also remind the reader of C.B. Macpherson's notions of developmental and extractive power, although they are not identical.

This is an interesting suggestion, but because it views the action-theoretical conception of power in the strategic terms of Weber's conception of action, it leaves out the constitutive features of some types of action. As we noted earlier, this is a difficulty in Arendt's position as well. In her distinction between action and speech she views action primarily as purposive. However, in the version of communicative action that we are employing, action is not simply purposive but is closer to what Arendt had in mind by speech. These intersubjective processes in which participants are engaged in mutual understanding are themselves constitutive or generative. They do more than create meaning; they also generate validity and authorize action. The ontological features that Saar tries to locate in a realm outside of action seem to be located *within* it.

These processes of intersubjective interaction are constitutive in another sense. They produce and reproduce, and even transform, the social world through acts of mutual understanding. We should distinguish between the strategic uses of power that influence and induce but are not *per se* constitutive, and communicative power that creates meaning and understanding. We have seen this problem in our earlier analyses of treatments of power that do not take account of the relation between strategic and communicative power.

More germane to our concerns, Axel Honneth has attempted to characterize power as the struggle for recognition between participants in the social world.[53] Like others, he has been critical of what he sees as an idealistic element in the theory of communicative action, which he sees as especially evident in an idealized conception of agreement and an overly cognitive notion of ethics. Hobbes saw social struggle as a war of all against all stemming from the competition for goods under conditions of scarcity. Honneth, by contrast, posits that social conflict is not merely over access to goods to satisfy our needs, but over who we are. We cannot realize our plans or interpret our needs without a sense of who we are and a sense of respect. These require a self-relationship that is acquired socially. Like Hegel did with his notion of interpersonal struggle, especially as developed in his famous dialectic of master and slave, Honneth gives priority to the struggle for respect and recognition. The injustice of the master is that he fails to recognize the personhood of the slave. The master's domination of the slave is rooted in an ethical struggle. Because the slave is reduced to something less than a person, the master can treat him in an unequal manner. For Honneth, this serves as the template for all social struggles. Subordination entails disrespect and lack of recognition of the humanity and equality of others, and he sees respect, and thus recognition, as central to social progress. He views history at times as an agonistic struggle for recognition between social groups in which we cannot necessarily appeal to an ideal goal.

Honneth's notion of struggle has some important elements that must be incorporated into a critical theory. However, he sometimes leaves out the other elements of communicative action that are relevant for power. For communicative power includes not just the formative power of personal identity but also a background understanding and sense of community regarding common norms forms of knowledge, as well as a widely shared stock of sentiments and expectations. Forms of power do not operate simply on the level of unequal respect; they also operate when expectations, norms, and forms of knowledge are shaped by strategies of power employed by dominant interests. They have a shaping effect on powers of constitution.

From this standpoint the model of mutual accountability can provide resources not available to Honneth's version of mutual recognition. Our conception retains from Habermas the model of communicative action as a form of consensual social action but emphasizes the contingent, post-metaphysical elements in consensual action. Because the lifeworld is always subject to contestation, it is always a possible site of social struggle. But it is not for that reason agonistic.

It is in this context that we consider Foucault's influential treatment of power. As we see it, his most significant contribution resides in his attempt to work out an alternative conception of generative power. As is well known, Foucault argued for a productive conception of power. He contended that power is not something that simply restrains or prevents one from doing something, it also produces or generates effects and unequal social arrangements. In one sense we can see how this operates. Strategic actions and strategic power, as we noted, can cajole, persuade, coerce, or otherwise influence or induce another to act. Foucault seems to have in mind situations of domination in which power is exerted over others. This is less clear, however, in the case of norms. In what sense can strategic actions generate norms? They can only do so in a *de facto* sense. Normative social action is consensual, not strategic. It requires the valid consent of participants. In contrast, Foucault comes to see this generative power as, variously, a world-disclosing force, a socializing force, or a strategic force. His inability to recognize the communicative aspect of generative power leads to ambiguities in his account of power.

Foucault's earliest work does not explicitly engage notions of power, but it does contain elements of a constitutive conception of it. His work here is associated with his archaeological phase. In the interpretive view he develops here, power constitutes knowledge, values, and norms. The strong version of constitution theory holds that power constitutes subjectivity and hence shapes domination. In some his earlier work Foucault conceived of constitution as a regime of truth. A regime of truth establishes a "general politics of truth ... the types of discourse which it accepts and makes function as true, the mechanisms and instances which enable one to distinguish true and false statements, the means by which each is sanctioned, the techniques and procedures accorded value in the acquisition of truth; the status of those who are charged with saying what counts as true."[54]

Here, in his archaeological period, Foucault gives generative power to these structural forces, which are independent of individuals. His work here is strongly anti-subjective. Regimes of truth form individuals – not the other way around. Discourses work to determine the limits of what can be said and understood. In opposition to subjective models of history, Foucault argues that the rules of a discourse are not shaped by logic or by deliberate action; rather, they represent an anonymous historical unconscious. He sees discursive formations as having a power to create structures and shape individuals. In some respects, Foucault's theory points to the same issue raised by interactionist theories such as those of Anthony Giddens or Pierre Bourdieu, and their accounts of social institutions. However, Foucault takes a different approach. Rejecting the idea that the subject or the ego speaks, Foucault argues that we are enunciated – or, more properly, articulated – by discourse. While he recognizes that as participants in a social world we are shaped by social forces, he does not seem at this point in his work to recognize the reflexive power of subjects.

Here, though, Foucault still has some elements in common with the repression model. Such regimes of truth deny reason to the other. Foucault sometimes refers to this in terms of subjugated knowledge, that is, knowledge that is considered insufficiently scientific in character or rationality.

At this archaeological level of analysis, the status of the inquirer is ambiguous at best: Is the archaeologist an objective observer who uses his method to grasp elements not accessible to participants, or is he a participant like others? If the latter, the theorist seems to enjoy a reflexivity that is unavailable to ordinary participants.

In his later work Foucault corrects this approach to a degree. He addresses several issues that are not sufficiently dealt with by the archaeological approach. The archaeological approach is mostly static. From this vantage point Foucault cannot explain historical change or the transition from one episteme to another. Nor, as noted, does he explain why subjects take up and are taken up by power. Although Foucault later comes to see continuity in all his approaches, in fact he makes a rather abrupt change. Rejecting the idea that he is attempting to go beyond the question of the subject, he later comes to see his work primarily as outlining three modes of "objectification." In addition to archaeology he employs genealogical methods that look at the formation of the subject from the viewpoint of both the individuation of individuals through institutions like prisons and schools in which a new form of individuation is practiced – something he calls dividing practices – and from the perspective of how subjects shape themselves according to this mode of individualization. Each of these is connected to the larger notion of governmentality. In both cases he is concerned with a modern form of pastoral care in a modern state that has taken over many forms of self-care. Modern care concerns itself not with saving the soul but rather with bodily health, mental health, punishment, and education. The state, in Foucault's view, has taken on these functions.

Here Foucault focuses on micro-processes through which compliance is secured. Rather than looking at the formation of subjectivity from the top down, so to speak, Foucault wants to study power processes from the ground up. He looks at how institutions like the family, organized medicine, and systems of punishment shape the individual. As in the model of confession, the subject is necessary to find the truth about the self. But as these confessional discourses are basically administered by the new social sciences, they are forms of objectifying and normalizing subjectivity. Foucault claims that we should oppose not just government power but the new forms of subjectivization that are brought into play.

In this genealogical approach, Foucault maintains that power is productive – that it creates meaning. However, he basically applies the Weberian notion that power, in the sense he wants to use it, is social. Against the view that power is always anonymous, Foucault now contends that power is exercised only over those who are free. It requires recognition that the other – that is, the one over whom power is exerted – is a person capable of a response. It concerns the power of A to get B to do something. In this sense, power brings about a certain state of affairs. It can also be influenced by institutional rules and settings. As Foucault's famous analysis of the panopticon shows, institutional practices are structured so as to strategically shape the responses of institutions as modes of control.

While Foucault's notion of strategic power as productive helps illustrate the ways in which others are influenced, persuaded, intimidated, or threatened into acting in a certain way, this notion, as noted above, falls short of illustrating how power works from the participant's perspective. We need to look at the ways in which strategic power impacts the communicative power of subjects. Without a fuller explication of this relationship, Foucault's conception of the nature of power and resistance remains incomplete. It is difficult to know how to understand the participant's perspective on power without accounting for her embeddedness in forms of communicative action.

The forms of strategic power that Foucault identifies do not simply want to induce people to act in a certain way. They also seek the consent or agreement of participants to the kind of norms that support the regimes of surveillance he identifies and the conceptions of the self he lays out. The forms of surveillance Foucault marks out, first with respect to prisons, but later in other institutions such as education and medicine, indicate new modes of accountability, both within the subject's relation to itself and in the rules and roles of social institutions. This involves changes in the background conditions and definitions of the situation within which people act. But there is considerable ambiguity in his treatment of these new forms of accountability.

Sometimes he adopts a model close that of Friedrich Nietzsche. Rejecting the idea that there is an inherent transcendental or ideal structure of morality or cognition in the subject, Foucault sees the creation of higher forms of subjectivity as a result of work on the self. However, this work is seen too often on the model of purposive or strategic labour. It becomes a form of self-objectification and a projecting of oneself onto the world through one's own will.

This conception, however, does not really explain the processes whereby we gain our identities by means of structures of mutual understanding and mutual accountability. It is not simply a matter of willful self-shaping. If we want to understand the pathologies of accountability that are brought about through the kind of colonization of the lifeworld that Foucault's analyses imply, as well as the modern self that he rejects, then we need to look at how the communicative power of subjects is shaped by institutional power. However insightful Foucault's analysis of modern institutions and forms of knowledge, his theory cannot fully explain these processes. Strategic power does not create meaning. The generative power that creates meaning is a matter of communicative action and communicative power. So we need to ask how forms of strategic power can shape or direct the generative powers of communicative action.

Post-structuralist Considerations

The legacy of the kind of analysis identified with the pivotal work of Michel Foucault, often labelled "post-structuralist," can clearly be seen in what have come to be called postcolonial studies. Writers in this field have been particularly concerned with the ways in which Western cultural imperialism defines the colonized as "other" – here meant as subaltern – in relation to Western cultures. In this respect they have not only questioned the supposed universality of these cultures but also formulated the most wide-ranging criticisms of the oppressive nature of "Western reason." Thus they play an important role in evaluating some of the achievements and failures of the post-structuralist critique of reason.

We cannot do justice here to the variety of perspectives that fall under the rubric of postcolonial thought. We are primarily interested in some significant proponents of post-structuralist thought who have applied their insights to this arena of struggle.

Using perspectives drawn from both Foucault and Jacques Derrida, Gayatri Chakravorty Spivak has argued that the "colonial subject" is constituted as radical "otherness" defined primarily by its lack of presence or pure difference. The colonial subject cannot be placed within the imperialist discourse and remains voiceless. Spivak has in mind a form of domination in which the colonizer's indigenous cultural forms of writing, speaking, and acting are devalued and sub-ordinated to the point that they can make no claims to validity. The colonized is defined entirely in the negative, that is, by a lack of reason and a lack of voice. He or she has no ability to speak or raise claims in the dominant discourse. The colonized may "speak," but what they say appears meaningless or irrational. In the context of colonial production, according to Spivak, those who are subaltern are without history or voice.[55]

Spivak interprets this process using Foucault's notion of "subjugated knowledge." Subjugation involves an act of epistemic violence against indigenous forms of knowing. As we have seen, these forms of knowledge are disqualified in relation to advanced models of reason. Moreover, their articulation is often met by opposition and suppression. Spivak does not interpret this form of structural violence through the lens of a theory of mutual recognition. Much like Ernesto Laclau and Chantal Mouffe, she sees the development of epistemic domination along the lines of a theory of hegemony. The hegemony of a social formation is the result of a central form or a transcendental signifier that organizes knowing and acting. Such an institution creates its own standards of right and wrong, good and evil, and this forcibly excludes all other forms of understanding. Dominant standards must, by definition, be closed or complete. From this standpoint, oppression is carved into the very act of creating standards of reason. Epistemic violence is inherent in any instituting practice.

Spivak's position has been taken to task for failing to conceive of resistance to domination. The thesis of epistemic violence as formulated by Spivak postulates a closure more radical than that of the onedimensionality of the Frankfurt School.

Not all of those who write in the post-structuralist mode agree that the transcendental signifier is fully closed or even that it exists. Against Spivak's argument, Homi K. Bhabha has argued that the epistemic structures Spivak describes must also allow for the possibility of resistance. Bhabha agrees with Spivak that the colonialist discourse amounts to a closed system that has its own forms of authority and recognition and that aims at transparency. Bhabha argues that "the acknowledgment of authority depends on the immediate – unmediated – visibility of its rules of recognition as the unmistakable referent of historical necessity."[56] Following the post-structuralist interpretation of the philosophy of the subject, Bhabha implies that the colonial discourse is rooted in a teleological philosophy of history in which Western society is the meta-subject. The colonized is by definition excluded from this teleology. It is not the subject, but only a justifiably subjugated outsider to this logic of development. Participation in history requires acceptance of these fated forms of "reason."

From these assumptions about Western reason it is easy to see how the colonized are interpreted as radically other. However, Bhabha dissents from the analysis given by Spivak in that he holds that this teleology is inherently ambivalent. The discourse of colonialism aims to impose a homogeneous form of "reason" onto the colonized; thus the colonized must disavow that homogeneous authority "as they articulate the signs of cultural difference." These articulated differences between colonizer and colonized means that the model of power used by Foucault to analyse bourgeois societies of the nineteenth century must be transformed. Foucault's account of the panopticon is based on an immediate and transparent model of authority. All power and all actions are made visible under the gaze of authority. According to Bhabha's reading, however, the panoptic model of authority fails since authority cannot be transparent in colonial societies. Colonial society cannot be rendered transparent. It is not a "stable unitary collectivity." In short, disciplinary power is not fully effective on the colonized because they are not subjects to begin with.

Like Spivak, Bhabha rejects the model of the "struggle for recognition" to explain this process and sees it as a structural version of psychic "doubling" or fragmenting as the "condition of subjection." If authority needs to be "essential" – that is, if it has to employ a unitary notion of a race or a nation or tradition to render its authority transparent – then the colonized are split from that unity. The notion of the double draws from psychoanalysis the idea of the hidden other. In colonial society the question of authorization involves the declaration (and naming) of a colonized other, who is not a member of a unitary race or nation. This ambiguous space is that within which the colonized can resist in much the same way that African Americans constructed their own roles and relations as a means to expose and in their own way resist authority.

Notwithstanding their differences regarding the nature of resistance, Spivak and Bhabha agree with Foucault that social formations are regimes of power/knowledge. As such, they provide authorized modes of validity exemplified by forms of transparent and immediate authority. Seen in this way they are internally impermeable. Spivak and Bhabha are correct when they point to communicative dimensions of domination and note that forms of power never operate purely though violence but employ communicative power to structure forms of truth and validity and to systematically exclude claims that might challenge the dominance of hegemonic groups. Nonetheless, Spivak and Bhabba short-circuit analyses of these communicative powers. That social formations are themselves essentially hegemonic and closed limits the communicative freedom of participants. As formulated by postcolonial theorists like Spivak and Bhabha, there is no essential distinction between domination and freedom. Resistance is based not on communicative power but simply on counter-hegemony.

The phenomenon of colonial domination could also be explained using the framework of the pathology of communicative freedom. This model would explain the power of resistance through reference to the freedom of participants to take a position on the interpretations imposed by colonial dominance. This power cannot be entirely suppressed so long as participants engage in some form of communicative action. Resistance is not just a form of counter-hegemony, it is also the power to affirm or deny, a power that is inherent in language. Rather than conceiving of radical otherness as the complete exclusion from discourse, a model of the suppression of communicative freedom would focus on the social mechanisms – such as socialization processes and institutional arrangements – through which colonizers excluded the colonized from participation in authority, as well as the power to develop their own interpretations in a context in which they could be taken seriously. It would focus on the uses of forms of power that restrict communicative freedom.

Here, some of the processes analysed by Foucault could be incorporated. These social practices might for example operate in the way that Foucault describes, as rules that exclude forms of knowledge as a whole, or they might more narrowly exclude specific kinds of claims, such as claims about collective goods. They might also operate through restrictive conceptions of social normality that label behaviours as criminal or deviant (among other things). In this way they can claim they have the consent, be it tacit or explicit, of subjected populations.

Finally, we want to briefly consider the contribution of post-structuralist feminist accounts of power. Judith Butler has provided one of the best-known and most influential defences of post-structuralist feminism.[57] Unlike some feminists who look to notions of the feminine as the essential basis for a feminist theory, Butler rejects any form of essentialism as rooted in a foundationalist conception of identity. All such attempts to find a fixed identity are metaphysical. They entail an independent notion of the self as an "agent" from whom acts originate.

The foundationalist reasoning of identity politics tends to assume that an identity must first be in place for political interests to be elaborated and, subsequently, for political action to be taken. Our argument is that there need not be a "doer behind the deed" and that the "doer" is invariably constructed in and through the deed.

In place of "metaphysical" theories of the self, Butler proposes a "performative" conception. The self is constituted in its performances. She also argues, however, that these instituting performances are forms of hegemonic power. But in her view, such hegemonic forms are transitory and changing. All forms of identity are fleeting; they represent the ebb and flow of power-driven interests.

Despite her seeming radical critique of feminism, Butler's position is not as radical as it appears. It does not cut to the core of questions of identity. While it is true in one sense that the doer cannot be separated from the deed – that is, that there can be no metaphysical self prior to the participant's perspective – this does not mean that the only viable solution is a power-based conception of "performance." Like her post-colonial counterparts, Butler neglects the dimensions of communicative freedom entailed in her own notion of performance.

Butler's work shares with communicative theory an emphasis on the formative power of language. However, her conception of language is too limited to account for the dimensions of communicative freedom. She argues that agency and selfhood are properties of "significations." Here, signification means the communicative power of the production of signs, which carry rules for usage, rather than a process of mutual understanding through which action in concert is coordinated. Butler sees the production of signs as form of "repetition," or, more properly, as a kind of repetition compulsion, whereby compliance with produced signs is induced.

Indeed, when the subject is said to be "constituted," this means simply that the subject is a consequence of certain rule-governed discourses that establish the intelligible invocation of identity. The subject is not determined by the rules through which it is generated because signifi-cation is not a founding act, but rather a regulated process of repetition that both conceals itself and enforces its rules through the production of substantive effects. Butler argues that agency is the possibility of varia-tion of repetition. Like Bhabha, she argues that systems of signification are imperfect or insufficient. They always leave room for variation.

While Butler aims to avoid charges of determinism, it is not clear that her notions of institution through signification are rich enough to account for identity-forming processes. While the exact identity of the subject may not be determined, one can say it is the product and never the producer of its structural articulations. In some respects, Butler thereby reintroduces the distinction between the doer and the deed. The systems of signification may not determine us but they do produce us and our performances. Our doing is not really a taking up but rather an inducement to act through signification.

If our conceptions of identity are to have any significant implica-tions for a theory of society, they need to be tied to notions of what we want to be and how we take up that identity in relation to the world we encounter. Identity and communicative freedom are linked. Unless subjects can critically take up their life histories and make them their own, they cannot be said to have social identities at all. Once again it is the power to affirm, deny, and otherwise take a position on this life history that allows us to form identities. The communicative power to develop these identities has to be employed in the context of communicative freedom if we are to take them up in a meaningful fashion.

The communicative theory we have advocated builds on the insights of pragmatic theorists and integrates these insights with hermeneutics. The self is clearly not a substance or an unchanging subject, but it *is* a point in a web of relations. However, identities do not simply represent temporary points of fixity, held in place by hegemony. They emerge out of the orientation of a person towards the social world. This indicates those important evaluations – what Charles Taylor calls strong evaluations – that a person holds. These do not come before the self. They *are* the self, which is brought into being and is renewed in its communicative relations with others.

Our account in this chapter of communicative reason and truth, and the related issues of freedom and power, is intended to pave the way for an engagement with the challenges of a critical theory of democracy itself. However, before we go on it is essential to relate key issues of critical theory to the contemporary socio-economic and political context in which this theory, and a theory of democracy, must be situated. This context is that of neoliberalism, its values, institutions, and practices. In the next chapter we treat the relation of critical theory to neoliberalism.

Chapter Three

Critical Theory and Neoliberalism

Critical theories of society are diagnostic. Rather than describing societies as they exist in a non-normative fashion, they have a practical and evaluative dimension. Critical theories identify the deformed subjective and intersubjective forms of life in modern societies along with the institutional and structural features that generate and maintain relations of domination and oppression, and that present barriers to realization of greater freedom, equality, and solidarity. Diagnostic theories evaluate impediments to human freedom in the conditions of modern life from the standpoint of emancipation from domination. The critic who diagnoses social pathologies is not like the doctor or clinician who diagnoses individual ills. The critic is less an expert observer than a co-participant who understands social pathologies through an involvement in social life that others share. Fellow participants are also able to interpret and assess, and often share, the diagnoses forwarded by the critic.

In its classic form, critical theory linked critique to a (primarily) political-economic analysis. Social pathologies stemmed overwhelmingly from the economic structure of society – that is, from capitalism. While the first generation of the Frankfurt School certainly recognized the intermediation of culture and even psychology with the economic, they still held that in the last instance, the economic was determining. More recent critical theories have emphasized the limits of the model of political economy formulated by Marx and have emphasized concerns rooted in the new social movements. Many of these attempts have formulated an independent line of development of subjectivity and intersubjectivity that is not strictly dependent on the economic sphere, but they have for the most part pursued commitments to justice, equality, and freedom. In the work of Jürgen Habermas and Axel Honneth this has led to the development of an independent logic of mutual understanding based on our capacities for intersubjective interaction and recognition. These elements have sometimes been interpreted as raising claims for inclusion and equality upon which questions of political economy are seen to have a limited bearing.

The diagnostic element of critical theory, then, is closely related to immanent critique. A critical theory takes the ideals that are internal to a society and confronts them with the diagnoses it has made of the pathologies emerging out of contemporary social structures, with the intent to invoke reflection. In carrying out this commitment to foster reflection it relies not on some ideal or utopian possibilities, but on those tendencies that while present in contemporary societies have yet to be fully actualized.

While questions of equal respect and inclusion continue to play a central role in critical discourse, the rise of neoliberalism has been accompanied by a new set of social pathologies that pose a challenge for critical theories. Such pathologies exacerbate problems of social and economic inequality, vulnerability, insecurity, and precarity not only among the poor classes but also among the middle classes. These conditions are having a decisive effect on the personal and political freedoms of subjects in neoliberal societies.

Thus a critical theory of contemporary society must establish itself against the dominant neoliberalism of our times. However, as we argued in the previous chapter, this cannot involve a straightforward retrieval of an unreconstructed Marxism, or a simple defence of or return to the welfare state. Of course, critical theories have been sensitive to the limitations of the welfare state and highly critical of the bureaucratic rationalization of social life. Critical theorists oppose the colonization of the lifeworld by bureaucratic imperatives and the education of citizens as clients who are to be shaped by experts. As we have also argued, critical theory must provide revised conceptions of freedom and equality; this is especially crucial if we are to understand the problems with neoliberal capitalism. The challenges of neoliberalism require us to formulate more complex notions that do not so easily fit into the Keynesian welfare state paradigm. A critical theory must do this while still recognizing the need for state action to regulate an economy rendered more unstable by neoliberal policies and practices.

The fall of the Soviet Union and the Communist Bloc in 1989 led to a triumphalist mood in the decades that followed.[1] The idea that there could be alternatives to capitalism, even to an unfettered capitalism, seemed hopelessly out of date. For example, Charles Lindblom argues that markets have come to dominate in almost all contemporary societies and are inherently superior to command economies.[2] Even some critical theorists have claimed to see no alternative. To take one example, Joseph Heath has attempted to fuse critical theory with rational choice. He rejects the view that there are viable alternatives to markets, specifically capitalist markets. His ideas about a market socialism are little more than capitalism under another name. He seems to welcome the end of ideology and even compares the contemporary work of Jürgen Habermas to Francis Fukuyama's paean to the triumph of market liberalism.[3] He contends that the primary if not only task left for social theory is to undertake a technical design of the game theoretical structuring of institutions to constrain behaviour in order to achieve the right outcomes.

Of course, this is an extreme version, one held by very few critical theorists. But the "third way" model associated with thinkers such as Anthony Giddens illustrates the dilemma of critical and social democratic theories in the post-1989 period. Giddens has tried to combine the social democratic commitment to justice and equality with market liberalization.[4] He believes that the traditional appeal to class politics is outmoded. Like critical theorists, Giddens recognizes that some of the consequences of the welfare state can be harmful, and he rejects what he deems an excessively statist conception in favour of decentralized economic processes. In the United States, President Bill Clinton's version of the third way tended to promote the agenda of neoliberalism. Pursuit of this agenda entailed the deregulation of major sectors of the economy such the media and the banking system, as well as a commitment to international free trade agreements. The welfare reform policies undertaken by the Clinton administration looked to replace government support of the poor with workfare programs that stressed the personal responsibility of participants for their fate. Far from liberating individuals from excessive and intrusive government monitoring and the consequent shaping of identities, neoliberal policies have made them more vulnerable and open to market manipulation. While purporting to promote the interests of civil society, third-way politicians and the policies they support have ended up weakening it.

Critical theorists such as Habermas have been slow to grasp the renewed role given to economic conflicts. Habermas, too, has at times embraced the view that the most viable alternative is not a rejection of the market, but the political restraint of it. In a 2009 interview he stated: "Since 1989–90 it has become impossible to break out of the universe of capitalism; the only option is to civilize and tame the capitalist dynamics from within."[5] Still, it would be a mistake to count Habermas among the triumphalists, as Heath does. Habermas recognizes that the fall of the Soviet Union did not represent the triumph of capitalism. The collapse of the Soviet Union and the demise of Soviet-style socialism did, however, give a boost to the dynamics of a neoliberalism that was already on the rise. And Habermas continues to view his legal/political theory as socialist – a point we take up in the following chapters.

Up to and including *The Theory of Communicative Action*, Habermas had argued that capitalism and democracy were in conflict.[6] He still appears to hold this view, but his conception of the role of markets makes the realization of his putatively socialist vision ambiguous. Part of the problem arises from his view that markets are a functionally necessary feature of modern societies. Thus the challenge for Habermas is to prevent markets and administrative functions from invading and colonizing the everyday lifeworld of participants, a lifeworld maintained through mutual understanding. His notion of the colonization and reification of the lifeworld remains a potent concept for analysing the pathologies of neoliberalism, but we think that his notion of the functional necessity of markets does not sufficiently recognize the extent to which democratic political processes impact what he sees as the independent logic of markets. He has been sceptical about democratic control of the economy, and unlike Macpherson and other theorists, he does not offer a clear statement about social property. His notion of taming the market remains too vague, in that he does not specify exactly which elements need to be tamed so as to align the market with his notion of socialist democracy. Would taming the market involve a fundamental reorganization of society so that control of the economy served social purposes, or would it merely require an extensive redistribution of goods as in social democracy? Can we conceive of notions of social property and social ownership that are democratic and decentralized and not simply a return to the *dirigiste* notions of Soviet-style socialism?

These ongoing tensions are found in Habermas's major statement on global capitalism, *The Postnational Constellation*.[7] Here he stresses the political consequences of globalization as a challenge to the sovereignty of the nation-state. He thinks that the problems of global capitalism can no longer be solved on the national level but require a regime of international human rights. Here, neoliberalism is primarily a movement that corresponds to the breakdown of state authority. For Habermas this development is part of a larger dialectic of modernity in which wider and more inclusive identities are shaped. Drawing on the ideas of Karl Polanyi, he characterizes this development as a dual movement. The opening of new markets frees individual identities for greater elaboration by breaking the bonds of provincial identities; but at the same time, it leads to new closures, that is, to new and more inclusive notions of solidarity.[8] Thus the major cleavage introduced by globalization has been the struggle for these larger forms of post-national solidarity combined with a transnational legal framework of human rights.

Perhaps from the heights of the theory of social evolution, such a perspective has merit. However, the kind of dialectic that Habermas identifies is by no means guaranteed. In fact, it does not seem to square with his earlier statements on the contradictions of capitalism and democracy, in which markets also erode the lifeworld. Although it may hold in a distorted way the potential for wider solidarities and identities, neoliberal globalization works primarily to diminish these potentialities. Habermas has not been sufficiently attuned to the serious pathologies generated by neoliberalism. Referring to the effects of neoliberal globalization, Habermas argued in *The Postnational Constellation* that "in themselves these trends don't imply any damage to the conditions for functional and legitimate democratic processes."[9] More recently, he has admitted that he was taken aback by the strength of the recent populist movements, and he now acknowledges some elements of new pathologies. Still, he does not see a general rise of authoritarian movements in the new populism.

We disagree with Habermas's formulation of the problem. We view contemporary neoliberalism as a social, political, and economic process that blocks the very democratic expansion of rights and solidarities that Habermas sees as extending the limits not just of the sovereignty of nation-states but also of individuals within nations or other groups. Neoliberal formations, then, seek to limit the political authority of citizens and tend to generate their own forms of illiberal democracy. This leads to the creation of versions of managed democracy that can go even beyond this to the establishment of quasi-authoritarian mechanisms. Increasing inequality fosters not only material deprivation but also social and political powerlessness. The loss of steady jobs and security generates an increasing sense of vulnerability. In advanced capitalist societies, neoliberalism limits the developmental possibilities of subjects and lowers the expectations of participants. Far from being libertarian, neoliberalism must actively eliminate the challenges posed by developmental and communicative democracy through rearguard and reactionary social and cultural policies that suppress developmental possibilities and indeed democracy itself.

There is scant discussion of the notion of property in Habermas's *Between Facts and Norms*, and the result is a certain lack of clarity in his view of how to tame capitalism. If markets – primarily capitalist markets – have a strong functional role, then some questions go unasked: Does the capitalist market model have the capacity to solve the problems posed by its own dysfunctional effects? Can this goal to be reached solely through the redistributive measures of the welfare state? Even if in principle this would be sufficient, is the rehabilitation of the welfare state viable in a period of restraint and retrenchment? Or does this reconstruction require a wider notion of publicly owned or social property to limit the concentrated power of large corporations? We agree that the model of political economy that sees the economic as determining all other spheres of life is theoretically and practically flawed; nonetheless, it remains true that democratic control of the economy requires that we consider the role of private property and not just markets.

What Is Neoliberalism?

As the devastating effects of neoliberalism have become more apparent, there has been a revival of criticism that focuses on its social and economic injustices. The renewal of interest in political economy has sometimes been associated with the rehabilitation of more traditional Marxist categories and a renewed emphasis on class. Thomas Piketty's massive study, *Capital in the Twenty-First Century*, stresses the inevitability of large-scale inequalities in capitalist society.[10] Piketty argues that the Keynesian era in which inequality was reduced was something of an anomaly. Over the course of its history, capitalism has tended to create increasing concentrations of wealth and social inequality. While he does advocate a global wealth tax, he is more sceptical than Habermas about the possibility of taming capitalism. Such scepticism has led theorist Sanford Schram to write of a return to "ordinary" capitalism.[11] Schram also thinks that the welfare state has not proven to be a permanent solution to the crises of capitalism, as in its wake we have witnessed not only a return to deepening economic inequality but also the increasing impoverishment of everyday life.

David Harvey provides what is the standard definition of neoliberalism: it is a form of governing that stresses individual initiative, property rights, unfettered capitalism, and limited government:

> Neoliberalism is in the first instance a theory of political economic practices that proposes that human well-being can best be advanced by liberating individual entrepreneurial freedoms and skills within an institutional framework characterized by strong private property rights, free markets, and free trade. The role of the state is to create and preserve an institutional framework appropriate to such practices. The state has to guarantee, for example, the quality and integrity of money. It must

also set up those military, defense, police, and legal structures and functions required to secure private property rights and to guarantee, by force
if need be, the proper functioning of markets. Furthermore, if markets
do not exist (in areas such as land, water, education, health care, social
security, or environmental pollution) then they must be created, by state
action if necessary.[12]

While helpful in identifying key elements of neoliberalism in practice, this characterization of it is too limited. Far from a return to a
pure free market system, neoliberalism exhibits a tension between
free market ideology and the corporate reality of neoliberal political
economy.[13] As American New Deal economists noted as early as the
1930s, corporate property is already a form of socialized property. The
corporate structure separates ownership from control. Stockholders
have little real control over the direction of the modern corporation.
Given its size and power, a corporation is often too big to fail, with
the result that risks are socialized and often redistributed to the worse
off. The state, then, not only creates the conditions for accumulation
but also guarantees these socialized risks. The government has been
the bank of last resort for enterprises too big to fail. Far from creating a realm of individual freedom, both corporate power and government regulation of the poor and vulnerable exert a coercive power on
individuals with the goal of shaping them into entrepreneurial selves:
"[Neoliberalism] is a self-consciously reactionary ideology that seeks
to roll back the status quo and institutionalize (or, on its own understanding, re-institutionalize) the 'natural' principles of the market. In
other words, it is transformative."[14] This contradiction between individualist ideals and corporate reality leads to dysfunction and crises,
including weakened growth, intense inequality, and coercion. Corporate control has eroded working conditions and created a sense of
contingency and precariousness that narrows the scope of individual
self-determination and self-realization.

More recently, some critical theorists have turned their attention to the
economic and political crises generated by neoliberalism. Nancy Fraser,
for example, characterizes third-way liberalism as species of "progressive neo-liberalism," which consists of an alliance between financial and
knowledge industry capitalism, and new social movements that cham-
pion diversity and multiculturalism.[15] Thus it combines privatization,
deregulation, and the reduction of the social safety net with a liberal
progressive outlook on diversity and social equality – but not economic
inequality. Fraser includes some forms of feminism in this process.
Those forms seek equality and diversity essentially for the social elites,

even while the life conditions of women in the rest of the population have grown more precarious.

Fraser agrees with many others that under the auspices of progressive neoliberalism and the conditions of post-1989 politics, the critique of capitalism has been replaced by forms of identity politics, that is, by struggles to strengthen the rights of groups long excluded from equal participation in both politics and social life. She thinks that with the election in 2016 of Donald Trump as president of the United States, this era has ended. We now face a transitional era in which the economic instability that has affected much of the population could lead in different political directions.[16] However, whether neoliberalism has in fact run out of steam has yet to be determined.

While Fraser welcomes the return of economic critique within critical theory, she holds, as we do, that this critique must be employed in a non-reductionist fashion. The political and social realms must be viewed as independent spheres with their own internal logic rather than as derived from the economic. They can interact with the economic in complex ways. Social, political, and legal norms and practices form the preconditions for the emergence and maintenance of the capitalist economy. As Max Weber noted, the development of normative religious structures preceded the formation of the economy. At the same time, however, these norms and practices can conflict with, and form the basis of, criticism of the direction and outcomes of the economy. At the same time, capitalist economic processes can have a strong impact on the direction of social and political practices as well, something that critical Marxists since Lukács have often pointed out. Such a position, however, challenges any neat and simple dichotomy between an economically oriented critique and a politics of recognition. A critical theory must be able to incorporate both dimensions.

Like Fred Block and Margaret Somers,[17] Fraser looks to the work of Karl Polanyi for a possible alternative. Polanyi argued that disembedding markets from social connections led to a social deficit. While the market claims it is self-regulating, historical evidence shows it is not. It requires support from the government, as well as a stable financial system established by the government. Furthermore, Polanyi argued, the market left to its own devices cannot provide for the basic social goods needed to sustain it, such as education, health care, the provision of social goods, or even work. He thought that the attempt to convert non-economic goods into market ones led to the creation of "fictitious commodities."[18] Fraser to be sure accepts much of Polanyi's critique, but as noted thinks that any return to a traditional welfare state risks the problems associated with bureaucracy.

Writing from a standpoint sympathetic to critical theory, Wendy Brown has attempted to assess the losses suffered as a result of the triumph of neoliberalism. In her view, in its all-encompassing rationalization and marketization of everyday life, one that goes beyond the scope of the late capitalist welfare state, neoliberalism is a sustained attack on the notion of the *demos*, the people. Using a Platonic analogy, she is concerned with the way that neoliberalism shapes the state and the soul. Neoliberalism, then, is a project concerned with eroding the foundations of democratic control in politics. The new political economy is attacking not only the structural features of the state but also the social and psychological setting in which participants operate.[19] Similarly, Sanford Schram sees neoliberalism as a project in which the state continues to support accumulation while submitting ever more areas of life to the logic of the market.[20] Rather than countering the market, the state supports it. Instead of protecting vulnerable individuals, it subjects them to monitoring and shapes them so that they are required to respond to the market's demands. However, neoliberalism is not simply a return to a laissez-faire philosophy. While it advocates deregulation, it also relies on government support for the conditions of accumulation and on the wielding of state power to shape subjects as entrepreneurial ones.

The Rise and Decline (?) of Neoliberalism

The transformation of neoliberalism from a philosophy with limited practical import to the dominant economic practice of our time was a response to the crises of the welfare state – that is, it was seen as the solution to the contradictions of democratic capitalism in the post-Keynesian period. Neoliberalism established itself as the dominant force in economic and social policy, but it has not proved to be a long-term solution to the problems of the welfare state. As we briefly noted, it is rent by its own internal tensions. Thus, neoliberal policies have resulted in a series of short-term solutions that have only postponed crises. If anything, the neoliberal era has been even more prone to crises than was its Keynesian predecessor.[21]

In the post–Second World War period from 1945 until about 1974, Keynesianism was the dominant economic outlook in Western industrialized countries. Keynes analysed the problems that led to the Great Depression as the result of structural instabilities in capitalist economies that classical theories failed to identify. Where classical economics postulated a stable equilibrium between supply and demand, Keynes held that demand could be unstable, especially in times of depression. The instabilities of the market required extensive government intervention, including monetary policy, government spending to stimulate demand, and industrial policy.

Keynes's theory, then, employed what was termed "embedded liberalism." It combined a commitment to free markets and free trade with state policies that focused on full employment, economic growth, and expanded social welfare protections for individuals. State power could achieve these goals either by supplementing or by substituting for market processes. In this respect states often intervened in industrial policy while promoting the idea of a social wage through social welfare policies that created national educational systems, health care, and other benefits.[22]

Keynesian economics was thus a political economics. In pursuing the goals of full employment, prosperity, a social wage, and protections against capitalist dysfunctions such as periodic unemployment, it supported social democratic aims and worked to pacify class conflicts. Keynesianism, then, was compatible with a kind of class compromise in which groups such as trade unions that represented the working classes had a voice in policy. "A broader consensus existed among economists and policymakers of the need for government intervention to stabilize the overall economy, prevent recessions, and maintain full employment."[23] Corporations accepted unions and collective bargaining, while unions accepted management's authority over production in exchange for wage increases and health and retirement benefits; the government protected citizens from the ravages of unemployment and other shocks and set up various forms of social security. The creation of governmental and bureaucratic agencies for the purposes of regulation, however, cut into profits, for those agencies required resources in order to regulate and stabilize the economy. Keynesianism was a form of corporate governance, with labour, business, and government collaborating to maintain prosperity.

The Keynesian compromise, however, also rested on a corporate-driven, elite democratic order. Elite democracy feared popular movements as essentially authoritarian and resisted those movements' demands for greater participation. It was social democratic only in a limited sense.

The linkage of the political and the economic in advanced capitalism led, according to Habermas, to a type of legitimation crisis not found in classical capitalism.[24] Once the state took on the tasks of managing and intervening in the economy, it had to justify those interventions on political, often social democratic, terms while maintaining a commitment to a well-functioning capitalist economy. Legitimation is a feature of all modern democratic societies. Authority does not stem from God or tradition but from the consent of the governed. This means that gov-ernments must justify their efforts to gain consent. While in classical capitalism such justifications often revolved around civil freedoms and the maintenance of the conditions for economic expansion and pros-perity, in late capitalism the state must also provide for the manage-ment of economic crises and social welfare functions. It needs to pro-vide resources to protect citizens from the side effects and dysfunctional consequences of the capitalist economy.[25]

While in classical capitalism it may have been sufficient for govern-ment to establish the legal conditions for a market economy and to pro-tect the rights of individuals to freely contract and reason, advanced capitalism is required to fulfil demands for social justice in order to compensate for the side effects and dysfunctional consequences of the capitalist economy. Claus Offe departs (as does Habermas) from the view held by the earlier Frankfurt School, which argued that admin-istrative control of the economy had successfully addressed and stabi-lized the crisis-filled nature of capitalism. Advanced capitalism must seek to balance legitimation with successful accumulation. While the Keynesian compromise rested on this elite consensus, it also generated political demands that went beyond this formulation. The rise of the new left, the civil rights movement, and the women's movement in the 1960s and early 1970s extended demands for political and social justice, greater participation in political decisions, greater social protections, and a more vital civic and public life. As we will discuss in chapter 6, the new left called for participatory democracy. The political and social demands made by the new left and the new social movements went beyond extensions of the social justice protections of the welfare state – they exceeded the bounds of elite consensus.

The crisis of the welfare state was both economic and political. Civil society is more than an expression of market relations. Normative struc-tures have a logic that in many respects is independent of economics. They also, however, provide the normative glue that allows the econ-omy and the state to act. Governments must foster loyalty and social cohesion in order to govern. They need the consent of the governed. Consent to a form of rule is based on ideals, on conceptions of a good or just life that are not simply contained by existing arrangements. Nor-mative conceptions of legitimate government, then, are not reflections of the economic system and indeed are often critical of them. On the other hand, they can be influenced by these systems as well.

The elite-driven political systems of the postwar period rested on forms of mass politics and the concomitant generation of mass loyalty. Mass loyalty so understood involves assent based on often spurious appeals to sentiments, such as patriotism or other values, to which in a passive and reactive manner people are expected to respond ("my country right or wrong"). Often such appeals draw on political symbols that condense experiences (the flag, an imagined past or future).[26] The use of symbols may not always be negative, but when they are used simply to arouse or reassure people without any further reflection or deliberation, politics becomes a mere spectacle, one designed to manipulate. Legitimacy requires some reflective assessment of reasons as well as active participation in political processes. Rather than gathering citizens together to deliberate and so form a public opinion, a mass politics of legitimation merely seeks to mobilize the population in support of policies formulated by elites, without input or evaluation by those so mobilized.

The tensions in legitimation also involve a conflict between mass democracy and more democratic involvement and participation. It seems that the developmental possibilities generated by welfare state capitalism have created the prospect not just of taming capitalism but of transforming it radically. Radical democrats criticized the consumerism of late capitalist societies and the civic privatism that pacified citizens in the name of a version of civic and public life that was generally missing.

By the mid-1970s the Keynesian compromise had broken down. The state could no longer successfully balance the claims for democratic legitimacy and capital accumulation, at least from the perspective of securing simultaneously economic growth, full employment, and social protections. The decline of the steady growth of the postwar period led to crises, for without sufficient growth the contradiction inherent in state regulation of the economy reaches a dangerous level. The very tools the state uses to stabilize the economy and provide the basis for accumulation can work as brakes on accumulation. These tensions were first manifested in the simultaneous rise of inflation and unemployment. The inverse relation between inflation and unemployment that Keynesians had postulated broke down, even as the rate of profit also fell. If profit was sufficient, then businesses would accept the costs of the welfare state; when profits declined, however, capital no longer agreed to the compromise. Hence, the tensions in the welfare state came to the fore. These tensions reflected the difficulty of balancing profitability and social welfare functions, that is, balancing administrative, economic, and normative imperatives in capitalism.[27]

The legitimacy of postwar capitalism rested on creating a standard of living that pacified the working classes. At the same time, it had to provide the conditions for successful accumulation of private profit by capitalist enterprises. In a capitalist economy firms must accumulate capital: they must make profits and reinvest them to maintain and expand operations. When firms either fail to make profits or have no incentive to invest, the economy slows and goes into a recession that leaves enterprises closed and people unemployed.

Administrative functions of government also conflicted with economic ones. Administrative agencies used tax revenues for what businesses came to see as unproductive purposes. These forms of regulation and taxation, as well as increased labour costs, were increasingly viewed a burden on businesses that limited accumulation. Businesses can fail to invest or to build due to limited profits. If governments are committed to the support and preservation of capitalist property, Claus Offe argues, these problems are always possible. Just as labour can go on strike for higher wages and better working conditions, businesses can engage in capital strikes by refusing to invest.[28]

The Neoconservative Interregnum, Democratic Deficits, and the Neoliberal Reaction

While the breakdown of the Keynesian welfare state compromise may have begun with economic issues, what came to be called neoconservatives mounted a political response. Critical analyses of legitimation crises in the 1970s were taken up by neoconservatives to explain the problems faced by the welfare state. They took this conflict between legitimation and accumulation in a very different direction – they sought *less* democracy, not more. In their view, capitalist democracies were becoming ungovernable. Samuel Huntington and his colleagues developed one of the best-known versions of this thesis in their report to the Trilateral Commission.[29] Huntington diagnosed the distemper of democracy as a consequence of excessive demands by groups for equality and social justice. These demands generated a crisis because they delegitimized authority and trust in government; they also undermined claims to expertise. The push for an unsustainable equality also put a fiscal strain on the economy. People demanded that resources be distributed for the purposes of social equity in areas such as education and social security, at the expense of defence spending and more productive support for capital investment.

From the neoconservative perspective, conflicts over resource allocation were not the product of economic contradictions, as Marxists argued. According to Huntington, they were the result of claims for greater participation and more democracy. Huntington took the left-wing critique of the difficulty – some might say impossibility – of combining capitalism with democracy (in the robust sense) and gave it a more conservative twist. He acknowledged the conflict between social justice and the economy but contended that democratic capitalism must be maintained despite this conflict.

Huntington described a situation in which the institutions of the welfare state were no longer fully effective. They lacked sufficient resources to carry out their normative imperatives. Because the political system in Huntington's view could not accommodate more radical demands for democratization, it constituted an internal limit of institutional structure. It was not an external force that could be eliminated. For Huntington, this meant that the expansion of political democracy had to be checked.

Huntington and his colleagues employed a functionalist notion of politics that limits its usefulness. They viewed the political system as a mechanism for processing subjective demands. They understood these demands, and the preferences that drive them, simply as interest positions involving claims for goods and services, or even for money and power. They do not involve questions of the good or the just. Once reduced to demands for scarce resources, issues of social justice can easily be dismissed as expressions of selfishness that need to be limited and contained.

Neoconservatism illustrated the inability of the liberal version of elite democracy to accommodate the developmental possibilities that had been given voice by the protest movements of the 1960s and early 1970s. Many neoconservatives, such as Daniel Moynihan, were chastened liberals who had supported the New Deal and the welfare state but felt threatened by popular democratic initiatives. Huntington was a lifelong Democrat who was liberal on many issues. These old liberals believed that the elite directed social change; when their science failed them, they became sceptical about social progress and so moved in a conservative direction.[30]

Neoliberals have taken the crisis identified by neoconservatives, and in one sense critical theorists, in a more reactionary direction. Neoconservatives wanted to tame democratic impulses but still supported some elements of the welfare state. Neoliberals, by contrast, strive to sharply reduce or eliminate the social safety net. They seek to change the legal structure so as to free a natural, spontaneous form of social order that has been blocked by government bureaucracy and to forcefully restructure both institutions and individual expectations. The idea of social rights rooted in a developmental understanding of freedom that is an achievement of advanced capitalist societies must be set aside. This will require social "unlearning," which is to be enforced by authoritarian measures and the administrative monitoring of individual conduct.

The neoliberal political economy has little use for popular democracy and has employed austerity to alter the nature of political accountability.[31] The demands of markets rather than popular initiatives have the upper hand in deciding what states do. Now that neoliberalism has consolidated itself, the state faces it with a diminished capacity to mediate between the rights of citizens and the imperatives of capitalist accumulation. Neoliberals generate their own form of legitimation crisis through the creation of an austerity state that is no longer accountable for a wide variety of government activities. The neoliberal "solution" to the legitimation problems of democratic capitalism seems largely to work to minimize forms of democratic legitimacy and the demands for accountability associated with the deliberative elements of democracy. In the process, individuals are overburdened with risk and precariousness.

Wolfgang Streeck has provided a convincing analysis of the trajectory of neoliberal economic development from the fiscal crises of the 1970s up to the present. The state has been the key battleground on which conflicts have been played out. Streeck sees a set of shifting policy commitments that have attempted to stabilize economies. Each, attempt, however, has created new barriers to the very stabilization it was intended to provide. Specifically, he sees a trajectory whereby the classical tax state, which reached a kind of pinnacle with the maturing of the Keynesian welfare state, gave way to the debt state as bourgeois resistance to democratic encroachments on market freedoms began to build. The resulting fiscal crisis led after the 1980s to the emergence of the consolidation state and its commitment to austerity; in various ways this form of state has remained in place down to the current era. This entire period has also witnessed the increasing financialization of capitalism, one element of which has been the explosive growth of private debt, both corporate and individual, that led to the global financial crisis of 2008 and after.[32]

The end of the Keynesian era was characterized by an attempt to use inflation to balance growth and rising wages. This strategy failed when the expected trade-off between inflation and unemployment no longer seemed to exist. In the United States, Paul Volker, chair of the Federal Reserve, instituted restrictive monetary policies that had a deflationary effect. In concert with attacks on unions, and along with deindustrialization, this policy shift represented the end of the era of rising wages.

A second strategy involved state fiscal crises. States wanted to maintain social programs and other spending, but the idea of increased taxes in times of wage stagnation was not politically appealing. Thus, in the 1980s states engaged in borrowing from capital markets, which they had previously liberalized. We might call this strategy "privatized Keynesianism." Streeck argues that this approach worked for a time to maintain social programs, but by the 1990s financial markets and private investors had rebelled and governments were forced to cut back. Privatization of government services and further deregulation were employed to balance budgets, but without tax revenues the state's power was reduced.

The third strategy that was employed in the later 1990s was the offloading of debt from public to private sources. Deregulated financial markets led to a massive increase in private debt, which along with speculation on tech stocks was responsible for the boom of the late 1990s. This strategy included the financialization of subprime mortgages that led to the crash of 2008. In the years since, central banks have bought up debt from failing banks and given out loans to these banks in order to stabilize markets and add cash. Austerity has kept inflation in check by restricting demand, and low interest rates and quantitative easing (i.e., the injection of money by central banks through the purchase of financial instruments) have been used to encourage investment. These have had a stabilizing effect and have produced satisfactory economic growth. Meanwhile, however, states plagued by debt, such as Greece, have experienced severe fiscal and social crises.

Each of these strategies has become exhausted, and it is not clear how much longer the current strategy will be effective as central banks have continued to embrace quantitative easing, which may bring back a certain amount of inflation. The stagnant wages of the last thirty years have not risen in any meaningful way.

Thus, Streeck sees an ideological shift that is not only transforming the social interests influencing the state but also creating a deeper democratic deficit. The debt-based state of the first stages of neoliberalism has been replaced by the austerity-centred consolidation state. The consolidation state places the needs of debt reduction over public services and the public good. It has in large measure transferred the costs of debt to private citizens in the form of taxes as well as reduced services (which must now be paid for through private expenditure). No longer is a balance sought between the needs of accumulation and those of legitimation; accumulation itself has become the primary justification for economic policy. (Elements of this transformation of accumulation into legitimation were already present in the 1970s, when what was called by neo-Marxists at the time the fiscal crisis of the state began to make itself felt.) The political demands for the correction or mitigation of the dysfunctional effects of advanced capitalism are economically (and politically) impossible to meet. Yet despite a series of measures

that have shifted the balance in favour of business – such as privatization, deregulation, outsourcing of debt to the public, low interest rates,
and the weakening organized labour – the economy has not recovered.
The austerity state is legitimized as a necessity, and this justifies the
impoverishment and punishment of the socially vulnerable.

Other theorists, agreeing with Wendy Brown and Sanford Schram,
emphasize the role of the state in neoliberalism. Werner Bonefeld and
Jamie Peck, for example, both stress the need for a strong state in neoliberalism, though it has taken different forms in different nations.[33]
Neoliberalism, as we noted above and discuss below, does not employ
a model of the state as simple nightwatchman. Neoliberals do not fully
endorse the idea of the invisible hand that would benignly shape the
market without intrusion. To the contrary, neoliberalism requires a
strong state to shape and guarantee the workings of the free market
and to defend the market against the dangers and challenges of socialism. The neoliberal state uses the creation of austerity and crisis to force
changes that benefit the interests of corporate capitalism even while
creating precarity and debt.

The construction of the strong state, and the priority it gives to economic over political freedom, is an important element in the authoritarian tendencies in neoliberalism. Bonefeld has used the term "authoritarian liberalism" to describe one version of neoliberalism.[34] Increasingly,
forms of political participation by ordinary citizens are being restricted.

Deregulation and Marketization as Political Interventions

The market, and especially the capitalist market, was far from a return
to spontaneous social order, as Hayek claimed; it did not arise spontaneously but rather through deliberate political action.[35] Capitalist market society, as theorists from Marx to Weber to Polanyi have shown,
was the result of a long struggle to implement the required institutions
and social norms. For the capitalist economic order to operate there
must be, at a minimum, state-sanctioned property rights, enforceable
contracts, and a currency of exchange. The state supports the capitalist
market society through economic policies, infrastructure, legal order,
and regulation of competition. It is in all respects an instituted order. Of
course, as Weber well noted, these initiatives must be accompanied by
cultural changes as reflected in religion, ethics, and personality structure. Though these developed in many ways independently of the market, they clearly work to support it. The world of individual freedom
in which we are free to pursue our economic self-interest in the market is one that has been created through social and political struggle.

Neoliberalism is not a return to spontaneous order but itself an instituted order founded on certain normative ideas. While we must follow the ways in which neoliberalism has rolled back forms of the welfare state, we also must be clear that neoliberalism is the result of deliberate policies – policies that are themselves the product of political forces and that by no means eliminate all types of regulation or government action.

If the capitalist market is not a natural phenomenon but one that is politically and socially constructed, it is reasonable to consider economic deregulation and marketization not simply as policies to restore profitability but simultaneously as political interventions. In the same way, the task of steering political decisions is partly privatized.

Deregulation and marketization shift decisions from the realm of public, political deliberation to a private realm where choices that affect the political fate of others are made without popular engagement. Especially in the United States, several sectors of industry have been deregulated, including transportation (airlines, railways, and trucking); energy (natural gas and electricity); communications (television, radio, telephone, the internet); and the financial and banking industry. In addition, many regulatory agencies have been captured by the industries they regulate and have become ineffective in carrying out existing rules.

Deregulation is aimed at reducing the costs of government action on business and supposedly allowing for greater efficiency. This has political implications. Deregulation means that, for example, decisions concerning the fairness of economic competition, the public interest obligations of radio, television, telephone, and now internet services, the health and safety of consumers (including protection from harmful or deficient products), and the safety of drugs and medical products are increasingly limited or eliminated altogether. Enterprises are no longer accountable to the populace for the side effects of capitalist economic activities.

A second neoliberal strategy is privatization. Publicly run business services and utilities are sold to private enterprises, while other sectors are opened to private competition. In Europe and in other places where there has been a history of public ownership, there has been more extensive privatization on the national level. In the United States, however, much of the impetus for privatization has taken place on the state and municipal level. Services from towing and garbage pick-up to social provision have been outsourced, and more recently this has extended to state institutions such as prisons. Charter schools, which are also licensed by the state, are another example of the outsourcing of public services to private enterprises. Such services are said to be more efficient and responsive to consumer demand. According to their proponents, deregulation and privatization, along with other measures such as reduced taxes, are supposed to unleash investment and innovation and create jobs. Deregulation, it is claimed, leads to lower prices and better and more efficient services.

Related to but distinct from deregulation and privatization, marketization refers to the conversion of non-market sectors to market imperatives. A prime example of this process is found in education.[36] The educational system no doubt has produced students who can fit into the economy in various roles, but it is their usefulness that provides the value. In addition, students have often developed critical capacities that may lead to dissent. The marketization of higher education is exemplified in the use of private sector management models at universities and the transformation of the student–teacher relationship into one between a service provider and a consumer. But more than this, universities are increasingly conceived as organizations whose main purpose is to facilitate profit-making, for both the university and private industry. Universities sell patents, provide consulting services, and launch private companies; in addition, they have become increasingly involved in leisure and conference services, much like private enterprises.

Marketization, then, is a process that brings to mind what Habermas called the colonization of the lifeworld. Here social relations, which are rooted in normative structures, become commodified. It is not just work relations that are turned into commodities, but relationships central to social reproduction. At this point, however, colonization becomes not just an economic process but a political one as well. As one observer notes, it is difficult to avoid concluding that marketization is as much about social engineering as economic concerns. In practice, a quasi-market in higher education propped up by state subsidies and micromanaged through government intervention coexists with genuine market-driven activities.

The Decline of Political Parties and Participation

Under the terms of neoliberal economics, governments have much less control over economic processes. The interests of finance and large corporations predominate over questions of social rights and welfare. As alternatives are increasingly dictated by economic interests, the manoeuvrability of political parties has become limited. In the United States, for example, the cliché that the two main political parties are largely the same comes close to reality. Under these conditions, faith in the democratic system as a force for change is diminished and participation in politics declines. Writers such as Colin Crouch and Jacques Rancière have used the term post-democracy to refer to a situation in which there are the formal conditions of democracy such as elections, congressional or parliamentary representation, and competing parties, but these institutions have little or no influence on actual political decisions.[37] Real policy is made in private. For Crouch, politics has become a "strictly controlled show, organized by professional experts and limited to a few topics chosen by these experts, while most inhabitants have only been assigned a passive role."[38]

Where participation is possible, it is relatively fruitless. Elites, especially economic elites, now almost completely dominate legislative affairs. Benjamin Page has noted the effects of this situation: even as public interest groups have arisen, it is the case that "contrary to what decades of political science research might lead you to believe, ordinary citizens have virtually no influence over what their government does in the United States." Martin Gilens and Benjamin Page have called this "economic elite domination"; Sheldon Wolin has characterized it as managed democracy.[39]

Wolin developed the idea of inverted totalitarianism to describe the notion of a market state ruled by an economic elite. While his historical analysis is somewhat flawed by a tendency to collapse postwar late capitalism into neoliberalism, he does capture something important about the structure of authority in contemporary politics. The possibility of democracy in America (and, as we are seeing, in Europe as well) has been significantly diminished. Indeed, we may have reached a crisis point from which we could easily lose any possibility of meaningful democracy for a generation or more.

Neoliberal Theory and the Problem of Popular Sovereignty: From the Threat of Totalitarianism to the Dangers of the Welfare State

Writing in the shadow of the Second World War and the ensuing cold war, Friedrich von Hayek and Karl Popper held that the central challenge facing Western democracies was the threat of totalitarianism. By this term they meant not only fascism and authoritarianism more broadly, but also communism, socialism, and even social democracy. Democracy could only flourish in a capitalist economy. The free market was the crucial buttress against these modern forms of tyranny, which in their collectivist orientation subordinated the freedom of the individual to a central authority. For Hayek especially, economic freedom was more crucial than political freedom.[40]

Here democracy was understood negatively. It was seen primarily as a protection against tyranny rather than as a positive achievement that ensured people's sovereignty. Neither Popper nor Hayek was enamoured of popular sovereignty. The former worried that the popular will would oppress minorities, that the majority would be undemocratic, indeed despotic. The latter felt that political authority was legitimated not by popular sovereignty but by unchanging natural laws that prescribed the fundamental norms of society. More than natural rights, these laws formed the basis of a permanent order of things, one that could not be superseded by the popular will.

For Hayek, social order is a spontaneous natural process, not a matter of social construction or central state action. Reminiscent of Adam Smith's invisible hand, his position held that order comes into being through the unintended coordination of intentional action. This idea of unintended coordination applies not only to the market but also to other aspects of social life. Thus, sovereignty does not arise out the deliberate actions of subjects but because of certain laws and structures that secure the freedom of spontaneously acting subjects. There is no common good for Hayek, only a set of formal conditions for freedom.

However, even given their reservations about or even hostility towards democracy, theorists of neoliberalism, such as Hayek and later Friedman, did not conceive of the state in classical nightwatchman form. They understood that the mid-twentieth century conditions required a different approach. The state has become the guarantor and protector of the economy. State power not only secures the conditions of successful accumulation through regulation of banking and trade but also has become the power of last resort that when called upon steps in to shore up the market against failures that have become all too common in the neoliberal era. The early neoliberals did not reject the use of state power even as they preached privatization and deregulation.

This commitment to a strong state buttressing a "free market" economy has both historical and theoretical roots. Ordo-liberalism, which developed in Germany in the 1930s, employed the notion of a social market economy that recognized the role of the state in creating the conditions of a market economy but combined this with a minimal notion of the welfare state. Rejecting pure *laissez-faire*, ordo-liberals wanted to use state power to oppose monopolies and promote some degree of social justice. They recognized that whatever its virtues, capitalism could have destructive effects. Such views were also held by postwar neoliberals such as Karl Popper and Isaiah Berlin, as well as members of the Chicago School, including Henry Simons, the teacher of Milton Friedman.[41] Even Hayek, who opposed the ordo-liberals, accepted

some limited forms of welfare. In *The Road to Serfdom* he argues that
"[t]he only question here is whether in the particular instance the
advantages gained are greater than the social costs which they impose.
Nor is the preservation of competition incompatible with an extensive
system of social services – so long as the organization of these services
is not designed in such a way as to make competition ineffective over
wide fields."[42] This somewhat vague statement was criticized by John
Maynard Keynes, who pointed out that this formulation failed to draw
a clear demarcation or limit on intervention. Hayek's position could
thus justify a wide variety of state interventions that he did not intend
to justify. Since in this period he was primarily concerned with opposing totalitarianism, he did not pay great attention to this problem. However, later neoliberals would take a more radical turn.

Although not totally opposed to welfare measures, neoliberals
rejected the New Deal and the Keynesian conception of social rights.[43]
Hayek, for example, viewed the state in legal rational terms. It could
only make general rules that did not favour ends. He echoed the criticism that the welfare state tried to guarantee substantive ends or goods
and thus distorted the free market. Like Berlin, he could only conceive
of a state that protected negative rights. Positive rights violated the
terms of the legal rational state. Social services would have to protect
negative rights or at least be compatible with them.

The next generation of neoliberals, led by Milton Friedman, was
much more concerned with the internal problems of the welfare state
than with the totalitarian threat to the open society. These neoliberals
departed from the assumptions of the earlier thinkers in several ways;
the most important for our purposes was that they accepted monopoly.
Unlike earlier theorists such as Ludwig Von Mises and Hayek, Friedman did not see monopoly as a problem for a market economy. The ills
of monopoly were explained away either as the result of government
actions or, if not, as insignificant. For their part, however, labour unions
were guilty of bad market behaviour: they restrained competition and
distorted market outcomes.

This later generation of neoliberals provided a rationale for the existence of large corporations that had enough power to influence if not
control markets. They did not seek to break up the large corporations
that dominated the economy. (Henry Simons, however, was a staunch
proponent of anti-trust measures; in this sense he was much closer to
the ordo-liberals.) Contemporary neoliberal theory is often quite com-
fortable with monopoly or oligopolistic conditions. Richard Posner
has argued that monopoly conditions do not lead to monopoly pric-
ing. Others have claimed that competitive conditions exist even under

monopoly or duopoly if the conditions of entry are not onerous. Thus, analysts ought to be careful about too easily assimilating neoliberalism to classical liberalism. The establishment and maintenance of market fundamentalism requires a more activist state than the classical liberals envisioned.

In 1951 Milton Friedman outlined the positive functions of the state. While rejecting what he called collectivism, like the ordo-liberals he argued that a pure *laissez-faire* approach fails as well. In addition to the functions of a nightwatchman, the state has an important role to play in economic regulation of, for example, the money supply. Though he accepted monopoly, he recognized that businesses could gain the power to coerce individuals and that in a complex society the government has a minimal obligation to aid the poor:

> Neo-liberalism would accept the nineteenth century liberal emphasis on the fundamental importance of the individual, but it would substitute for the nineteenth century goal of laissez-faire as a means to this end, the goal of the competitive order. It would seek to use competition among producers to protect consumers from exploitation, competition among employers to protect workers and owners of property, and competition among consumers to protect the enterprises themselves. The state would police the system, establish conditions favorable to competition and prevent monopoly, provide a stable monetary framework, and relieve acute misery and distress. The citizens would be protected against the state by the existence of a free private market and from each other by the preservation of competition.[44]

While Friedman accepted charity for the poor, for him this did not entail an acceptance of social entitlements.

Where the earlier neoliberals saw some role for social services, Friedman saw little. His fundamentalism extended to marketizing social services. He was a strong supporter of school vouchers and the privatization of all social services – for example, through housing vouchers and work-for-welfare programs. Friedman argued that such private services are inherently more cost-effective and responsive to consumer demand. These reforms, however, still require a strong state – not a mere watchman. The state must still administer programs and enforce compliance. Individuals or groups must be monitored, measured, and shaped to conform to the idea of market subjects who display the appropriate motivation and work discipline.

Freidman also doubts the power of popular sovereignty. Since economic freedom is the precondition for political freedom, capitalism is the necessary condition of personal and political freedom. Where there is no economic freedom there can be no political freedom.[45]

In giving priority to economic freedom over political freedom, Friedman argues that under certain historical conditions there can be free markets without subsequent political freedoms. He cites Bismarck's Germany, Japan before the First World War, tsarist Russia, fascist Spain, and fascist Italy as examples of capitalist markets without political freedoms. Whatever their limitations, Friedman considers these societies superior to "totalitarian" societies in which there is no economic freedom: "Even in those societies [i.e., authoritarian states] the citizenry had a good deal more freedom than citizens of a modern totalitarian state like Russia or Nazi Germany, in which economic totalitarianism is combined with political totalitarianism."[46]

As examples of this "freedom" Friedman cites tsarist Russia and other countries where one could change jobs. Private property provided a check on the power of the state. This sort of freedom, however, is a purely private. Even the role of civil rights is unclear. Public freedom, which includes the ability to act in common and deliberate with others, is ignored. We can see here the basis of Friedman's statement that he preferred dictatorship to socialism – recalling his view of the 1973 coup in Chile. Structural adjustments imposed by outside powers can be defended because they create the conditions for freedom.

Capitalism for Friedman is thus the basis of the good life. It guarantees prosperity and freedom for all. In fact, Friedman predicted that when neoliberal policies were put in place, prosperity for the common worker as well as for the plutocrat would result. (Thus far his prediction has not been fulfilled.) Friedman sees the primacy of the economic as a way of decentralizing authority and taking it out of the orbit of state control. Because he is tone deaf to the effects of concentrated economic power, he has no sense of its inequality-generating force.

Friedman employs a limited notion of freedom. The subject is the private individual who chooses alternatives in the context of the choices of others. Social order is the coordination of these choices. Yet this notion of freedom is incapable of accounting for the very ends that Friedman supposes: the creative entrepreneurial subject who creates new ideas or products; and the democratic subject that he claims is the result of economic freedom. What Friedman provides is a form of freedom without autonomy. It privileges the freedom to exchange and choose over the freedom to reflexively guide one's own life. It lacks any conception of the notion that social and public–political freedom is central to autonomy.

In the postwar period, the emergence of neoliberalism as a political force was closely related to the rise of rational choice theory. Of course, rational choice and neoliberalism are not equivalent. Yet they both shared a concern with welfare economics and with the problems of popular sovereignty. Economists and political scientists such as James Buchanan, Gordon Tullock, and William Riker expanded the market assumptions of rational choice economics to political theory.[47] They drew on and extended the work of Nobel Prize–winning economist, Kenneth Arrow, who held that no model of collective choice could be derived from the premises of individual choice. Like earlier neoliberals, Arrow held that his conception of the sovereignty of consumer choice was a vital buttress against the threat of collectivism. Arrow's theorem posed a real challenge to Marxist and republican theories like that of Rousseau, which stress the importance of a popular will.

These premises had great appeal to political scientists who sought to put their discipline on a secure scientific basis and at the same time counter the challenge of "collectivist" or socialist political and economic thought. Using Arrow's theorem, they rejected theories of the general will or popular sovereignty as the basis of political legitimacy. From the standpoint of rational choice theory, William Riker was very sceptical of ideas of the general will – for him, the latter was simply an illusion. In line with Hayek and Popper, rational choice theorists equated such conceptions with socialist and totalitarian systems that put the group ahead of the individual. The basic legitimating principle for politics was the same as that of economics – individual consumer choice. The conditions of democracy could be fulfilled or only when individuals were afforded the freedom to choose.

However, this whole edifice rested on a questionable first premise: the idea that individual consumer choice can serve as the basic feature of politics. It provided the equivalent of a logical *simple* in this system, which was unchanging and unaffected by other conditions. It was in a sense a purely independent variable.

We believe this premise is incorrect. Our choices and preferences are not independent of social arrangements but are affected by a whole set of conditions, such as the normative background and structures of power in society. Moreover, as a social theory it flounders on the problem of order. It cannot explain how individuals are bound together as members of a society. The systematic aims of rational choice theories mean that they cannot avail themselves of Hayek's notion of spontaneous social order but need to construct the bases of social order from the ground up. They cannot account for the intersubjective bases of social life rooted in mutual accountability that we discussed in chapter 2.

Neoliberal and rational choice theories question the bases of democratic legitimacy. Voting is seen as an essentially irrational act and popular deliberation as irredeemably collectivist. Gordon Tullock and James Buchanan reconceive the constitutional system as a market transaction. Following a social contract model, they claim that people give their obedience to government because they benefit from the rule of law. The amount of authority they surrender is the subject of cost–benefit analysis. They interpret this as a form of consumer sovereignty and reject notions of social welfare altogether. In opposition to majority rule, which they find inefficient and unjustified, they believe that basic rules need unanimous consent.

William Riker ultimately argues that voting is only irrational as a form of populist expression designed to establish a common will. It can be rational, however, when exerted as a veto power, that is, as the negative liberty to vote someone out. Rational choice sees this as a constraint on the behaviour of leaders who will not want to lose power.[48] This exerts constraints on the coercive authority of government. Such a theory does not seem to explain, however, the workings of power both in the formation of leaders and in the capacity to change the rules and rig the system.

By contrast, James Buchanan interprets the rise of bureaucratic power in a neoliberal manner. He argues that legislatures have limited control over bureaucracies and holds that we should view government as a competition between prospective monopolists (parties) that seek to maximize their own ends instead of serving sovereign consumers, as would a purely competitive market system. Seen in this way, government is not a mechanism for citizens to obtain collective goods and services, but an exploiter. Government has gotten out of hand. Buchanan thinks that constitutional limits must be placed on it. He viewed his own work as providing an important major contribution to the process of establishing such limits.[49]

Even these constructions, which are aimed at limited government, seem to us to leave questions of the scope and extent of authority in the lurch. The notion of consumer sovereignty leaves a great deal open for arbitrary authority. Neoliberalism in practice requires a larger and more ominous source of political power than most of its proponents realize, or, if they realize it, than they are prepared to admit.

Both positions discussed here reject any idea of popular sovereignty as the ground of democratic political authority. These theories accept notions of individual choice but are incapable of addressing questions of *how* individuals create binding social relations through intersubjective action. Many of the active characteristics of citizenship are lost in the process, such as the ability to deliberate and act in concert. Individuals are little more than isolated consumers who are at best aggregated as choosers without a common orientation. This is the neoliberal perspective on democracy. Citizen-consumers are passive spectators presented with alternatives brought forward by elite providers of political goods.

Neoliberalism and Authoritarian Liberalism

While elite democratic theories held that voters choose leaders who then formulate policies initiated by elites, they also retained a pluralistic conception of pressure groups that influence policy. Of course, elite democrats, like the neoliberals, rejected the notion of widespread participation in political deliberations and decisions. Pressure groups were understood in terms of self-interest, and widespread participation ran the risk of encouraging the growth of populism, whereby the uneducated masses would rule. Elite theorists were not, however, necessarily opposed to the welfare state.

The neoliberal conception diverges from the elite pluralist model in that it fundamentally rejects the notion of pluralism associated with democratic elitism. In contrast to pluralist thinkers, neoliberal theorists move in the direction of a more aggressive, disciplinary liberalism, whose origins can be traced to the political, economic, and social crises of the Weimar Republic in Germany in the 1920s and early 1930s. The legal scholar Hermann Heller used the term authoritarian liberalism to refer to Carl Schmidt's conception of a state that was both strong and weak: strong when required to protect capitalism and private property from popular, pluralist democratic forces pursuing redistribution; but weak insofar as it permitted the market as an ostensibly self-regulating and self-directing source of freedom and prosperity to function with little or no political intervention, even though political authority was essential for the institution of market relations themselves.

Thus, authoritarian liberalism clearly supports a strong state when it comes to the regulation and control of subjects. As Wolfgang Streeck notes in his commentary on Heller,

> the freedom of the market from state interference that defines a liberal and indeed, a liberal-capitalist economy is not a state of nature but is and needs to be politically constructed, publicly instituted and enforced by state power. The depoliticized condition of a liberal economy is itself an outcome of politics, in the sense of a specific use of the authority of the state for a specific political purpose – it is a political construction that must be politically defended against the possibility of political authority

falling into the hands of social forces that might use it for non-liberal, market-subverting objectives.[50]

The market economy was, then, a social construct. For authoritarian liberals, it did not exist independently of state power but was the *creation* of that power. At the same time, the strong state was needed to guarantee that those who might wish to undermine or subvert the market through redistributive policies, or who threatened private property, were kept at bay.

For authoritarian liberals, the state must exercise coercion to suppress and shape the behaviour of those who pose a threat by advocating for democratic reforms that would also regulate the market. Neoliberal authoritarianism is more subtle: cloaking themselves in calls for freedom, neoliberals seek to reward winners and punish those who lose in free market competition. In this respect, it suggests similarities to Wendy Brown's account of the shaping of the state and the self. Streeck detects a similar outlook in German ordo-liberalism, which we discussed earlier – although its idea of the social market would seem to provide some room for a limited welfare state, just as Hayek had done. Streeck sees this as a development that runs counter to the position developed by the earlier Frankfurt theorists, who as we have seen believed that the emergence of extensive state intervention to address the problems and contradictions of capitalism meant there could be no return to a market-guided economy.

The contemporary version of authoritarian liberalism, according to Streeck, is found in neoliberalism. And although ordo-liberalism has been broadly more accommodating of state intervention in the capitalist market economy to secure some measure of social protection, Streeck nonetheless still views it as crucial for the rise of neoliberalism, in both theory and practice. In his view, ordo-liberalism has built "a bridge from the authoritarian liberalism of interwar Germany, as conceived by Schmitt and analysed by Heller, to the neoliberalism that began to dismantle the post-war political economy in the 1980s."[51] So for Streeck,

[t]oday's post-democratic, or better perhaps: a-democratic Hayekian capitalism, after the victory, or almost-victory, of neoliberalism, may be regarded as a historically updated version of ordo-liberalism. What it has in common with it is the insulation of a politically instituted market economy from democratic politics, an insulation because of which both the neoliberal state and the neoliberal economic regime qualify as authoritarian in the sense of Schmitt and Heller ... [T]he language of authority being out of fashion in today's Europe, it must be replaced with a mixture of

technocratic claims to superior expertise and resigned submission to the "realities" of globalization.[52]

What is particularly disturbing for Streeck is precisely the fact that, as noted above, Hermann Heller developed his account in response to the position of Carl Schmitt. More specifically, Heller identified authoritarian liberalism as Schmitt's counterpoint to what Schmitt saw as the Weimar "total state" with its strongly interventionist and in his view potentially dangerous democratic presence throughout the economy and society. Ordo-liberalism and (now) neoliberalism thus have unsettling historical antecedents in fascism. Indeed, as Streeck sees it, with the rise of Nazism Schmitt himself in effect abandoned the authoritarian liberal model, which with the triumph of fascism was no longer needed. And Schmitt's critique of the "total state" foreshadowed comparable attacks on excessive state intervention that accompanied the emergence of neoliberal opposition to the postwar Keynesian welfare state – yet another disturbing implication of Schmitt's position.

The political character of economic distribution that characterized the Keynesian era is reversed but still held in place by political structures, while at the same time individuals are subject to market discipline. The idea of a totally "free" market, a kind of pure state of nature, is a chimera. However, to get at the processes that operate in contemporary neoliberalism we need to examine how initiatives such as privatization and deregulation create an increasingly risky and precarious situation for individuals.

Guy Standing provides a more precise definition of the what has come to be called the precariat: it refers not just to the vulnerability that many people feel, but to the formation of a new social class that differs from the traditional proletariat. The traditional working class lacked ownership of the means of production and thus was required to sell its labour, whereas the new "class" is characterized by permanent and structural underemployment and forms of unpaid work.[53] The precariat can include workers displaced by globalization, or those with no skills and no future, as well as young professionals in highly industrialized societies with scant chances for employment in their fields. But it can be found in all parts of the global economy, even in developed industrialized societies where access to a profession increasingly requires unpaid apprenticeships or other low-paid forms of work, and social connections besides. Possession of formal academic or technical credentials often means little.[54]

For Standing, the problem lies in the new ideas about work in the neoliberal era. Not just neoliberals but even welfare state liberals adopted the idea that "labour market flexibility" was required to keep costs down and to prevent capital from fleeing to low-cost countries. But this meant that labour conditions became more insecure. Here Standing's ideas call to mind the notion of fluid modernity, although he has a narrower focus. The precariat is not simply a more flexible middle class; rather, its members have no security or benefits. With Ulrich Beck he sees the risks in social life being passed down to those who must somehow find by themselves the resources needed to mitigate these risks. For Standing, this insecurity is the result not of technology but of economics.

From Authoritarian Liberalism to Reactionary Populism

Neoliberals have difficulty accepting democratic authority. Since they see economic freedom as prior to political freedom, they will sacrifice the former to the latter. However, consent for neoliberal initiatives requires a new form of mass politics in which the underclass, immigrants, and other outsiders are used as scapegoats to justify anti-democratic policies. Far from a simple return to a state of freedom, whereby the removal of restraints and government programs will lead to a spontaneous and free order, neoliberalism adopts revanchist or reactionary mass politics to win approval.

American politics is becoming more authoritarian and less open to public deliberation. The political system is no longer a vehicle for citizen participation. Many observers have noted the increasing polarization of political parties in America. For example, a recent survey by the Pew Foundation suggests that the increasing polarization of political views is reflective of other social changes.[55] Citizens with different political viewpoints are becoming more and more polarized; they get their news from different sources and live increasingly segregated lives. Up to half of all committed conservatives get their news exclusively from one source: Fox News (liberals seem more likely to use multiple sources). Most analysts see more ideological division and a declining centre. They see fewer points of contact between opposing groups. Rather than a public sphere in which people are exposed to diverse ideas, they see restricted and indeed almost privatized publics that get information only from outlets expressing and legitimizing similar perspectives.

Morris Fiorina provides a forceful dissent to this thesis.[56] He argues that if there were polarization there would be more Democrats and Republicans; but in fact, there are more independents. Thus, he claims that most individuals' preferences have not changed. However, Fiorina makes a problematic assumption: that those who are independent are necessarily in the middle of the political spectrum – which is not always true. The bigger problem arises from the fact that Fiorina focuses on the majority of populace and not on the elite; thus, he misses the power of elites to set the agenda for politics. In Christopher Lasch's phrase, we face a revolt of the elites.[57] Significant elements of these elites have essentially given up on the vision of a democratic America and have increasingly separated themselves economically, culturally, and politically from the lower classes.

It is here that analysts see a significant change in politics and in the psychological bases of politics. For Marc Hetherington and Jonathan Weiler,[58] these developments are the correlate of world views, sets of value orientations, and beliefs that are "connected to a visceral sense of right and wrong." In other words, we should look at the lifeworld of the participants, and their sense of that world, to get a grip on contemporary forms of polarization. That sense includes not just politics but other social practices, such as childrearing and gender roles. Hetherington and Weiler argue that it is not just the beliefs of partisans that determine the extent of authoritarian politics; it is also the style of these world views and the ways they orient people to the world. They see an increasingly authoritarian style, especially on the right, one that is driven by fear and insecurity. Authoritarians see the world as a fragile and besieged place and often see their supposed opponents as radically "other" and thus threatening. Authoritarians tend to separate the world into "in" and "out" groups and to be hostile towards those others who do not share their views. Thus they tend towards more combative relations with enemies, who must be destroyed or put down. They also tend to lack affect and sympathy for those in subaltern groups who do not share their views.

American political scientists and historians has tended to focus on the authoritarian potential of mass democracy and populism. For Richard Hofstadter, writing with a post–Second World War sensibility, all populism is linked to the threat of dictatorship.[59] One of the greatest threats to the political system is that the less educated masses will, through their fears of "status anxiety" and irrational thinking, respond to populist appeals and open themselves to demagogues like Joseph McCarthy (and, presumably, Donald Trump). Hofstadter identified a paranoid style in politics, a mindset in which conspiracies abounded. While he was by no means a pure apologist for liberalism, he underestimated the progressive potential of populism in American life, as well as the potential strength of elites.

Elites exhibit a greater tendency and need for ideological coherence and greater interest in, and involvement in, government. In the process of becoming political activists, participants often must take on a more explicit ideology – and for conservatives, increasing ideological rigidity. In Europe and the United States, significant elements of these elites with authoritarian sympathies have been attracted to the ideologies of the new right. Others, less radical, have nonetheless moved towards a more coherent version of activist conservatism that seeks to restrict popular participation in the name of economic freedom.

Yet Hofstadter, who was also influenced by more progressive thinkers like C. Wright Mills and Theodor Adorno, has turned out to be correct in one respect.[60] A conservative form of populism that manifests elements of the paranoid style has become a feature of mainstream politics in America. The everyday experiences of significant segments of the population have been shaped by the declining fortunes of the middle and working classes, whose increasing vulnerability and precarious status have led them in the direction of a reactionary populism. People in this situation can come to feel powerless and alienated from political institutions and to blame their problems on elites who ignore them. Along with many on the left, they object to the negative effects of neoliberal policies on the economy – in particular, they object to "free trade" agreements and the concomitant export of jobs.

The crises of neoliberalism are not just economic. The precarious character of contemporary life and the offloading of social risks onto the backs of the middle and under classes has led to a sense of grievance, powerlessness, and danger among segments of the population. Some have reacted to the situation with an awareness of the power relationships that are at the root of these problems. For other groups, however, the vulnerabilities that have been magnified under neoliberalism are not just economic; they also trigger often unconscious cultural anxiety about pollution and purity, about threats posed to national or cultural identity by external forces and internal enemies. The sense of powerlessness leaves segments of the population open to the appeal of demagogic leaders.

The members of the first generation of the Frankfurt School were aware that authoritarian tendencies were found not only in Germany but also in democratic countries such as the United States. In the work of agitators like Father Charles Coughlin, who, based in a Detroit-area church, built a following in the 1930s using radio, they saw many of the main themes found in fascist rhetoric.[61] While such agitators remained decidedly on the margins of American society, the Frankfurt theorists worried that this could change. Writing in 1970 with Richard Nixon and George Wallace in mind, Herbert Marcuse warned that the tactics of such agitators were now part of the mainstream. This seems true today as well.

What does increasing polarization mean for the political system? The notion that the "vital centre" is being lost is perhaps too much of a hangover from the days of liberal consensus. It is not simply the fact of polarization but its style and what the polarization represents. We argue that polarization is a serious problem in the political system but that it is merely a symptom of the larger conflict – some might say contrast – between neoliberalism and democratic self-government. Neoliberalism as a response to the neoconservative crisis of governability has simply deepened this crisis rather than resolving it.

Democracy and Civic Life

Questions about the nature of civic life illustrate the conflict between the economy and the scope of democratic social life. Neoliberals and rational choice theorists tend to reject, or at least are sceptical about, any notion of a common interest or public good. From their vantage point, civil society and civil life must limited in scope for the market to fully operate and thereby guarantee freedom and efficiency. Yet capitalism rests on a background of legal norms, common understandings, and social sentiments and solidarities that underpin social life. Unrestricted capitalism tends to impoverish the very civic life it requires. Thus civic life offers a key vantage point from which the conflicts and contestations of a neoliberal economy can be viewed.

The notion of civil society has become an important element in contemporary discussions of political life. Civil society represents a sphere of intermediary, often voluntary, non-governmental institutions that stand between government authority and citizens. It represents a sphere in which social interests take shape and political will is expressed. Institutions of civil society include clubs and voluntary associations, sports groups, churches, and educational bodies, but also political parties, private foundations, and policy groups and even social movements, such as environmental and consumer groups.

For some theorists, civil society is simply an expression of a liberal social order. It represents the sphere of private life that is separated from government and public life. Here, as in the liberal conception, civil society is a bulwark against interference in the freedom of subjects to pursue their goals. By contrast, the republican understanding, which is exemplified in the work of Hegel, sees civil society as a space for creating social bonds and solidarity.[62] It protects individuals and also creates social relations and possibilities. It is the source of the communicative relations among people.

Broadly speaking, there are two distinct ways that the second (Hegelian) version of civil society is approached. One approach stresses the formation of sensibilities conducive to solidarity and identity. The other stresses the deliberative democratic and political nature of the public sphere. These two approaches are not necessarily opposed and can even be complementary. Both address the lacuna in classical liberalism. The first emphasizes the socially integrative elements of civil society that shape sensibilities and create moral bonds. On this reading, civil society can include our interpretations of others and our own identities. The second identifies civil society as a source of political deliberation and contestation. The emphasis here is on the role of social movements, political parties and clubs, and extra-parliamentary debate in the public sphere.

According to Robert Putnam, civic life is in decline.[63] As is well known, Putnam looks at the decline of common social activities, such as bowling, in which individuals from different walks of life can participate. Like Alexis de Tocqueville, he sees the unique core of American life and its democratic ethos in widespread participation in the voluntary associations of civic life. Participation in groups and associations leads to greater reciprocity and cooperation, as well as stronger trust and solidarity – in other words, social integration – among members of a community. But Putnam, unlike Tocqueville, does not include politics as an element of civic life, seeing it instead as a divisive force. Thus he does not view political parties and social movements as components of civic life. Social capital in contemporary society is declining not because of changes in the economy and work or related social conditions, but because of television.

Robert Bellah's analysis of civic life takes the second path; for him, it is a source not only of social integration but also of political legitimacy. Civic virtue does not simply provide the moral support for society. Because the norms of civic life often conflict with the demands of the market, they raise issues related to the political justification for market pressures and outcomes. Therefore, in his account of civic life, Bellah stresses not just voluntary associations but also the moral dimensions of social and political rights. The creation of civic life requires moral and political obligations to others that cannot be fulfilled by market forces – for example, our sense of justice and fairness and concern for the welfare of others.[64] These norms are part of a shared American ethos or a civil religion that unifies the nation.[65] In this respect, Bellah is closer to Tocqueville than to Putnam. He fears that individualism rooted in a market mentality erodes civic life. He retains a republican standpoint of a single shared ethos (however weak), an American civil religion that reduces the pluralistic quality of modern societies. In contrast, much political debate seems to centre on the conflicting ideas of the good and just life and does not always suppose a shared ethos.

Still, there is an element of truth to the republican version of the public sphere. It highlights crucial elements of social and personal integrity of the lifeworld that need to be maintained. It is often overlooked that Jürgen Habermas in *The Structural Transformation of the Public Sphere* also analysed the literary public sphere.[66] This was a space within which sensibilities and solidarities could be formed. Later, these concerns re-emerged in Habermas's analysis of the lifeworld. We need to be careful, however, in separating the notions of reason and emotion arbitrarily. The formation of sensibilities is intersubjective. Sensibilities are not merely inner emotions that rest wholly within the self; rather, they represent an orientation towards the world – a judgment on it. They must be grasped though forms of mutual understanding. Our ways of being in the lifeworld are central to our ideas of the good life, our conceptions of solidarity with others, and our identities. Given the decline in reading, the literary public sphere is withering. It is however reasonable to speak broadly of a cultural public sphere. This would involve the mass media, including television, radio, movies, and now the internet and other digital forms; but also, much of what is called popular culture. Popular culture helps define the scope of the lifeworld and consequently our engagement with questions of the good life, its meaning and purposes.

Studies of economically besieged Middle American towns illustrate the cultural and social disintegration generated by the impact of neoliberal economies on public life. Arlie Hochschild in her study *Strangers in Their Own Land* shows how families and communities have become fragmented and destroyed by stagnant wages, deindustrialization, and loss of a sense of community and place.[67] They have become alienated from an American Dream that no longer holds the promise of a better life. Bellah's notion of the American civil creed has become emptied of meaning. Far from voting against their own interests, individuals seek ideologies and views that make sense of their situation, in which the common strands of culture in the lifeworld are beginning to snap. The lifeworlds of working classes are becoming fragmented and desiccated, and their attempts to make sense of this are leading to alienation from those they see as big government liberals who benefit from a state that has abandoned them and crippled industry. To be sure, the conclusions they reach in making sense of their situation are not always well founded. Hochschild gives the example of Mike, a supporter of the right-wing and ostensibly populist Tea Party, who lived near a sinkhole caused by the activity of a lightly regulated company. He decried government regulation and doubted that global warming existed. He berated big government even though his state was receiving among the highest per capita levels of support from the federal government. His understanding of his own lifeworld was filled with paradoxes.

Similarly, in *Hillbilly Elegy* J.D. Vance describes the tangle of pathologies facing poor families who move from Appalachia to the Midwest to find jobs.[68] Instead of finding the American Dream, they face difficult obstacles, including their own past of spousal and substance abuse. They live in a culture of despair, hopelessness, and, sometimes, denial. While Vance writes from a conservative point of view that stresses character flaws rather than structural power, we can give his observations a more generous reading: these are problems of social disorganization that stem from the impact of the loss of industrial and agricultural employment. Such disorganization recalls Gaventa's work *Power and Powerlessness* to which we earlier referred, which traces the sense of acquiescence in an Appalachian town.[69] Forty years later, the situation is worse. Now, with few jobs available, their culture is mired in drug abuse, disorder, and deeper despair.

Neoliberals are sceptical about the ideals of public service and voluntary sector activity. They cannot for the most part conceive of motives that are altruistic or even deontological. Only self-interest counts. Thus they cannot make sense of the social solidarities or ethical motives of actors in the public sphere and the voluntary or not-for-profit sector. Public choice theorists James Buchanan and Gordon Tullock argue that there is no distinct set of ethical motives that public sector actors have. Like market-based actors, they only pursue self-interest.[70] Similarly, they see public servants as self-serving bureaucrats who act to maximize their interests by increasing their salaries and the scope of their power. From the standpoint of public or rational choice, of course, ideas of social welfare and other social objectives are incoherent.

The social solidarities that Putnam and Bellah identify fit uneasily in the neoliberal framework. Attachments that bind members of a society through mutual respect and understanding are viewed as either pre-political or irrelevant. For rational choice theorists and neoliberals, it is sufficient that actions are coordinated through self-interest. Yet as we have seen, a capitalist economy requires a moral substructure to support it, one that places accumulation and profit over other goods and puts a value on work as a vocation. The terms of morality under the conditions of an advanced capitalist economy cannot simply be a reinstitution of the Protestant ethic – the side effects and contradictions of this economy are grasped tacitly or explicitly by all. There is an expectation among many that government must intervene to protect society against these side effects.

Civil Society and Communicative Power

When civil society is conceived as a pluralistic public sphere, structures of mutual accountability through which participants can reach understanding on matters of public concern assume a central place. As outlined in the work of Habermas and others, the public sphere emerged as an arena in which citizens met in clubs and coffee houses to read newspapers and discuss the issues of the day, in the process forming their political and social views. This was a sphere of independent public opinion that could be critical of existing authorities. Over time the public sphere has come to include social movements, political parties, and other informal vehicles of democratic discussion. It is a forum for political debate, not just for the creation of an ethos. It takes up questions of the good and just life that are in dispute in pluralistic societies. We do not always have to share ideas of the good to engage in public debate. To the contrary, it is the condition of plurality that brings us to debate and deliberate on these matters. Citizenship on this view requires the capacity for participation in the public and political affairs of the community. Civil society is one source of the communicative power that is generated when participants come together to form the will to act in concert on an issue or problem. But forms of communicative power – albeit weak – can also be found in situations where agreement is achieved. Even when it does not result in agreement, discussion about public issues can foster cooperation or engender trust that individuals can carry on interaction in the face of disagreement.

To be sure, the extent and adequacy of the public sphere in capitalist societies can be contested. The actual character of the public sphere has been far from ideal. It has often excluded groups from participation and can be found in multiple forms that do not always work in concert. Nonetheless it still represents an important structural element of modern politics that needs to be realized in democracy.

Rational choice theorists do not see deliberation as a central feature of public life. They lack a notion of communicative power that is intersubjectively generated. They cannot conceive of a political will created through acting in common, but only a concatenation of individual choices that can be aggregated. Rational choice theories can at best establish a market model of political initiative: elite political actors are the producers of alternatives and programs, while ordinary citizens are consumers.

Neoliberal attacks on the public sphere take two distinct but related directions. The first is the conversion of the social relations of the public sphere according to the demands of market rationality. Human activity is reduced to issues of profitability and, as we will see in the next section, the constriction of the rational economic subject. To the extent that the public sphere is reduced to calculation and self-interest, however, those elements of mutual accountability and deliberation needed to form both common sensibility and public opinion disappear. When decisions are based on economic imperatives, public reasons or common sentiments have little place. As we will discuss at the end of this chapter, neoliberalism is characterized by the colonization of the lifeworld and the replacement of communicative processes by economic imperatives. In eliminating these elements of communication, neoliberalism has introduced pathologies into civil society. The conflict between the social, political, and cultural rights of development has led to crises in social and cultural integration. Individuals no longer see themselves as part of common society or a cultural tradition.

From the State to the Soul: The Fate of the Individual

Contrasting the embedded liberalism of the welfare state with forms of disembedded liberalism, critics have noted that liberalism so understood destroys the reservoir of social welfare (in the broad sense) and trust and solidarity in every sphere of social life. However, contemporary versions of disembedded liberalism have to establish dominance in different contexts. Calling to mind once again the work Wendy Brown, disembedded liberalism promotes the use of the disciplinary power of the state to construct an entrepreneurial subject.

Neoliberal arguments about the superiority of the market as a mechanism for distributing all social goods often flounder on the realities of income inequality and unequal distribution of the risks and benefits of social life.[71] Deregulation is central to neoliberalism because in its view it frees businesses to respond to the new conditions of global capitalism. This "new" capitalism requires flexibility to quickly meet changing market demands and conditions throughout the world. In the eyes of both its defenders and its analysts, this fast and agile capitalism requires constant change. It must shift priorities and resources quickly to find supplies and new markets. It constantly seeks new opportunities.

The individual also must learn to adapt to the world of fast capitalism. She must be flexible. She must adapt to the changing job market and be willing to change jobs or move to meet the market demand. Richard Sennett draws on Zygmunt Bauman's notion of liquid modernity to describe this feature.[72] The world of seemingly solid jobs and stable conditions has given way to more unstable conditions of personal life.

This new constellation of subjectivity has fostered the fragmentation of everyday life in the neoliberal era. Since a significant amount of work in neoliberal times is contingent employment, it requires constant adaptation. According to Sennett and Bauman, we learn to ignore our past identity so that we might "go with the flow." Stable identities become more difficult to maintain. In short, "liquid modernity" implies both economic insecurity and social instability. Neoliberalism creates new risks that are financial, social, and ecological and then distributes them asymmetrically since many of the wealthy can insulate themselves from some risk and privatize the risks for the less well-off. Individuals must negotiate a new environment in which they face new constraints on time based in short-term relationships and marketing of the self as a "brand" for potential economic gain. These developments have destabilized the sense of a narrative of the self so that a continuous identity is difficult to establish.

Neoliberalism promises prosperity and freedom but has created its opposite – a state of constant social insecurity and unfreedom. As the conditions of work in neoliberal society have become casualized and contingent, individuals have lost their stable mooring in the social world. This new "flexible" world in which people are required to constantly adapt to labour markets and changing conditions benefits few. The modern economy has taken on a "winner take all" character. The winners get big rewards, the losers little or nothing.

Just as jobs have become more unstable, elements of the social safety net have been shrunk or restructured. The costs and risks of social life that are the result of forces the individual did not create have become burdens the individual has to bear. Privatized education is a good example of this. When education becomes financed primarily by student loans, for example, what is essentially a social good in redefined as a private risk. The costs of education become mostly a private matter. If the public system of K–12 education is dismantled, individual families will be forced to accept substandard education or pay exorbitant costs. The rhetoric of personal responsibility often means that individuals are cast aside to bear the side effects and even unintended consequences of a capitalist economic system over which they have little personal control. The downloading of the risks of social life often makes individuals feel more vulnerable and renders their lives more precarious.

A related argument has been made by French sociologists Luc Boltanski and Eve Chiapello in *The New Spirit of Capitalism*.[73] They, too, have noted the shift from a production system based on relatively permanent industrial jobs and a hierarchical workplace to a flexible workplace that champions individual initiative. This type of capitalism has incorporated the critique of the conformism of corporate culture developed in the 1960s and created a new, more or less hierarchical, collaborative and project-driven workplace. This new form of capitalism is best embodied in the ethos of Silicon Valley and in corporations such as Google. Boltanski and Chiapello see the rise of a new ideal – a new spirit of capitalism in the vision of the unencumbered individual who is free to create his or her own life. Of course, this formulation is limited in scope. The rise of flexible corporate culture has been accompanied by hyper-exploitation in the less developed world as well as the degradation of work for those who have lost industrial jobs. While beneficial for a few in the short run, such developments have greatly increased the precarity of the clear majority. The people studied by Hochschild and discussed by Sennett are quite alienated from the fluid entrepreneurial self. They seek community, continuity, and security in permanent jobs to counter the meaninglessness and vulnerability of their lives.

What Marx once wrote characterizing the power of capitalism – namely, that "All that is solid melts into air" – has been reinforced dramatically in neoliberal capitalism. The individual under neoliberalism is not the optimistic and self-interested actor of classic liberal theory who creates a harmonious social order; rather, she is constituted through insecurity and fear. The entrepreneurial subject is not a construct of nature but requires a kind of negative individualization, which rather than establishing identity within a community separates the individual from social connections and from public life. The project of using one's time and freedom to create a coherent plan of life through which to express one's own deeply held commitments is far more difficult when subjectivity is circumscribed in a world of risks that threaten to overwhelm our ability to cope with them.[74]

Michel Foucault similarly argued that neoliberalism was not a theory that sought a return to a natural state but rather a social construction of subjectivity, in this case an entrepreneurial self. In his interpretation, the classical idea of economic man is based in the satisfaction of needs and rooted in a productivist model. Wendy Brown notes: "We come to the market to offer what we have (labor and goods) for what we need." The entrepreneurial self is, in contrast, a mode of subjectivization, the creation of a subject who sees himself as "being for himself his own capital, his own producer, the source of his earnings."[75] Whatever his role, whether producing, selling, or consuming, he produces his own satisfaction. Foucault, however, does not link this entrepreneurial self to the offloading of social risk or to the increasing sense of precarity that many people are now experiencing. To be sure, he speaks of "responsibilizing," a circumlocution for the internalization of personal responsibility; but at times he seems to embrace the sense of risk.

Foucault's distaste for governmental intervention in personal life and his assumption of the necessity of risk lead him to oppose much of the modern welfare state. He does not distinguish clearly between those elements that convert citizens into clients and those that provide necessary conditions for human flourishing and compensate for the effects of the capitalist market. This has led some commentators to think that Foucault, who wrote his lectures on neoliberalism in the late 1970s, was enamoured with the libertarian elements of the doctrine as an alternative to Hegelian Marxism.[76] Whatever the limits of his analysis, however, Foucault did recognize that neoliberalism is a social formation distinct from classical free market economics.

The precariousness of everyday life is reinforced by the increasing disciplining of subjectivity.[77] For example, to qualify for welfare in the United States it is no longer sufficient to be in distress; one must show the proper attitude towards work and be actively seeking employment, no matter what the situation. In the United States, large groups of men – especially African American men – are incarcerated for minor offences that seem to represent resistance to this discipline. Instead of eliminating bureaucracy, these new disciplinary practices create new bureaucratic structures. In many areas of life, individuals are increasingly monitored and shaped to conform to the demands of neoliberalism and to accept the risks inherent in the culture of the new capitalism. Information is monitored and mined for data that is then used to shape subjectivity. Some of the organizations engaged in information mining are not government bureaucracies, yet the vast power they exercise is as invasive as that of any government.

The disciplinary state created under neoliberalism illustrates the dilemmas raised by its moral standpoint. The supposedly libertarian element that preserves personal freedom requires a punitive morality that eliminates freedom for many. The undeserving poor must be disciplined, monitored, and punished, not given freedom to choose. A good illustration of this is the debate over a neoliberal approach to welfare that took place in the later 1980s.[78] The neoliberal approach takes the position that welfare causes dependency by removing the incentive to work. Reflecting the view that the Clinton administration adopted in part, Lawrence Mead in *Beyond Entitlement* argued that the welfare state placed too much emphasis on rights and entitlements at the expense of duties.[79] If the latter were emphasized over the former, receiving benefits would depend on carrying out work obligations and adopting drug hygiene. Mead contended that once welfare was linked to work, necessary changes in character would follow. Charles Murray, for his part, argued that for moral as well as fiscal reasons, the welfare state should be more extensively dismantled.[80] Individuals in need would be thrown back on the voluntary sector – on churches, families, and not-for-profit organizations. He thought these would be more likely to influence the moral behaviour of individuals. Any unequal outcomes would be a private matter and not the concern of the government.

Both Mead and Murray see the poor as constituting an underclass, one that exists below the traditional working class and is characterized by inadequate living and working conditions, low-paying jobs, and lack of education – although others note that the underclass can contain well-educated but discouraged people. In the work of these theorists, however, the underclass becomes a moral category. The members of the underclass lack character and self-control as well as basic life skills. For example, Mead contends that

> [t]he underclass is most visible in urban slum settings and is about 70 percent non-white, but it includes many rural and white people as well, especially in Appalachia and the South. Much of the urban underclass is made up of street hustlers, welfare families, drug addicts, and former mental patients. There are, of course, people who function well – the so-called "deserving" or "working poor" – and better-off people who function poorly, but in general low income and serious behavioral difficulties go together. The underclass is not large as a share of population, perhaps 9 million people, but it accounts for the lion's share of the most serious disorders in American life, especially in the cities.[81]

Mead's remedy for welfare dependency would require extensive government control and bureaucratic monitoring. Thus it would run into problems typical of all administered programs. Many neoliberal initiatives to discipline the poor suffer from this problem. Murray's policy proposals, for their part, are descriptively inaccurate and are restricted by the limits of private charity. Charities no longer depend on a few donors, nor are they run privately. They deliver outsourced government social welfare services, and the dependence of not-for-profits on both governments and corporate donors for funds has led to significant changes in operations – they, too, have become marketized and are appraised by market and corporate standards of fiscal accountability and measurable outcomes.

New Forms of Reification

The emergence of social and political pathologies within neoliberalism poses a challenge to Jürgen Habermas's claim that we can still – even in the current situation – tame capitalism. Repairing the rifts in the social fabric, and rebuilding reserves of trust and solidarity, under conditions of increasing inequality and the decreasing political power and influence of the population at large would seem to require at the very least radical reforms to the neoliberal order that are not currently on the horizon. Instead, we see the rise of authoritarian elements and moral dogmatism. These are being reinforced by the inculcation of the entrepreneurial self throughout the population and by a strengthening of the disciplinary state. Nonetheless, the developmental possibilities and competences generated by late modernity remain latent resources to draw upon for political change. We still believe there are possibilities for change. However, the reforms needed will go beyond what we think of as taming capitalism. Habermas's political theory can provide a conception of radical democracy, but his analysis of the market and its role seems to limit the kinds of changes he wants to make.

We suggest, however, that Habermas's analysis in his earlier work can show the limits of his more recent work. Specifically, his diagnosis of social pathologies in modern societies as developed in his *Theory of Communicative Action* points to the contradictions between capitalism and democracy and so can provide an alternative critical framework to that at play in his recent writings. More precisely, we think that the notion of reification, to which he devoted significant attention in the earlier work, can illuminate not just the problems of the welfare state but the pathologies of the neoliberal era as well.

The concept of reification has a long history in Western Marxist thought. Georg Lukács adopted Max Weber's notion of rationalization as a central process in modern societies.[82] Production processes that rely increasingly on science and the demands of modern administration also require a calculative rationality. In a society driven by capitalism, science and technology, reason was primarily viewed as instrumental rationality, a form of rationality that was concerned primarily with efficient means to reach pre-established ends. Reason was largely a matter of calculation and of strategy. By contrast, forms of value rationality that rested on the validity and worth of the ends were subordinated. Weber famously warned that the predominance of instrumental reason would create an iron cage in which humanity would become imprisoned, a victim of its own mechanisms for carrying out its purposes.

Weber felt that the capitalist economy was the unsurpassable basis of human freedom and held that socialism was inimical to freedom. By contrast, Lukács recognized that the commodity form of capitalism was becoming generalized throughout society and that it structured social relations. Weber stressed the interplay of culture and economy in the formation of rationality, while Lukács stressed the role of the capitalist economy in rationalization. He used the term reification to describe the processes whereby relations between humans were reduced to commodity relations between things.[83] Under Lukács's conception of reification, far from providing the basis of freedom, the fundamental processes of capitalism impede autonomy.

Reification disembeds and separates individuals from those concrete social relations that Hegel and his followers identified as the core of ethical life. However, more than simple alienation, reification is a transformation of human action into a mechanism that restricts if not eliminates freedom.

Max Horkheimer and Theodor Adorno took up Weber's diagnosis in the form of a critique of instrumental rationality.[84] For Horkheimer and Adorno, modern instrumental rationality was primarily subjective reason. It reduced reason to the status of an instrument for achieving arbitrarily chosen ends. It eliminated the critical facility of humans to reflect on their ends and purposes. Reason was no longer guided by ends that pointed beyond the isolated subject. As we argued in chapter 2, in positivism we find the clearest example of a philosophy that views reason simply as an instrumental logic and the choice of ends as irrational and emotive. The rationalization of society extends to the bureaucratic rationalization of social life. For critical theorists, then, the welfare state did not represent the extension of social democratic ideals; rather, it was an intensification of the reification in advanced capitalism. By directing the economy, the state meant to eliminate the economic crises that had plagued capitalism; but this also meant that areas such as education and public opinion fell under state control and bureaucratic regulation.

Habermas takes up the question of reification from a standpoint that recognizes more complexity than did earlier theorists. He does not equate rationalization with reification; instead he recognizes dimensions of rationality within capitalist modernity that are not grasped in earlier theories.[85] He also challenges the idea that we can re-embed the market in social relations in the way that Karl Polanyi, for example, believes is necessary to counteract the destructive consequences of disembedded markets.

In opposition to the idea that reason has become primarily instrumental in modern societies, Habermas took up the spirit of Weber's value rationality and, as we have already seen, developed the notion of communicative rationality as a rationality that seeks mutual understanding and mutual accountability, each with its own logic. Against the idea that forms of understanding and normative reasoning have been eliminated, Habermas holds that capitalist economies still require sources of mutual understanding for the legitimation needs of the welfare state. Capitalism must maintain the assent of citizens. Moreover, against Horkheimer and Adorno, Habermas argues that welfare state appeals to notions of social rights, no matter how limited, indicate possibilities for social change, even if they do not and cannot point beyond the welfare state itself. Thus rather than a simple unidirectional course of rationalization leading to instrumental reason, there are contradictory processes of rationalization occurring in capitalist modernity: one leads to greater normative rationality and awareness of social rights, while another reifies forms of social action and turns communicative processes into instrumental or strategic imperatives. We must to avoid a one-sided critique of the welfare state that views it solely as a form of state power and control. The protection of human life from some of the vulnerabilities of industrial capitalism is also a condition for the development of social freedom and personal autonomy.

We can get a better sense of the genesis of these contradictory processes by examining the second criticism that Habermas levels against the earlier theories of reification. Along with Weber, Habermas sees the differentiation of society, and the separation of the economy from other forms of social life, as developments that cannot be reversed. Differentiation is more than simply a matter of instrumental reason or strategic reason. It also marks the emergence of the relatively self-contained economic spree that characterizes capitalist modernity. There is a limit to the ability to re-embed the economy in the social world.[86] Of course, Habermas holds that the economy can be regulated and shaped by norms and values; however, he thinks there is a limit to this process.

The differentiation of the economy from social life also has positive features. When we are relieved of some of the burdens of material reproduction and of the requirement to produce more goods, both developmental and communicative possibilities are released. New forms of self-realization, as well as new forms of autonomy, emerge. Put in more traditional Marxist terms, capitalism represents an achievement over the older, feudal mode of production. But this achievement does more than increase material wealth, it also heralds the possibility – to be sure not always realized – of greater freedom.

For Habermasian critical theory, then, reification is not a matter of rationalization *per se* but the illegitimate extension of forms of instrumental and strategic action into realms of social life that can only be successfully regulated communicatively. When the processes of mutual understanding are reduced to instrumentalities, the social world is subject to pathological developments that limit the freedom and autonomy of participants. These can be political, social, or (in many cases) psychological. Reification creates contradictions between the developmental tendencies of late-modern societies and the demands of a profit-making economy that seeks to submit more forms of life to instrumental imperatives. Habermas calls this impinging of instrumental (and later system) imperatives on the lifeworld the colonization of the lifeworld. And like political colonization, it entails forms of domination and oppression.

Thus, Habermas's demarcation of the boundary between a differentiated economic sphere and the lifeworld is both a normative and a critical standard. The role of the economic sphere is limited by the need to protect the autonomy of citizens, but also by the integrity of the lifeworld, which provides the conditions under which human freedom can flourish. The imperatives of economic rationality must not intrude on the developmental possibilities, conditions for human flourishing, that the lifeworld incorporates and that should ultimately govern the economic realm.

Habermas may have formulated his diagnosis of social pathologies to account for the contradictions of the welfare state; in turn, that state can provide a resource for grasping the social processes that created the pathologies of neoliberalism. Neoliberalism can be seen as increasing the pressure for the colonization of the lifeworld. It extends the intrusion of economic imperatives into lifeworld settings.[87]

Critical theories must pay attention to those struggles over the integrity of the lifeworld that have emerged in neoliberalism in the form of populist movements of the right and the left. By replacing normative coordination with a continuing expansion of the commodity form, marketization impacts the boundary between system and lifeworld, to once again use Habermas's terms. Marketization emphasizes cost–benefit analysis, that is, the use of price or quasi-price mechanisms and standards of measurement such as return on investment. At the same time, the social structure of the norms governing an institution or process needs to conform to the behavioural expectations of markets – that is, the forms of socialization change. These could lead to political struggles over the nature and scope of that expansion and the changes in normative structures, or they could be absorbed by bureaucratic institutions as a means to restructure policy goals. For example, the privatization and marketization of prisons in the United States has led to a situation in which they are evaluated not so much according to whether they are good or bad but whether they are cheap, safe, or legal; that is, marketization imposes the goals of bureaucratic rationality in place of normative ones.[88] No doubt this occurred to some extent even with respect to public prisons; the point here is that once detached from political processes of deliberation, the private prison is less open to intervention by citizens. For that reason, they may serve other policy purposes that have become associated with the carceral state as a mechanism for the segregating and disciplining of segments of the population, without much public discussion or debate once the aims of public institutions become private. At the same time, of course, prisons and prison populations can also become commodities and treated like marketable goods.

The Problem of Markets in Habermas

In accepting Weber's notion that the economy had become independent of normative and moral regulation – that is, a norm-free sphere of action – Habermas has often been viewed as arguing for an acceptance of the capitalist market. David Ingram exemplifies this view. While Ingram thinks that *The Theory of Communicative Action* contains a critique of capitalism, he contends that in his subsequent work Habermas has become "a liberal defender of the rule of law and its functional base: an efficient market-driven economy that accords individual freedom pride of place."[89] While Ingram's analysis has a point, we think he overstates the case. As we argue, Habermas sees markets and administrative rationality as ideally having a limited sphere of operations. To the contrary, his notion of the colonization of the lifeworld refers to the reification of spheres of social action that are impinged upon by economic or administrative imperatives. To recall, for Habermas societies are held together by structures of mutual understanding and accountability. Moreover, social integration in Habermas's terms requires social solidarity, which is threatened by colonization. Thus the invasion of the lifeworld by economic and political imperatives is pathological. With its tendency to reify spheres of everyday life the capitalist market has inherent pathologies. Colonization means that citizens are turned into consumers of goods and clients of bureaucracies. Clearly, then, Habermas is not simply a theorist of liberal or libertarian individualism. He recognizes the vulnerability and dependency characteristic of human action as well as its potentials for autonomy. These capacities need to be protected.

Yet despite these qualifications, Habermas's theory still leaves us with questions about the extent to which he hopes to limit market intrusions into everyday life. Obviously, he believes that markets are superior to command economies. In his view they are more efficient and effective in producing goods and services. In addition, he is sceptical of workers' control of production and management. He has little to say about the new forms of organization and hierarchy in the workplace analysed by Luc Boltanski and others. Although he clearly thinks that capitalism needs to be restrained, he apparently is not concerned about the increase in rapacious behaviour on the part of business and corporate leaders. He thinks that capitalists are simply being rational in seeking to maximize profit.

Can the limited version of the market that Habermas proposes provide the protections of the lifeworld that he proposes are necessary for a non-reified social order – one that advances developmental possibilities instead of impeding them? While we realize there is no absolute theoretical resolution to this problem, we remain sceptical whether the restrictions Habermas proposes are sufficient to provide the protections his theory requires. Even the augmented and regulated market of the Keynesian era rested on democratic elitism and a kind of state corporatism, not to mention an intrusive welfare state that frequently turned citizens into clients. In the end it failed to successfully balance accumulation and legitimation. A renewed Keynesianism would require more intervention into the economy and greater democratic participation. It is hard to see how this would not entail another pushback by capital. Even if it were possible, short of another Great Depression it is hard to see how it would overcome the great accumulated power of global capital in the twenty-first century. A revised notion of property is also needed to address the concentration of economic power.

We think that a suggestion made by C.B. Macpherson could help. Macpherson realized that conceptions of property are neither natural nor essential; they are *political* formulations.[90] Property, he noted with Morris Cohen, is not a thing but a relation between persons (often about things). It is normative and legal in character; it is a creation not of nature but of the state. Property relations are either themselves justifications for human flourishing or are indissolubly linked to these.

The form of private property typically used by classical economics was developed by John Locke. He thought that private property was based on labour. Property was created by mixing one's labour with the products of nature. The ideal of the possessive individual found in Locke's theory was well suited to justifications for the capitalist economy. Property was the exclusive domain of the individual, who had the right to dispose of what he owned and to exclude others from the use or benefit of it. This understanding of property was also considered central to the notion of a private sphere in which the individual was free to choose his own course of action without interference by other individuals or by the state.

This image of the isolated individual who has rights in a state of nature is a convenient fiction, and its assertion of natural right neglects the socially constructed character of law. Property is a form of power and sovereignty. The "free labour contract" is asymmetrical.[91] The worker who needs a job to pay rent or feed a family and is dependent on an employer has little choice about the conditions of employment. The modern regime of private property is in Macpherson's terms a system of extractive power – that is, power over others – rooted in the exclusive ownership of property.[92] What Macpherson indicates with this idea is something like what Weber meant by domination: "Extractive power points to the ability to use, along with one's own power, the power of others to achieve one's purposes."[93] An unregulated market economy leads to forms of domination and oppression, not the individual freedom it promises. In capitalist societies an exclusive focus on private property leads to the extraction of power from the least well-off by the most well-off and to the creation of inequalities of wealth and power and the ability to use and exert capacities. Macpherson also viewed extraction as moral activity, and one by no means free from evaluation. In a developed capitalist economy, property involves more than just production. In financialized capitalism, stockholders depend upon returns on investment to gain wealth, not on direct ownership of production or material property. This form of property fits uneasily with the labour theory of acquisition.

There is, however, no logical or other necessity for conceiving property primarily as exclusive ownership, that is, as the right to exclude others from the use or benefit of something. Macpherson suggests that a theory of property can be tied not simply to individual ownership or possession but also to the ability to use and develop one's powers – and, we suggest, to communicative rights as well. This would entail a very different notion of property, one that included private property and even state property as well as common or social property. There is a crucial difference, however, between social property and state property. The former represents property held in common; the latter can be state-owned property, with the state functioning in a capitalist fashion. Looking at property relations as social constructions that are creations of the state reminds us that systems of property are embedded in justifications for forms of human life, conceptions of the good life. Property relations can be modified as social needs change.

Market fundamentalists argue that a private property system and the market are the optimal institutions for allocating goods and services, yet these institutions have failed to fulfil this promise. In a post–welfare state environment, allocation is not simply consigned to private individuals or to the market. The state has a large role to play – even the professions are not allocated through the market but rather through standards provided by the state. These matters lead to another issue in Habermas's conception of markets. While he clearly would endorse extensive reallocation and redistribution of resources in society, he also clings to the idea that markets are the most efficient way to produce goods.

Habermas does acknowledge in some of his more recent interviews that the problems of a financialized capitalism are significant ones and that capitalism has "taken on a life of its own."[94] Yet he still does not see the changes in the economy as the main issue. Referring especially to the European context and to the development of a supranational European union, which has become largely a technocratic instrument, Habermas feels that the central problem is political: it is the failure of political elites to have the courage to assert universal human rights against the forces of nationalism. While this argument has elements of truth, we think Habermas neglects the changes in economic outlook that are necessary to bring about the universalism or cosmopolitanism that he desires. Conceptions of social and collective property are based on a universal notion of justice and access for all, and not just political considerations. Habermas fails to resolve the tension between his critique of the pathologies of capitalism and his acceptance of markets. In the conclusion to this study we will revisit the question whether Habermas's positive view of certain features of markets is as defensible as he believes it to be.

Conclusion

We have emphasized the need for an account of the pathologies of neoliberalism that addresses the lacunae in Habermas's later work. If a critical theory is to maintain its relevance in the contemporary setting, it needs to confront the dominant pathologies of the time. While some critical theorists have taken up this task, Habermas has not developed their insights, and his own, into a critical theory of neoliberalism. To the contrary, he has appeared surprised by the emergence of these new pathologies.

In one sense, Habermas's account of pathologies remains tied to his earlier analysis of late capitalism. While economic crisis remains a

problem, the major issues concern the political legitimation of the welfare state compromise. When he does address neoliberal globalization,
it is in the context of the need for a transnational universalism. Once the
political compromises of the welfare state broke down, economic insecurity and instability increasingly became the rule. The economic instability of many, however, has been accompanied by de-democratizing
tendencies and individual fragmentation and cultural alienation. While
this is not just a return to ordinary capitalism, it requires more focus on
the political-economic dimension of critical theory.

These pathologies, we argue, entail a more profound threat to democratic life and forms of developmental and communicative freedom
than Habermas seems to recognize. It not likely that a universal identity
will emerge under the conditions of neoliberalism; nor is it likely that
we can return to the compromise of the welfare state without addressing the problems of democratic elitism and administrative control.
Addressing these problems would require that we take a more radical
approach to changing capitalism. Preserving democracy requires more
fundamental economic reforms then he is willing to formulate. These
include much greater democratic control over production and social
property that can be used to produce collective goods.

At the same time, we believe that Habermas's later writings, particularly *Between Facts and Norms*, can serve as a basis for radical democratic
reforms of law and politics if suitably conjoined with radical economic
reforms. In the next chapter we turn to the ways in which Habermas's
communicative theory formulates an alternative to neoliberal notions
of reason and their conception of the social world, and thus provides an
alternative to the dominant discourse of self-interest in political theory.
These considerations set the stage for chapter 5, in which we examine
more fully Habermas's version of democratic theory.

Chapter Four

Towards a Critical Theory of Democracy: Deliberation, Self-interest, and Solidarity

At the end of the previous chapter we noted that the pathologies of neoliberalism are especially evident in the anti-solidaristic and anti-communicative marketizing of cultural spheres. For thinkers who highlight such pathologies, challenging them requires the equivalent of a de-reifying critique of neoliberal values. However, for another group of theorists, who have been influenced by the post-1989 collapse of "really existing" socialism, the problem is different. These analysts view criticisms of the anti-solidaristic character of neoliberalism as reflecting republican or neo-republican nostalgia for a fused community. They also believe that self-interest, or in other cases dissensus, is necessary to keep at bay the dangers of a fused community that would stifle plurality. These criticisms have a point in stressing the necessary role of self-determination and disagreement, which would be threatened by a fusion of wills under a unitary common good; even so, they can be said to miss the forest for the trees. In assimilating the critique of a fused community to that of communicative reason, they fail to see how individuality and community are integrated in communicative reason. They miss the biggest threat to a democratic social order posed by neoliberalism's attack on the necessary sources of both social freedom and solidarity: the creation a new form of reification in place of the old one.

In this chapter and the next, we explore how a critical theory of democracy can confront the challenges of neoliberalism – and, more specifically, why the implicit and explicit theoretical commitments and assumptions of such a theory provide a uniquely powerful way of re-establishing and reinvigorating the case for a radical democracy with developmental aims and aspirations. At the core of our analysis in these chapters is the work of Jürgen Habermas. As he approaches his ninth decade, and even as other critical currents have sought to supplement if not challenge his positions, Habermas remains a central and important

figure. His ideas continue to provide a focus for reflection on the possibilities for democracy in the face of neoliberal ideas, institutions, and
practices. They remain informed by the prospect for a better future
even in the face of those contemporary forces that call into question
the very possibility of a radical democracy that, in the words of C.B.
Macpherson, would enable all individuals to equally develop and exercise their distinctively human capacities. In what follows we highlight
the strengths and limitations of Habermas's work and how this work
requires supplementation by a renewed emphasis on political economy
and a reconsideration of the powerful and insightful ideas of his predecessors and teachers, Horkheimer, Adorno, and Marcuse.

Habermas's theoretical work, up to and including the theory of communicative action, always admitted its debt to a Marxian framework,
albeit a fundamentally revised one. He saw a contradictory relationship between democracy and capitalism. The realization of democracy
required a rejection of capitalism. As will see in the next chapter, there
is no indication that Habermas has abandoned this view, but his formulation of the problem has become more ambiguous. At the least, it is
consigned to the background. However, we think that a reconsideration
of this work, which incorporates some of the insights offered by Axel
Honneth and more recent criticisms, could provide another direction.

If democracy can be defined broadly as a political order in which
the people exercise rule or sovereignty, a critical theory of democracy
potentially provides a distinctive way of confronting both the question
of who "the people" are and by what means, and for what purposes,
they are to "rule." This is particularly crucial when popular sovereignty
is linked to a conception of radical democracy whereby individuals are
enabled to freely and equally develop and exercise their distinctively
human capacities, as opposed to one in which democratic participation
is limited to elections and voting, perhaps with interest group activity
serving as a supplement to electoral politics. From the perspective of a
critical theory of democracy, we need to look at the implications of communicative action for democratic thinking through the lens of a theory
of society that is not final but provisional and historical. It is in this context that we seek to explore questions of freedom, justice, and solidarity
and so attempt to chart a path beyond neoliberalism.

Deliberative Democracy and Communicative Action

The theory of communicative action that Habermas developed, and
which we treated briefly in our discussion of reason and rationality
in chapter 2, rests on the idea that we coordinate our actions through

mutual understanding. Our knowledge and our sensibilities are formed in this intersubjective context. As George Herbert Mead argued, mind is social.[1] In social life we are actors who inhabit a lifeworld of shared understandings and mutual expectations. We can give accounts of our actions to others when commonsense understanding breaks down or our expectations for action are not fulfilled. These can be reasons for actions, explanations or even excuses that we may be challenged to justify, with the result that we may even revise our views. This element of rationality in everyday life means that our interactions have not only a dialogical but also a deliberative structure. Individuals do not act solely out of instinct or naked self-interest. They also have frameworks of understanding that incorporate their values through which they make sense of the word they inhabit. They monitor their actions in life situations with a certain degree of everyday reflexivity. Thus, what we call discourse is really a more formalized and elaborated practice of mutual accountability. When we reflect on problematic knowledge claims, norms, or the authenticity of actions, we attempt to reconstruct the conditions and elements of mutual understanding. In this respect, although theories of discourse use idealizations, they are not idealist. They require neither a transcendental subject nor a social world based on full agreement.

Questions of mutual understanding also have a bearing on issues of political sovereignty. For the forms of mutual understanding are not simply means of discussion; they also generate a communicative power that is the basis for a democratic notion of sovereignty. While not every instance of communicative power generates political sovereignty, democratic sovereignty always involves communicative power. When individuals act in concert to authorize public action, they generate this power. Neoliberalism fails to recognize either the importance of mutual understanding or the generative power of communication to establish sovereign political authority.

In chapter 2 we briefly mentioned the concept of deliberative democracy. Habermas's theory of communicative action has been one of the most influential in the formulation of such deliberative theories. For deliberative theories, democracy is a consensual process whereby participants come to discuss alternative possibilities under conditions of fairness – that is, conditions of freedom and equality. Participants in deliberation are to have an equal chance to discuss all issues and are free to present any alternatives or considerations. Of course, this is an idealized situation that is difficult to fully meet, but it does provide a critical standard for evaluating public and private argumentation and deliberation. For example, if a manager and an employee discuss a matter of work policy, implicitly or explicitly the manager's reasons may be given more weight by the parties in the discussion. If so, the agreement they might reach about work policy could be open to criticism and revision because the employee (or employees) did not have an equal chance to put forward their own reasons or to challenge the reasoning of the manager. Similarly, public debate in a democratic political order should include all relevant participants and ensure they have a chance to propose ideas or policies, give reasons for their positions, and criticize the reasoning of others. Such a debate would also include evaluating the norms that guide them in the formulation of policies or proposals, the sincerity or honesty of participants, and even unconscious mechanisms of self-deception.

The notion of deliberative democracy, however, also rests on a conception of communicative freedom. As we noted, the participants in a deliberative process are not self-interested actors who pursue their own ends or purposes. Although deliberation contains an element of self-development and identity – which as we shall see is crucial in some circumstances – it also requires a third notion of freedom that is inherently linked to our relations with others. On the one hand, communicative freedom means the capacity to freely use symbolic means to make sense of and reason in the world. It involves the capacity to transcend a particular understanding or even self-conception in interaction. On the other hand, communicative freedom also requires a relation of self and other, a relation of mutual recognition. We recognize the other as a potential partner with whom we can reason and discuss, but also as a source of otherness with whom we can experience discord or difference. Communicative power consists in the ability to find sources of consent through dialogue and to authorize actions among individuals who deliberate together.

Communicative power is a binding force. It is not just cognitive but volitional as well. It is a generative force that motivates action. Like communicative freedom it has a self-constitutive element. Individuals create themselves and their social world through both ordinary interactions and specialized discourses.

The communicative model offers more than an account of democratic deliberation. It can also provide an element of a critical theory of society. A discourse theory deals not only with a situation in which participants enter into discourse to address a dispute or disagreement but also with the conditions and capacities that participants possess when they enter a discussion. While an agreement that is fair is always possible, for there to be a society in which such democratic deliberation is widespread, individuals require not just the capacity for self-determination but also and equally the possibility of self-realization. (Habermas raises this issue in his later work.) To be useful for the practice of democracy, self-realization must be linked to some notion of a good society or an institutional structure, if only in outline.[2]

However, consensual understandings about action that participants reach are also practical. They generate communicative power. In the political realm, as Habermas notes in his appropriation of Hannah Arendt, communicative power is an intersubjectively constituted authorization to act. It creates motivations, not just intellectual agreement. While discussion may suspend the connection between action and understanding, an agreement creates communicative power in the form of a will to authorize action.

Less attention has been paid to Habermas's use of the notion of solidarity. Morality is derived in part from the situation of individuals in society. It is not, as some argue, just the biological vulnerability of individuals that brings them together into society; also, and indeed more importantly, it is social and cultural vulnerability and dependency. Individuals are not self-sufficient: they only become individuals through socialization, that is, through participation in an intersubjectively shared lifeworld. Yet this lifeworld is also reproduced through the actions of individuals. From the beginning, individuals need at least a minimal degree of reciprocal regard as one element of mutual recognition. As Habermas interprets this, it requires both equal respect for others as beings capable of individuality and a certain care and concern. This comes out of an awareness of the conditions of vulnerability, in oneself and in others.

To get at the core of Habermas's notion of justice we must note how he differentiates it from the ethical standpoint.[3] The ethical standpoint is a conscious plan of life based on orientations to deeply held values – that is, a conception of human flourishing. An ethical standpoint is constituted through reflection on a life history through which we locate our identity as an authentic expression of who we are and who we want to be. This standpoint cannot be seen simply as a form of prudence or an expression of preferences, as both can suggest an essentially egocentric point of view. Ethical life, as Hegel well understood, is a social creation. An individual's life history should be seen in the context of a shared set of traditions in which that person finds a unique identity. Thus, against rational choice theories our preferences and our goals are embedded in our social and ethical lives and are subject to deliberation. They are elements of self-understanding that can be altered as our own sense of who we are changes through experience and reflection.

The limits of the ethical standpoint emerge, Habermas believes, when we encounter those with fundamentally different conceptions of the good life. In such cases, conflicts cannot be resolved within the boundaries of a shared conception of the good. Nor does he think that any overarching conception of the good can or will be found. He thinks that such a conception would fail because it would either be excessively paternalistic (e.g., Westerners' assumptions that their values are the ones that should and must be accepted by others) or too empty of content (e.g., theories of basic needs). Here he thinks that ethical considerations become transformed and incorporated into higher-level moral thinking; this is what he means when he argues that questions of morality are impersonal. Questions of what is good for all transcend questions of what is good for us or for me. We must suspend or bracket our own shared conception of human flourishing so that we may ask what is good for all, including for those who are not part of our community.

In this light, Habermas wants us to ponder what principles we can employ when considering issues of justice that are, in Kant's fashion, moral as opposed to ethical. Habermas thinks that for this purpose justice must take priority over any conception of the good we may hold. He conceives of this priority in the strong sense of a duty-based moral theory. In moral reasoning our understanding of what is right and our duties to others always count more than any conceptions of our own good. Matters of justice are never just one element in our ethical repertoire but are pre-eminent.

Habermas thinks he can draw the principles that a theory of justice requires from the features of communicative action rather than from any specific notion of human flourishing. We cannot avoid the moral point of view when we confront certain problems, even if our interpretations of these problems diverge. Habermas, however, contends that we can derive general and universal principles of morality from the basic conditions of intersubjectivity and mutual recognition. Here his claim that his theory of justice requires an impersonal standpoint has sometimes been criticized for taking an outsider's perspective. By abstracting from our ethical commitments and attachments, it is argued, the theorist transgresses the boundaries of the participant's perspective and takes the role of a detached observer.

We do not think this interpretation is warranted, although we suggest that finding a term other than "impersonal" could more fully clarify Habermas's position. Here we must address the linkages between justice and solidarity. In Habermas's argument the moral point of view does not leave the participant's perspective behind but *redefines* it. When we adopt the moral point of view, he argues, we still maintain some remnant of the ethical commitment. The good for all is an ideal-izing extension of the ethical standpoint, one that applies to all members of any community. Rather than standing outside of community and commitment, it *enlarges* community and strengthens the bonds that link individuals together. Here justice and solidarity are connected. The basic situation of justice concerns the vulnerability and dependency of humans who win their identities in social interaction through mutual recognition. These relations of recognition can be disrupted and need to be protected. Principles of justice are therefore also critical standards to which we can appeal and that are not fully bound to a notion of the good.

Not enough attention has been paid to questions of solidarity in Habermas's work. Justice and solidarity are complementary, but the claims of solidarity imply that we see the other person from the perspective of an inclusive and non-dominating otherness where we can also take the position of the other:

> If we interpret justice as what is equally good for all, then the "good" that has been extended step by step to the "right" forms a bridge between justice and solidarity. For universal justice also requires that one person should take responsibility for another, and even that each person should stand in and answer for a stranger who has formed his identity in completely different circumstances and who understands himself in terms of different traditions. The remnant of the good at the core of the right reminds us that moral conscience depends on a particular self-understanding of a moral person who recognizes that they belong to a moral community. All individuals who are socialized into any communicative form of life at all belongs [*sic*] to this community.[4]

From this perspective the standpoint of justice retains, if in a weak fashion, a version of the participant's perspective. We are involved in recognitions of others insofar as they are participants in communicative interaction. Justice can never transcend the intersubjectivity involved in mutual recognition and *cannot* be understood from the vantage point of an objective observer. The notion of an impersonal standpoint only refers to the denial of any privileged conception of the good.

Axel Honneth proposes a complementary notion of solidarity, one that he derives from a threefold account of social relations and forms of recognition. As opposed to love, which requires intimacy, solidarity reflects a broader social pattern of intersubjectivity. In the first instance, solidarity emerges when members of a status group see themselves as having equal honour or respect. Honneth thinks this first develops collectively when individuals identify themselves as members of a group who share a similar identity. In late-modern societies, however, such respect is individualized (i.e., as self-respect). We are esteemed, and we esteem ourselves, because of our accomplishments, not those of our group, and we feel damaged when we are not respected. Solidarity extends in an egalitarian way to all members of society, although Honneth does not specifically say that this must be in the direction of respect for persons. We can respect people even if they fail, especially if social conditions make success difficult. But more generally we respect persons regardless of who they are or what they are. We recognize a universal component of mutual recognition that extends to all.[5]

This account of Habermas's notion of solidarity can address several persistent criticisms of the communicative approach – in particular, the main objections to his version of deliberation. For communitarians and other strong contextualists, Habermas's conception of justice is "impersonal" – that is, it does not allow for any consideration of the theory of the good.[6] On its face, the idea that justice is impersonal seems to contradict the theory of communicative action. In terms of the theory, action is committed in nature. We have the capacity to understand others only because of our involvement in the world as participants. We can never take the position of an observer in relation to others. It appears to critics that Habermas, like John Rawls, steps outside or above the position of the participant and sees justice from the standpoint of an external judge or impartial spectator. One could make a case for this in Rawls's theory, but a more sympathetic interpretation of the deliberative standpoint would hold that in considering questions of justice our notions of the good are taken up in relevant ways. Habermasian theory is different from Rawls's account on this point. It does not argue (as Rawls does in his first formulation of the original position) that we can have no knowledge of the good of others. Questions of justice arise at the point where theories of the good life conflict and people need protection from domination and oppression. We protect people in such cases by recognizing the condition of any individual and their inherent vulnerability. For example, all are entitled to equal rights, but this is not because of any specific notion of the good – it is because they are participants. However, this does not fully solve the problem, since (among other reasons) it assumes that even within cultures or subcultures, individuals learn to consider questions of justice from this expanded awareness and enlarged horizon. Whatever the logical structure of deliberation, it still rests on practical conditions that cannot be reduced to the formal requirements of deliberative interaction.

Communicative Action and the Problem of Solidarity

Because we are participants in common social worlds, we are always already bound to one another through often taken-for-granted forms of mutual understanding. A second set of related problems concerns the relation between justice and solidarity: Why is there any motivation to enter into discussion at all or to continue it if understanding is not reached? In the abstract it appears that individuals have no special motive to engage in discussion. They must bring their motives from another source. In his discussion of discourses, Habermas often spoke of a rationally motivated consensus. The rationality of the process yields a normative commitment that is itself binding upon participants in a discussion. We think that Habermas's later usage of communicative power as an authorizing power is a more fruitful way of understanding this point, for it is communicative power that is generated by such agreements. However, this still leaves open questions with respect to situations where no agreement is reached: Why would individuals enter into such a procedure with no guarantee of agreement?

Habermas's more recent reflections on solidarity provide a basis for dealing with this issue. Participants already have attachments and social relations that allow for forms of solidarity. These constitute what Durkheim called the pre-contractual foundations of the social contract.[7] In order to engage in a contract, one must trust that the contract will be upheld.

We can construct a similar scenario with questions of discourse. To enter into a deliberation, individuals must suspend their ordinary frame of actions and reflexively consider contesting claims that may upset their received understanding. We could even end up alienated from those with whom we enter into discussion. Deliberation could more than break down – it could result in conflict or withdrawal from interaction.

We think that participants who come to discourse must do so with at least a weak sense of solidarity. They must have a willingness to carry on in the face of disagreement; they need to trust that their partners in discourse want to continue to seek agreement. This trust is complemented, as Habermas notes, with a sense of justice. When we treat others as free and equal participants we consider them not just as formally free subjects but as members of a moral community worthy of our respect. However different they may be from us, we treat them as worthy of inclusion. Here we assume that they have been or can be capable of gaining and holding our respect and recognition, and we theirs, even when we are unable to reach agreement. Respect requires a higher generalized ability to identify with others even if they hold fundamentally different perspectives and may even seem to be radically "other." In this way discourse comes close to the idea of dialogue in which co-participants are seen as "concrete others" with whom we form wider intersubjective bonds.

By contrast, we can think of cases of mistrust in which claims that are reasonably established through discussion and inquiry are denied by others. This seems to emerge in discussions about climate change. In such cases some parties lack trust in the claims of those defending the idea of potentially disastrous climate change and refuse to engage in discourse when challenged. When employed by those with power, this kind of refusal can be a form of oppression. However, when it becomes a facet of ordinary communication it entails a breakdown of trust and solidarity.

In contemporary democratic societies like the United States, the weakening if not collapse of solidarity presents a radical threat to democratic practice. This is not, however, simply or primarily about a loss of common values, as both left and right communitarians sometimes argue. The anti-solidaristic tendencies in these societies break down the discursive and deliberative mechanisms whereby we create communicative power. Individuals lack the willingness to engage others as equal participants who are sincere is their commitment to the truth. In situations where many get their information from selective sources, they are likely to seek confirmation in a non-discursive manner and so reinforce already fixed positions. Such individuals view the world through the lens of self-interest and tend to mistrust the motivations and reasoning processes of others.

Towards a Democratic Notion of Solidarity

The notion of solidarity can be employed in both democratic and non-democratic contexts. An authoritarian populist state could be characterized in certain circumstances as having a high degree of solidarity; so could a fundamentalist religious group whose members see themselves as having a common religious/political mission. However, the most significant challenge to the scope of democratic solidarity comes from the republican tradition. Its version of solidarity rests on the ideal of a unified community. Solidarity here does not, however, involve merely an ethical bond. On the one hand, it refers to relations of reciprocity and mutual expectations. In situations of interdependence or conditions of vulnerability we have obligations and expectations of mutual aid and support, although we typically do not use the term solidarity to refer to close relationships between family members who may have strong ties to us. However, Émile Durkheim did use the term mechanical solidarity to refer to less complex societies integrated though kinship relations. For modern societies Hegel characterized these kinds of relationships as *Sittlichkeit*. They refer to a common ethical bond that applies not just to the family but to the nation seen as an ethical unity. This bond has its roots in a pre-existing community that is linked to the past.

The modern understanding of political solidarity has roots in the French revolutionary notion of fraternity but even deeper roots in monotheistic religious traditions. Since Weber, we have recognized that these religions rest on conceptions of the brotherhood of all believers and in the possibility of a universal community that transcends national or ethnic boundaries. During the Enlightenment this impulse was transformed into a secular notion of the unity of humanity. The revolutionary idea of fraternity shares with the religious tradition a redemptive dimension. The humanity that would constitute human solidarity does not yet exist and must be brought into being though deliberate human action. This notion of solidarity is of course weaker than kinship or ethnic obligations, yet it remains central to political bonds and legitimacy in modern societies. It is both future-oriented and inclusionary. It can serve in this context as a critical standard. It stands in opposition to the tendencies of market-based societies to erode solidarity and prevent its development in the universal forms foreseen by the revolutionary tradition. In chapter 6 we will return to the ideal of fraternity as it emerges in Axel Honneth's attempt to rethink and reimagine the socialist project.

To be sure, we cannot return to the understanding of pre-modern solidarity. The very processes of capitalist modernization are also a condition, albeit an external one, for the expansion of our understanding of fraternity. In capitalism we are linked in ways that were not possible in pre-capitalist societies. But the same modernization processes that create the social (though not the cultural) conditions of a universal society also create a universal bond in the form of a market society.[8] Thus it has a contradictory set of effects.

The kind of communicative solidarity we outline is in many ways analogous to the political concept of solidarity outlined above. It is not based on the trust, a shared ethos, local attachments, or ties of kinship. It is based instead on the universality of linguistic understanding, which links all who participate in dialogue. Like democratic solidarity it is future-oriented and based – albeit more weakly than its political analogue – on common humanity. Such a common humanity does not exist at all times and in all discourses, but when we do engage in deliberation and dialogue with others, especially those who are socially and culturally distant and with whom we disagree, we must employ weak solidarity in communicative action.

In this conception we are close to the idea of solidarity among strangers that also is employed in a political context. Democratic solidarity involves ties among strangers that are created in democratic citizenship. Citizens gain solidarity through participation in democratic processes in a democratized public sphere and a democratic civil society. Notions of solidarity no doubt take hold in lifeworlds and cultural traditions, but they are also embedded in democratic practices based on equal respect for all:

> The counterpart to this social-theoretical program in moral and legal theory is a universalism that is highly sensitive to differences. Equal respect for *everyone* is not limited to those who are like us; it extends to the person of the other in his or her otherness. And solidarity with the other *as one of us refers* to the flexible "we" of a community that resists all substantive determinations and extends its permeable boundaries ever further. This moral community constitutes itself solely by way of the negative idea of abolishing discrimination and harm and of extending relations of mutual recognition to include marginalized men and women. The community thus constructively outlined is not a collective that would force its homogenized members to affirm its distinctiveness. Here inclusion does not imply locking members into a community that closes itself off from others. The "inclusion of the other" means rather that the boundaries of the community are open for all, also and most especially for those who are strangers to one another and want to remain strangers.[9]

To be effective in a society, however, this notion of democratic participation and solidarity cannot be legally compelled. Participation in democratic processes should be mobilized through the guarantees of communicative freedom. Individuals must be motivated to act politically. This requires cultural norms and practices that respect democratic processes and ensure that individuals can both participate in democratic will-formation and enjoy basic protection, not only of civil rights but of social rights as well. Habermas sees this kind of solidarity as a constitutional patriotism, one in which citizens are willing to sacrifice for those they do not know but with whom they share a bond of equal respect. We can also see this as a type of weak reciprocity based on a suitably limited notion of mutual aid. This broad respect for individuals is the precondition of solidarity.

Deliberation and Self-interest

As we indicated in the introduction to this book, our view of deliberation and of democracy itself is different from that of Jane Mansbridge
and her colleagues. They contend that theories of deliberative democracy oppose strategic actions such as bargaining, negotiation, and the
exercise of power. In contrast, they contend that "self-interest, suitably
constrained, ought to be part of the deliberation that eventuates in a
democratic decision."[10] For Mansbridge, situations where deliberation
is incomplete or disagreement is intractable call for a different set of
procedures. Non-deliberative mechanisms such as voting, aggregation, and bargaining have to be used, and these involve coercive power.
Mansbridge and others who stress self-interest believe that recognizing
its central place is a way of incorporating plurality and diversity into
deliberation. At the heart of this argument is the view that the discourse
ethics of Habermas are based on a conception of the common good or
social unity, that a discourse theory favours a model that seeks conver-
gence on a single answer.

The situations Mansbridge takes as paradigmatic involve questions
about how to act in the circumstances in which agents find themselves
in conflict over courses of action. Mansbridge gives the example of a
discussion in the 1960s over the protest tactics adopted by faculty at a
school. While the group thinks that a certain course of action is correct,
one participant objects that he is afraid to carry out this action for fear of
being fired. So the members pursue another tack. In another example, a
couple face a situation in which they have competing job offers, one in an
East Coast city and another in the Midwest. They cannot decide what
is good for them as a unit (the family), and they must also consider their
self-interest – or, more properly, their well-being. Mansbridge sees these
sorts of arguments, among others, as undermining the logic of agreement.

Mansbridge's examples do not establish the priority of self-interest in
these situations, and thus pinpoint issues that a Habermasian theory of
deliberation would fail to consider. In other words, these examples do
not simply involve pure self-interest; they also raise ethical issues that
can become thematic in discussions. This is even clearer in the case of
collective action. The example of the faculty protest involves not just the
self-interest of the wavering participant but also the question of existential commitment, which is at heart an ethical issue. As Mansbridge
ought to know from the protest movements of the 1960s, standing up
to authority requires such a commitment and is not without risk. It
involves not just a participant's self-interest but his or her identity and
personal integrity as well. We cannot say in advance of a discussion

whether all will have the courage or will want to take the risks that necessarily accompany some forms of protest. Thus, consideration of risks and consequences is not outside the scope of discourse ethics as Habermas originally formulated it. There are many possible decisions that could be made. Members could decide on an action that all could undertake. They could pursue an option that leaves out the dissenting member, or they could ask the participant who harbours concerns for his well-being to reconsider his existential commitment. Perhaps the injustice in the situation is so great that it requires an existential risk. In this specific case, the members decided on a less confrontational option that would allow all to participate. In so doing they showed respect for the participant who feared the action.

Let us look now at the second case now, which also seems to involve the ethical self-understanding of the participants. The questions facing the couple are not just about self-interest but also about identity. They raise questions of what kind of person we want to be and how elements of our social situation support or do not support our aims. Is our commitment to our partner the more important element? Can we maintain our career commitment in some way other than by moving, or will we have to give up on our ambitions? We may feel that we cannot give up our career without losing elements of our identity and that will make our life together unhappy and unfulfilling.

This case, then, involves a situation in which the couple's common expectations are called into question. Their sense of solidarity and mutual care is challenged if not threatened. Their expectations must be renewed or revised if the shared sense of the relationship is to be sustained. But of course, one's own sense of who "I" am is also called into question. While such issues of identity and even shared identities are self-regarding in some sense, it is a strain to call these manifestations of self-interest or to see conceptions of our identity as rooted in preferences. Rather, they are ways by means of which we establish our relationship to the larger social world as distinct individuals within the group. Such an example would be a challenge to theories of discourse such as that of Habermas only if one assumed that all social relations and all deliberative processes followed the model of impersonal deliberations on justice. But there is no indication this is true. To the contrary, Habermas recognizes that issues of identity and even self-interest play a role in social life and places a good deal of stress on questions of individuation via Mead and German Idealism. Questions of justice apply to only a small, albeit crucial, set of issues.

These arguments and the examples provided by Mansbridge and her collaborators seem to imply a rigid and moralistic version of deliberative reason. We can distinguish between deliberations that are concerned with establishing correct moral or ethical principles and those that are concerned with the right thing to do in a situation.[11] To elide one with the other is to make a serious mistake.

Let us say we are faced with a policy question around equal pay for work of equal value. According to analysts, women receive about 78 per cent of the wages of men for the same jobs. The first question is one of justice: Is it fair? When we engage in a moral discourse we are called upon to inquire into the principles of justice or fairness that stem from the recognition of equality and equal respect for all; it is not just a question of material gain. At least for Habermas, issues of justice are not based on a notion of the common good of a community but rather on principles that apply to all. Such principles of course require that equality and freedom be recognized in all deliberations for participants to reach a fair agreement. Moral discourses aim at establishing valid norms, not social policies or practical problems of action in concrete situations.

The principles of justice are not, however, rigidly applied in all circumstances. We concur with Habermas's position that only in "their application to particular concrete cases will it transpire which of the competing principles is the most appropriate in the given context." Moreover, Habermas identifies three different forms of practical reason: moral, ethical, and pragmatic. While the first deals with questions of justice and the second with questions of the good life, the third deals with strategic and technical means to reach a pre-established end. There is no debate over proper norms or goals here. In this case we have a fixed goal and we seek to realize it. Returning to our example, a group of people agree that equal pay for equal work is a desirable goal. While they could try to raise consciousness and shape identities, they could also seek strategies to get a law passed. Here deliberation might be concerned only with strategic action around how to get a bill before a legislative body and how to lobby or convince legislators. Of course, some lobbying might involve appeals to justice as well, but there is no reason to think that such actors either eschew conflict or deny the presence of strategic elements. Getting a bill passed might require compromise or negotiation. We might not win all we wanted but we could come to feel that we have obtained a reasonable bargain. This is all perfectly compatible with a critical theory of deliberation.

A second line of argument concerns the problems of coordination through self-interest. Following game theoretical approaches, Mansbridge and her associates want to argue that coordination can be carried out through self-interest alone. This type of coordination would be independent of mutual accountability in almost all respects. The reflexive sense of order is achieved through a reconciliation of preferences. These preferences are ultimate units.

Mansbridge gives the example of a hypothetical policy decision in which the common good is achieved through a set of discrete group or individual preferences. The hypothetical legislator supports the decision, not out of normative concerns but because it benefits her constituency. But this position too has weaknesses. Even here, where the focus is on material benefits, the legislator refers to some form of human flourishing that the constituents share, not just unmediated self-interest.

Aggregation, Deliberation, and Coordination

The question of the binding character of rational choice theories was the topic of a debate among thinkers who to varying degrees were committed to rational choice assumptions and analysis. Neo-institutionalists rejected rational choice fundamentalist arguments that the aggregation of choices could yield a stable order. This problem had already been raised though examples showing the irrationality of voting and ordering of preferences. Arguments around the rationality, or irrationality, of voting are well-known and will not be restated here.[12] Neoclassical theories assume a well-functioning if imperfect market system; they also assume widespread acceptance/compliance with this system and with the basic structures of economic and political life, including presumably stable property rights and intact media of exchange. As we noted in chapter 3, markets are not spontaneous occurrences; they require background conditions that both make possible their existence and maintain their stability.

In focusing on just those questions that neoclassicists have taken for granted – that is, the establishment of market conditions and institutions – rational choice theorists address the genesis of and change in institutional design. Here, questions of cooperation and coordination of action are central. Neo-institutionalism aims to explain how institutions lead actors to work together and why there are stable sets of rules. For neo-institutionalists, these are normative questions. Focus on the coordination of action connects them to the problems of traditional moral theory as well as to sociological questions about the rise of normative structures. Jack Knight and Itai Sened note that the "key to understanding the importance of social institutions lies in the role they play in the formation of expectations and beliefs. The problem here is one of establishing expectations about the actions of the other players in the game: the formation of such expectations is a prerequisite for making a rational choice."[13]

Although some neo-institutionalists try to derive institutions from self-interest, they too must acknowledge beliefs that are derived from mutual understanding and the trust between participants. It is difficult to defend the creation of order through aggregation. The order that Mansbridge presupposes rests on prior institutional arrangements that can be called into question in deliberation.

Furthermore, it is not even clear that the example of aggregation – voting – that Mansbridge employs can be seen simply as raw preference. If in fact voting is a result of some deliberative procedure where one considers the reasons for voting, then it becomes a normative action, an expression, however muted, of a collective process. Voting is also a means whereby we can express our membership in a political community.

Democracy, Disagreement, and Rational Choice

Employing a pragmatic interpretation of rational choice theory, James Johnson and Jack Knight take the criticisms of Mansbridge and her colleagues further.[14] Rather than seeing strategic action as an element of deliberation, they view discourse *in toto* as a form of strategic action: its basic aim is to persuade or induce others to undertake an action. They do see that certain specific forms of action and the stability of democratic institutions do not rest simply on preferences expressed through voting. These also require discussion, which plays a crucial role in forming preferences and in limiting the scope of alternatives. However, they are at pains to divorce their position from that of deliberative democrats (especially Habermas) who base deliberation on a strong notion of agreement and achieved consensus. This, they claim, is unrealizable and unrealistic. Johnson and Knight seek to redefine the distinction between communicative and strategic action to the benefit of their notion of strategic action.

For Johnson and Knight, social action is not primarily consensual. In place of a notion of consensus based in mutual understanding, they believe deliberation is simply a matter of argument. As they see it, consensual action reflects a failure to accept conflict and indeterminacy, while, by contrast, strategic action aims to limit (rather than end or avoid) disagreement. Political argument is strategic: it includes persuasion, cajoling, negotiating, and providing incentives. It does not rely on the force of the better argument. Johnson and Knight contend that self-interested modes of argument are sufficient to coordinate action. Reaching the outcome we desire does not depend on "agreement" over norms.[15]

Like other theorists of rational choice, Johnson and Knight employ a desiccated notion of social action. For them, cooperation is only desirable because it is personally profitable. To be sure, they do not actually want to reject all norms, although their attachment to a strategic model makes comprehending norms difficult. Like Mansbridge and her colleagues, they want to solve problems in which a plurality of norms do not admit of consensus. However, in one respect they go further: they promote the idea that we can and should try through incentives to induce or persuade others to do what we want. This does not, however, solve the problems of social order they pose.

Imagine a social world that is coordinated entirely through incentive and inducement. While Johnson and Knight see a happy outcome where all cooperate strategically, or at least where cooperation is sufficient, what happens when these incentives fail or if some people begin to gain substantial advantages over others? Then it would become difficult to trust others or to maintain an unproblematic notion of strategy as non-antagonistic. What happens when someone is in distress, ill or troubled, or lacks resources? We need to invoke questions of justice or even ethical notions of the good to understand and approach these problems.

When we see argument and deliberation as essentially strategic, we lose the bases of social order in mutual understanding. We lose the capacity for solidarity. Neither norms nor practices of solidarity are means for strategically achieving ends; they are instead modes of relating to others. They express who we are as individuals, as well as the social identity of participants. We do not just seek to fulfil preferences or to relate means to ends that are merely given. We strive to realize purposes and to create conditions that are compatible with the kind of person we believe we are or would like to become.

When I view another from the point of view of strategic action, I regard this person not as one with whom I am bound by ties of accountability or solidarity, but instead as a means to my ends, even if those ends are themselves benign. Even when we are trying to induce cooperation or to find incentives that avoid domination, the other person is still not one with whom we share bonds of respect and care, who needs to be treated as free and equal. So long as we stay within the horizon of strategic action we have no way to make the distinction between good and bad uses of such action. Thus, the proposals by Mansbridge for the incorporation of strategic action and the more radical position of Johnson and Knight are caught in a dilemma. Either they are unable to explain the non-dominating elements of strategic action or they are forced to incorporate assumptions from the communicative use of deliberation.

For once we consider the other person as worthy of enough respect to deliberately avoid dominating via the resort to strategic action, we have left the realm of strategy and have begun to employ norms that require and shape reasoned agreement. Once we see the other as a free and equal participant, and not merely a strategic partner, we consider that individual as someone who is both due just treatment and accountable for her actions. This type of ethical or moral accountability is not possible within the framework of strategic action.

We cannot generate a theory of democracy based entirely on strategic action. Strategic action is not sufficient to generate a normative social order on its own. Arguments employing strategic action often tacitly draw upon the background conditions of the social lifeworld in order to circumscribe its legitimate scope. This form of action relies on the prior existence of norms of accountability as well as on the trust and solidarity, however weak, of the members of that world. Try to imagine a world in which solely strategic actions were the basis of order. How would we deal with questions of unjust distribution of goods or distribution of power? It could deal neither with questions of personal and social identity, nor with the ways that preferences are formed in the context of these background conditions.

Antagonism and the Basis of Politics: Against Consensus

The idea that liberal politics is either apolitical or anti-political has a long pedigree in twentieth-century political thought. The critique of behaviouralism developed by the Caucus for a New Political Science in the United States in the 1960s held that this approach eliminated politics from political science. In seeking a value-free social science, behaviouralism lost sight of the significance of problems and was guided simply by methodological concerns.[16] A value-neutral social science left out questions of the good life. As a result, behavioural approaches, whatever the political outlook of their practitioners, were inherently conservative. They provided no tools for opposing the existing order.

In addition, liberalism has often been criticized for its interest group politics, which like behaviouralism lacks any overarching conception of the good life. If political actors act largely in terms of private interests, questions of the public good are difficult to address. Especially as seen in rational choice theories, there can be no conception of the general will or common interest.

Postmodern thinkers extend the criticism of the anti-political character of political theory to the very conceptions of the good life that earlier theorists used to criticize behaviouralism. In their view, it is not just a value-free or interest-based approach to politics that generates an anti-political conception of politics. Postmodern theorists reject the very notion that there are norms of order or ideals of the good life. They consider any attempt to establish such norms as a means of promoting conformist attitudes and practices that fix behaviour and deny conflict. As they see it, theories of deliberative democracy stand on the side of conformity. They rely, according to this critique, on forms of consensus that eliminate politics. Radical democracy requires the acknowledgment of the inevitability and permanence of conflict, struggle, disagreement, and dissensus that transgresses existing orders and generates radical change. For these thinkers, politics is essentially agonistic. To think otherwise is to deny politics altogether.

For Bonnie Honig, much of contemporary political theory denies or displaces politics. She finds this tendency in a wide variety of contemporary positions from liberalism to republicanism to communitarianism, which "converge in the assumption that success lies in the elimination from a regime of dissonance, resistance conflict, struggle."[17] These theories are essentially conformist because they reduce forms of politics to settled terms. They are concerned with stability, order, regulation, and law. They eliminate conflict. In contrast, Honig's version of agonism proposes a politics of destabilization and transgression as a form of permanent contestation. This politics aims to upset fixed political norms and identities. Only such a "transgressive" politics can unleash the freedom-creating potential of human action to begin anew and create new forms of social life.

William Connolly develops a related version of agonism.[18] A democratic ethos, he argues, must encompass a permanent agonistic struggle of conflicting commitments. He sees the conflict over viewpoints to be undecidable and resistant to any closure or finality. Following Friedrich Nietzsche, he sees agonistic struggle as guided by the mutual respect of adversaries. Much like the idealized *agon* of Nietzsche's thought, the great men of the *agon* strive for glory in the competition of great ideas against the tragic backdrop of finitude.

Chantal Mouffe, sometimes in collaboration with Ernesto Laclau, differentiates her version of agonism from those of both Honig and Connolly.[19] Mouffe begins from a rejection of Marx's idea of a non-antagonistic society. According to this position, Marx eliminated politics. He employed the idea of a harmonious post-capitalist society without division or conflict. Antagonism was only a feature of class-divided societies. Because Marx saw civil society as little more than a reflection of bourgeois power, he had a limited notion of public life, one that ironically echoed the very liberalism he subjected to critical attack.

For Mouffe, recovering the political involves overcoming Marx's harmonistic and economistic assumptions. Unlike critical theorists, Mouffe takes the postmodern route to the return of politics. She follows Carl Schmitt's earlier critique of liberal politics without rejecting all elements of liberalism. Schmitt rejected liberal theories of deliberation and discussion as empty and politically impotent. Parliamentary democracy operated via the mediation of plural interests though compromise and indecision. It was incapable of dealing with a crisis by protecting the commonality of the nation. Mouffe accepts Schmitt's delineation of the friend/foe distinction as at the root of politics. She rejects universalist notions of right. Politics is always rooted in antagonism. Being "for" something always means being "against" something or someone. Conflict is thus an ever-present possibility.

In place of consensus, then, Mouffe holds that the basis of social order lies in relations of power. Contrary to the views of Honig and Connolly, for Mouffe there is no standpoint of mutual respect among antagonists that keeps struggle within bounds. Instead, power and order are founded in hegemony. There must be a dominant power that precedes rationality. The dominant forms of understanding that define what is right and wrong, good or bad, are established through hegemony. While this position borrows from Gramsci, unlike Marxian views it rejects any notion of rationality with which forms of hegemony can be evaluated. The establishment and acceptance of norms is based on "persuasion" rather than conviction. Mouffe thinks that the rationalism of theorists such as Habermas and Rawls occludes the emotion and sentiment at the heart of citizenship. She thinks that political theory must be concerned with shaping the *feelings* of citizens so that they have a sense of solidarity with others. Here, however, she seems to employ a sense of virtue that Honig would reject.

Coming at the question of politics from a somewhat different though related angle, Jacques Rancière views politics as dissensus.[20] His focus, however, is on a specific form of disagreement. Disagreement always occurs as a break with order and conformity. It is a rupture that creates a new world, a different outlook. Politics, then, is an extraordinary activity that is distinct from ordinary ones, and in fact Rancière gives it a privileged ontological position. Politics is distinct from policing. The latter is a consensual form that reinforces the exclusion and division that always exists in ordinary life. Politics comes into play when a group that has been excluded asserts that it is in fact equal, that is, when it breaks with the existing order of domination. Thus, politics always involves a wrong; it breaks from the consensus that excludes and puts in its place a dissent in which a group that is excluded declares it has an equal place.

Rancière's view of democracy is a radical one.[21] Democracy is not just a form of social life or a specific form of government, but the form of politics itself. The political is a creative force that has the power to institute new forms of social life. Democracy thus does not refer to a specific community constituted through exclusion; rather, in counting the uncounted it creates a space in which the included and excluded are one. Such a process generates a new public, a new sense of a "we," that includes the oppressed and those who stand in solidarity with them. The sense of "we" is in Rancière's view created when a collectivity asserts its equality. It also relies on a new sensibility that allows these new social identities to arise. Paradoxically, this inclusion of the other occurs only through dissensus. Contestation is not simply a conflict of interests or values but a dispute over what is given and about the frame within which we sense that something is given. It encompasses both who we are and how we understand who we are.

Sheldon Wolin takes up some of the problems that Rancière raises through a less ontologically tinged and more historically oriented notion of boundary-breaking experiences.[22] Wolin too sees the political embodied in the extraordinary experiences in which political actors unite to revolt against domination. The major threats to political action are not so much ontological as historical. Wolin is concerned with the survival of democratic initiatives in the face of state and administrative powers that tend to overwhelm them. As Wendy Brown correctly notes, his approach is neo-Weberian.[23] He is more concerned with Weber's notion of the rationalization of power than with, for example, that of Marx. He is however a *neo*-Weberian who does not accept Weber's strictures about the need for representative democracy. For Wolin, like most radical theorists, representative democracy is limited. This bureaucratically circumscribed form of politics is primarily concerned with management of behaviour. We will return to this issue in the next chapter.

In a manner reminiscent of Max Horkheimer, Wolin is concerned with a persistent Cartesian influence that reduces the search for social practice to a form of natural science. Instead, the emphasis in participatory democracy on local decision-making makes clear that Wolin sees politics as located basically in conflict or in contestation over power.

Wolin is concerned primarily with democratic processes as forms of renewal that are meant to break the boundaries of existing politics and reinstitute democratic demands. His normative model is a form of radical and popular democracy that transcends the bounds of the managerial politics that characterize late-capitalist societies. In protest movements such as the civil rights and environmental movements, and in groups such as Solidarity, the Polish trade union, he sees social forces that seek to reinstitute popular sovereignty and thereby renew the promise of radical democracy inherent in that idea. However, Wolin thinks this process is limited in modern society. Democratic popular actions emerge only sporadically and in response to social problems, and to inequalities and injustices. Democracy here acts more as a corrective or even a renewal of a republican spirit, but it still seems to acknowledge limits to radical democracy.

Radical critics of deliberative democracy see the quest for consensus in metaphysical terms. They often see order in terms of a permanence and certainty that is ontologically ensured. However, the post-metaphysical conception of reason and action that we develop here does not require that mutual understanding be identified with the certainty or even harmony that critics claim to find in it.

If, however, we begin from the perspective of participants in a social lifeworld, then we base our analysis not on a metaphysical certainty that things are fixed but rather on the institution and reproduction of the forms of mutual understanding, recognition, and accountability that are central to social order. We look at deliberative democracy not simply as a decision-making procedure but as a key element within a theory of society. While participants in the lifeworld do assume that what they believe is true and that the norms they hold are correct, they are also reflexive participants who can provide accounts of their actions when called upon. Seen from this angle, the process of mutual understanding in the lifeworld is not simply based on the need to decide but is part of the process of constant renewal of the social world though mutual understanding. As reflexive participants in this social world, however, individuals are capable of critically understanding the norms they follow.

An ontological notion of the social order as a fixity that is opposed to dissent and disagreement reifies the open character of communicative action, which presumes a reciprocal relation between reproduction and renewal. What we more formally call discourse comes into play not primarily in situations of social order and maintenance but when norms or other features of social life are called into question. Of course, it is true that social forms can become ossified and difficult to change. Individuals too can form rigid identities and authoritarian personality structures. These challenges, however, are as Wolin argues historical, not metaphysical. Radical democracy no doubt implies openness to social transformation. It always holds out the possibility of new forms of social relations; but that openness is an element of ordinary understanding and cannot be ontologically opposed to order.

Nor can we see norms or forms of social order simply as policing or disciplining subjects. Clearly some forms of social life and some institutions can be enabling, if not always so. Families can be both oppressive and supportive; educational institutions can promote conformity, or they can foster critical reflection. As long as we human beings are vulnerable and dependent, we rely on personal and institutional arrangements to develop and use our capacities. While there is no doubt that politics is distinct from administration, citizens do act in concert not only to reject or rebel against rules but also to bring about new forms through authorization. The communicative power exercised by citizens acting in concert can both create new institutional forms and bind individuals together. Again, order and transformation are not ontologically separate. They create a new consensus. From this standpoint, it is difficult to see politics as constituted solely by struggle or by agonistic conflict. For example, if a legislature passes a law guaranteeing equal pay for equal work, creating a society in which this is accepted may not be a matter of policing or administrative rationality alone. It still requires a political commitment to equality, not just technical or instrumental reason.

Against post-structuralist arguments, contemporary critical theory seems to accept the plurality of values and conceptions of the good life. Theories of justice, then, are called into play when conflicts over values or the good life affect the basic rights and capacities of subjects as participants. To be sure, the notion of pluralism employed by such theorists does not satisfy all agonistic thinkers; nonetheless, it is an exaggeration to speak as if pluralism is denied. However, there are points of contact. For example, where William Connolly speaks of the mutual respect that contestants have in the *agon*, he draws on the same sources of respect and recognition that critical theories of justice employ. In his view the contest between participants in the *agon* for recognition and glory is itself limited by these principles of respect for self and others. Similarly, critical theories of justice are based on conceptions of solidarity that entail the inclusion of others in ways similar to what Rancière and some post-structuralist theorists argue. Theories of "consensus" are rooted in these conceptions of a consensual social order that require a broad reading rather than a narrow one.

The most widespread criticism of the discursive account is that it is unable to deal with situations of conflict.[24] Mouffe argues that such situations are constitutive of politics and involve more than just disagreement – they also involve opposition. In such cases the opponent is treated not with respect but rather, as in cases of war (hot or cold), as an existential threat. For Carl Schmitt the idea of the enemy as an existential threat was the basis of a politics that saw the executive, not the legislature, as the true authority and sovereign. The popular will is replaced by the will of the dictator, who embodies the pre-thematic unity of the people.

Mouffe does not adopt Schmitt's proposal for a unitary power through which friend/foe relations are defined; instead she tries to recast it in terms of a tempered antagonism within a democratic society that is an "agonistic (rather than antagonistic) public space in which there is the possibility for dissensus to be expressed or different alternatives to be put forward."[25] She sees social formations as necessarily bounded. A democratic society conceives of itself as a body of equals within a social order that is defined as different from others. Even within democratic societies, however, there is an irreducible plurality of positions that never cohere into a single unity. Mouffe believes hers is a conception of radical democracy because it extends democratic practices into all areas of social life, but without any "transcendent" notion of unity.

This theory runs into difficulties, however, in determining where and how sovereignty lies. While a radical theory would seem to say that sovereignty rests with the people and with the communicative power of creating understanding, the theory of hegemony that Mouffe and Laclau develop leaves the status of sovereignty uncertain. For authority is in some sense constituted by the hegemonic powers from which notions of good or bad, right or wrong, come into being. Subjects, then, do not come to an understanding about matters of importance; rather, they are persuaded in the rhetorical sense of the term. It is a matter of creating emotional commitment, not mutual understanding. To be sure, Mouffe looks to the establishment of public spaces in which contesting views are aired. However, to the extent that social order is a matter of hegemony, the question of sovereignty remains dependent on strategic rather than communicative power.

It is, we think, a mistake to see mutual understanding, as Mouffe often does, as a rationalist conception that operates from the top down. Rather, rationality is built into mutual understanding from the ground up through notions of mutual accountability. Subjects who engage in understanding are caught up in a world of involvements and commitments. Once we begin to see rationality as internal to processes of social life, the rigid opposition between reason and emotion or justice and solidarity gives way to a more complementary set of relations.

Axel Honneth provides one helpful account of the dynamic relation between private and public that casts into relief the important questions involved here. The key is to recognize that, like freedom and autonomy themselves, "private" and "public" are not so much properties as practices. They are forms of social interaction. Basing his position on pragmatist themes in the work of John Dewey, Honneth writes:

> Social action unfolds in forms of interaction whose consequences in the simple case affect only those immediately involved; but as soon as those not involved see themselves affected by the consequences of such interaction, there emerges from their perspective the need for joint control of the corresponding actions either by their cessation or their promotion ... The term "public" is attributed to that sphere of social action that a social group can successfully prove to be in need of general regulation because encroaching consequences are being generated; and, accordingly, a "public" consists of the circle of citizens who, on the basis of a jointly experienced concern, share the conviction that they have to turn to the rest of society for the purposes of administratively controlling the relevant interaction.

For Honneth, then, following Dewey, the "public" is "a discursive medium of cooperative problem solving under democratic conditions," in effect a form of rational practice rooted in and reinforcing a communicative form of freedom.[26]

Here we can see that the practice of policy deliberations necessarily implicates us in a public at the point at which it becomes a matter of concern to us that the effects of these actions have bearing on us. The point is that private concerns become public issues. The "public" should not be understood as involving a prior ethical substance existing independently of its relational character. Such relations form and reform in the context of a "relevant interaction" that generates "encroaching consequences."

Honneth's position is part of a larger argument that seeks to establish the basis for social cooperation in the division of labour and the practical encounters that associated individuals as problem-solvers have with the constraints of nature and social life. This larger argument need not concern us here. However, his definition of the "public" and its implicit relation to the "private" suggest core elements of both self-reflexivity and a critical diagnosis of the present in the face of social pathologies. On the one hand, where those involved see the consequences of others' actions as affecting them and thus call for more general regulation in the "public interest," there is the commitment to publicize, as it were, these interactions. This involves mobilizing others who may also be affected but who may not notice it. But it also entails engaging with those whose "private" interactions have triggered public consequences. The possibility of doing both defines the conditions for rational self-reflection, where there can be no assumed natural harmony of interests but rather the potential achievement of agreement that responds to the needs and interests of each and all. Both those interacting and those affected by these interactions can enrich their appreciation of the multiple dimensions of social conflict and cooperation: the original agents, by coming to a recognition of the (perhaps originally suppressed or obscure) public quality of their acts; and those affected, by seeking to make public their position and thus implicitly engaging the actors as communicative equals whose private autonomy must be respected (as opposed to simply "muscling" them as opponents in a process of making their own narrowly private interests prevail).[27]

Honneth and Social Freedom

Honneth's account of social freedom, to which we will return in greater detail in chapter 6, highlights a central idea: that since participants in everyday life are mutually accountable, they must accept at least minimal obligations to others. We have shared expectations that regulate how we respond to them. Of course, not all of these expectations are directly connected to rationality. We expect that when we say "hi," the other person will greet us in return. However, in most areas reason is central. We believe that others will act in accordance with what we see to be true or normatively right. When our mutual expectations are violated, we seek an explanation. We might initiate a discussion, or at least a conversation, and find that we have strong disagreements about a norm, for example. As we have argued, what allows us to continue or even pursue discourse at all is that we share at least a certain amount of trust and a weak solidarity with others – we need to believe that the other person will be sincere and willing to carry on with the discussion. This is not to devalue the quest for validity or truth, but rather more specifically to indicate that trust and solidarity are complementary.

These same two elements are central, too, in cases where we do not reach agreement. In the face of diverging expectations on the part of participants with respect to the way they carry out actions and plans of life, we need to retain a certain amount of trust in order to continue interaction where there is a significant disagreement. We can think of many examples of this in social life. A husband and wife may disagree on some important issues such as money, childrearing practices, or even politics and still maintain their relationship. We frequently interact with others of diverse political and social views in a cooperative spirit. We do not have to agree completely to have a functioning social order. However, when trust breaks down, cooperation in the face of disagreements can be difficult. In the United States, to take an example, this trust is badly frayed.

For these reasons we do not think that strategic action is sufficient to generate trust. The examples given by Jane Mansbridge and others rest on the creation or maintenance of trust and solidarity as background conditions. For example, a political situation in which individual interests and not general interests are considered rests on the prior sense that we respect the individual's right to pursue a good life – that is, that individuals are due equal respect and consideration. This consideration extends to their choices of the good life, though such plans can be criticized. Without this moral element individual plans do not gain the recognition needed to make them elements of an agreement.[28]

Moral understanding and solidarity are also closely linked. They require a wider understanding of and identification with others. We do not have to use the term "empathy," but clearly the idea of, for example, equal respect requires something like empathy as a precondition for the kind of universalistic moral framework that theorists of justice – including and perhaps especially critical theorists – require. These forms of moral consciousness and solidarity can even be part of our identity,

The above considerations also require a modification of Honneth's (and Dewey's) conception of politics as collective problem-solving. No doubt this is a central feature of politics. But politics also involves the creation of a common will to act and an accompanying social identity; indeed, Honneth's more recent elaboration of the idea of social freedom and its relation to socialism, which we also examine in greater detail in chapter 6, seems intended to take the issues of a common will and social identities more fully and explicitly into account. It is we who must act together and authorize the group and in some cases provide the motivation to act. This "we," however, is not a stand-alone entity or essence that exists apart from its articulation through the very process of generating a common will.

The securing of the conditions of rationality for this kind of social order, one of cooperation and interdependence, is thus at the core of democracy. The key point, which can only be outlined here, is that this rationality is inextricably tied to the articulation of a common will that must be viewed as a practical accomplishment of individuals bound together such that the freedom and autonomy of each is tied to that of all. Democracy is the realization of a Hegel-like system of "right": "the steps needed to be taken for the free will of each individual to attain its actualization in the present"; or "the social preconditions for the actualization of the free will" under conditions whereby "the specifications of morality and law can only be considered justified to the degree that they bring the individual autonomy of human self-determination to expression."[29]

From this vantage point, negative and positive liberty – liberalism and democracy – would be not antagonistic but rather complementary elements of a complex practice of freedom, where freedom would consist in the ability both to be left alone and to be with others. To use Jürgen Habermas's formulation of this relationship, democracy understood in terms of a rational social order would maintain and respect both private and public autonomy – that is, the securing of a personal space free from interference *and* the provision of opportunities to participate in collective will-formation (i.e., the determination of the laws under which one is governed). The autonomy of each is dependent on the autonomy of all, and vice versa.

But if negative and positive liberty are not inherently incompatible, they are not naturally harmonious, either. (This was a key flaw of orthodox Marxist conceptions of democracy: eliminating the conditions alleged to both necessitate and establish negative freedom as freedom from the community does not automatically secure the well-being of each and all.) Hegel famously identified "concrete" freedom as being with oneself in another, where "we are not one-sidedly within ourselves, but willingly limit ourselves with reference to another, even while knowing ourselves in this limitation as ourselves."[30] Determinacy and indeterminacy, universality and particularity, are necessary for full freedom; but neither can absorb the other without destructive consequences. To be sure, Hegel himself may have thought they could be readily reconciled in a concrete and perhaps even self-evident ethical life of "objective spirit" (interpretations around this issue are diverse, to say the least; again, Honneth's work on social freedom contributes to a clarification of the issues involved). We cannot be so confident about this. So the question of how to be at home with another, which might be considered another way of addressing what we view as the key elements of democracy – rational solidarity and autonomy – might better be framed in terms of something like what Hannah Arendt called "bearing with strangers." To be oneself means to engage others in ways that are neither purely instrumental nor overwhelmingly fraternal, and that involve neither hostility, nor indifference, nor benevolence.[31]

Understanding the conditions and prospects for solidarity and autonomy in this light suggests that a key link between private and public autonomy and democratic political forms, institutions, and practices is the shifting character of the relation between private and public spheres of activity. In effect, this is Habermas's way of formulating under contemporary conditions Hegel's claim that freedom consists in being with oneself in another. Both public and private spheres always and already exist as mutually determining: the context and content of each refer to those of the other. (In Arendt's case, of course, there is a third, mediating dimension: the social, itself a complex intermingling of the public and private.)

Other critical theorists try to either criticize of defend a deliberative concept of democracy without elucidating its basis in the lifeworld. This creates misunderstanding. James Bohman, for example, seems to think that deliberation is purely formal – that it does not provide any substance for a democratic theory. By contrast, Nadia Urbinati and Maria Paula Saffon want to defend deliberative democracy strictly, using the principles of freedom and equal respect, and to detach these from the requirements of rationality.[32] Urbinati relies on what might be called a "top down" reading of Habermas's theory of the conditions of deliberation as developed in his early account of the ideal speech situation. The conditions that provide fair deliberation are given only in the ideal case. A more "bottom up" approach to Habermas's theory begins with the condition of subjects in the lifeworld. Our capacity for mutual accountability does not stem from ideal conditions; rather, ideal conditions are rooted in the interactive capacities of subjects. We operate in daily life with the capacity both to reason and to discuss our concerns with others. We hold a set of ideas or assumptions about the world that we believe to be true, as well as norms we believe to be just or right. We are reflexively aware of participation in the world. Thus we can assess and evaluate not only the claims that are made about the world but also events within this world that we encounter. Similarly, our mundane interaction is characterized by concerns and involvements. We have moral conceptions that we use to evaluate the institutions, practices, and persons we encounter.

When called upon to do so in everyday life, we can give an account of our actions, using our reasoning capacities. We do not abandon these when we enter into discourse. The conditions that Habermas calls idealized presuppositions are refinements of the conditions of ordinary interaction. We assume that people are capable of reasoning and that the reasoning process leads to conclusions that are true or valid. Habermas does not have in mind here a situation in which anything that people agree to must conform to a process of validation. He simply says that for a discourse to be reasonable, we must strive to achieve those conditions, and that the elements of idealization are not alien to everyday life. When we read a text that seems alien or find another person difficult to understand, we try to make sense of what they say. We assume people make sense until we are convinced otherwise. If we did not assume that speakers and texts are comprehensible, we would be unable to speak a language at all.

Just as in situations in which expectations are not fulfilled, or we do not understand why someone is acting in a certain way or holding something to be true and are thus entitled to ask for an account, in deliberation and discourse we are similarly justified in asking for an account. It seems to us that this structure of accountability guarantees that an element of rationality is necessary in all deliberation, Thus trust, solidarity, rationality, and communicative power are all elements of discourse.

In contrast to discursive or deliberative processes, reification can be characterized by a diminution or even elimination of communicative power. The problem with Marxian models of reification is that in the past they have been modelled largely on a concept of subject-centred reason of an expressive subject.[33] As we've noted, in Georg Lukács's formulation the relations between humans are reduced to relations between inert things. He saw that the capitalist forms of reification treated everyone as a commodity, that is, as goods to be bought and sold. Today, intensified marketization has extended the process of converting human relations to market form. From the standpoint of a theory of communicative reason and communicative action, reification manifests itself as the removal of human actions from the sphere of public deliberation and authorizing will, and subjects them instead to quasi-automatic regulation though instrumental and strategic imperatives. When, for example, education is governed by market considerations, the standards of evaluation are based on those of profit and loss or benefit to industry, not on the creation of free and equal persons who create a common way of life. Bureaucratic imperatives related to education have pushed it towards a regime of high-stakes testing in which students' progress is constantly monitored and measured. The standards are based on the abstract mastery of skills geared to job performance, without any reference to the students' agency. Equal and respectful treatment of students is subordinated to the testing regime.

Reification also extends to personality formation. As critics have noted, educational regimes, which have always been slanted towards business, now function like factories in which students are devalued. High-pressure competitive testing is discouraging many students, who in addition have low economic status. Schools in marginalized, disadvantaged, low-income areas are being targeted for privatization or radical reform, with local control ceded to governments. As pawns in this power struggle, students learn mostly that they have little chance to get ahead in a world in which job prospects are weak and the poor are increasingly marginalized.

The Limits of Participation?

Mark Warren contends that we should take a more circumspect view of what a transformative politics can do.[34] The basis of politics is social groundlessness and contestability. Politics is essentially agonistic. It is a domain of struggle in which norms, practices, rules, and identities are contested. Where there is no disagreement, there is no politics. Politics emerges out of social groundlessness because when there is contestation, one loses one's identity and sense of belonging with others; in order to express disagreement, one has to take a stand apart from others, which risks conflict.

Warren further contests the classic Aristotelian notion of politics. The Aristotelian tradition sees participation as a virtue-creating activity, one in which participation builds character and indeed is necessary for realizing our potential. Warren, by contrast, sees politics as a risky, anxiety-promoting activity, which because it sets us apart from others exposes vulnerabilities and creates hazards. To be sure, political action has a transformative character. Warren uses examples of isolated individuals confronting a system that is rigid and in so doing exposing its flaws and limits. His model is one of a politics that creates no common good or "we" relation.

The problem with Warren's analysis can best be explicated using a counter-example that shows that the political does have some of the qualities he denies. One of his examples involves a woman who finds the language and atmosphere of her workplace oppressive. She has to decide whether to contest this environment or leave it be. In the former case she risks being labelled difficult or a troublemaker. She faces a condition of social groundlessness where she is at odds with prevailing norms. As an actor she is isolated and at odds with the behavioural expectations of her workplace. She rightly considers those norms to be flawed and takes a stand against them.

Consider this other example taken from the news. The state of Indiana enacted legislation allowing businesses to discriminate against LGBT people on religious grounds. Many groups reacted negatively to this, including businesses organizations and professional associations, as well as individuals and groups that either represent or support LGBT rights.

The first thing to notice is that political issues have an unavoidably public character. While someone may choose to avoid LGBT persons in private life, this matter becomes problematic when it involves the public sphere – that is, institutions such as businesses, schools, and governments, all of which necessarily deal with the public at large. Public issues are generally created when private troubles become public issues. This is not to say that the example Warren gives is of private troubles – only that his account leaves out the link to larger public concerns. It is not the nature of an issue as contestable that makes it public or political. It is, rather, the type of concern we have where what is often precisely at stake is the question of the right to say "we."

It seems to us that in this situation we are looking at the creation of a "we" relation as this represents a will to act in concert. With respect to the state law restricting the rights of LGBT individuals, the central question raised by the law concerns the right of individuals on the presumptive ground of religious conviction to exclude some from equal consideration and respect under the law. That equal consideration and respect have been the result of long struggle is an important part of what defines us a group. What Warren sees as social groundlessness is in this case what we have identified as the diminution, if not loss, of equal respect. But it is not clear how far this alienation extends. When we are treated in a differential way in important public arenas, our self-respect can be diminished.

However, it is also true that political discussion is carried out collectively. I may find I have been treated unfairly or in a demeaning way by one possibly dominant group. I may join with others who believe similarly and so organize to transform such issues into public ones. As citizens we can appear together to deliberate about a shared situation.

The arguments of Mansbridge and Warren provide a rather restricted view of political action, especially in the face of neoliberalism. The thrust of the neoliberal project is to reduce or eliminate features of strong democracy, that is, precisely those possibilities for transforming what seem to be exclusively personal into political questions.[35] This is particularly the case with respect to the apparently nature-like qualities of a capitalist market economy, qualities enhanced by neoliberal values, institutions, and practices. A strong, radical democracy must raise issues around the creation of solidarity and strong participatory relationships and in turn must link these to a critique of the domination inherent in the capitalist economy. It must, in other words, promote the autonomy of subjects.

The project of creating a strong, radical, and participatory democracy thus also requires at the very least a radical reform of the current welfare state. But it also needs to recognize the importance of a welfare state, that is, the necessity for a social safety net in capitalist societies. The existence of welfare measures at the least recognizes the side effects if capitalism.

The reification/marketing of forms of life runs up against immanent limits. If we were to eliminate all possibilities for the exercise of communicative reason, we would not have socialized individuals who can function in the reified world – they would be unable to develop the ability to challenge it. We cannot completely eliminate forms of mutual recognition, though the power of recognition can be minimized by forms of subordination. While open to vast change, human life is not infinitely malleable. Critical theorists should be sensitive to the points at which these conflicts emerge. However, the agents of the process should be seen not as strategic actors but as communicative participants.

We therefore should seek institutional practices that enhance individual autonomy. By "autonomy" we do not mean simply freedom to choose, but more fundamentally a sense of a strong identity and an ability to resist domination. Autonomy might well include the formation of more autonomous publics and alternative institutions, including social movements. The latter have been central to raising questions of social justice. In other words, we need to raise questions of social rights – a key element of social freedom.

Another important area of conflict is the workplace. Here, traditional socialism, including of course Marxism, has emphasized the condition of the working class under capitalism, something that remains central to any theory of radical democracy. Our everyday lives are becoming more exploited, while the power of unions is declining. Much paid work is largely meaningless and at the same time is becoming more contingent and insecure. Any conception of justice must include the need to move beyond distributive questions, which are to be sure important, to the exploitation of work relations under neoliberalism. The hyperexploitation of workers has created a situation in which the loss of power and autonomy is extensive. Any theory of justice must address these features of the contemporary work situation. One example of hyper-exploitation is found within the confines of the academic world. At many universities, teaching is increasingly conducted by adjuncts or temporary faculty who lack the security and benefits enjoyed fulltime, permanent employees. Of course, this example can be generalized across all spheres of employment under the current conditions of neoliberal capitalism.

Neoliberalism and Crisis Revisited

In this context, there is thus the question of whether capitalism, particularly in its current, neoliberal stage, is at all compatible with social justice, and if it is not, whether then it might be vulnerable to crises or crisis tendencies. Some analysts of neoliberalism see an irresolvable conflict between capitalism and democracy. Unregulated capitalism creates "savage inequalities" that send tremors throughout the political system. Today this has reached the point where even supporters of capitalism have taken note. Works like Thomas Piketty's have garnered widespread attention.[36] Piketty's principal contention, which most accept, is that unfettered capitalism does not lead to the diffusion of wealth throughout the economy. Left to its own devices, in producing inequalities the "free" market tends to move in the direction of an anti-democratic oligarchy. It is thus hard to see how the unfettered market can be the best guarantor of individual freedoms and liberties. On the contrary, it has become the site of an ongoing conflict between democratic rights and conceptions of the good life, on the one side, and the deepening rationalization of forms of social life, on the other.

While Piketty seems to think that measures such as progressive taxation and wealth redistribution can remedy many ills, analysts such as Wolfgang Streeck seem to think that these contradictions cannot be fully reconciled, even in welfare capitalism. Rather, they represent an endemic and essentially irreconcilable conflict between capitalist markets and democratic politics that, having been suspended for the historically short period immediately following the Second World War, has forcefully reasserted itself since the waning of economic growth in the 1970s.[37]

For Streeck the financial crisis of 2008 was indicative of permanent instability in the capitalist economy; it signalled that tensions between the demands for democratic rights and liberties and the requirements of continuing accumulation were becoming more acute. Here, he was updating the conflict between accumulation and legitimation identified by Claus Offe and Jürgen Habermas in the 1970s. Offe and Habermas thought that the breakdown of the Keynesian welfare state would raise new challenges to legitimacy, challenges most strongly and visibly raised by new social movements. Their assumption turned out to be faulty – in fact, the political economy of the post-Keynesian era would come to be dominated by neoliberal market assumptions. Rational choice theory, which in various guises came to predominate in academic/intellectual circles and even to some extent in popular journalistic quarters, attributed economic crises to unnecessary and ultimately damaging state and political interventions, which distorted the economy. For proponents of rational choice, as for those neoconservatives who wrote of the threat of an economically destabilizing democratic "overload," calls by social justice proponents to redistribute goods and maintain social rights represented excessive democratic demands.

Given the criticisms made by Piketty, Paul Krugman, and others, all of whom have highlighted growing inequalities as well as the weakening of democratic institutions and freedoms, the key points of conflict in neoliberalism seem to revolve around the question of social rights. Neoliberals typically argue that social justice, if it exists, should be based on merit. Redistributive policies should be discouraged, market-friendly initiatives should be pursued vigorously, and fiscal austerity should be applied to rein in "excessive" demands for social protection. In this regard, Wolfgang Streeck notes that participants are still vigorously resisting challenges to the social welfare net. He claims that at least so far, non-market notions of social justice have not totally given way to efforts at economic rationalization, forceful as they may have become, especially in the era of an advancing neoliberalism. Apparently, people stubbornly refuse to give up on the idea of a moral economy under which they have rights as people or as citizens that should take precedence over the outcomes of market exchange.[38]

In addition to challenging social justice, neoliberalism pursues an anti-solidaristic approach that seeks to devalue the experiences of individuals and their connections with others. In the United States, at least since the Reagan era, recipients of government aid have been labelled as deviants (welfare queens) and leeches on the system. In this context the anti-solidaristic direction of neoliberalism extends far beyond an intellectual argument about the limits of intervention; it extends too into the sentiments and personality structures of individuals. Social democratic notions are widely held in society, so they must be forcefully suppressed in a multitude of ways. Their basic worth is now under siege, as is the value and even legitimacy of union membership, among teachers or anyone else. There is a growing authoritarianism in American society and a hardening of political divisions and conceptions of the "enemy."

In contrast to Streeck, Claus Offe seems to recognize that such tendencies are present. Instead of a conflict between neoliberalism and social justice, in which context the latter is holding its own, Offe stresses the pathologies of liberal democracies: declining rates of participation and the potential for a rise in right-wing populism.[39] In America, at least, the growing power of seemingly right-wing forms of populism, funded and driven by oligarchs, appears to be succeeding in destroying social welfare institutions. If they have not triumphed entirely on the national level, they have had notable successes on the state level, where gerrymandered legislative districts have yielded conservative majorities and super-majorities that have sometimes in a blitzkrieg fashion passed regulations against labour and reproductive rights and have also moved to defund and privatize education. Even beyond the sphere of education, key features of government administration have been privatized and outsourced. The transformation of American politics has been so fundamental that one group of researchers has not hesitated to call the political system an oligarchy.

The conflict between democracy and capitalism has taken some new forms. As Streeck has observed, "it seems clear that the political manageability of democratic capitalism has sharply declined in recent years, more in some countries than in others, but also overall, in the emerging global political-economic system. As a result the risks seem to be growing, both for democracy and for the economy."[40]

Since the financial collapse of 2008, the economic situation has stabilized to a degree. However, the crisis tendencies of neoliberal capitalism have by no means disappeared. The financial sector has not been adequately reregulated and continues to move towards new bubbles and ruptures. Banks remain too big to fail, but popular opinion may militate against any future bailouts. Inequality has increased, and despite some degree of recovery, growth remains slow, debt is high, and demand remains flat. It is becoming more possible that, without any remedial action on the horizon, capitalism will experience decline and even the possibility of a more extensive breakdown.

Here too the conflict between capitalism and democracy is intensifying. As claims of increasing debt are being used to impose austerity, redistributive policies are being further limited and citizens are losing faith in government as an agent that can improve their lives. As the power of labour unions and other social movements declines, analysts such as Wolfgang Streeck have pointed out that the economy itself has become increasingly insulated from popular and democratic initiatives for reform. "For the time being, the neoliberal mainstream's political utopia is a 'market-conforming democracy,' devoid of market-correcting powers and supportive of 'incentive-compatible' redistribution from the bottom to the top."[41] In these conditions the legitimation of capitalist democracies seems to be fraught with difficulties. If democratic equality and freedom are to be preserved, the economy must be transformed.

Adding to this analysis, we would point to the increasing presence of authoritarianism and undemocratic political rule exercised to stabilize this contradictory set of forces. As we have seen, the inequalities of neoliberal capitalism have had an impact on democratic life. For some critics, Karl Polanyi has provided the framework for confronting neoliberalism and its threat to democracy; we think the ideas of C.B. Macpherson can add to this discussion as well. Particularly valuable here is his account of the central place of possessive individualism in those forms of democracy most fully tied to the triumph of capitalist market relations and values: protective and equilibrium democracy, especially the former in its current incarnation as neoliberal politics and government.[42] In this situation the calls for social justice must include re-establishing solidarities, as well as increasing needs and possibilities for participation.

Neoliberalism not only limits developmental freedoms and pursues anti-solidaristic aims; it also rejects the efficacy of most forms of communicative freedom and communicative power. Thus, one set of strategies for reform should centre on enhancing the communicative power of participants. This would no doubt include strengthening the public sphere through non-governmental institutions. Some writers focus on the creation of institutional supports, but non-institutional forms of communicative action, as embodied in social movements and protests, are important as well. It is unlikely that capitalism will tolerate the development of new institutional forms without significant opposition. More participatory institutions will be established only through conflict. Participation in and identification with social movements could also promote forms of solidarity. In addition, critical theories need to enter the debate about economic inequality and the quality of work, especially the increasing predominance of precarious and casual labour.

Finally, a critical theory must make an issue of the present day's rising authoritarianism and willful ignorance of information; both have been prevalent at the level of personality and identity structures. In his account of communicative action, Habermas discusses briefly the notion of a defensive preservation of the lifeworld whereby bureaucratic rationalization and reification would foment a critical response that attempts to preserve tradition in the face of disorganizing forces. We are not sure, however, that those who adopt a traditionalist defensive posture to threats to the lifeworld would respond to deliberative measures because they might not be amenable to the kind of persuasion involved. To be sure, appeals to sensibilities may work in such circumstances. But the limits to a purely deliberative approach are encountered when individuals are incapable of basic trust and deliberative competence.[43] If they believe others are so tainted that they are incapable of a cooperative endeavour, then trust and deliberative competence are threatened. In this case a critical theory has to consider what reparative measures would be needed to establish deliberation and to deal with bigotry and authoritarianism. We do not say this in the sense of some cliché, such as "being nice to everybody." Conflict of some sort would likely be unavoidable. However, the nature of this conflict would be decisive: conflict involving solidarity around issues of equality and social justice could reinforce rather than undermine the transformation of private woes into public concerns.

It seems to us that for any consideration of a robust critical and radical theory of democracy, it is essential to raise the various issues and concerns we have tried briefly to address in this chapter. But before we directly explore what such a theory might be – in our view, this would be a theory of participatory democracy – we return in the next chapter to the Frankfurt School and a more detailed account of its significance for grasping the challenges of democracy.

Chapter Five

Towards a Critical Theory of Democracy: The Frankfurt School and Democratic Theory

In this chapter we build upon our discussion in the previous chapter and attempt to lay out what we believe are central elements of a critical theory of democracy. This raises the obvious question of what such a theory would entail: what elements of critical theory as we explored it in previous chapters; and what kind of democracy for which such elements could provide a solid basis. More specifically, we need to show how to connect (a) a theory that in its focus, structure, and concepts offers a critical diagnosis of the pathologies of the present from the standpoint of a possible future society that secures social freedom and solidarity, with (b) a conception of democracy that emphasizes not just present forms of democratic politics and government, nor even necessary institutional reform, but also the normative requirements of a democratic social order capable of fostering and sustaining an emancipated form of life. As we argued in our first chapter, this would be a radical, developmental democracy within which all individuals would have the equal right and ability to use and develop their distinctively human capacities.

To explore the question of what a radical, developmental democracy would involve, we focus primarily once again on the claims and concepts of Jürgen Habermas, specifically as he developed these in *Between Facts and Norms*, which we discussed in chapter 1, and which represents his most systematic treatment of what he calls a discourse theory of democracy. But we also return to the ideas of the first generation of Frankfurt School critical theorists. We noted in previous chapters that these thinkers, most notably Max Horkheimer, did not systematically explore the idea of democracy, much less work up an explicit theory of it. In part this reflected their belief that liberalism and capitalism were, if not identical, certainly indissolubly linked. But as Albrecht Wellmer has recently reminded us "the very term *critical theory* was coined in a secret reference to Marx's critique of political economy."[1] The task was to overcome capitalism and its pathologies; issues of politics, including democratic politics, took a back seat. At the very least the theory assumed the possibility, and not just the necessity, of replacing capitalism with socialism. With the transcendence of capitalism, the class antagonisms endemic to bourgeois society, which precluded the achievement of the common will essential to democracy, would be overcome: a classless society would *inter alia* be egalitarian and thus democratic.

Historical developments outwitted such hopes and aspirations. It became clear that the economic base does not determine the political superstructure, and that abolishing private property was not equivalent to establishing to a solidary common life, nor did it automatically lead to it. The question of socialism and the issue of democracy had to be treated separately: the political had an autonomy that demanded an autonomous form of political thought.

Yet as necessary as it has been, the turn to political theory and an autonomous theory of democracy has had a paradoxical implication. The reality that politics cannot be reduced to economics has frequently led to a diminished concern with the unified political economy that characterized traditional Marxism, upon whose assumptions Horkheimer had relied even as he recognized the need to revise these assumptions in the face of historical circumstances. The securing of an autonomous political theory raised issues of power, citizenship, and public life that often came to be seen as legal and governmental and that were treated from either a descriptive/institutional or a normative perspective. So-called economic questions were acknowledged as factors influencing the political process and even shaping the policy concerns of governments. However, this approach failed to take on board what classical socialist political economy had understood – that economic and political power and identity were intertwined, even though the political could not be reduced to the economic. As C.B. Macpherson presented it, possessive individualism was an account of agency that manifested itself in all spheres of society, not just the economic or political as these might be narrowly conceived. That political behaviour could not be completely reduced to supposed economic motives and interests did not preclude or eliminate the need to link democratic possibilities to overall social dynamics in a society that remained resolutely capitalist. What Macpherson called the economic penetration of political theory still needed to be acknowledged, even if in a non-reductionist way.

We agree. In this chapter we attempt, through an exploration of the work of the Frankfurt School, both first and subsequent generations, to approach the question of a critical theory of democracy on the basis that political economy and critical theory must be rejoined. So that there is no misunderstanding, we want to be clear that the necessary turn to political and democratic concerns by critical theory has generated much of continuing value. As should be apparent from our account to this point, we ourselves have been influenced by these currents and believe them to be fundamentally important for a radical, critical democratic theory and practice. Critical theory has no doubt been enriched by second and subsequent generations of thinkers who in different ways have sought to maintain the currency of the paradigm in the face of changing social and historical conditions and challenges. Yet we think that the shift has frequently come with a cost: the failure to provide an adequate analysis of the pathologies of neoliberalism has meant that critical theory has lost some of its broader cultural resonance for a wider audience that the original architects of critical theory hoped would be drawn to their work.[2]

We continue here to explore the ideas of Jürgen Habermas because he is the thinker whose thought most fully expresses the turn to autonomous political and moral theory, its contributions, but also its limitations. However, to fully grasp the concerns that motivated Habermas, and his approach to critical, democratic theory, we must first examine in some detail the thrust and impact of the first-generation Frankfurt School thinkers and the problems and dilemmas – but also resources – they bequeathed to those who followed. We can then offer an appraisal of Habermas's thought and his legacy, including efforts by theorists such as Axel Honneth to build on this thought while addressing its shortcomings – including the limited place it allows for political economy.

Our account in this chapter is intended to pave the way for the next one, in which we examine various attempts to produce theories of democracy that we believe are at least open to the reconnection of political economy with political theory. These will be developmental and participatory accounts, especially as laid out in the work of C.B. Macpherson, Carol Gould, Carole Pateman, and Axel Honneth. In their respective ways these theorists have attempted to link issues of democratic practice to social critique, political theory to political economy.

What Is Democracy?

The term democracy has had a wide variety of meanings, from minimal and formal to rich and substantive. As noted above, in its broadest sense democracy may be considered a theory of sovereignty in which the power to rule lies ultimately with the people. However, this leaves much room for interpretation and even constriction of the scope of democratic institutions and practices. In the post–Second World War era, theories of elite democracy, or competitive elitism, saw democracy simply as a method of choosing those elites that would rule. Hannah Pitkin called this conception the "authorization" position. As the central feature of representative democracy, representation is "seen as a grant of authority by the voters to the elected officials."[3] We elect leaders and then authorize them to do anything they wish. Such restrictive notions of representative government often prevail in Western and capitalist democracies; the populace at large plays a limited role. Of course, this view is short on democratic accountability. It does not specify how or why the decisions that are authorized have be representative of the public or the public interest.

Often this elitist view was combined with a rational choice perspective. As we have seen, rational choice theorists claim that in authorizing those who are to govern them, citizens are "choosers" who have to decide between two or more alternatives. As we have indicated, many rational choice analysts reject any notion of a common will or of the active formation of common goals through deliberative selection.[4] Politics is seen as fundamentally an aggregation of choices created through a competition for goods – in this case, competition among leaders.

A broader perspective would see democracy as the ability of citizens to influence and "have a direct political impact on the choices and actions of those who govern."[5] This is certainly more comprehensive than the first definition, but it too has several drawbacks. It makes democracy a function of the choices and actions of those who govern, not an expression of popular sovereignty. Questions around agenda setting and initiatives from below are not sufficiently clarified. A fuller notion of democracy might include the ability to initiate action, in concert with others, in a wide variety of spheres of public and private life. Of course, acting in concert also means that in the public sphere, democracy involves more than just the power to initiate – it includes as well a public process of discussion and deliberation in which questions of justice, the good, and legitimacy are central.

In the classical notion of politics, democracy was identical to self-governance. Only those individuals who ruled themselves, albeit in concert with others, were considered free. Citizens were full participants in society and were expected to take positions of authority and to engage in deliberations with other citizens. Of course, the Greek *polis* differed from our society in vital ways. In the first place, the freedom of the citizens rested largely on the labour of unfree individuals and groups (i.e., slaves and women). Second, the Greek *polis* was smaller in size than modern democracies, which are both large and diverse. We cannot always expect to have citizens who share a common world view. Nonetheless, the idea of a democratic politics needs to retain the idea of self-rule through participation to guide its reflections.

Democratic Deficits: The Frankfurt School, Capitalism, and Liberalism

The early Frankfurt School's legacy for political theory is ambiguous. At least in the work of its major figures, Max Horkheimer, Theodor Adorno, and Herbert Marcuse, critical theory often had a "democratic theoretical deficit."[6] Horkheimer's earlier works were more concerned with the psychological, social, and philosophical aspects of critical theory than with politics. There were, however, several intra-theoretical reasons why Horkheimer did not develop a systematic theory of politics. On the one hand, he seemed to employ a model of politics and political economy derived from Marx. Politics, for him, was a form of antagonistic conflict that would disappear when capitalism was superseded. Thus, if politics was little more than a function of class rule, there was little to be found of the Greek notion of politics and participation. What was important was conflict over control of the economy. To be sure, Horkheimer claimed in his earlier works that an emancipatory social theory would have to replace determination by blind social forces with conscious human direction. But he never moved towards what we could call political theory.

Horkheimer assumed that classical capitalism and liberalism were, if not identical, nonetheless intimately linked. Liberalism was the theory of private property. By the early 1930s, critical theory had developed an account of capitalism according to which it had exited its liberal phase and had entered a new, authoritarian one. Herbert Marcuse in his 1934 essay "The Struggle against Liberalism in the Totalitarian View of the State"[7] more fully developed this theme and hence illuminated key assumptions about liberalism inherent in the Frankfurt School's view.

Marcuse defined liberalism purely and simply as the defence of private property. As he saw it, the other features of liberalism could be modified based on the constellation of forces:

> Liberalism was the social and economic theory of European industrial capitalism in the period when the actual economic bearer of capitalism was the "individual capitalist," the private entrepreneur in the literal sense. Despite structural variations in liberalism and its bearers from one country or period to another, a uniform foundation remains: the individual economic subject's free ownership and control of private property and

the politically and legally guaranteed security of these rights. Around this one stable center, all specific economic and social demands of liberalism can be modified – modified to the point of self-abolition.[8]

Classical liberalism, however, had been superseded by a new stage of capitalism – monopoly capitalism – in which the competition of forces was replaced by a concentration of power in large conglomerates and corporations. While the foundation of liberalism in the centrality of private property was maintained, there was the need for a more holistic conception of society, in terms of which acceptance of authority had to be a core element. The rationalist conception of reason with its stress on the critical power of the individual had to be replaced – a move that anticipated to some extent Habermas's later analysis of the decline of the bourgeois public sphere, whereby free discussion was replaced by an authoritative disclosure of the whole. Marcuse, like Horkheimer, did not draw a sharp distinction between societies that were fascist and those that were corporate but democratic. The liberal democratic nature of the capitalist state was absorbed into the totalitarian formulation.

Horkheimer did not in his earlier work take up the question of the form of the state under monopoly capitalism. He did, however, see political forms as dependent on economic ones in the manner of base and superstructure, an antagonistic relation that would disappear when capitalism was transformed.[9] In this light, political institutions had no independent function. Later, when Horkheimer was more concerned with the structural changes made by monopoly capitalism, he loosened this analysis somewhat. In late capitalism the political had come to dominate the economic. By this formulation he meant that the state had taken over socialization processes, such as education, previously carried out by the family or civil society. For Horkheimer this meant, as it did for Marcuse, the decline of the independent individual who could at least to a limited extent assess knowledge on his or her own.[10] Here Horkheimer also employed Pollock's analysis of state capitalism.[11] Pollock thought that because the state was capable of stabilizing capitalism through intervention and regulation or the co-opting of labour, the crisis tendencies of capitalism had been muted. To be sure, he did not strictly equate democratic and totalitarian variants of this process. But in Horkheimer's analysis the distinction between the two became blurred. This was not so much, however, a problem of an apologetic approach to a post-liberal capitalist society as it was the denial of any crisis tendencies in state capitalist formations.

In *Eclipse of Reason* and *Dialectic of Enlightenment*, Horkheimer to a considerable extent replaced his critique of political economy with a critique of instrumental reason. Even here, however, he presented liberal theory as a form of subjective reason, exemplified particularly in Lockean liberalism and, later, in pragmatism and positivism. Reason was no longer a critical reflection on the conditions of human life, but a way of calculating means to pre-given ends. In the process, however, lost were any vestiges of liberalism or even republicanism as elements of a political formation capable of criticizing society. Reason for Horkheimer was self-liquidating.[12] The very processes that had led to increases in social rationality had come to undermine that same rationality.

Franz Neumann and Otto Kirchheimer were somewhat outside the main circle of the Frankfurt School. Their early work was influenced by Carl Schmitt's conception of the political and his critique of liberalism.[13] For Schmitt, recall, parliamentary democracy was ineffectual and impotent. It was rooted in endless and fruitless discussion and deliberation between competing interests and was unable to produce or maintain legitimacy. In his first work, Neumann accepted this criticism of liberal parliamentary government, but he also tried to maintain a socialist theory of the rule of law, which was in his view being impeded by liberal capitalism. Later, he moved in the direction of a social democratic conception of the rule of law that recognized its importance in restraining bureaucratic power.[14]

Both Neumann and Kirchheimer felt that Horkheimer's and Pollock's notion of an administered society underestimated the conflict potentials of state capitalist societies. Whereas Horkheimer claimed that the rise of fascism and totalitarianism was a developmental tendency of capitalism that was not affected by events, Neumann took the view that it was historical and contingent and that it could have been averted if the correct actions had been taken. He struggled, rather unsuccessfully, with the task of developing a notion of political freedom and the rule of law that could accommodate the gains of the welfare state. Both he and Kirchheimer were critical of the nascent neoliberal theories of the time associated with thinkers such as Friedrich von Hayek and Milton Friedman and wanted to defend some version of the welfare state.[15] Neumann's attempt suggests some links between his essentially legal theory and a political theory along the lines of that of C.B. Macpherson. A developmental theory based on the exertion of capacities could provide a basis for the social rights of the welfare state as well as a way of identifying those conflict potentials that had not been completely neutralized under late capitalism. It also could provide an alternative theory of freedom that emphasized the organization of society around the protection of social rights and social and economic freedoms.[16]

The development of an adequate critical theory of democracy has been one of the central aims of Jürgen Habermas's reformulation of critical theory. He has taken a less orthodox approach to politics than did Horkheimer and Marcuse and has been more sensitive to elements of liberal and republican theory than were his predecessors. Habermas has also located crisis potentials in advanced capitalism that Horkheimer and Adorno failed to find. In what follows, we focus primarily on the first aspect, namely, Habermas's attempt to formulate a radical democratic theory and his attempt to combine it with the rule of law.

The Early Habermas and Radical Democracy

As we have argued, Habermas broke ranks with the first generation of the Frankfurt School – at least with Max Horkheimer, Theodor Adorno, and Herbert Marcuse – in his treatment of the emancipatory possibilities of modern politics and liberalism. Whereas the first-generation theorists saw liberalism as closely, if not internally, linked to capitalism and the reification of social life, Habermas argued that liberalism also contained the idea of a public sphere of free discussion that was not linked to possessive individualism but instead represented a realm of discursive will-formation. Possessive individualism was only one possible outcome of the development of liberalism. To be sure, Habermas did not think that the dominant form of liberalism was sufficient. His notion of the public sphere was not intended to be official liberalism by other means; rather, it drew implicitly upon republican notions of communicative or discursive interaction. However, unlike republican theory, which tends to link discussion to the idea of a single nation, to a body politic unified along a shared dimension, Habermas's conception was tied to a cosmopolitan realm of public discussion. In addition, Habermas, at least early in his career, accepted that capitalism and democracy were contradictory. In what remains one of his most powerful works, *The Structural Transformation of the Public Sphere*, he essentially agreed with the early Frankfurt thinkers that late capitalism had created a mass society with monopoly control of media of communications and the consequent manipulation of public opinion.[17]

As Jean Cohen pointed out some time ago, Habermas's subsequent work did not fully develop this insight.[18] Indeed, he did not begin to fully analyse the relation between liberalism and republicanism until he had reformulated his intersubjective perspective in *The Theory of Communicative Action*. But his fullest attempt to work out this relation came in *Between Facts and Norms*. As noted in chapter 1, in that book Habermas lays out a theory of democracy that he believes could bridge the gap between liberalism and republicanism; in this respect his position demonstrates similarities to Macpherson's attempt to fuse liberalism and socialism.

Habermas's earliest work took up questions of democracy in the context of a Frankfurt Institute study of students' political attitudes. While he found that many students had authoritarian attitudes – which is similar to what earlier Frankfurt School studies on authority had found – he also contributed an introduction to the collection about the concept of political participation that provided a theoretical overview of the problems of democracy. Habermas employed the idea of participatory democracy associated with both the Greek *polis* and the radical democratic movements of the bourgeois era. The basis of democracy was popular sovereignty, not the parliamentary forms of capitalist democracy. Both contemporary parliamentary democracy and the welfare state could be seen as attempts to restrict participation by the populace.[19] Here, as Douglas Kellner notes, Habermas employed, in contrast to parliamentary forms, a notion of strong democracy as found in the work of John Dewey and that of later writers such as Benjamin Barber.[20] At the time he wrote his *Habilitation* on the public sphere, Habermas, like Horkheimer and Adorno, saw late capitalism as a closed system that had successfully managed crisis tendencies and muted opposition.

It was in his work on the public sphere that Habermas began to develop a model of radical democracy that went beyond the analysis of the earlier Frankfurt School. Here a radical democracy meant more than simply participation in government. It also involved a separate realm of civil society in which public opinion could be formed. This was a model more adapted to a modern bourgeois society in which, unlike in the Greek world, state and society were separated. The formation of a sphere of public opinion expanded the social elements of democratic theory. Radical democracy also required the democratization of the institutions of civil society.

It is no doubt true that Habermas's formulation of the public sphere has limitations, which he has acknowledged. However, regarding the inclusion of women, minorities, and the working class in the bourgeois public sphere, it retains importance because it identifies structural possibilities for freedom that were not effectively identified by the earlier Frankfurt School. Habermas sees the public sphere as a social realm that resists and is opposed to the imperatives of capitalist rationalization. It represents a counter-sphere of democratic will-formation within capitalist development.

Habermas agrees with the earlier Frankfurt theorists that late capitalism forecloses possibilities for action. However, he does not share their view that critical reason has been completely supplanted by instrumental reason. He worked out this line of thought over the course of a decade, from his essays in *Theory and Practice* to his rehabilitation of crisis theory in *Legitimation Crisis*. In his earlier work he still adopted a conceptual perspective reminiscent of the early Frankfurt School. This position, however, could not always accommodate his insights into modern democracy – insights that have allowed him to maintain a commitment to radical democracy while taking on and exploring the possibilities of the liberal and republican traditions.

In the essays on the classical doctrine of politics and natural law, Habermas develops a distinction between practical and technical reason. While the latter is a kind of instrumental reason that entails the development of efficient means to achieve selected ends, practical reason refers to consciousness, will, and understanding. At this point in his work he sees the distinction as between control and action, or forms of purposive and communicative action. The classical notion of practice derives from Aristotle's conception of practical philosophy and is opposed to technical control. The former is a notion of practical deliberation about questions of the good.[21] For Aristotle practical philosophy was *phronesis*. It did not seek theoretical certainty of the order of things but rather practical knowledge of the right thing to do. By contrast, the tradition that starts with Hobbes sees the problems of politics as capable of objective scientific solutions. The laws of politics could be derived axiomatically from first principles. This system of laws derived by the theorist could be applied by the ruler independently of the consent of the governed. The only consent needed was for the original agreement. For Hobbes man was no longer the social animal of Aristotelian thought. Society was an arrangement for ensuring commodious living and the protection and security of citizens. It was the application of scientific knowledge of the mechanisms of social order – mechanisms that are timeless and permanent.[22]

We can see this construction in elements of Horkheimer's approach to Cartesianism in "Traditional and Critical Theory," although it also closely connected to the critique of instrumental reason that Horkheimer and Adorno formulated in the 1940s. However, Habermas did not see instrumental reason in the totalizing fashion of his predecessors. He thought that instrumental reason had a role in social action. However, when technical claims take the place of processes of democratic deliberation, instrumental rationality oversteps its bounds. In their attempts to replace the normative orientation of the classical notion of politics with a technical conception, Hobbes and his successors essentially bypassed a politics that featured active citizen participation.

Habermas's notion differs in some other important respects from that of his predecessors. First, it provides a source of non-dominating reason and action. Horkheimer's distinction between objective and subjective reason left little room for a notion of praxis. The concept of mimesis, which Adorno and Horkheimer developed in *Dialectic of Enlightenment* as an alternative, is primarily negative: it does not deal with processes of deliberation, discussion, and consent that are central to the formation of political will.[23] Habermas's use of an independent notion of praxis fills that lacuna. There is an independent capacity for forming a political will that can persist even under the conditions of late capitalism. The notion of practice gives some substance to the capacities identified in the public sphere. The second issue is related to the first. The concept of practice also provides the space in which democracy can take root and grow. The idea of an intersubjective formation of political will – that is, popular sovereignty – requires something like the concept of praxis if it is to have any possible grounding.

As some critics have noted, however, Habermas's conception of practice seems to incorporate an unresolved tension. His use of the Aristotelian model of praxis is based on a world in which the modern distinction between state and society is absent. At the same time, the existence of a viable public sphere requires the separation of state and society, as well as the maintenance of those autonomous institutions of public media and discussion that Habermas emphasizes. He therefore needs a concept of practical reason that more adequately fits modern societies than does the Aristotelian notion. In his essay on the classical conception of politics, he argues along with neo-Aristotelians that Aristotle's notion of practice persisted through the nineteenth century until the rise of positivism and a modern "political science" brought about its final defeat. This neo-Aristotelian version of course stressed virtue as its normative basis, not rights and freedoms.

The problem of natural law is, however, capable of a more radical interpretation. Modern natural law has been uncoupled from its ties to a substantive or material basis in the ethical structures of the good life. In the process, it has become formal. Still, it retains some element of normativity as expressing basic rights that all humans inherently possess. In the rationalism of the modern era, these rights were permanent and often given prior to society. As such they were applied, albeit in different ways, to the revolutions of the modern era, both the American and the French. In Habermas's reading the revolutionary character of these rights was less apparent in the American Revolution because they took the form of an essentially Lockean notion of property. As opposed to Hobbes, Locke saw the basis of self-preservation in the property-owning individual and the attainment of goods. In the state of nature this was the fundamental right. To recall our earlier discussion, for Locke property was owned when an individual mixed his labour with the resources provided by nature through gathering or, later, farming or craft production. In the state of nature the individual had the right to enforce natural law; a state only became necessary in a market economy, when production allowed us to store and trade beyond our immediate needs. At that point a state was needed to regulate the market order.

Natural law was seen as a "revolution" of property owners, yet it signified no more than the recognition and reclamation of those rights that were already assumed to exist. Even more than Locke, Thomas Paine thought that while it was essential to establish government, such a government needed to be restrained so that individuals who owned private property could peacefully create a successful social order in a market society. In each of these formulations, the bourgeois character of the American Revolution was clear. It was already based on the common sense, the public opinion, of the bourgeois class. Thus, America was far from an ideal public sphere. The public there was limited to one group and the views it held. It fell short of a notion of popular sovereignty.

A very different understanding of the people and popular sovereignty emerged during the French Revolution. In France, revolution meant the construction of a new society that included those who were not part of the propertied order. Here Rousseau was a better guide than Locke or Hobbes.[24] Rousseau, too, employed the fiction of a state of nature that led to war; however, he saw the resulting society not as peaceful but as inherently conflictual. Market societies were rife with egoism, greed, and inequality. Thus a social contract could not merely trade the rights of nature for civil rights of the state. It needed to create these rights anew within society. A notion of popular sovereignty was embedded in Locke's and especially Paine's version of revolutionary change; but notwithstanding Paine's nod to the poor, this was largely the sovereignty of the property-owning classes. This was not true for Rousseau, for whom the central problem was the inequality of society, which had to be addressed not transferring rights to society but by reconstructing society and state.

To be sure, Habermas believes that Rousseau's version of the general will is inadequate.[25] It is not based on the idea of public opinion formation and discussion, but rather on a common feeling; Habermas calls it "unpublic" opinion. Still, Rousseau's work stands at the inauguration of another conception of rights, a positive conception derived from the new formulation of natural rights as a product of a constitution that forms both state and society.

In revolutionary France, rights were no longer seen as pre-political and as having a purely negative function. The new rights were positive – they were posited by and through the act of constituting the new state and society. These rights included the right to political participation and to equality, not just as a private citizen but also in public life. Individuals also had justified claims to social welfare provisions. As Habermas notes, these rights were by no means developed fully in the revolutionary constitution, which still assumed that they could be protected negatively, but they nonetheless became the basis for the guarantees of the welfare state.[26]

This second dimension of positive rights is not really integrated into the earlier formulations of critical theory. To be sure, notions of free human development arise frequently in the work of Horkheimer and Marcuse. These derive, however, from Marx and are strongly indebted to his early writings, which were rediscovered in the 1930s. But the main theorists of the Frankfurt School all concurred on the central role of a certain line of development. The liberal order with its assumption of a rational individual consciousness was being replaced by the totalizing state of late capitalism. The welfare state did not represent a new source of rights but was part of a system of intensifying control. However, as earlier noted, the emerging developmental interpretation of natural rights came to include rights to participation and equality that had gone unrecognized in classical notions of individual, negative rights. Here the rights guaranteed by natural law went beyond the protection of bourgeois property and extended to those who could oppose it.

This reading has an explicit as well as an implicit relation to the work of C.B. Macpherson. It is explicit in that Habermas draws on Macpherson's reading of Hobbes and Locke. It is implicit insofar as he anticipates Macpherson's later work on developmental democracy. Habermas in his early writings is more pessimistic about the possibilities of democratization, but he does not fully close off these possibilities. He notes that the concepts of rights formulated in the welfare state still maintain the possibilities of participatory democracy even as the welfare state tends to suppress these claims because of its ability to mute crises.

Transforming the Theory of Democracy:
Legitimation Problems and Beyond

Some of the issues raised by the Marxian notion of crisis are given a more sociological – one could say more political-economic – reading in Habermas's account of legitimation crises. This marks a further break from the analyses of the first generation of the Frankfurt School.

Whereas the critical theories of late capitalism held that capitalism had largely succeeded in staving off crises and exerting almost total control over social affairs, Habermas, who wrote in the shadow of the civil rights, antiwar, and student protests of the time, was aware that late capitalism was not as successful in staving off crises as Horkheimer and Adorno had thought. In part this was due to the limits of its inner development as a technical system. Postwar liberals, especially proponents of the American version of the "vital centre," thought that pluralist democracy had put in place the best system of government, which only needed technical refining and correcting to function properly. In short, liberals thought that normative questions had been settled. Thus, as Habermas and others were later to point out, they had little understanding of or sympathy for social movements that raised these normative questions anew. However, standing behind the social and technological assumptions undergirding welfare state democracies were the earlier questions raised in the second version of natural law and developmental democracy, namely, those relating to the demands for greater democratic inclusion and participation linked to the idea of popular sovereignty. No doubt these questions are recast in the welfare state, but they remain available for participants. Rights no longer can have a transcendental basis but must be justified through communicative reason. Protest movements raised questions not only about civil rights but about these positive rights as well. They called into question the ways in which Western democracies understood and justified their own project. Similarly, late capitalist societies were seen to have failed to provide motivations for its citizens not just to participate in society but also to accept the work discipline central to their economies.

In making this argument, we do not mean to leave out the major revisions that Habermas was making to Marxian theory. We simply mean to highlight some of the assumptions that he carried over from his earlier work. *Legitimation Crisis* both elaborates and modifies the earlier formulations in the context of a new approach to a theory of society. To begin with, Habermas increasingly gives an independent status to normative considerations. This independence was already evident in the role he accorded to practical rationality in his earlier work. This role was not, however, anchored in a theory of society. Now, Habermas conceives of different concepts of social action. Normative questions have an independent logic in that they represent dimensions of social interaction that are basic to all societies. Societies are held together not only by the requirements of an economic order but also by forms of mutual understanding. In Habermas's terms this involves communicative action. Such action is oriented to agreement among the participants.

Habermas sees this kind of action as different from purposive rational action, which like social labour and natural science is oriented to success or the achievement of ends. The logic of norms in the social lifeworld is not simply dependent upon the structure of social labour or purposive action. Of course, while independent, these dimensions are closely related. The economy still plays a dominant steering role in his theory of society. Economic problems are still central to the crises of late capitalism. Writing at the end of the Keynesian era, Habermas has been much more aware of its tensions and limits than were the earlier Frankfurt theorists. He sees Keynesian theory as having failed to solve the accumulation crises of late capitalism, which was presumptively in the process of dissolution.

However, it seems to us that Habermas still provides space for a radical democracy that can steer the economy and provide more widespread participation. The tensions in late capitalism keep these possibilities open. Certainly, Habermas sees contradictory forces at play in the competing spheres of accumulation and legitimation. In seeking legitimation, capitalist societies draw on the reservoir of traditional meanings created in pre-capitalistic social orders. Paradoxically, such traditions have been eroded by capitalist rationalization. Like Weber, Habermas sees traditional meaning as being emptied in modernity. However, in his later work, beginning with *The Theory of Communicative Action* and especially in *Between Facts and Norms*, he argues that modern societies themselves have an independent generative power, a communicative power, that creates an intersubjective will and binding force.

We cannot go into a full-blown analysis of Habermas's discussion here. But central to his claim is the idea that the relations of production are depoliticized in late capitalism. In the liberal capitalist era the state guaranteed the conditions of production but was independent of it. However, as the dysfunctional elements and side effects of the capitalist market become apparent the state has come to assume some of these functions. It is called upon to regulate the economy in various ways through active interventions. For Habermas, as for the earlier Frankfurt theorists, the political comes to predominate over the economic. However, political intervention into the economy leads to new conflicts and problems. The performance of the state in directing and intervening in the economy becomes subject to legitimation questions and open to contestation. It creates needs for legitimacy that Horkheimer and Adorno either did not recognize or did not accept.

Here we must shift focus. Habermas extended his notion of practice as developed in his earliest essays in the direction of the theory of communicative action that we discussed earlier. More broadly, the need for legitimation derives from his claim that societies are held together by forms of social integration – consensual forms of mutual understanding that bind subjects. Social interaction in his view is oriented towards standards of truth or normative validity. When these agreements break down, individuals need to renew, repair, or replace their understandings if they are to maintain consensus. Of course, we do not have to rely on a notion of complete agreement here; societies can no doubt maintain their integrity with fair amounts of dissensus. But when an institution like the state no longer acts in a way that is consistent with its core values or principles, it can lose the trust of the populace, which no longer gives its consent. We can become alienated from our solidarities and our identities as citizens; or we can engage in resistance. In advanced capitalism the state takes on the burden not only of managing the economy but of providing for basic welfare needs and social equality. These clearly make the state open to claims that it is failing either to properly manage the economy or to fulfil the normative expectations of participants.

What stands behind these legitimation crises are the norms of equality and participation that are central to the developmental view. At the same time, late capitalism attempts to create *de facto* legitimation through mass loyalty. The latter is more a form of administratively created acceptance of authority through exchange for material goods and services. Central to this dynamic is a kind of civic privatism, in which individuals focus on family, private life, and material goods. Habermas also includes parliamentary democracy as a form generating loyalty. It limits the participation of citizens to periodic voting and restricts the accountability of public officials and administrators. And it often reduces political problems to technical ones.

In adopting a systems framework, which for many critics is problematic, Habermas in some respects moves away from the political-economic perspectives that are central to some of his earlier work. He contends that the changes in late capitalism have significantly altered both the way we understand the social system and the kinds of crises that can occur. The exploitation and domination of the working class has been partly mitigated by the welfare state.

Nonetheless Habermas retains some important elements of Marx's analysis. For our purposes one question is important: Are democracy and capitalism compatible? In the full sense of democracy that Habermas employs, they cannot be. The limits of reform within late capitalism are given by this contradiction. Habermas maintained this position up until *The Theory of Communicative Action*. There he wrote: "Between capitalism and democracy there is an indissoluble tension; in them two opposed principles of social integration compete for primacy."[27] He cited Offe's interpretation of this conflict as the contradiction between the drive to privatize the means of production and the countervailing drive in late capitalism to politicize or socialize them. Habermas saw a series of dilemmas in the fact that politicians must simultaneously appeal to investors and to the masses; public opinion is both an expression of the popular will and the product of the engineering of consent.

Whatever we think of this analysis, it showed the changes in Habermas's conception of the possibilities inherent in late capitalism. Instead of a one-dimensional rationalization, which foreclosed possibilities and eliminated contradictions, while class conflict was muted, there had emerged other zones of conflict and other contradictions.

During the period following *The Theory of Communicative Action* and culminating in *Between Facts and Norms*, Habermas largely developed the paradigm of communicative action in the realms of both ethics and political/legal theory, and with this, indirectly, a theory of democracy. This later work essentially expresses the assumptions and commitments he continues to hold. There is far less discussion of political-economic issues and how these bear on democratic theory. On the one hand, Habermas develops his political theory in the light of a lifeworld-based conception of interaction. Ethics and politics are discursive and deliberative. The constitutional state, he contends, is anchored in "the *higher-level* intersubjectivity of communication processes that unfold in the institutionalized in parliamentary bodies, on the one hand, and the informal networks of the public sphere, on the other. Both within and outside parliamentary bodies geared to decision making, these subjectless modes of communication form arenas in which a more or less rational opinion-and will-formation concerning issues and problems affecting society as a whole can take place."[28] This idea of the communicative basis of will and authority is meant to serve as a counterweight to the systemic imperatives of the economy and administrative rationality that attempt to insulate political decisions from collective will-formation. The nascent political theory evident in this position still points to a notion of democratic popular sovereignty that underlies his critical theory.

Popular Sovereignty Revisited

However, Habermas has returned to the concerns of the public sphere from his earlier work to ground a communicative alternative to both liberalism and republicanism. He argues that the discourse conception of law is meant to suggest a bridge between the rule of law associated with liberalism and popular sovereignty. The parliamentary system of democracy needs to be supplemented by a strong public sphere that surrounds metaphorically the parliamentary and bureaucratic processes. This would provide a normative basis for the participation of all in the political process. Citing Ingeborg Maus, Habermas argues that the communicative theory of law entails the mediation of legal institutions and non-institutionalized popular sovereignty: "Here the social substratum for the realization of the system of rights consist neither in spontaneous market forces nor in the deliberate forces of welfare state but in the currents of communication and public opinion that, emerging from civil society and the public sphere, are converted into communicative power through democratic procedures."[29] Habermas has in mind here a robust and democratically structured public sphere that includes plebiscites, grassroots party organizing, and open political participation, as well as a democratized media. The idea is that the public sphere is the space in which democratizing impulses are generated.

To be sure, as we have argued, there has been a shift from political economy to political and legal theory over the course of the development of Habermas's thought. Nonetheless, with respect to the idea of a democratic public sphere there is still a strong continuity between Habermas's account as it was formulated in his earliest work and the theory he develops in his later writings. This later treatment upholds the ideas of popular sovereignty and political participation, albeit in a new theoretical framework. The theory of communicative action provides a framework for grasping the consensual nature of social action and the deliberative bases of understanding.

However, it is not clear whether Habermas provides the socio-political resources for such a program. We can get at this issue first by asking why the impulses that originate from below in the communicative substructure of society do not enter further into the structure of the state as such. Because Habermas sees the lifeworld as limited by system imperatives of money and power that structure action non-communicatively, economic and state structures are removed from any forms of mutual accountability. It should not be impossible, however, for participants who are reflexively aware of their own situation to act together in order to put the economy and even the bureaucracy under more democratic direction – or even to take certain types of actions regulated by the market out of market regulation, that is, place more elements of the economy under democratic control.

A more radical form of democracy would involve more than the distinction between system integration and social integration, or between the internal perspective of the participant and the external perspective of a social system. This relation is far more fluid than Habermas argues. Consider, for example, the question of higher wages. Businesses argue from a system point of view that higher wages are a brake on accumulation and affect competitiveness. These are objective requirements. But actors form groups to advocate for change in the public sphere. These could be seen on the one hand as system imperatives for mass loyalty, which in a bureaucratic administrative/corporate social formation promotes labour peace and thus long-term profitability. It is also, however, an element of social integration, that is, it represents a norm derived from the expectation of fair treatment on the part of those who work in the marketplace. Having a decent living standard is an expectation held by of a large part of the citizenry of a democratic country. The point here is that ordinary actors engaging their situations from the internal perspective of the lifeworld are capable of reflexively monitoring and incorporating knowledge of system imperatives. They can assess whether and how they can act in relation to these supposedly objective conditions, those that can be modified by collective action, and others that are resistant to change, at least in current historical and social situations.[30] By contrast, the externalist perspective tends to see these system constraints as objective conditions, necessary requirements of the economic and administrative systems in terms of which fundamental change is largely ruled out.[31]

The second question that emerges from a consideration of Habermas's theory of discursive, constitutional democracy, particularly as laid out in *Between Facts and Norms*, is whether and to what extent his proposals could be realized within an essentially capitalist society. In his earlier work, as we have noted, he saw capitalism and democracy as incompatible. Are the proposals for greater equality and participation likely to wreck on the barriers in capitalist societies? Are the barriers high enough to make the kind of robust democratization of public life that Habermas desires beyond reach?

Finally, Habermas bases his theory on a strongly universalist program that is linked to a transnational world and transnational identities. This would seem to entail a socialist or social democratic understanding widespread throughout the larger transnational society that Habermas seeks.

While this ideal is indeed worthy, it needs to be combined with additional, more elaborated analysis of the conditions of the neoliberal constellation. This becomes evident from a closer examination of the key elements of Habermas's theory of democracy, to which we now turn.

Radical Democracy Revisited

Habermas presents his democratic theory as a form of radical democracy. It retains the project of a democratic self-organization in which participants decide on the laws that will govern them. However, this project takes a different shape in contemporary society. It no longer involves the realization of a specific form of life. Rather, it points to an understanding of democracy and socialism as a set of formal qualities that lead to greater emancipation: "If, however, one conceives 'socialism' as the set of necessary conditions for emancipated forms of life about which the participants *themselves* must first reach an understanding, then one will recognize that the democratic self-organization of a legal community constitutes the normative core of this project as well."[32]

Here Habermas retains the idea of popular sovereignty but interprets it procedurally though his notion of communicative rationality. Popular sovereignty is embedded in the communicative power of participants in social interaction. It is constituted by the creation of both understanding and the practical will to act in common. There is a necessary discursive and dialogical element of practical reason that is linked to the central elements of political sovereignty through mutual understanding and mutual accountability. These ideas form the core of what Habermas sees as a post-metaphysical notion of democracy. However, he also acknowledges the limits of this model under the conditions of modern societies. These conditions affect what is in many respects a Hegelian/Marxist understanding of democracy. Democracy and democratic society can no longer be considered, at least potentially, as a totality.

Habermas feels that the utopian energies of the Marxian project centred on the emancipation of labour are exhausted. They were always in any case too concrete. In its classical form Marxism provided a holistic notion that interpreted society as a meta-subject or unity. In his view, Marxism took from Aristotle and Rousseau the idea that society was a settled or concrete form of life rather than a set of necessary conditions for freedom and emancipation about which the participants themselves could decide.[33] Thus he finds the notion of revolution untenable. Rather, Habermas sees communicative freedom and power as the repository of any utopian energies left in society: "Instead of the rationality of productive forces, including natural science and technology, I trust in the productive force of communication."[34]

Habermas's essay on popular sovereignty as procedure revisits the concerns of his earlier work on popular sovereignty and political participation, but now addresses these concerns in the context of his lifeworld/system distinction. At least one of the issues raised by the

French Revolution retains its significance for Habermas: the creation of popular sovereignty through a discursive process of will-formation. The model employed in *Theory and Practice* is continued in one dimension. The notion of radical democracy that combines human rights and popular sovereignty is based upon the idea that both rights and sovereignty are founded within society. We cannot consider basic rights as external to or prior to society.

However, Habermas now rejects several versions of his prior formulation. Specifically, he rejects what he sees as the totalizing elements that characterized traditional ideas of sovereignty. Sovereignty cannot be conceived as a unitary will or the expression of a people. In one sense this is because of the pluralist character of modern societies, which cannot be unified by a pre-existing ethos or will. Habermas is dubious about conceptions of the nation-state that view it as a carrier of a unified will that expresses the spirit of the people.

Nor does he see the idea of revolutionary transformation as necessary in the current constellation. As noted above, the productivist orientation he associates with the French Revolution and the Marxian tradition is exhausted. We can no longer speak of a workers' utopia that will overthrow capitalism in one stroke and bring in a totally emancipated society. To the extent that as with Marxism we could organize a society through rational economic planning and administration, Habermas sees this vision as flawed: economies are crisis-ridden, and administration is often irrational. Instead, he sees human rights and sovereignty as potentially capable of fostering reform, perhaps even radical reform.[35] Thus for Habermas the deliberative processes that could engage members of democratic societies implicitly include ideas – and ideals – of popular sovereignty in terms of which citizens can discuss and deliberate about collective decisions. In other words, Habermas is sceptical about notions of national identity as the basis for a revolutionary consciousness.

These claims are linked to a third idea. Habermas does not think the notion of a self-directed society, whereby society is viewed as a collective totalizing subject able to give itself its own norms, is any longer plausible. Rather, he believes that in modern societies elements of the economy and the state are organized in a functional manner. They have been detached from normative moorings and can act independently for essentially instrumental reasons. For example, administrative rationality is concerned with order and the stability of the system and not with its normative functions. For Habermas, both administration and the market have the tendency in modern society to take over or "colonize" more and more elements of social life that need to be norm-governed.

The marketization of elements of social life, such as education, provides good examples of how the lifeworld is colonized. In the circumstances such forms of consensual action and popular control are no longer effectively able to facilitate social integration. In Hannah Arendt's terms the colonization of the lifeworld and the expansion of, and strengthening of, administrative and economistic values and practices represents the increasing predominance of behaviour – potentially measurable and predictable responses to the unquestioned demands of hierarchical, authoritarian bureaucratic apparatuses – over action – the capacity to intervene in ongoing social processes by means of new initiatives undertaken in a vibrant public realm that embodies and furthers civic freedom.

Habermas's more formal notion of democracy sees it as placing a limit on the power of economic and bureaucratic imperatives. In contrast to his position in *The Theory of Communicative Action*, in which these system imperatives seem to have greater independence, here he believes that these imperatives should be subordinated to democratic considerations. The aim of radical democracy is to place the economy and bureaucracy under popular control. However, subordinating and controlling the economic and administrative apparatus does not mean transforming society into a unitary entity in which the differentiation of separate spheres would be overcome. Habermas thinks this differentiation means that economic and administrative spheres cannot be structured by forms of mutual understanding. They can only be regulated; they cannot be reintegrated into a social whole. But even if we were to accept Habermas's conception of modernity, it is not clear exactly what form this democratic control of the economy would take.

This issue highlights a key element of Habermas's democratic theory, namely, its incorporation of a strong rights discourse and his adoption of a legal parliamentary model of political will-formation. This has led some to think that Habermas has regressed to a form of liberalism that defends the status quo. But such a view is misleading. If liberalism represents a theory that sees rights as prior to society and as based in self-interest, the task of government in those circumstances is to protect the individual's interests and property from intrusion. Habermas rejects this version of liberalism to the extent that a liberal political theory sees politics as the aggregation of individual interests and the protection of these interests. Habermas's position is more clearly sympathetic to republicanism and its emphasis on popular sovereignty. Republican theory stresses the virtuous citizen who engages in public participation to determine the common good. In the republican view, law does not simply protect the individual, it also expresses the ethos of the community. Habermas is uncomfortable, however, with the notion of a common ethos or political community. His communicative theory attempts to combine the best elements of both theories. His synthesis is not a return to liberalism but rather an attempt to link the notion of rights to popular sovereignty. We will return to this issue later in this chapter. At this point we wish to focus more explicitly on Habermas's specific understanding of rights.

In one sense Habermas's conception of rights is a new elaboration of his concerns with the dual foundations of democracy as he laid these out in his early essays, although his position on rights is not identical to his earlier perspective. For democracy, including radical democracy, must be built on a foundation of human rights *and* popular sovereignty, in which members of a society take on a form of self-organization. These human rights represent the basic conditions for the institutionalization of discourses in democratic societies. We might extend this argument and say they represent the basic conditions for communicative freedom. In this view, then, rights are not claims that derive from a natural law or moral law prior to society. Rather, they are both internal to society and state basic conditions that transcend partiality and apply to all. Here popular sovereignty and rights are complementary in character and not in conflict. If one accepts democratic rule as a discursive process in which individuals acting in concert decide on and implement rules, policies, and practices through deliberation (what Habermas calls the discourse principle), this requires an institutionalization of basic rights that protect the conditions of communicative freedom of individuals. Only if they are legally free to participate as equals can they discursively determine their shared conditions of political life. These rights associated with communicative freedom and action cannot be just moral rights, as some might argue. They need to be legally enforceable if they are to serve as bulwarks against unjustified coercion and domination.

As we saw with Habermas's earlier reflections on the genesis of modern political theories, the relation between rights and popular sovereignty is not fully clear. This disjunction is more straightforward in a thinker such as Thomas Hobbes, who detaches sovereignty from rule. But of course, the Hobbesian solution is unavailable to Habermas.

Habermas then thinks he can avoid some of the problems of earlier theories. Against Marxism and to some extent the earlier Frankfurt theorists, he believes that rights are not just a creation of capitalism and bourgeois society, expressions of an atomistic individualism. Rather, they are rules and laws that enable social action. He does not envision a society in which all antagonisms are eliminated and all politics is abolished. A legal constitutional framework is needed to regulate these antagonisms and conflicts.

Thus, as we have seen, Habermas rejects the idea of a nation or community as unified by a single ethos or sense of moral uniformity. He does this for two distinct reasons. On the one hand he thinks that notions of the good are local, not universal. Conceptions of the moral good cannot by themselves be sufficient to found basic rights or legal order. Since modern societies are inherently pluralistic, we cannot have a purely ethical/moral reading of human rights independent of legality. Otherwise a single understanding of the good would be imposed on others, without discursive redemption. On the other hand, the impulses of human rights are certainly moral. We view infringements of human rights as violations of our moral sense. Nonetheless these moral impulses are insufficient for a constitutional state unless they have a legal foundation.[36]

The second limit on the idea of a unified moral community involves a theme we discussed earlier: the idea that modern societies are based on the imperatives of money and power, that is, the market and bureaucracy. Modern societies are too large, complex, and pluralistic to be run on the model of direct democracy. However, Habermas argues that despite these features a theory of democracy based in popular sovereignty still has force. Such a theory, however, must accept the reality of a market society and administrative state as well as the conditions of plurality. This sets a difficult task: how is a socialist conception of popular sovereignty to be reconciled to a constitutional state with a market economy?

Rights and the Claims of Welfare: Reconsidering Social and Economic Rights

Another element of Habermas's theory of democracy that is clarified in his work is a conception of the legal status of welfare state norms. A tradition of thought that moves from Weber through the early Frankfurt School, and that undergirds the distinction between formal and material law, has been used to criticize welfare state measures. Legitimate law according to Weber is formal, that is, general. Weber criticized laws that treated different groups or classes unequally, as welfare measures have done. Among the Frankfurt School theorists, Franz Neumann adopted this perspective. The deformalization of law was in this view anti-democratic and a precursor to fascism. Neumann carried this line of thought and influenced Habermas in his earliest work.[37] However, Habermas's conception of formal law is not only abstractly formal but also tied to a discursive procedure of justification. Law is based on communicative power, and it is that, rather than its formal quality, which gives it legitimacy. One could enact welfare state measures that deal with specific groups if they passed the test of reasonable acceptance by all parties.

Habermas believes that rights and popular sovereignty are linked through the discourse principle, and in a similar fashion he thinks that public and private rights are co-originary. Private rights are necessary to protect the autonomy of the individual from interference so that she has the private freedom to say "no" to prevalent social norms and take her own path. This is the source of a context-transcending power that can make possible new forms of mutual understanding. At the same time, rights protect the equal opportunity of all to participate in discourses as free and equal citizens. An individual who lacks the private freedom to say no also lacks the ability to be an independent individual and form his own plans. Moreover, individuals are participants in a larger world. Their private freedom is based on public freedom.

In casting rights in this fashion, Habermas intends to resolve the dilemma found in Kant and Rousseau. Kant saw basic rights as the foundation of a legal political order, but he conceived these as *natural* rights and hence prior to society. Thus he recognized and highlighted the central place of individual autonomy and self-determination but was unable to account for the idea of popular sovereignty that he drew from Rousseau. By contrast, Rousseau saw rights as emerging from processes internal to society, but he also came to view sovereignty only as the creation of a unified order – a conception that was insufficiently attuned to autonomy and plurality. It is Habermas's claim that his account can do proper justice to both individual autonomy and popular sovereignty.

Habermas develops an alternative to direct democracy in his idea of a two-stage process of democratic deliberation, a process that is meant to preserve in large measure popular sovereignty. He sees the necessity of an open and wide-ranging public sphere in which there is unrestricted discussion and debate of issues. In this public space, new issues are raised, new structures of relevance are created, and new agendas are debated. The public sphere, recall, is intended to incorporate an institutionally unbound process in which "wild" communicative reason is to prevail. This is still, however, seen as a deliberative or quasi-deliberative process in which the force of good reasons prevails. Habermas sees his proposal as the communicative theoretical translation of the idea of popular sovereignty.[38]

Following once again the ideas of Ingeborg Maus, Habermas views the democratic genesis of law as indeed resting with the ultimate authority of the people to formulate the problems and the direction of society – but only if, and insofar as, popular self-determination is understood not as a single will that can be ascertained, but rather as a web of communicative and action structures that can permit citizens to unite on specific themes, goals, or norms. To be truly feasible, however, this proposal would also require a large-scale democratization of all elements of society – a true social democracy. Habermas does intend his account to represent a "bottom-up" approach to democracy. His approach is broadly pluralistic but is not intended to be simply another variant of interest group liberalism. He sees competing groups not as the centre of a politics oriented strictly towards the contentious quest for power but as a series of decentred processes for forming and discussing of problems, processes that are aimed at reaching agreement on the salience of these issues.

The second stage in this account requires a more formal democratic element involving legislatures and government agencies, formal elections and even courts. Habermas, like many others, recognizes that in societies the size and scope of our own, a direct democracy is impossible and only some form of representative democracy is feasible. He sees these institutions as keyed to a deliberative assessment of proposals and issues formulated from below. Legislators and others are supposed to make such assessments through impartial deliberation about the fairness of legislative proposals; or, in the case of courts, they are supposed to offer reasonable appraisals of the results of legislative enactments.

Habermas thus offers a challenging and thoughtful solution to the problems of popular sovereignty in complex societies. Several questions are yet to be answered, however. There is the matter of formal institutions serving as a translation process that could under certain interpretations become elitist despite the nod to popular sovereignty. The problems and concerns raised in the public sphere cannot simply be handed off to the legislature and left for it to decide. Habermas's conception of the role of the legislature tends to support the idea that law-making processes are more rational than everyday discussions. This would seem to violate the reciprocal interaction of everyday and expert discourses that Habermas has formulated elsewhere. The transmission process cannot just be one-way. There need to be ways for citizens to criticize these deliberations and participate in them, even if only virtually; and for this to be effective, there need to be strong democratic media through which citizens can be informed about legislative deliberations, and they must have the means to effectively criticize those deliberations.[39]

Even if we were to accept Habermas's proposal at face value, a second problem arises for its employment as a critical theory of law and justice. Real deliberative processes, especially as conducted in legislatures, hardly qualify as ideal exercises in deliberation. In many respects, legislative deliberation – if indeed it could be called that – is less rational than discourses of the sort one finds in the public sphere. Indeed, where they have been captured by corporate economic interests, as has happened in the United States, state and national legislatures have worked to *restrict* popular input and have thus become reactionary instruments of conservative revolution, not expressions of popular sovereignty.

On these grounds, and understandably so, progressive and radical scholars and thinkers have criticized Habermas's discourse theory of democracy. However, we want to be a little more precise than some critics have been in specifying the nature of our own criticisms. As we noted earlier, many have viewed *Between Facts and Norms* as a surrender of radical principles, especially Marxism, and as an embrace of conventional liberalism. We think this view is mistaken. While Habermas as we noted above clearly rejects the model of revolutionary transformation of society that Marxists have traditionally defended, he nonetheless thinks that radical reform can bring about the realization of the ideals Marx desired, even if in a changed form. Habermas believes, however, in the power of the constitutional state to serve as a vehicle for this radical reform. As Matthew Specter has observed, Habermas's mature work can hardly be characterized as a document of political resignation. In *Between Facts and Norms*, constitutionalism is imagined as capacious enough to absorb the full force and breadth of "the revolutionary project of the French Revolution."[40] Habermas contends that the constitutional state preserves the ideals of the French Revolution, and of Marx, with regard to freedom, equality, and solidarity. He argues for a notion of constitutional patriotism that is based not on simple loyalty to country but on loyalty to the idea of the realization of the democratic project.

Thus for Habermas the constitution, very much like modernity itself, represents an unfinished project based in a fallible learning process. Certainly, there is some evidence in favour of the idea of radical reform within a constitutional order. In the United States, for example, some have seen three waves of progressive reform in the twentieth century: the Progressive era, the New Deal, and the Kennedy–Johnson Great Society. These periods of reform involved expansion of the democratic franchise and the generation and extension of social rights and freedoms. Yet even these are ambiguous: the Progressive era often looked to an expert culture to reform society, and the New Deal's establishment of the foundations of the welfare state was largely the creation of an inner circle of bureaucrats. Still and all, the initiatives associated with these two periods in American history *did* represent significant and progressive changes within a constitutional democracy.

These considerations do not invalidate Habermas's achievements in formulating a discourse theory of law and democracy. They do, however, point to its shortcomings as a critical theory. The latter, to recall, is also concerned with the ways in which these popular democratic developments nonetheless proved inadequate to the challenges of a social world still very much in the thrall of domination, unfreedom, and irrationality. In short, Habermas's account, like other theoretical initiatives shaped by its contours and concerns, lacks a thoroughgoing discussion of the pathologies of neoliberal society and its profound threats to the ideals that Habermas holds and defends.

Perhaps this is too much to ask of a work the scope and breadth of *Between Facts and Norms*. Nonetheless the book was published in Germany in 1992, at a time when the spread of neoliberal ideas and practices was already becoming apparent. In the intervening quarter century, Habermas has not really developed or presented a complementary analysis of the pathologies of neoliberalism. In some respects, his recent remarks on Brexit and the rise of Donald Trump in the United States, and on the emergence of right-wing populism more generally, show too much faith in the power of existing liberal democracies to deal with the serious problems of neoliberalism. At least up to now, his focus on the need for transnational institutions of justice has failed to recognize the force of the reaction against existing institutions and practices, and the crises created by neoliberalism. The question is whether the kind of full-scale democratization of society envisioned by Habermas could come about within a capitalist social formation. How far can radical reforms be carried out under capitalism? Is there some point at which a clear shift towards a socialist society becomes necessary? It may be true, for example, that the ideals of freedom and equality are the liberal core of the socialist ideal, but what conditions are conducive to the realization of those ideals?

The Problem of Administrative Rationality

A major issue raised in debates over the radical potential of *Between Fact and Norm* is the relation between public spheres and administrative systems. Some critics think that, despite his commitment to radical democracy, Habermas assigns too great a role to administrative rationality and not enough to democracy. He does not, it is argued, allow sufficient scope for popular control of administrative decisions. He holds that administrative decisions often require a level of technical expertise that ordinary citizens do not have – for example, in areas of medicine or science, or economics. For that reason, expert professionals in such areas must be granted a certain scope and autonomy. However, this does not mean that administrative decisions are completely insulated from public opinion or debate. Ordinary citizens as well as legislatures and other formal deliberative bodies must have normative and even legal control over the direction of policy. The average citizen is not going to be able to carry out tests to decide on the safety of a new drug or medical device, but they could – as the case of HIV/AIDS research shows – exert pressure to bring new drugs to ill individuals more quickly. Individual citizens may not have the technical expertise to assess research on climate change, for example, but once aware of its effects, the public has a crucial role to play in the direction of policy.

Habermas argues that with the exception of specialized functions, technical problems are not independent of the public sphere. Members of the public are sufficiently cognizant of their own their health and of the environment that they might play a role in guiding decisions. In matters like these, problems arise less with expert opinion and more with a public sphere that may come to be dominated by corporate interests that are able to apply their own money and influence to shape and restrict public discussion.

To differentiate among organized bodies of opinion formation and exchange, Habermas writes of strong and weak publics. Although the term is somewhat misleading, Habermas defines weak publics as informal public spheres such as private associations and the mass media as well as, it seems, sites where citizens in their everyday lives come together to discuss ideas. As the first stage or, as it were, "ground floor" of discussion, these weak publics are most sensitive to emerging issues and problems in society. They have the burden of creating and renewing the normative frameworks within which problems are defined outside of and prior to their treatment in a bureaucratic/administrative legislative context. By contrast, strong publics are formal bodies such as parliaments, legislatures, executives, and courts. These institutions possess the ultimate decision-making power in society and are also responsible for applying formal standards.

If Habermas were to give extensive authority to bureaucratic and administrative rationality, it would not be consistent with some of his earlier positions. In addition to defending the public sphere, he inveighed against the dominance of politics and society by technological reason, which is exercised independently of the reflective capacity of subjects. Most important for our purposes is Habermas's view on the reciprocity of participants and observers in social inquiry, an issue we discussed earlier. We have argued that this formulation leads to a dialogue between participants and observers. But in these reciprocal processes, participants and experts are capable of mutual critique. Claims of expertise are never justified in advance and can in fact be criticized. And as we have become aware, the social function of expertise can be challenged. Medicine provides a good example of this. In recent years, the model of the doctor or medical professional as the ultimate authority in all decisions has been ceded to the patient or the family. Often, the model of the patient as simply a physical body to be diagnosed and treated by the doctor has given way to alternatives that allow more scope for the human factor.

Similarly, the role of expertise in administration and bureaucracy, as well as the scope of parliamentary authority, must be carefully limited. The idea that parliaments are filters that can judge laws and policies in ways that take greater account of fairness and equality seems to represent a rather idealized picture. In the current climate, legislative decision-making often does not always create greater fairness or equal treatment; indeed, it very often produces the opposite. Habermas assumes a set of conditions that, while desirable, require more specification. We must ask what kinds of arrangements and cultural conditions are required to achieve the types of deliberation Habermas defends as essential for democracy in the present day.

However, even under these conditions there needs to be a more reciprocal relation between weak publics and strong ones. Ordinary citizens have the capacity to pass judgment on legislative deliberations and to criticize them while they are happening. They have the reflective capacities to make judgments about such policies and legislative processes. They need to have a vital role in shaping these deliberations in a reciprocal way. It is not outside the scope of ordinary understanding to make sense of major legislative initiatives. And it is the responsibility of the media and government leaders to make information available to the public and ensure it is widely disseminated.

Habermas's idea of weak publics would seem to require a widespread democratization of all aspects of society. Citizens who have extensive experience with participating in deliberation at all levels of society are more likely to have developed their reflective capacities where there have been efforts to democratize the family, educational institutions, and workplaces, just to name a few.

Habermas does not treat property extensively in *Between Facts and Norms*. He does speak of collective goods, though not in a way that helps clarify his views. We can infer, however, from his conception of basic rights that he does conceive of a notion of rights that would limit private property. This can be seen in his commitment to the protection of civil rights, but also and especially in his defence of the right of all to participate as equals in meaningful processes of democratic will-formation, which, as Habermas indicates, requires social rights in the form of social and economic security. These latter rights are what C.B. Macpherson and others might call developmental rights. They would secure those conditions that allow individuals to realize their purposes and form their identities. Habermas also recognizes self-development and self-realization as central to the development and protection of social rights and thus democratic deliberation. Conceptions of both can be and have been used to critically assess social and economic conditions, such as inequality and exploitation.[41]

If rights have a developmental component then the line between negative and positive, civil and developmental, rights is not hard and fast. Just as Habermas sees the co-priority of public and private rights, questions of self-determination and self-realization are connected. Being truly free to make one's own choices means that one has the resources and capacities to make those choices and to form one's own identity. These in turn no doubt require at least some minimal notions of a decent life. Gross levels of inequality, of political and social domination or oppression, of cultural invasion and colonization seem incompatible with Habermas's conception of rights. Habermas does not think that the welfare state satisfies these considerations, nor does the state socialist version of the legal state. But neither does he advocate a return to a free market.

Between Liberalism and Republicanism: Deliberative Democracy in a Wider Perspective

If our analysis to this point is correct, it is in the context of both the aspirations Habermas holds for his account and the challenges posed by the neoliberal constellation that his appraisal of alternative forms of democracy must be understood. For Habermas, liberalism and republicanism represent two models of democracy, neither of which is sufficient by itself.[42] Liberalism starts from the model of a market-like competition of interests for the control of state power. On this model, political power is seen primarily as administrative or strategic power, which is then employed to achieve politically chosen goals. Subjects are viewed as independent bearers of rights protected by the state. This is the classic understanding of negative freedom or liberty. Political choices are essentially an aggregation of individual private choices. These in turn shape the use and direction of political power.

By contrast, republicanism develops a theory of popular sovereignty. Politics and ethics are fused. Politics is not an aggregation of private interests; rather, it takes form around a collective ethos that possesses a quasi-objective character. Citizens of good character are formed through political participation, and in this respect republicanism bears affinities to the developmental liberalism of thinkers such as John Stuart Mill.

The form of ethical life specific to each community creates elements of political solidarity. Through sharing this ethos, individuals become aware of one another as citizens, as free and equal co-participants in the shared life of a common world. Citizens are primarily public persons whose rights of communication and participation are prior to private rights. Politics is not primarily administrative or strategic, but a way of acting in concert whereby the deliberations of citizens determine the aims of politics.

While liberalism largely lacks any sense of the solidarity that republican political thought emphasizes, and hence has a limited notion of the social world, republican conceptions fail to recognize the independence of rights claims from a specific ethos and tend to underestimate the role of administrative power. Liberalism employs an exclusive notion of private interests; republicanism holds an exclusive notion of public freedom. For Habermas, like Macpherson, an adequate theory of democracy must recognize the co-priority of private and public freedom.

Habermas's conception of deliberative, or discursive, democracy is meant to provide the basis for such a theory. Deliberation is here conceived as a structural property of human interaction and justice is seen in the first instance as procedural. Deliberation and its possibilities emerge from the basic structure of mutual understanding prior to any specific human rights or concrete sense of community. Our basic capacities for deliberation and action are derived not from a particular content but rather from our ability to deliberate together to reach understanding and to act in concert.[43] Thus basic rights to equality, freedom, and communication are drawn from the core conditions of mutual recognition and not from isolated individuals.

Because Habermas formulated the intersubjective bases of communicative rationality and its notion of mutual recognition, he could employ this analysis to show the relation between public and private freedom that liberals and republicans had failed to achieve. He argues that this "reciprocal relation is expressed by the idea that legal persons can be autonomous only insofar as they can understand themselves as authors of just those rights which they are supposed to obey as addressees."[44]

For Habermas, human rights are required to ground the universal public right of reason. They need to be institutionalized if public reason is to be free and accessible to all. At the same time, the public use of reason, and republican freedoms, require the assumption that there are independent individuals who are free to accept, reject, or modify these rights. They have a context-breaking and not just a context-dependent quality.

And this capacity can only develop intersubjectively and dialogically, in relation to others. Thus Habermas's specific procedural conception of democratic will-formation distinguishes his position from that of, for example, John Rawls or Immanuel Kant. In contrast to the original position of Rawls's or Kant's transcendental subject whereby individuals are fundamentally unconnected to one another, Habermas's intersubjective starting point interprets human rights and discourse as requiring a higher level of solidarity – a solidarity with others.

This understanding of solidarity indicates that while it is generally seen as Kantian, even by himself, Habermas's account nonetheless has a significant if latent Hegelian quality – a point we emphasized in chapter 1. To remind, *Between Facts and Norms* has an architectonic structure reminiscent of Hegel's *Philosophy of Right*. In place of Hegel's account of abstract right, morality, and ethical life, Habermas presents the system of rights, the constitutional state, and procedural (deliberative) democracy as a system of public opinion and will-formation. Instead of absolute spirit by which a substantial ethical life is realized as objective spirit, there is communicative reason (the discourse principle) by which an inner connection between the system of rights and the constitutional state, the rule of law and popular sovereignty, is secured. And a similar basis for the critique of the *Philosophy of Right* of the kind offered by Marx can be established for *Between Fact and Norms*: just as Marx argued that in reality the state as a concrete ethical community was subordinated to civil society and its class-based antagonisms, so it could be argued that communicative rationality is subordinated to instrumental rationality via the spread of relations that convert moral/practical into technical questions (to use Habermas's earlier formulations), which are posed in such a way that their inescapable moral/practical dimension is occluded.

Habermas intends his ideas to represent a critical diagnosis of the present in a post–Frankfurt School, post-Marxist, post-socialist context. Specifically at issue is the nature of a viable democracy that retains a connection with the normative/egalitarian impulses of classical democratic theory and classical socialist doctrine, while acknowledging the realities of societal complexity and a pluralism that generates multiple concrete life plans and motives.

At one level, this account targets various self-declared realist theories of democracy that dismiss the possibility of any substantive conception of popular will-formation. Such theories are rooted in the recognition of the evident asymmetries of power in society, on the one hand, and the existence of social complexity, which makes discursive will-formation and normative direction by self-conscious, acting individuals unrealistic, on the other. Habermas wants to challenge such "realism" while acknowledging the significance of issues it raises. (We more fully examine realist theories of democracy in the next chapter.)

Thus, at another level, Habermas is attempting to distinguish his view from "classical" Marxist and social democratic conceptions of the state, as well as from the neoliberal revival of classical liberal accounts of the relation of the state to (free market) society, a revival that shares ground with the realist position. The cornerstone of his argument here is his account of the legal paradigms he identifies with alternative conceptions of democracy: formal liberal, material welfare state, proceduralist. This argument too exhibits a Hegelian structure: the relation Hegel drew between abstract right, morality, and ethical life is here recast in terms of the relations among these three paradigms, with the proceduralist paradigm performing the role of ethical life. It does so because it embodies the claims of communicative freedom in the same way that ethical life embodied those of objective spirit. Of course, communicative freedom is not the equivalent of objective spirit, nor can it be. Spirit takes on its distinctive characteristics only within the framework of a philosophy of consciousness whereby as a totalizing power it "makes" society. No longer tenable, the philosophy of consciousness needs to give way to an account of intersubjectivity *qua* communication and communicative rationality: the procedural legal paradigm is the "spirit" of a plural universe in which the mutual recognition of subjects guaranteed by Hegel only at the level of the fully realized universal reason of ethical life now takes the form of legal guarantees of private and public autonomy as a system of rights among equal legal consociates who must order their relations under the framework of this-worldly positive law. The "spirit" of proceduralist law informs and rationalizes the institutions of political opinion and will-formation in light of the securing of a functional separation of powers "which, at a different level of abstraction, governs the availability of various sorts of reasons and how these are dealt with.

This logic requires the institutionalization of various discourses and corresponding forms of communication that, *regardless in which local context*, open up possibilities of access to the corresponding sorts of reasons."[45]

Hence "the social substratum for the realization of the system of rights consists neither in spontaneous market forces [i.e., formal liberal law *qua* abstract right] nor in the deliberative measures of the welfare state [i.e., material welfare state law *qua* morality] but in the currents of communication and public opinion, emerging from civil society and the public sphere, that are converted into communicative power through democratic procedures [i.e., proceduralist law *qua* ethical life, here understood as establishing the identity of the modern democratic constitutional state in terms of which there is a necessary inner connection between private and public autonomy, justice and popular sovereignty]."[46]

Habermas's conception of the interpenetration of private and public freedom provides a starting point for a critical theory of democracy, one that, as noted in chapter 1, has considerable similarities to the developmental democratic theory of C.B. Macpherson. This relation again entails going beyond the Kantian notion of critique as the illustration of the limits of knowledge to a conception that links concrete forms of life that are historical and social in nature to the pathologies of late-modern forms of capitalist globalization – that is, towards the key concerns of Frankfurt School critical theory. As Macpherson and others have pointed out – and, to a considerable extent, as Habermas accepts – the liberal idea of basic rights is both atomistic and easily transformed into possessive individualism. It fails to account for the impediments to public freedom generated by an exclusive reliance on the market model. This model significantly restricts the public realization of freedom because it generates deep inequalities of power and money. Unequal power leads to unequal public freedom – a key insight that informed Macpherson's conception of the net transfer of powers. The achievement of equal private rights requires equal public freedoms and social rights. Habermas argues, however, that public freedom requires not just the interventions of the social welfare state, which can in isolation lead to welfare paternalism, but also appropriate and supportive cultural conditions. Such conditions must incorporate a radical egalitarianism. While Habermas has not fully developed this idea, particularly in his more recent work on human rights, it points to the need for an extensive network of public and private spaces that could in turn enable a much more robust participatory democratic politics.

Radical Democracy and Democratic Autonomy

Habermas's theory, in other words, points in the direction of a radical democracy that requires a wide variety of well-developed public spheres within civil society that can sustain a democratic autonomy. So understood, autonomy is a complex process that interweaves self-interpretation, self-development, and self-determination with a robust freedom of communication in an intersubjective context. A network of public spheres would provide more than simply a means of organizing private interests to influence state power. Such spheres would also facilitate active participation whereby citizens could form themselves through their involvements in the world. According to Habermas, this would be possible only in a radically egalitarian society.

Habermas's conception of a radical egalitarian society could thus suggest important elements of a critical theory of democracy. Unfortunately, as noted at the beginning of this chapter, in his more recent writings on global cosmopolitanism, neoliberal globalization, and the contemporary crisis of the European Union, he does not adequately develop these elements in his own work.[47] But a more developed version of Habermas's insights could provide a powerful critique of the barriers that limit the emergence of egalitarian global justice. The unregulated expansion of global capital has led to increased exploitation and the passing on of social risks to subaltern and even middle classes. Capitalist globalization increases the vulnerability of life plans and forms of life. It generates ever more massive inequalities and a greater concentration of wealth and power. While undermining some of the achievements of the social democratic welfare state, it creates new forms of socio-cultural colonization that restrict the cultural freedom and integrity of exploited groups.

This is another way of making the point we highlighted in the introduction to this chapter: that critical theory needs to re-engage with critical political economy if it is to be faithful to its own insights. The strengths, possibilities, and limitations of Habermas's position highlight this need.

Nonetheless, Habermas's attempt to reformulate the grounds of moral and political theory in response to the challenges of neoliberalism, neoconservatism, and postmodernism raises important themes. These include of course his substantive theoretical principles and commitments. But there are also methodological issues important for our own analysis in that they suggest a basis for a plausible radical and developmental theory of democracy, one that would meet the criticisms usually levelled against developmental theories in general. We would identify these issues with an intersubjective perspective that draws on Habermas, while hopefully going beyond the limitations of his position. The core of our perspective in this respect includes the following claims:

- Neoliberal and rational choice theories revive a form of methodological individualism based on an economic conception of rationality. The individual is seen as a strategic actor who aims to maximize happiness, wealth, or some other utility. Here, social order is achieved through the coordination of choices in the market. The problem of individual consent is reduced to the aggregation of such choices to create a social equilibrium.
- Republican or communitarian accounts see social order as an ethos or tradition that exists prior to individual preferences or freedom – that is, it has a quasi-objective quality. While many communitarian thinkers share a republican outlook compatible with developmental theories, they employ strong notions of context that limit the scope of community.
- Ironically, many post-structuralist theories recapitulate certain elements of communitarian thinking. Post-structuralist theorists posit social order as a unitary structure that discloses prior to the individual conceptions of truth, reality, and selfhood by means of which these individuals find themselves defined. Power-interpretative theories argue that order is not a function of reason or tradition; rather, it is established through a will to power. Because of its capacity to define situations, interpretation is a mechanism for dominating others. By contrast, other interpretative theorists hold that social forms are a given, or represent a dispensation, but are never completely produced by anonymous force. None of these theories captures the dialectic between individuals who take on rules and the social order into which they are born.

This somewhat circuitous route into questions of social order is necessary to illustrate the context in which we can rethink developmental theories. As self-interpreters who take up, renew, and sometimes transform the world, we come to be accountable for the ideas we accept as valid. Here self-determination means that we can choose among alternatives and formulate our own purposes, and beyond this, construct through these purposes a core of our own identity, our sense of place in the world, and our projects within it. In this context, self-understanding refers not just to an individual who externalizes and realizes an inherent *telos* or goal but also to social processes through which we form a sense of the world. Thus, developmental theories need not posit fixed individual ends or a fixed human nature. Rather, in a way that recalls Jean-Paul Sartre, it is a matter of making oneself, and in the course of doing so renewing humanity. This should be at the core of a contemporary critical theory of democracy that is both radical and developmental.

Chapter Six

Towards a Critical Theory of Democracy: Participatory Democracy and Social Freedom

In this chapter we consider participatory democracy as a model of democracy that is most compatible with the main themes and concerns of a critical theory of society and an account of radical democracy that could emerge from it. Indeed, the link between participatory democracy and critical theory would seem obvious. Critical theory aims to identify the barriers within existing social structures to the realization of freedom and reason, where this realization would involve those norms, practices, and institutions that facilitate the achievement of both individual self-determination and social solidarity – what Jürgen Habermas calls the inner connection between private and public autonomy, and what Axel Honneth understands as social freedom. At the heart of a theory of participatory democracy is the idea that democracy should not be limited to current electoral and representative forms; rather, it must be broadened to incorporate a more direct, active, and extensive engagement by citizens as they collectively determine their social relations. This in turn requires that the range of issues and the forums within which those issues emerge be expanded so that any and all – or at least all possible – areas of social life within which power is exercised and where prospects for the fullest use and expression of human capacities are at stake are subjected, at least in principle, to collective will-formation.

So understood, participatory democracy occupies common ground with deliberative democracy; indeed, some theorists now consider the two equivalent.[1] However, it is important to specify which approach to deliberation is most compatible with the commitments of a critical and radical participatory theory. As we have already indicated, notions of deliberative democracy run the gamut from weak versions to strong ones. Weak versions cast deliberation as a decision-making procedure to be employed primarily, if not exclusively, in formal political settings. So conceived, a deliberative procedure is designed to ensure free and equal access to sites of deliberation, where political decisions would ideally result from the fullest and freest exchange of good reasons on the part of participants. Where deliberative democracy is understood in this way, it differs significantly from participatory approaches. Participatory theorists tend to be concerned not just with democratic decisions but also with the ongoing arrangements that facilitate democratic social and political values and practices. In other words, they see the role of participation in democratic institutions not simply as a way of making decisions, but as a way of life.

A participatory democracy, then, looks to democratic organization as a mode of development, a vehicle for becoming who we are. Taken in a narrow sense, deliberative democracy need not imply anything specific about participation in sectors of society beyond the political arena, and it says little about the self-constitution of subjects or the development of individuals.

The situation appears different, however, when we take a stronger and broader notion of deliberation. A strong version of deliberative democracy is closely linked to a theme we have discussed and emphasized in previous chapters: mutual recognition and mutual accountability, that is, the nature of the self and the social constitution of participants. It involves the reflexive capacity of participants to understand and critically assess social arrangements and plans of life. Deliberation is here understood more broadly. It is seen not just as a decision-making process, but as an element in the formation of the reflexive capacity for intersubjective relations.

The connection between a strong version of deliberative democracy and participatory democracy is considerably tighter. As we see it, participatory democracy is linked to the extension of the capacities for communicative reason and communicative freedom throughout a wide range of social relations. Hence the developmental account we have earlier discussed, which has been formulated largely in Aristotelian terms, must be supplemented by a more Hegelian approach that stresses the modern conditions of subjectivity realized through intersubjective ties. We become who we are through our relations with others. But these relations are themselves constituted through a rationality that is elaborated in the giving and taking of reasons. An emphasis on forms of participation that facilitate the development of communicative freedom seems compatible with a strong notion of deliberation. The extension of participation to all important dimensions of social life entails the institutionalization of discourses along those same dimensions.

With this understanding of deliberative democracy as a backdrop, in what follows we examine the core elements of participatory democracy as developed by Carole Pateman, C.B. Macpherson, and Carol Gould, three key thinkers long identified with participatory democratic theory. These thinkers share significant concerns – notably a critique of liberal individualism – and at times they cite each other's work. At the same time, each provides a distinctive focal point for a critical appraisal of existing liberal democratic forms that serves as a basis for their alternative conceptions of democracy: Pateman, with a critique of the social contract as a basis for liberal democracy; Macpherson, with an account of the contradictions of capitalism and the need for individuals to move beyond their self-consciousness as limitless consumers and appropriators if a participatory democracy is to be at all possible; and Gould, with a distinctive social ontology and an intersubjective theory of human rights. Throughout, we attempt to indicate that although somewhat marginal to recent theoretical work, participatory democratic theory, as spelled out by Pateman, Macpherson, and Gould, offers a unique perspective that deserves a more significant place in current discussions.

We then follow up and further elaborate a theme we discussed in chapter 4 by seeking to demonstrate that from the point of view of critical theory, a key component of participatory democracy as a form of radical democracy – and a common if implicit element in the work of the three thinkers treated here – is the idea of social freedom. We believe that social freedom could represent an important dimension of a reinvigorated participatory democratic theory – one that is adequate to the demands of democracy in the current era – because it is uniquely equipped to address the challenges of neoliberalism and the constrained understanding of democracy associated with it. To this end we discuss and appraise the recent work of Axel Honneth, who as we indicated earlier has devoted considerable effort to highlighting the key elements and critical significance of social freedom for contemporary social and political thought.

To be clear, although we offer a detailed treatment of the ideas of Pateman, Macpherson, and Gould, our aim in this chapter is not to undertake a complete survey or analysis of participatory democratic theories or theorists *per se*. Rather, we wish to highlight what we see as important and suggestive elements of such theories that illuminate key concerns central to a critical theory of democracy.

Participatory Democracy and the Critique of Democratic "Realism"

Wherever and however it is defined and carried out, for theorists of participatory democracy, participation is a central element of individual and social identity; indeed, it plays a powerfully formative role in the establishment and flourishing of this identity. In short, participatory democracy and developmental democracy are intimately linked. Given this connection, participatory democratic theory poses a key issue that we have raised throughout this study: how classic developmental themes defined in terms of the flourishing and exercise of human capacities can be related to communicative reason and action.

In turn, the idea that participatory and developmental democracy are, if not identical, tightly intertwined suggests that when so viewed, the range and scope of democracy, its nature and extent, raises at the same time the question of politics itself, *its* nature and extent. That is, under modern conditions and especially in the context of the emergence and development of capitalism, democracy defines the scope of collective will-formation and decision-making in both state and society. In this light, John Dryzek has usefully identified three criteria for defining democracy and its extent, and thus the range of politics: *franchise* ("the number of participants in any political setting"), *scope* ("the domains of life under democratic control"), and *authenticity* ("the degree to which democratic control is substantive rather than symbolic, informed rather than ignorant, and competently engaged").[2]

In a similar vein, Jeffrey Hilmer distinguishes between *modes* and *sectors* of political participation. A sector has to do with the physical location of participation, while a mode represents the form or forms of political action that take place in various sectors. Thus, a sector "includes social, civil, and economic realms: the household, classroom, neighbourhood, associations, or ... the workplace; and also governmental realms: local and regional seats of political power and bureaucratic administration." By contrast, a mode "might include deliberation, cooperative ownership and management, collective decision-making, administration, and so on."[3] Theorists of participatory democracy may emphasize one or the other of these dimensions of democratization, but all of them address each one, be it explicitly or implicitly.

From yet another perspective, Frank Cunningham has explored the meaning of democracy through an analysis of different "degrees" of democracy in different social settings. Cunningham draws upon the ideas of John Dewey, who viewed democracy as more than a narrowly political phenomenon identified almost exclusively with voting and elections. Dewey also conceived it as a broadly social idea in terms of which people possess the capacity to regulate the activities of overlapping social groups to which they belong. Democracy, for him, involved determining, shaping, and conducting the affairs of multiple "publics," with each "public," or site of collective activity, posing distinctive challenges and prospects for participatory engagement. Thus, "rather than regarding democracy as a quality that a social site either has or lacks, one should focus on 'publics' to ask how democratic (or undemocratic) they are, how democratic they might (or ought) to be, and how democracy within them can be enhanced."[4]

Cunningham clearly includes within the scope of his analysis not only representative and formal political bodies but also other social and economic institutions; contemporary questions of identity along the lines of class, race, and gender would likely fit here as well. In this light he expresses sympathy for the position of Dewey and Macpherson "that a democratically functioning group is to be valued especially for liberating development of the potentialities of all the individuals in it," and he also notes favourably "the view of each theorist that egalitarian, and in Macpherson's case socialistic, policies are required for approximating this goal."[5]

Dryzek, Hilmer, and Cunningham suggest the tight link between individual autonomy and social solidarity, as well as the need to take on board not simply issues of political philosophy but also questions of political economy and social analysis. Each of their approaches is essential for a robust theory of democracy faithful to its deepest commitments to equal citizenship and social equality. Although not specifically laying out a model of participatory or developmental democracy *per se*, their accounts identify key elements that such a model would incorporate. And inasmuch as the boundaries of democracy and the range of politics are understood as dynamic and historical, there is yet another link to a critical theory of society, for which the idea of the historical and dynamic character of social phenomena is indispensable.

Interest in participatory democracy as an alternative to electoral, representative democracy began to take shape in the 1960s in the face of increasing dissatisfaction with existing structures of power and authority. These were often viewed as unresponsive or irrelevant at best and as corrupt at worst – or even as deliberately designed to thwart the emergence and expression of a popular will for social and political change. (This was perhaps most succinctly expressed by the pithy and ironic new left barb that if elections could actually change things, they would be made illegal.) The conditions of its emergence highlight those historical and dynamic features of participatory democracy that link it to critical theory.

But there is another equally significant connection between participatory democracy and critical theory that is particularly important for our purposes. Although it is insufficiently noted or appreciated, at least in contemporary discussions of democracy, the emergence of the theory of participatory democracy coincided as well with the challenge mounted by progressive and radical political and social scientists to the dominant paradigm of democracy within academic and intellectual circles, namely, the pluralist–elitist–equilibrium model. This model, which was both an empirical and normative one, viewed democracy as, in the words of Macpherson, a mechanism for choosing and authorizing governments. The democratic process was driven by self-organized political elites, or parties, which competed for voter support in elections. Voters authorized one of the competing parties to govern in their name, eventually passing judgment on the performance of this government in a subsequent election. Given the realities of society and human nature, this was the best that could be expected of a democratic system. To press for more extensive popular engagement or participation beyond the casting of a ballot, or some degree of involvement in interest or pressure group activity, was to court the threat of political instability, mass upheaval that in the extreme could threaten liberal values and indeed potentially unleash totalitarian forces. The Cold War setting within which this account came to prominence was decisive here as its proponents generally assumed a world-historical struggle between (liberal) democracy and (communist) totalitarianism.

In the words of Lane Davis, a critic of the elite model and its assumptions, there is a significant cost to the "realism" it claims to express. Counterpoising to this dominant paradigm a conception of "classical" democracy along the lines of the Athenian *polis* or the New England town hall meeting, he argued that that the pluralist–elitist–equilibrium understanding of political democracy

> sharply reduces the extent and the intensity of necessary individual participation in democratic politics. This permits the abandonment of the classical notion that general attainment of the ideal of rational, active, and informed democratic man is essential to the realization of genuine political democracy. Political democracy is now considered to be a complex system within which apathy and ignorance as well as activity and informed reason have a part to play. Thus, the reality of irrational mass emotion, self-interest, group egoism, and the prevalence of oligarchic and hierarchical social and economic organizations need no longer be denied in the name of democratic values ... Popular participation is reduced to the manageable task of periodic choices in elections. This kind of participation is, at best, a pale and rather pathetic version of the responsible and active participation which was the aspiration of classical democracy. It is hard to see this sort of thing, intermittent in time and marginal in importance for an overwhelming majority of the public, as the central means to educate the intellectual, emotional, and moral capacities of the citizen ... By limiting

238 Critical Theory, Democracy, and the Challenge of Neoliberalism

the moral possibilities of political activity, contemporary democrats reflect
something of earlier Whig suspicions of political power.[6]

It is worth noting that the issues raised by both the critique and
its target would not seem out of place in the contemporary world.
Today's combatants are various forms of centrist liberalism, on the
one hand, and so-called populisms of the left and right, on the other.
And the fear of "unreasoned" mass, potentially destructive opposition to governments and "elites" that exercised so many academics,
commentators, and political actors during the Cold War resonates
with those who have followed in the footsteps of the proponents of
the elite model and become self-appointed defenders of civilized liberal values. For example, former British prime minister Tony Blair, a
key architect of the "third way," argues that "the modus operandi of
[right-wing] populism [which, according to Blair, left-wing populism
has to some extent unfortunately emulated] is not to reason but to
roar. *It has at times an anarchic feel* ... The question is, will this be a
temporary phase, perhaps linked to the aftermath of the 2008 financial
crisis and Sept. 11, *and will politics revert to normal,* or has a new political age begun?"[7] The history of suspicion that democracy is always
potentially liable to descend into mob rule and thereby threaten or
even destroy civilized values and institutions is a lengthy and by no
means unfinished one.[8]

Our point here, however, is that the earlier critique of elite democratic
theory, and of its architects and defenders, embodied what might be
called the driving force of the critical theory of society: that (scholarly)
method and (social) object are connected; that forms of thought and
social life, and conceptual and social structures, are intimately linked.
Social analysis not only describes (or purports to describe) social and
political phenomena but also helps constitute them.

Lane Davis's critique of behaviouralism and the elite theory of democracy that we summarized above offered a defence of robust popular
participation against the limited conception of participation associated
with elite theory. In effect, an alternative model of participatory democracy emerged immanently from the critique of the dominant theory. It is
an articulation of those values and practices to which democracy points
but which it rarely achieves.

To be sure, the critics of behaviouralism in politics were not usually
critical theorists.[9] Meta-metaphysical and self-reflexive thinking – that
is, developing concepts while at the same time attempting to account
for them in relation to rationally defensible insights about historically
emerging human social challenges and possibilities – did not explicitly

shape their criticisms and reflections. Critics of "apolitical politics" tended to juxtapose the ideal of "classical" democracy to the (false) "reality" of pluralism. This largely abstract counterpose of the "ought" to the "is" made the critics easy targets for conventional political scientists, who could defend the "realism" of their own claims and easily dismiss their critics as utopian and "unrealistic" proponents of a classical democracy that never was, nor could be.[10]

But the critics were on to something that they could not or did not explicitly articulate. The Hegelian–Marxian impulses of the Frankfurt School and critical theory supported the claim that the real and ideal interpenetrated in a historically evolving, dialectically accessible synthesis, whereby a decisive social concept or category – in this case "classical" democracy – represented a rational universal; that is, it was not merely an abstract notion but rather an articulation of real and ideal possibilities. Such possibilities were tied to deeply entrenched human aspirations, whose partial realization over time demonstrated genuine potential for human fulfilment and flourishing through the medium of ever-evolving wants, needs, and purposes. Wants, needs, and purposes have varied in relation to the ongoing development of human productive powers, both material and intellectual. These powers are manifested not simply in the command associated individuals come to exercise over external nature, but also in the expansion of moral and ethical insight – that is, mastery over human nature. From Horkheimer, Adorno, and Marcuse to Habermas to Honneth, this understanding of the human condition has endured in one form or another as a central dimension of critical theory.

Thus, participatory democracy should not be viewed simply as an abstract model. Rather, it is itself a form of critique, whereby a way is indicated or suggested for realizing human purposes in the sphere of political life such that the fate of democracy and the fate of politics are inextricably linked.

But as with all critique in the tradition of the Frankfurt School and critical theory, the connection between thought and world, or thought (critique) and historical actuality, is not fixed. (The failure to grasp or explore this connection was another limit of the critical response in the 1960s to behaviouralism and pluralist–elitist–equilibrium democracy.) Participatory democracy emerged in the 1960s and 1970s as essentially a global project, both geographically and socially/institutionally. It was tied to a sweeping critique of capitalist (and "really existing," Soviet-style socialist) political-economic forms. The prospect that capitalism could be radically transformed, and socialism made more humane, seemed both realistic and imminent.

Subsequent developments dashed such hopes and expectations. A scaled-down conception of historical possibilities for change generated a scaled-down approach to alternatives. Participatory democracy has not been immune to this development. Its recent revival, at least as a standard of critique, is instructive.[11] As Antonio Florida has noted in a very interesting and extensive account of the "genealogy" of participatory democracy, this new theoretical turn has tended to emphasize the local and communitarian, focusing on initiatives such as the popular participatory budgeting process in the Brazilian city of Porto Alegre.[12] Such local experiments clearly have value. But are they and the theoretical reflections associated with them sufficient?

We think it is necessary to reimagine participatory democracy in the more comprehensive sense associated with its original aspirations in the 1960s, while at the same time acknowledging that conditions and circumstances have indeed altered. In this light we want to argue that a theory of participatory democracy could be reconsidered on basis of the idea of social freedom: the notion that our freedom and thus our identities are not secured independently of our social bonds, but rather in and through them.

Participatory Democracy, the New Left, and After: Carole Pateman, the Sublimation of Politics, and the Quest for a Radical Alternative

As is well known, a key expression of the core ideas of what came to be called the new left in the United States was the Port Huron Statement produced by Students for a Democratic Society in 1962. Challenging the stifling orthodoxy of the dominant Cold War liberalism, the document promoted a new, more vigorously democratic politics in the service of fundamental social, political, and economic change. This politics would express and reflect the reality that humans "have unrealized potential for self-cultivation, self-direction, self-understanding, and creativity" – in other words, what we have throughout this study identified with developmental and communicative individualism and thus developmental and communicative democracy. Building upon a non-egoistic individualism – "the object is not to have one's way so much as it is to have a way that is one's own" – the statement proposed an alternative that "would replace power rooted in possession, privilege, or circumstance by power and uniqueness rooted in love, reflectiveness, reason, and creativity; … the establishment of a democracy of individual participation, governed by two central aims: that the individual share in those social decisions determining the quality and direction of his life;

that society be organized to encourage independence of men and provide the media for their common participation."[13]

This alternative, then, was to be a participatory democracy in which all major social institutions – political, economic, cultural, educational, rehabilitative, and others – "should be generally organized with the well-being and dignity of man as the essential measure of success." Participatory democracy would be rooted in several core principles, chief among these the idea that individuals should have the opportunity to participate in public groups that could collectively create acceptable social relations through arrangements under which it would be possible for these individuals to emerge out of isolation and into some relation of community. Echoing the ideas of C. Wright Mills, which exerted a powerful influence on Tom Hayden, a key author of the Port Huron Statement, the document called for the creation of political channels that "should be commonly available to relate men to knowledge and to power so that private problems – from bad recreation facilities to personal alienation – are formulated as general issues." And because the economy was of such critical social importance, "its major resources and means of production should be open to democratic participation and subject to democratic regulation."[14]

Clearly, powerful and ambitious words like these call for more exact specification if they are to be fully effective as elements of critique. In this light, David Held has offered a lucid and helpful further clarification of the core justification for participatory democracy. Drawing primarily upon the ideas of Carole Pateman and C.B. Macpherson, he states that an "equal right to liberty and self-development can only be achieved in a 'participatory society,' a society which fosters a sense of political efficacy, nurtures a concern for collective problems and contributes to the formation of a knowledgeable citizenry capable of taking a sustained interest in the governing process." Among other things, a truly and fully participatory system requires the direct participation of individual citizens in the key institutions of the society; democratization of the internal organization of political parties; the provision of participatory opportunities directly within state structures, including legislative and administrative bodies; and an ongoing openness to experimentation in expanding participatory opportunities in response to both citizen experience and shifting and evolving social challenges.[15]

If the Port Huron Statement represented an early clarion call for a radical transformation of existing liberal democracies to make them more robust and egalitarian, it is the ideas of Carole Pateman and C.B. Macpherson that are most often associated with the theory of participatory democracy, to be sure supplemented and expanded upon by thinkers such as Carol Gould. At the core of the work of Pateman and Macpherson are questions of freedom and equality. In contrast to the restriction in the neoliberal understanding of freedom to negative (economic) freedom, and of democracy to a state that at best aggregates individual preferences, Pateman and Macpherson emphasize positive or developmental freedom and a broader conception of democracy and politics that encompasses issues of state *and* society. Democracy thus has to confront questions of power that are not limited to formal political or state power.

Carole Pateman has been perhaps the most widely cited analyst and proponent of participatory democracy. Partly this reflects the fact that she has thoroughly explored issues of democratic participation for more than four decades – from her now classic study from 1970, *Participation and Democratic Theory*, to her presidential address to the American Political Science Association in 2011.[16]

But even more significantly, her work on participatory democracy has both drawn upon and informed her sweepingly broad critique of liberal and existing liberal democratic theory from multiple perspectives – from her trenchant analysis of patriarchal domination and the rendering invisible of, and exclusion and subjugation of, women via the "sexual contract" to her signal treatment of the contradictions and elisions of norms and practices of political obligation.[17]

In other words, in her approach to participatory democracy she makes clear that a meaningful and compelling account of democracy and its possibilities necessarily raises the question of the extent and nature of politics itself. While obviously critical of the sexist assumptions that have always haunted mainstream political theory, including most versions of democratic theory, she holds what amounts to an Aristotelian understanding of politics as central to human development and not simply as a concession to and check upon human weakness and potential for evil. Dominant liberal and liberal democratic theories are caught in a contradiction between a stress on the importance of political authority to reconcile the competing goals and aspirations of putatively free, self-interested individuals, and at the same time the fear of any political expressions that engage the whole community in managing and regulating its common affairs, wherever those affairs might emerge. This contradiction is clearly reflected in the fact that while the liberal state and its theorist-proponents emphasize political *obligation* with its assumption of free, voluntary commitment to political order as the centrepiece of the social contract that binds free individuals together in a political body, in reality they are defending political *obedience*. Pateman writes:

If "obligation" is taken seriously, and examined critically, it becomes clear that the practice of political obligation is not, and more importantly, cannot be, given expression in the liberal democratic state. The dilemma for liberal theory is that it cannot afford to abandon hypothetical voluntarism, and talk merely of political obedience, or the liberal state is deprived of a major ideological support. But nor can it really afford to retain voluntarism because the concept of "obligation" is a standing reminder that the liberal state is being presented as something other than it really is, and that there is a democratic alternative to liberal theory and practice.[18]

The idea that current liberal democratic theory and practice is contradictory – that is, the claim that its core assumptions and commitments point beyond their current embodiment in political institutions and values – gives Pateman's analysis a dynamic dimension that is also the hallmark of critical theory. And the suggestion "that there is a democratic alternative to liberal theory and practice" likewise indicates that democracy as an alternative to liberalism in its current form emerges immanently from liberalism's contradictions: it manifests and transcends the tensions that define the historical meaning of liberal values.

But in our view an even more significant foundation for Pateman's reflections is her argument that the limits of liberalism – limits that point beyond it to (radical) democracy – represent what she calls the reification of politics in the modern age. This argument merits attention because of its potential for opening up issues central to participatory democracy as a form of critical and radical democratic theory.

Although not every model or theory of participatory democracy incorporates direct democracy – that is, a system within which citizens govern themselves or render political and social decisions in an unmediated way without others deciding on their behalf – the question of direct versus representative democracy has always informed reflections about what kinds of participatory initiatives and institutions are both desirable and possible. Since representation in whatever form has at its core a paradox in that it makes present something that is not literally present,[19] it has always raised the question of whether representative government and democracy as popular rule or sovereignty are or can be compatible. Especially in the United States, such doubts have only been reinforced by contemporary circumstances, which encompass among other things the enhanced and increasing role of money in liberal democratic political systems and, associated with this, evident limitations of the electoral franchise: "hollowed out" political parties, diminished voter turnouts, political gerrymandering, and legislated voter restrictions that are supposedly designed to guard against voter "fraud" but that in reality limit the political rights of minorities and the disadvantaged. The decay of representative bodies has also contributed to an increasingly authoritarian involution in many political systems as executive power has been consolidated and increasingly insulated from legislative and popular control and direction.[20]

The limitations of representative liberal democracy provide a central point of departure for Carole Pateman's conception of participatory democracy and what must be done to establish and maintain it. In an article from 1975 that remains important and valuable because of what it conveys about her key assumptions, then and now, Pateman plays off Sheldon Wolin's well-known claim that at least since John Locke, what had been the autonomous realm of politics and the authentically political has under modern conditions been sublimated. By this claim, Wolin meant that those unique activities that historically addressed the common good or interest of the community have been displaced and consequently distorted. As Wolin put it, in the age of large public/governmental and private/corporate bureaucracies,

> [n]o longer do legislatures, prime ministers, courts, and political parties occupy the spotlight of attention in the way they did fifty years ago. Now it is the "politics" of corporations, trade unions, and even universities that is being scrutinized. This preoccupation suggests that the political has been transferred to another plane, to one that was formerly designated "private" but which now is believed to have overshadowed the old political system. We seem to be in an era where the individual increasingly seeks his political satisfactions outside the traditional area of politics ... The problem is not one of apathy, or the decline of the political, but the absorption of the political into non-political institutions and activities.[21]

The result has been a kind of anti-political politics of private interests and the consequent diminution of citizenship and civic life.

It should be noted that Wolin offered this view in the original (1960) version of *Politics and Vision*, his comprehensive survey of the history of Western political thought. His thinking changed dramatically over the ensuing decades. Although he left the original text intact, including his discussion of the sublimation of the political, the lengthy addition he made to the original work in the expanded edition of *Politics and Vision* (2004) reflected a sweeping change in his outlook. He presented this change as "the journey from liberalism to democracy" and as an increasing concern about what he called "the emerging divide between liberalism and democracy." He argued that liberal thinkers – Wolin

highlights Karl Popper and John Rawls – have accorded little importance "to democratic ideals of shared power and an active citizenry"
and have failed "to grasp the political significance of capitalism, not
merely as a system of power but as one with totalizing tendencies."[22]
In revising his position Wolin essentially moved to one much closer
to that of Pateman, who argued that his notion of sublimation did
indeed reflect a liberal understanding of the genuinely political in that
it assumed the unavoidability of the contemporary state and existing
forms of representation.

Nonetheless, there is still value in treating Pateman's analysis and
her response to Wolin's position at the time. For one thing, it tells us
something important about Pateman's argument; it also raises general
questions about participatory democracy. But beyond this, while this is
not our focus here, the idea of sublimation might still illuminate certain
features of contemporary political life and debate, although perhaps
not quite as Wolin originally envisaged. The idea that the political has
been absorbed by private interests has figured in criticisms of certain
progressive political initiatives and is evident in a wide range of conservative views, from the critique of "rent seeking" by rational or public
choice economists and political scientists to the opposition to "political correctness" and the allegedly improper use of the state's coercive
authority in ways that threaten personal and political freedom. One
element of such criticisms is the idea that, for example, the politics of
gender and anti-racism reflect the psychic disorder of rights proponents
rather than the "real" interests of the community: what should be private or personal is now illegitimately rendered political.

In any case, Pateman challenges Wolin's position as an explanation
for the contradictions and problems of liberal democracy. Drawing primarily from Jean-Jacques Rousseau, Karl Marx, and Hannah Arendt,
she argues that reification, not sublimation, better explains the status of
the political in liberal democratic theory and practice. Both Wolin and
Pateman see the origin of the decline of or suppression of the political
in Locke's account of the state of nature and the transition via a social
contract to civil or political society. They agree that Locke's strategy –
whereby individuals cede the right to enforce the law of nature or freedom to the political community and its standing rules as determined
by representatives who serve as an umpire for the whole community –
works to avoid the demands of a radical democracy. For Wolin, Locke's
approach was grounded in his account of the state of nature as already
political because it was essentially social. Autonomous politics had so
to speak "disappeared" into or been sublimated into social relations
rooted in private property and individual interests such that political

power as collective power was dispersed and equally shared among these individuals.

By contrast, Pateman takes another tack. She argues rather that Locke includes among those rights that individuals enjoy in the state of nature "a natural, *political* right" whereby "each individual has to perform the task that, historically, has been performed by a monarch [in the state of nature] or, in civil society, by a representative government, of 'deciding,' interpreting and enforcing the rules necessary if social life is to be carried out in an ordered and peaceful fashion ... The exercise of the natural political right requires that each individual judge 'directly' what is the right and good thing to be done to preserve communal life, and then act on that judgement."[23]

This situation establishes the basis for the reification of the political. For Pateman, reification involves the emergence of the liberal (later, liberal democratic) state as an institution that supposedly embodies and acts on behalf of the interests of the community but that in fact stands as an external force over and against society, in which individuals conduct their lives within their everyday material relations with one another. As Pateman reads Locke, he identifies the political right as of a piece with other natural rights that individuals enter civil society to protect – except that in contrast to those other rights, individuals must give up their political right as the price for protection. Specifically, this political right is yielded up to their chosen representatives, who form a body that by majority vote enacts laws that secure individuals in their lives, liberties, and estates. Representatives do so by standing in for the associated individuals – but on this reading of Locke it is not clear how they could do so since those individuals no longer have political selves, if indeed they ever did have them. For having "given up" her political right, the individual could plausibly be seen as never really having enjoyed it in the first place. Another way to view this situation is that it involves a kind of splitting off of the political side of the individual's make-up, "the natural political aspect of their selves":[24] the individual retains the right of direct judgment and action in all other spheres of life outside the political.

Hence the reification of the political in the received account of liberal democracy, to which Locke made such a crucial contribution: the political is not sublimated so that it essentially disappears into social relations; on the contrary, it is accorded an elevated status above society. Ironically, if the political is "hidden" or displaced, this happens in plain sight. (Pateman indeed argues that despite Wolin's criticisms of liberalism for destroying the autonomy of the political, the establishment of a reified public realm suggests precisely that autonomous domain whose resurrection he so vigorously promoted.)[25] The restrictions of the political to formal institutions of government and the state masks the reality of power in other supposedly private and non-political spheres. This of course is at the heart of Marx's view, to which Pateman specifically refers, that in bourgeois society individuals live heavenly communal lives as public citizens, but profane lives as private individuals who use others as means to achieve their self-interested ends. For these individuals their political selves are little more than the equivalent of rather threadbare political lion skins.[26]

Thus, for Pateman, liberal democratic theory – and society – and the reified conception of politics and the political both enshrine depend upon and sustain two fictions: the fiction of citizenship and the fiction of a social contract. Illuminating these fictions and their consequences has over the decades continued to play a central role in Pateman's work on existing liberal democratic exclusions and the need for a genuinely participatory democracy. The two fictions in turn rest on the paradox that the natural individual political right always has to be given up and thus becomes a fiction as well, "posited only to justify a certain kind of political authority in a specific manner. The individual's political right has no *actual* expression either in the ... state of nature or in civil society. It is a conceptual hypothesis that serves to justify the exercise of political authority by one man, or a few representatives, given the liberal starting point of the 'natural' freedom and equality of all individuals."[27]

If the natural political right, which has as its object the preservation of all and not just oneself, cannot be carried by individuals into civil society, then it is unclear what citizenship, which also must involve the preservation of all, can amount to. This in effect is the basis of Pateman's claim that citizenship is in liberal democracy a fiction. And since the social contract was supposedly intended to establish citizenship as the right to participate as a legal and, with the achievement of (putatively) universal suffrage, political equal in the constitution of a civic order with the power and authority to preserve and sustain the whole, it, too, must be seen as fictional. Thus, the fiction of the social contract is not simply historical. More importantly, it is a fiction that sustains another one: that of citizenship itself. According to Pateman, the establishment of universal suffrage, whereby the liberal state devoted to the protection of individual interests – which in the state of nature had become increasingly contentious with the growth of private property along with the introduction of money – became democratic, did not fundamentally change the fictional nature of citizenship. Citizenship in liberal democracy represented the achievement of formal political equality overlaying substantive socio-economic inequality – the heavenly domain that was the target of Marx's critique. And although Pateman does not quite put it this way, in the measure that democracy threatens to bring the issue of social inequality into the political arena in a way that could lead potentially to the transformation of social relations, the state, as we earlier noted, increasingly tends to insulate its operations from popular pressures – yet another way in which citizenship becomes "fictional."[28]

Fictional citizenship, even where there is universal suffrage, in turn points towards the paradox we noted at the outset of our discussion of Pateman: the paradox of representation:

> Citizens vote for representatives, but they do so precisely so that representatives can make political decisions on their behalf; once again the right of political judgment is being given up. The representatives now become, as it were, the embodiment of the political selves, the citizen selves, of the members of the community. These selves can then be "viewed" by those members in a separate, autonomous sphere, the political sphere. The task of the representatives is precisely to represent the interests of all the citizens, i.e. to represent the political or public interest, not the separate, conflicting interests of individuals. This means that representatives, on entering the political sphere, put on their own version of the "political lion skin." As Locke stresses, private judgement is now excluded; representatives do not judge privately but politically. They make political decisions which are not so much matters of principle as of procedure or technical expertise, that of the umpire of conflicting interests in the game of the market. But what is the collective, political interest of citizens who are bound together by only a formal status? This is difficult, if not impossible, to answer.[29]

Pateman goes on to note that

> [the] giving up of the fictional right by actual private individuals leaves the political sphere with no concrete or actual embodiment in the community. Individuals have nothing in common to bind them together, so what is "common" to society ... can only be seen as something over and above society, something abstracted from the actual social relationships of private individuals ... Citizens can only look at such a political sphere and not act in it ... The political sphere appears as a "thing" – "the state" – objectified and external to the members of society.[30]

Representation and reification are linked at the source of liberal and liberal democratic conceptions of politics and the political. Thus, "[l]iberal theory ... is based on the paradox of a 'natural' political right

that has no actual expression, and this forms the basis for the justification of an allegedly 'autonomous' political sphere, reified in Marx's
'heaven' of the liberal democratic state." Pateman goes on to note what
she sees as the key contradiction: "Thus, on the one hand, liberal democratic theory mystifies the realities of political life. On the other hand, it
also contains, buried within itself, an important truth about the liberal
democratic state and contemporary citizenship: namely, the latter is a
fiction and that the state is in fact external to and out of the control of
its citizens."[31] Her account of a "natural political right" that is neither
natural nor a right suggests, however, an ambiguity in her account that
we will discuss presently.

For Pateman, what is required is an alternative participatory conception of the political, one that involves "moving beyond the liberal
democratic state to a political community composed of a multiplicity of
participatory or self-managed units (perhaps to be called councils)."[32]
Here she turns to Hannah Arendt and Jean-Jacques Rousseau. From
Arendt, Pateman takes up her account of the emergence during modern
revolutions of popular, self-managing councils that assumed the political initiative by inserting themselves through word and deed into the
affairs going on around them. In the process they established a public
realm and thereby altered the course of events. According to Arendt,
establishing such councils under contemporary conditions would
require that the councils form a federal system as an alternative to the
existing state. In a federal arrangement, political power "moves neither
from above nor from below, but is horizontally directed so that the federated units mutually check and control their powers."[33]

From Rousseau, Pateman takes up his famous alternative version of
the social contract. As is well known, in Rousseau's view if the political
order is indeed to be based on a social contract (and it is not altogether
obvious that it can be, or that he thought it could be), this contract must
be of a certain sort. It must be one under which (putatively) free individuals leaving behind the state of nature can somehow simultaneously
unite with all yet remain as free as before. (The freedom achieved by
means of this contract would be a form of social freedom, which we discuss below.) Under Rousseau's social contract, individuals give themselves up or alienate themselves totally to the community and are then
in turn received as equal, indivisible members of the whole. The whole
is nothing other than the relations among these equal members. The
contractual bond is one whereby an individual in effect makes an agreement with himself. He is thereafter doubly committed: "as a member
of the Sovereign he is bound to the individuals, and as a member of the
State to the Sovereign."[34]

For Rousseau, although the community and its members are sovereign this does not mean that private individuals, as private individuals, now legislate, relying on their private judgment as for Locke they had done in the state of nature. To give this a contemporary gloss, Rousseau is no libertarian anarchist *à la* Robert Nozick. While individuals take on a new life as citizens – and as members of the sovereign body their citizenship is potentially very robust – they are still as they were in their "natural" condition: self-interested and competitive. To permit particular individuals in their particularity to act politically would be to continue the state of nature, its "inconveniences" and potential for war of all against all, when the point is to transcend it. (Again, there is some doubt whether Rousseau himself believed this transcendence to be likely or even plausible.)

So there still must be representatives. However, Rousseau famously distinguishes between the sovereign and the government (i.e., representatives). Government is not sovereign but rather serves as an "intermediate body set up between the subjects and the Sovereign, to secure their mutual correspondence, charged with the execution of the laws and the maintenance of liberty, both civil and political."[35] Governments, that is, representatives, cannot have or develop private interests at odds with the common interest of the community. (To be sure, Rousseau doubted private interests could be held at bay for long. The government, or the "prince," would usurp the sovereign and so destroy the common good or the general will. Thus, *The Social Contract* concludes on a pessimistic note, with Rousseau pondering the perhaps inevitable need for censorship and a civil religion, that is, an authoritarian state.)

Thus from Rousseau's point of view, representatives "are not the bearers of the alienated political right of the citizens, nor are they parties to the contract … These representatives are strictly accountable for what they do. It is citizens collectively who alone retain the right to make political decisions and who, therefore, are not merely spectators of their representatives but the active creators and controllers of their own political life."[36]

A radical, self-managing democracy formed through a federated network of popular councils does not rule out the presence of representatives; nor does this presence necessarily contradict the radical ideal. Pateman's view is that representation as such is contradictory only from the perspective of the reified liberal understanding of the state: "The alternatives, then, become either a – clearly absurd – assembly of millions, or a – clearly realistic – giving up of citizens' political right to a few representatives who assemble to make decisions, representatives who embody the political interest of the community."[37] By contrast, "representatives are strictly accountable for what they do" when "an enlarged and actual citizenship in a multiplicity of participatory units" provides "concrete experience of the complex inter-relationships between different social spheres, roles and capacities."[38] (We will see this idea surface again in Axel Honneth's account of social freedom and a democratic way of life.)

Even given that representatives are likely to be required in any organization, self-managed councils not excluded, the scope of political action would in a participatory system be widened dramatically. For democracy to be realized it would have to include, beyond traditional governmental institutions, what are now deemed private organizations, especially economic and industrial (and now, presumably, financial), that make collective decisions and allocate resources. Indeed, Pateman's *Participation and Democratic Theory* devoted significant attention to the question of industrial democracy and offered empirical support for the proposition that a participatory politics in the workplace was both feasible and workable, and that enhanced participation facilitated the development of civic capacities and thus political efficacy.[39]

However, according to Pateman, that the *private* could potentially be political does not mean that the *personal* should be – even though she recognized and sympathized with the feminist claim that the personal was political. Making the personal political and the political personal would simply assimilate the two spheres and thus serve only as a mirror opposite to the liberal position. Assimilating the two would replace technocratic rationality with personal morality; neither is sufficient for a participatory democratic order:

> The interrelationship of the personal and the political spheres can be recognized, as can the fact that any relationship can, in certain circumstances, have political effects, but this is not the same as arguing that the criteria and principles that should order our interactions and decision-making as citizens should be exactly the same as those that should underlay our relationships with friends and lovers ... A public or political morality, principles of political right on which members of a self-managing democracy can self-consciously draw to order their political practice, has also to be developed along with a participatory conception of the political.[40]

Both the personal and the political need to be reconceived and transformed if participatory, self-managing democracy is to be possible – not in order to assimilate them but rather to preserve a deeper and richer meaning for both, since each suffers from the effects of reification.

In "Sublimation and Reification," as well as *Participation and Democratic Theory*, Pateman outlined key themes that have been central to discussions and debates about participatory democracy: the scope and purposes of politics and the political; the relation of "private" institutions, notably economic and financial ones, to public institutions and bodies and thus the interplay of private and public power; the nature of political representation; the character of individual agency and the relation of political life to identity formation; and the meaning and practice of freedom. These issues in turn reflect the key commitments and assumptions that inform her conception of participatory democracy:

> The theory of participatory democracy is built round the central assertion that individuals and their institutions cannot be considered in isolation from one another. The existence of representative institutions at [the] national level is not sufficient for democracy; for maximum participation by all the people at that level socialisation, or "social training" for democracy must take place in other spheres in order that the necessary individual attitudes and psychological qualities can be developed. This development takes place through the process of participation itself ... Therefore, for a democratic polity to exist it is necessary for a participatory society to exist, i.e. a society where all political systems have been democratised and socialisation through participation can take place in all areas.[41]

Pateman has carried these and related themes, commitments, and assumptions forward into subsequent work down to the current time. This is evident from her 2011 presidential address to the American Political Science Association, in which she revisited the issue of participatory democracy in light of contemporary challenges and possibilities. What is of particular interest and value is her attempt to relate participatory to deliberative democracy; in doing so, she addresses what is arguably the most significant current model, one that proposes an alternative to or at least a modification of existing liberal democratic institutions. Her treatment of this relationship is key to her appraisal of the state of participatory democracy as we find it today: while she acknowledges certain recent developments and advances that at least potentially could address and inform participatory initiatives, she is by and large pessimistic about the current situation.

In reconsidering participatory democracy, Pateman lays out its key features as she now sees them, and her account here demonstrates significant continuity with her arguments from forty years earlier. She continues to stress that a democratic theory that is both participatory and developmental must address the interrelation of individual capacities, skills, and characteristics, on the one hand, and democratized authority structures, on the other. In other words, there need to be "opportunities for individuals to participate in their everyday lives as well as in the wider political system." Ultimately, as before, the goals are to create a participatory society and to reform undemocratic institutions.[42]

Pateman re-emphasizes these elements because of two recent developments in the worlds of political theory and political practice. One of these we have already indicated: the emergence of deliberative democracy as the dominant form of alternative democratic theory. Because deliberative democracy stresses non-traditional forms of civic participation, such as citizens' juries and assemblies, it can readily be assimilated to participatory democracy. That both juries and assemblies, or "mini-publics," have been utilized in real policy settings – she offers an account of assemblies established in the Canadian provinces of British Columbia and Ontario to consider alternative electoral systems – has even led some thinkers (as we noted in the introduction to this chapter) to claim that deliberative democracy represents a regeneration of participatory democracy.

Pateman challenges this view. Deliberative democratic theory, which contends that "individuals should always be prepared to defend their moral and political arguments and claims with reasons, and be prepared to deliberate with others about the reasons they provide," would certainly play a role in a participatory system: "Deliberation, discussion, and debate are central to any form of democracy, including participatory democracy." However, she goes on to argue that "if deliberation is necessary for democracy it is not sufficient" or "synonymous with democracy itself." This is because "the primary interest of its advocates lies in the process of deliberation inside deliberative forums. They are not usually concerned with structural features of the wider society. This means, for the most part, that 'democracy' in the wider society and political system is outside their purview; it is largely taken for granted as an institutional background of the forums."[43] Beyond this, exiting institutional structures have not been particularly hospitable to deliberative initiatives. As Pateman notes, while the Canadian citizens' assemblies undertook their activities in the context of referendums conducted simultaneously with provincial elections, their visibility in the electoral campaigns prior to voting day was limited, their roles marginal. Faced with daunting thresholds for success that had been set by governments – in effect, super-majorities were required – the referendums in both British Columbia and Ontario failed. Moreover, the fact that such mini-publics are temporary means that "they are not integrated into the overall system of representative government or democratic institutions, nor do they become part of the regular political cycle in the life of a community."[44]

By contrast, the recent upsurge in participatory budgeting practices would appear to suggest at least some hope for participatory democratic alternatives. The participatory budgeting process that has been in place in the Brazilian city of Porto Alegre for more than a quarter of a century has been the most prominent example. And as Pateman acknowledges, it has demonstrated "how central components of participatory democracy can be institutionalized successfully in what is conventionally seen as an expert, technical area." In this way, "citizen participation in decisions about the municipal budget is established as a *right* of citizens." The pyramid structure established, with neighbourhood assemblies at its base, has encouraged extensive popular engagement: "In a very significant reversal of the usual pattern of political participation, poor citizens form a large proportion of participants," although "the very poorest are much less likely to participate, excluded by the costs of transport and loss of earnings."[45] It is nonetheless noteworthy that Indigenous and African Brazilians, as well as women, have participated significantly.

The system has seen redistribution of resources from wealthier to poorer areas of the city, and participants have recognized the connection between participation and outcomes and experienced enhanced political efficacy. However, participatory budgeting in Porto Alegre does not extend to the entirety of the municipal budget; rather, it is restricted to capital projects. For Pateman, "if democratization is to be strengthened, serious thought needs to be given to ways in which PB can be used for a much greater proportion of municipal budgets."[46]

The actual reach of participatory practices is an especially important issue in light of the adoption of participatory budgeting practices by, according to one estimate, three thousand cities around the world.[47] With respect to actual democratic control of budgets, even at the municipal level these models by and large fail to go as far as Porto Alegre. They are typically justified as mechanisms for improving governance, accountability, and transparency or for enhancing responsiveness to citizen preferences. Thus, existing participatory models for the most part "fit very easily within existing authority structures, and citizens are not participating, as a matter of right, in decisions about their city's or town's regular budget." For Pateman this means that "we are seeing an expansion of participation and an extension of citizenship, but not the beginnings of democratization and the creation of a participatory society."[48] Indeed, the extension of what is called participatory budgeting is not only compatible with current neoliberal practices but can in fact serve to further legitimize them. Extending participation without substantive democratization so that citizens "have the right to public provision, the right to participate in decision-making about their collective life and to live within authority structures that make such participation possible" can be readily fitted "to a minimalist, 'realistic,' Schumpeterian conception of 'democracy' that sees citizens as merely consumers in another guise."[49]

If enhanced participation and citizen engagement by themselves are understood as an extension of democracy – even as the essence of participatory democracy itself – then from Pateman's perspective it is clear why participatory democracy could be understood as a form of deliberative democracy. Both would involve greater citizen consultation. Depending on the circumstances they might even enhance governmental responses to citizen concerns and thereby establish a wider range of policy options. But neither would address the broader patterns of power within the state and the economy that shape the life chances of individuals and prospects for human flourishing. Issues of, for example, economic inequality, which shape individual conceptions of one's possible social choices, and which can even distort cognitive capacities through "epistemological warping" and thereby generate value irrationalities (as Michael Thompson argues), can slip from view.[50] In other words, the transformative possibilities of developmental individualism and communicative rationality would go unrealized or, at best, be given largely symbolic expression. The question of what kind of democracy is possible and desirable in current circumstances, and in foreseeable future settings, remains on this account unsettled – and unsettling.

In reminding us of the importance of posing the question of the meaning of democracy, of what kind of democracy is consistent with its humanist claims, Pateman has over the decades made an important contribution.[51] Recall, though, that she specifically presented her theory of participatory democracy as decidedly non-liberal. While it is clear what she meant – she had in mind the identification of liberalism with private property and the market, as well as "indirect" government with limited and largely passive citizen engagement – there is nonetheless an ambiguity in her argument about the reification of the political in modern liberal democracy. This ambiguity is the product of her reading of John Locke's account of the state of nature. Pateman based her defence of an individual political right that individuals always had to give up in order to enter civil society on Locke's claim that "[p]olitical power is that power, which every man having in the state of nature, has given up into the hands of the society, and therein to the governors, whom the society hath set over itself."[52] She interprets this literally, as meaning that every individual has specifically political power in the state of nature and that this is what is ceded in the move to civil society. It is therefore a key element in her effort to refute Sheldon Wolin's claim that Locke's theory involves the sublimation or disappearance of the political under modern conditions.

Yet this does not seem to be a totally obvious reading of Locke's position. Locke could also mean that although the power of the commonwealth created by the agreement of associated individuals can only be the combination of each one's power, it is the very combination itself that constitutes properly *political* power. If this is so, then there is no political power in the state of nature and consequently no such power for individuals to lose when they leave.

If our reading of Locke is accurate, this does not mean that Pateman's account of reification (and the theory of participatory democracy it undergirds) is thereby invalidated. It remains an important and incisive contribution to critical reflection on democratic possibilities. And she might well respond that, of course, individuals never had any "real" power in the state of nature to lose, but that nonetheless it was essential for Locke to argue as if they did – this is what sustains the fictions of both citizenship and the social contract itself.

But what in Pateman's terms might function for Lockean liberalism as an ideological conceit that sustains reification simultaneously serves for her as a critical standard that points to what individuals require for a genuine political life. Her position thus implies an unbridgeable gulf between the free individual who holds a political right (which is always already alienated) and the liberal and liberal democratic society that results from the social contract. Her participatory democratic theory, radical and substantive, seems to require that individuals retrieve or reconstitute a power of self-government that under no circumstances can be enjoyed in the existing social order. But this leaves open the question of how to get from here to there. Although muted, there must be developmental and communicative possibilities in the present. However distorted, there remain potentials for the development and exercise of communicative freedom; indeed, Pateman's effort to lay bare the ideological character of the state of nature and the social contract relies on it. Without these potentials it is difficult to imagine how to move towards a more genuinely participatory system that would enhance developmental possibilities and opportunities.

It may well be that the political, as well as political power, does indeed exist in the state of nature. But it inheres not in an individual political right but rather in the impersonal pressures of the market, which imposes an order and structure on relations between property (or commodity) owners. In this respect Wolin's conception of sublimation is insightful. Certainly, it is the case that from the point of view of liberalism, the state of nature is fraught with uncertainty, and even danger, and requires that individuals contract to establish a formal political society. But the political dimension of the state of nature is not lost. It is carried over into civil society.

However, Pateman's notion of reification also comes to the fore. Just as she argues, the political-economic power inherent in capitalist market relations is obscured by the attribution of power exclusively to government and the state. Highlighting the political dimension of exclusively private relations is central to the critique of existing liberal democracy that is at the core of participatory democratic theory. Both reification and sublimation accurately capture important elements of political systems that are liberal democratic and capitalist.

That a theory of participatory democracy can critically build upon and not completely repudiate liberal values and practices is at the core of C.B. Macpherson's account of participatory democracy. While Pateman argues that a radical theory of participatory democracy must in fundamental ways be non-liberal, Macpherson believed that a radical participatory democracy could be a liberal democracy, at least where liberalism involved the equal right of all to develop and exercise their distinctively human capacities rather than the right of the stronger to do down the weaker using market rules.[53]

Liberal Democracy beyond Capitalism?
C.B. Macpherson's Participatory Alternative

For Carole Pateman, the liberal notion of the "free and equal individual" represents an "abstractly individualist perspective" that "enables the position of the middle class male to be generalized, while the actual social position of other individuals is never seriously considered."[54] Liberalism from this perspective fails to adequately account for relations of gender, race, and ethnicity, as well as class. If universal liberal rights and freedoms are to have concrete content, we must be aware of how the asymmetries of power in social life distort the capacity of people to enjoy freedom and equality in their everyday lives. For Pateman, as we have seen, "private" matters, and especially gender relations, are shot through with issues of power and so must be brought into view if claims on behalf of freedom and equality are to be realized. The reification of the political means that the extent to which the state is itself embedded in supposedly private spheres is hidden behind claims of an autonomy that is simultaneously genuine and spurious.

As we have also argued, this situation poses the issue of what democracy means and indeed what politics can involve. Classical Marxism raised this question but mistakenly assumed that representative or parliamentary institutions, elections, party competition, and the rest were themselves the problem – get rid of these "bourgeois" covers for capitalist class power and all would be well. This was a tragic misunderstanding. On the other hand, the Western-style social democracy that emerged as an alternative to Eastern Marxism-Leninism was in its own way seriously flawed. Its commitment to minor reforms of existing social and political relations led to the growth of a bureaucratic state that in its own way stifled prospects for democratic political action and thereby undermined its purported moral vision. Each model reinforced rather than challenged the process of reification that Pateman had identified.

Given the limitations of "classical" socialism and social democracy, what other possibilities might exist? According to David Held, the new left, to whose ideas about participatory democracy we have already alluded, emphasized two sets of changes: "the state must be democratized by making parliament, state bureaucracies and political parties more open and accountable, while new forms of struggle at the local level (through factory-based politics, the women's movement, ecological groups) must ensure that society, as well as the state, is subject to procedures which ensure accountability."[55] Citizen rights in the political arena needed to be complemented by similar rights in the family, the workplace, and the community at large.

Macpherson addressed these concerns through his own account of participatory democracy.[56] A participatory democracy depended upon a radical (but not in his view implausible) political and social transformation, one demanded by what he saw as the ethical requirements of democracy itself. In her account of reification Pateman contended that citizens were for the most part passive spectators of a political process in which they played virtually no role beyond the casting of a ballot. In a similar vein Macpherson argued that in existing liberal democratic (capitalist) societies the capacity for political activity had been stifled by structures of power that generated apathy, particularly among the lower strata. Through democratically organized political parties, each with a pyramid-like structure of accountability and anchored in a "base level" democracy that was further buttressed by workplace and community organizations promoting engagement in social spheres outside the formal political arena, people would be far more able to achieve the benefits of active citizenship, including the equal right to liberty and self-realization. Individuals could as a result develop a greater sense of political efficacy as well as the capacity to appreciate collective problems and act in response to them.

For Macpherson, radical participatory democracy builds upon and extends the insights of John Stuart Mill regarding the importance of political participation for individual self-development. This is the claim that only as active agents (doers and exerters of their human capacities, as Macpherson put it) do individuals have the opportunity to develop their potential for freedom and solidarity. Thus the sphere of democratic politics must include areas of "private" life: only when individuals are empowered in all aspects of social life that impinge on their life chances can they realistically be prepared and willing to assume the challenges – but also the joys – of active citizenship. For Pateman, especially, this is vital, because, taking a cue from the democratic elitists, she (and likely Macpherson as well) accepts the unavoidability of elite leadership and more limited opportunities for citizenship at the national level (as opposed to more local ones). Representative institutions would still be required because of social complexity and the inevitability of competing interests and competing conceptions of appropriate resource allocation. Such institutions would also be needed to address the challenges of establishing mechanisms for decision-making that could facilitate social cooperation and coordination of activities, and for reconciling democratic participation with the demands of efficiency and leadership. Nonetheless, more extensive and meaningful participation at local and sub-national levels would allow citizens to more fully develop their civic capacities, which would better equip them to monitor the work of representative bodies in order to ensure that popular views and perspectives were meaningfully considered. Even given its limitations, the experience of Porto Alegre with participatory budgeting testifies to the positive effects of more substantial popular involvement at the local level.

Macpherson believed that a genuinely participatory system would require fundamental social change on behalf of equality. Furthermore, any serious movement in the direction of participatory democracy would demand a transformation of consciousness. By this he meant there was a need for the majority of the population to change their values: from their current preference for affluence of the sort capitalism has until now been able to provide, at least to enough people living in advanced liberal democratic societies, to a desire for community and solidarity.[57] Without such a change, liberal democracies would remain saddled with a contradiction: formal, individual political equality clashing with class-based, substantive economic inequality.

This contradiction has been nicely captured by two American theorists of democracy, Joshua Cohen and Joel Rogers.[58] They relate the problems involved in moving towards a more radical and participatory democracy to two "constraints" or barriers thrown up by the existing institutions and culture of liberal democratic capitalism: the "resource" constraint; and the "demand" constraint.

The "resource" constraint refers to the reality that while highly valued and valuable, the formal political rights found in liberal democratic, capitalist societies – the right to vote and form political parties, and the freedoms of speech and association – have a limited ability to help the disadvantaged organize on behalf of social change – a point Pateman also makes. This is because material inequalities make such rights unequal in practice. For example, trade unions have far fewer resources than do corporations to make their voices heard and heeded.

The "demand" constraint specifically addresses the problem of consciousness that is central to Macpherson's position. This constraint involves the tendency for individuals to view themselves as primarily limitless desirers and acquirers. Where this view is deeply embedded, it facilitates the ability of capitalist society to create, promote, and satisfy interests in short-term, material gain, where such gains are achieved by means of narrowly defined, or instrumental, calculation.[59] This state of affairs reinforces highly individualistic perceptions of who we are and how we relate to others. One way to put this: there is a tension in "possessive" individualism. On the one hand we believe ourselves free and responsible for achieving our ends, particularly our acquisitive ones, and that the world is strictly the product of our individual actions added together. On the other, if things do not work out – and they do not for large numbers of people – one must accept the consequences of the decisions of others (i.e., "the market") as if they truly were one's own.

Each of these constraints reflects the emphasis that Pateman and Macpherson, respectively, bring to their accounts. The constraints are related, and this explains why Macpherson put so much stock in the idea that for there to be a more radical, participatory democracy we must come to see ourselves less as infinite consumers and appropriators and more as creative doers and exerters of our distinctively human capacities. Nonetheless, they point out the complex challenges posed by any plausible ideal of participatory democracy: it must avoid any fixed model or blueprint that, whatever its commitments to freedom and equality, risks becoming an instrument of oppression.

Participatory Democracy and Human Rights: The Social and Developmental Ontology of Carol Gould

This is perhaps why some theorists of democracy, and participatory democracy, have made human rights and securing such rights both the cornerstone and the key accomplishment of a robust radical and substantive democratic system with developmental intent. Human rights would seem to provide a standard by means of which models for political change, including those representing a move towards a participatory democratic society, can be appraised.

Macpherson hinted at such a reading in his reflections on participatory democracy. To be sure, his most explicit discussions of human rights occurred very late in his life, after he had laid out his account of participatory democracy. However, he appeared to have something like human rights at least partly in mind in his treatment of the possibilities for participatory democratic development. For him the key question was not how to run a participatory democracy – and the idea of a blueprint suggests this is the only question – but how to reach it. He identified two key barriers to this. One of these we have already noted, namely, the predominance of consumer consciousness, the overwhelming tendency for people to view themselves as competitive, self-interested, infinite consumers and appropriators rather than as exerters of their own human capacities. The other, to which we have also alluded, is structural and significant (and, we might add, ever intensifying) social and economic inequality. These two barriers are inextricably linked and are essential to the reproduction of capitalist social relations. Each is inimical to the attainment of participatory possibilities. Consumer consciousness reinforces an anti-solidaristic outlook and practice. Inequality results in the exclusion of substantial numbers of people from meaningful participation. Unless these hurdles are removed, no participatory system is truly possible, and any model will have to be imposed by what is essentially a vanguard. As a result, Macpherson ruled out a classical Marxist revolutionary project, for which in any case the requisite working-class revolutionary consciousness was absent. A reformist liberal alternative such as that of John Stuart Mill was also unlikely given the limited political engagement and widespread political apathy that resulted from both inequality and consumer consciousness.

Writing in the late 1970s, after participatory democratic theory had reached its high point, Macpherson argued that its proponents were confronted with a vicious circle: transforming consciousness and eliminating inequality required extensive and intensive participation; but such participation could only result precisely from the transformation of consciousness and the elimination of inequality. Macpherson pointed out then contemporary developments that he believed offered at least some hope for and prospects for breaking out of this circle. His specific account of those prospects does not concern us here. However, his approach does suggest that we view his treatment of participatory institutions with great care. Always more cautious and even pessimistic than his writings might suggest, or most analysts of his work recognize, Macpherson implied that any participatory system not based on overcoming or at least reducing the barriers to such a system was bound to fail – or, just as ominously, serve up the pseudo-legitimation of a managed plebiscitarian state. (The contemporary emergence of right-wing populism indicates that Macpherson was prescient here.) It would, in short, risk becoming precisely the kind of abstract model that could only be realized by forcible imposition, and not by the actions of free and equal individuals exercising their distinctively human creative capacities.

Since Macpherson offered his account, human rights discourses, along with theories of deliberative democracy, have come to occupy centre stage in contemporary political and social theory, often in conjunction with proposals for strengthening or establishing global or international mechanisms for the defence of these rights. In chapter 5 we explored the relation between rights, positive and negative, and the critical theory of the Frankfurt School, particularly in relation to the position of Jürgen Habermas as he developed it in response to the blind spots of the original paradigm. Here we approach the question in the context of the reality that much analysis from a human rights perspective, if not at odds with democracy, nonetheless assumes a gulf between democracy and human rights. Indeed, reflecting the long-standing fear that popular majorities could trample on the rights of both individuals and vulnerable minorities, human rights discourses typically assume that these rights require above all protections against legislative bodies and mobilized publics. This would go double for a participatory democracy. In fact, some proponents of human rights would likely reject participatory democracy as potentially if not inherently tyrannical, or at least as a species of that populism that these days so exercises many analysts.

However, there is a way of conceiving human rights as not *opposed* to popular engagement but rather as dependent upon and even essential for such engagement and hence for participatory democracy. As we have argued, in this view human rights must include, beside and beyond traditional liberal and individual rights, social, economic, and communicative rights and freedoms. Without specifically identifying it, or developing an account of it, Macpherson indeed seemed to, and needed to, assume the possibility of communicative freedom and rationality.

Carol Gould builds upon this implied commitment to a broader conception of social rights and uses it to work up an account of democracy that fits well within the participatory framework. Drawing on "the traditions of political philosophy and critical social theory, and on more recent feminist theorizing," Gould argues for a theory that "entails an expansion of democratic modes of decision making and of human rights themselves, not only internationally, but also beneath the level of politics, so to speak, in social, economic, and even personal life." She anchors this in a social ontology that "gives priority to a conception of human freedom and to socially understood *individuals-in-relation*s as the basis for the extension of democratic decision making to all contexts of human activity, whether political, economic, or social." Social ontology gives rise to a specific understanding of human rights: these rights "reflect the basic claims people can validly make on each other for the conditions that can make each one's freedom achievable." Furthermore, "feminist approaches to the idea of care and empathy as important values, to women's equal rights and the corollary critique of domination, and to the idea of embodiment importantly suggest ways to personalize, and in this sense, to transform both democratic politics and human rights doctrine."[60] Hence Gould in effect incorporates and synthesizes the ideas of both Pateman and Macpherson even as she takes issue with certain elements in the work of both.[61] And as she acknowledges, her account also demonstrates explicit affinities with key themes from critical theory.

What makes Gould's position particularly instructive from the perspective of Macpherson's analysis of the challenges of reaching as opposed to running a participatory democratic system, and how to respond to those challenges, is her conception of social ontology. Macpherson thought that individuals could themselves generate insight into the painful contradictions of life within late capitalist society and so move away from consumer consciousness and its social basis and consequences. He viewed this as possible even if we make the minimalist assumption that people reason only in terms of a cost–benefit analysis (he clearly believed they were capable of more than this). Gould offers an account that suggests how individuals might gain this insight. She argues that the evidence for what she calls "a social-ontological characterization of human action and of human beings" is "experiential or phenomenological; that is[,] it presents itself to us in the structures of everyday action and social interaction." On this reading, human rights are anchored in "the daily and recurrent recognition by individuals of others as beings like themselves, namely, as agents with claims to the conditions for their self-developing or self-transformative activity ... [I]n asserting one's own right, one acknowledges the validity of the other's claim as a right by virtue of reciprocally recognizing it as like one's own."[62]

Rights are thus viewed as accomplishments and not statuses. They result from the joint political action of the individuals claiming them. In the words of James Ingram, "the politics of human rights should be understood as a democratic politics of universalization, based on the political activity of those they are to protect." The achievement of rights, he further argues, suggests "a notion of the politics of rights that decouples it from the state and law ... Rights politics can be thought ... as the active, cooperative practice of those who recognize one another as equals."[63] Viewing rights as politically claimed and secured entails the idea that they are both universal and democratic, with both elements indelibly linked. This in turn indicates that the liberalism of human rights, and democracy with its commitment to equal rights of participation in key social decisions and thus popular self-rule, can be rendered compatible through a radically participatory politics. This, at least, is the claim and hope of both Macpherson and Gould.

As we have indicated, in our view the key to a democratic conception of human rights lies in the need to expand the standard liberal political and individual rights to include social and economic rights. Both sets in turn require and give substance to communicative rationality and freedom whereby the mutual relations of trust and reciprocity essential for both human rights and democracy can be maintained and deepened. Human rights matter in the context of activities that matter, with each defining the other.

This is the focal point of Gould's analysis of radical and participatory democracy with a cosmopolitan intent. A cornerstone of her position is precisely that human rights must include social and economic rights, along with civic and political ones. These rights express and embody the demands of justice, where the core principle of justice is what she calls equal positive freedom. Equal positive freedom requires that the material and social conditions of individual self-development be secured. The right of equal positive freedom tied to the establishment and maintenance of the conditions of self-development is crucial for the exercise of our capacity to be agents capable of making and acting upon choices. The individual right to self-development and the conditions that make it possible are dependent upon the reciprocal or mutual recognition of individual agents, all of whom are entitled to equal positive freedom and hence justice. Such reciprocity is not limited to formal discursive practices – thus Gould's criticisms of deliberative democracy – but include as well norm-governed non-discursive activities (which to be sure may include discursive elements): "individual action and joint action oriented to the realization of goals, such as work; expressive or creative activity, such as in the arts; scientific activities of discovery and invention; as well as the range of caring relations among family, friends, and citizens, even across borders."[64] As we have noted, these relations of reciprocity are tied to everyday patterns of interaction – they are at the core of Gould's social ontology.

The tie between justice, or human rights, and democracy is a product of what this social ontology articulates and demands:

> The principle of justice thus conceived as … equal right to the conditions of self-development requires *democracy* as the equal right to participate in decision making concerning the common activities in which individuals are engaged. For engaging in such common activities involving shared goals is itself one of the main conditions for individuals' self-development, the opportunity for which requires that they be self-determining in this activity. If, instead, an individual's actions were determined by others in such contexts, it would not be an exercise of the agency that is required for self-transformation. However, since such common or joint activity necessarily involves acting with other individuals, the exercise of individuals' agency in this context must take the form of codetermination of the activity, that is, rights to participate in decision making about it.

Furthermore:

> Rights of democratic participation arise from rights to self-determination in the context of joint activities. At its root, it can be argued that people should be equally free to control the conditions of their own activity and that, where their activity is social or common, this gives rise to rights to codetermine it if they are not to be under the control of others. Common activity can be defined as activity in which a number of individuals join together to effect a given end. To the degree that they choose for themselves the end of this activity and the good it serves, it essentially involves the cooperation and coordination of many individuals in the realization of their joint projects or purposes. Yet such common activity can be seen to be among the conditions that people need for their own freedom as self-development, in that it provides a social context for reciprocity and makes possible the achievement of ends that cannot be achieved by an individual alone.[65]

If this conception of common activities and its implications address the issue of democratic participation, matters of justice and human rights can according to Gould be addressed by a version of the "all affected" principle: the idea that everyone affected by the decisions of a political or social institution should have meaningful input into the decisions in question. For Gould this sweeping and overly general principle could be made more specific by determining whether such decisions have an impact on the possibilities for individual agency and hence self-development that are inextricably associated with their freedom, needs, or core interests – in other words, their basic human rights and the realization of equal positive freedom:

> Given the status of these human rights as valid claims that we each make on others for the conditions that we need for our freedom and dignity, it follows that social, economic, and political institutions, including those in the international sphere, need to be designed to make it possible for all to fulfill these basic rights ... Because of the centrality of democratic participation in people's having the ability to realize and protect their human rights, including economic and social ones ... it follows that they should have substantial input into those decisions that affect rights fulfillment.[66]

Over the years Gould has increasingly shifted her focus to the question of how to create trans-border and international forms of democratic participation and practice in the face of intensifying globalization. She has specifically attempted to show how human rights, along with the principles of common activities, can be made viable in the face of the increasing impact of bodies such as the World Trade Organization, the International Monetary Fund, and regional entities such as the European Union, to say nothing of transnational corporations. She has also sought to explore how the growth of cross-border communities and transnational associations could offer new possibilities for realizing democratic norms in ways that do not require a world government or *demos*. Again, the specifics of her proposals do not concern us here. It is her conception of human rights tied to individual agency as the development and exercise of human capacities, and the social ontology that as an immanent critical standard grounds this conception, that we believe represents Gould's important contribution to participatory democracy as a critical theory of democracy.

Starting from existing (liberal) democratic theory and practice, Pateman, Macpherson, and Gould explore the limits of the assumptions and commitments of this theory and practice and their failure to realize the promise of democratic life. Pateman begins with the social contract, a key source of legitimation for the existing liberal order, and traces out its contradictions and exclusions. In doing so she points to potential sources of a reified politics that sustains a passive citizenship and undercuts democratic potential. Breaking through reification required movement towards a non-liberal form of participatory democracy. More sympathetic to liberalism and its contradictory heritage, Macpherson argued that for both liberalism and democracy to be faithful to their deepest commitments to individual development, democracy needed to be transformed from a mechanism for choosing and authorizing governments into a society in which individuals were equally able to use and develop their distinctively human capacities. For this transformation to occur the massive inequalities intrinsic to capitalism had to be overcome, and, just as importantly, individuals had to see themselves as doers and exerters of their capacities rather than as self-interested and competitive infinite consumers and appropriators.[67] Gould picks up on this latter theme by way of a distinctive social ontology, in terms of which individuals should be understood as always and already embedded in a multiplicity of relations within which they develop wants, needs, and purposes that define their possibilities for self-development. Self-development requires that individuals enjoy both the equal right to the material and social conditions that facilitate it – equal positive freedom – and the equal right to participate in decision-making with respect to those common activities that themselves form a significant element of this self-development. In other words, it requires both justice, or human rights, and democracy.

In their similarities and differences, all three thinkers elaborate core elements of a substantive and participatory theory of democracy. Each thinker makes central the assumption that the individual should not be understood in an atomistic way, but rather as embedded in social networks and contexts.[68] On this view, narrowly individualistic conceptions of democracy based on the maximization of individual preferences or interests understood discretely must give way to a broader and richer understanding that acknowledges our social nature. Each thinker argues that democracy must be extended beyond the formal political arena into all areas of social and economic life that impinge upon individual life chances and prospects. Each is therefore concerned with issues of modes and sectors of democratic engagement, as suggested by Jeffrey Hilmer, as well as questions of franchise, scope, and authenticity, as outlined by John Dryzek. Moreover, Pateman, Macpherson, and Gould all strongly stress the need for robust publics anchored in those radically egalitarian social conditions that are essential for autonomy and self-development, and thus for a democracy that is genuinely popular and solidary; in this respect they touch base with the position of Frank Cunningham. And if currently existing representative and electoral institutions cannot be and should not be completely replaced, at the least they should be reinvigorated and further supplemented by more direct forms of participation. These could include popular assemblies of the kind associated with participatory budgeting initiatives and with forms of deliberative democracy more generally.

What might unite these distinctive if related conceptions of a radical democracy that put self-development and self-determination at their centre? In defining her position Carol Gould gives us a clue. She writes that "the common root or common foundation that normatively grounds the conceptions of both justice and democracy is freedom, understood as the crucial or distinguishing feature of human action." She goes on to claim that such freedom is complex: "It is, on the one hand, a bare capacity for choice among alternatives; on the other, it is the exercise of this capacity – individually or together with others – in the realization of long-term projects and the development of abilities. In this sense, freedom is an activity of self-development or self-transformation as a process over time, and I interpret this as the characteristic mode of human agency or life activity."[69]

We agree with Gould's account here and believe it links her treatment of democracy, and the analyses of Pateman and Macpherson, with the core commitments of critical theory. More specifically, it highlights the significance of *social* freedom – the idea that individual freedom is attained in and through, and not outside or against, our relations with others and their needs and purposes; that freedom and a certain kind of mutual trust and obligation are linked – for a critical theory of democracy. In the final section of this chapter we return to the issue of social freedom by once again exploring the recent work of Axel Honneth, a key contemporary Frankfurt School theorist.

(Participatory) Democracy as a Way of Life: Axel Honneth, Social Freedom, and Socialism

Axel Honneth has developed his conception of social freedom on the basis of an extensive engagement with and reconstruction of the philosophy of Hegel, and in particular Hegel's complex account of freedom as he laid it out in his *Philosophy of Right*.[70] Eschewing historical teleology and the metaphysics of spirit that underpin Hegel's position, Honneth argues that the *Philosophy of Right* "can be understood as a draft of a normative theory of those spheres of reciprocal recognition that must be preserved intact because they constitute the moral identities of modern societies."[71] The freedom secured in these spheres is thus communicative because it presupposes that individuals are always and already linked through intersubjective relations. Why and how our ties to others are not restrictions on our freedom, or what Hegel calls the "free will," but preconditions for it – namely, "those social conditions under which each subject is able to perceive the liberty of the other as the prerequisite of his own self-realization"[72] – is for Honneth the key insight we can reclaim from Hegel's account.

As Honneth sees it, Hegel recognized that although essential for the realization of the free will, two components of our modern understanding of individual freedom – abstract right, whereby individuals, as holders of subjective rights, exercise legally secured, free personal and potentially arbitrary choice unencumbered by others; and morality, in terms of which we appraise our actions according to principles that spell out what we ought to do and thus exercise inner, reflective self-determination – are not by themselves sufficient to fulfil the demands and requirements of individual autonomy. This is because on their own they are indeterminate. They fail to provide a sufficient basis for establishing our aims, purposes, and aspirations, which, as moderns no longer acting under the constraints of tradition or the demands of the sacred, we are now called upon to responsibly undertake. For this we require (re)engagement with others that respects the demands of autonomy without a re-submergence in a quasi-natural, organic community that under modern conditions could only be oppressive. We need relations with others in order to confirm and enact our freedom, but this must be consistent with what, following Hegel, Honneth calls being with oneself in the other.[73] We must have the capability to "withdraw" from our social bonds as bearers of both personal and moral freedom. However, we must also return to those ties, which in any case are always and already there, in our very withdrawal. We need confirmation by others in determinate roles, connections, and activities if our freedom, which is communicative and interactive, is to be actualized as constitutive of our identities. Otherwise we will be threatened by a kind of anomie that Honneth calls "suffering from indeterminacy." Taken in isolation, our personal choices push out against those of others who thus appear instrumentally as either barriers to or facilitators of our efforts at satisfaction. Resistance to our efforts, or even unintentional facilitation by others, is insufficient to confirm our freedom and thus our selfhood. Conversely, our moral self-reflection lacks purchase in the external world.

The problem of indeterminacy lays the groundwork for Honneth's conception of social freedom, which completes and sustains what he defines as negative and reflexive freedom, his versions of abstract right and morality. He puts the problem this way: "While the idea of negative freedom ... must fail because the 'content' of action cannot itself be grasped as 'free,' the idea of reflexive freedom is insufficient because it opposes the actions it views as free in substance, viz. as self-determined acts, to an objective reality that must continue to be regarded as completely heteronymous." Hegel's great accomplishment was to recognize that "individual freedom unfolds only within institutions of recognition" – that "the kind of freedom he has in mind can only be realized through participation in concrete institutions."[74]

Social freedom addresses the limits of both negative and reflexive freedom. According to Honneth, and following Hegel, for modern subjects

> it is obvious that our individual freedom depends upon the responsiveness of the spheres of action in which we are involved to our own aims and intentions. The more we feel that our purposes are supported and even upheld by these spheres, the more we will be able to perceive our surroundings as a space for the development of our own personality. As beings who are dependent on interacting with our own kind, the experience of such a free interplay with our intersubjective environment represents the pattern of all individual freedom: The schema of free activity, prior to any tendencies to retreat into individuality, consists in the fact that others do not oppose our intentions, but enable and promote them ... Our dealings with others, our social interaction, necessarily precedes the act of detachment captured in relations of negative or reflexive freedom. Hence we must define that antecedent layer of freedom located in the sphere in which humans relate to each other in some way. If we follow Hegel at this point, freedom signifies our experience of being free from coercion, of unfolding our personality – a kind of freedom that results from our purposes being promoted by those of others.[75]

For Honneth, social freedom under modern conditions can be and must be realized in the spheres of personal relationships of romantic love, friendship, and family; in the market economy, as consumers and producers; and through democratic will-formation in a public realm and constitutional state. As domains for the articulation and exercise of freedom, these spheres incorporate important dimensions of recognition that are essential to the formation and development of coherent individual personality structures: personal affirmation through love and intimacy; egalitarian cooperation in the service of social production; and civic and legal respect.

Honneth developed this notion of social freedom in detail over the course of several works, most fully in *Freedom's Right*. In our discussion here, we focus on his 2015 study, *The Idea of Socialism: Towards a Renewal*. There are two reasons for our choice. First, it is the most recent iteration of social freedom and the central place it holds in his political and social thought. More specifically, it extends his analysis in *Freedom's Right* by attempting to more fully develop its implications for transformative social change. Second, in raising explicitly the question of socialism and linking it to the ideal of a democratic form of life, which as we have noted represents for him a vital sphere for the realization of social freedom, Honneth touches base with key concerns of Frankfurt School critical theory as well as with the issues we are attempting to explore in this chapter. We believe his ideas resonate with those of Pateman, Macpherson, and Gould and enrich our appreciation of the demands of participatory democracy.

In *The Idea of Socialism*, Honneth identifies the source of both socialism and social freedom, and the tight connection between them, in the recognition of an internal contradiction in the principles and normative ideals of liberty and fraternity that along with equality had emerged from the French Revolution. Early socialists such as Robert Owen, Charles Fourier, Louis Blanc, and Pierre-Joseph Proudhon believed that a narrow liberal, legal interpretation of liberty precluded the achievement of fraternity. As they saw it, the "aim of fraternity, of mutual responsibility and solidarity, cannot even begin to be realized as long as liberty is understood solely in terms of the private egotism characteristic of competition in the capitalist market ... The contradiction in the moral demands of the French Revolution could only be removed if individual freedom was no longer understood as the private pursuit of interests, but rather as a relation in which the pursuits of individual members of society complement each other in the economic power-center of the new society." The need, in other words, was to interpret liberty "in a less individualistic and more intersubjective manner."[76]

The reconciliation of individual freedom with solidarity became and remains the core of social freedom. Emerging as a normative demand bequeathed by the French Revolution, and not only from the desire to re-embed the capitalist economy in society to facilitate a more rational and just distribution of resources, the idea of a new kind of freedom in solidarity required not merely that each individual supported the other in pursuit of their goals. It also demanded that the freedom of one became a condition for the freedom of the other. The challenge from the outset has been to establish how this could be done – how, in other words, to echo Jean-Jacques Rousseau, it could be possible for each, while uniting with all, to remain as free as before – indeed, freer. The key question might be whether individual freedom, however understood, is a property of individuals as such, taken discretely, or exists only in and through mutual relations of fraternity or solidarity: "whether a free act can be regarded as already having been completed prior to being supplemented by others, or whether it needs the supplementation of others to count as a completed act."[77] (This is comparable to the question whether human rights should be conceived as statuses or accomplishments.)

In responding to this issue Honneth points to Daniel Brudney's claim that social communities can be distinguished according to whether their members relate to one another by means of overlapping or intertwined aims. Individuals with overlapping aims might pursue these together, but common action is not the point. Market relations have this character. But it *is* the point for intertwined aims: unity is *itself* the purpose so that individuals act not only *with* but *for* one another: "In the first case, that of overlapping aims, the fact that my actions contribute to the realization of our shared aims is a contingent effect of the pursuit of my own intentions; in the second case, that of intertwined aims, the same result arises as a necessary consequence of my conscious intentions."[78]

Honneth sees this account as crucial for Marx's Hegelian approach to the reconciliation of liberty and fraternity: Marx's conception of solidarity, as least as laid out in his early writings, involves not merely the implementation of our aims but, more fundamentally, their formulation. The needs of others and their satisfaction become conscious sources of our fulfilment and not, at best, by-products of our quest for gratification, or, at worst, vulnerabilities to be exploited for our own egoistic ends. This is the case under capitalism, where we anonymously exchange products in the market with the aid of money in a system that, according to the young Marx, pitted isolated individuals against one another in a relation of "mutual plundering."[79]

Society, then, is to be organized as communities of solidarity, of mutual, shared sympathy, trust, and respect. Possessive individualism would give way to developmental, social individualism; purely negative freedom would be incorporated into, and transformed into, positive or developmental liberty. Thus: "Social freedom therefore means taking part in the social life of a community whose members are so sympathetic to each other that they support the realization of each other's justified needs for each other's sake ... If subjects practice mutual sympathy, they will necessarily treat each other as equals and thus refrain from exploiting or instrumentalizing each other in any way."[80] Social freedom, then, "would eliminate not only the opposition between freedom and fraternity, but also the distinction between rich and poor, for members of society would then regard each other as partners in interaction, to whom they owe a certain measure of solidarity for the sake of their own freedom."[81]

As we have seen, Honneth attributes the key insights that served to establish the idea of social freedom to the early socialists, including the young Marx, who took the community of solidarity, rather than the individual, as the bearer of freedom. This community, however, was understood not in opposition to the liberal or bourgeois demands for liberty, equality, and fraternity, but rather as the fulfilment of these via the resolution of their internal contradictions. Hence the community of solidarity is not conceived as existing above and beyond the individuals who comprise it, but in and through their interactions. Individuals come to consciously recognize this because, insofar as their aims and purposes are intertwined and mutually determined through the exercise of communicative reason, they no longer view their freedom as sacrificed to the demands of fraternity, which in a capitalist market society imposes itself on them as external compulsion exercised by either social pressures or state action – that is, by means of the reified politics that so concerned Carole Pateman.

Moreover, the fact that socialists have built upon the ideas and ideals of freedom, equality, and solidarity – the very same ideas that anchored the bourgeois revolution and have subsequently served to legitimize the liberal social order – has always made it difficult for the forces of the status quo to wholly expunge the threat of a radical alternative claiming a common heritage. The ferocity with which the forces of order defend neoliberalism, even in the absence at this time of serious organized opposition, testifies to the always present sense that something like a socialist alternative could always emerge – at least as long as the heritage of the French Revolution continues to shape the self-understanding of citizens.[82]

Based on his conception of social freedom, Honneth attempts to reconstruct the idea of socialism in order to see how it could be made relevant to a global capitalist era increasingly characterized by economic stagnation, deepening inequality, and financial instability.[83] Indeed under these conditions socialism ought to have a place, given increasing discontent in the face of the social and political consequences of largely uncontrolled and apparently uncontrollable market forces. But for socialism to gain a renewed vitality as a vehicle for the realization of social freedom, it is essential to revisit the core commitments it has historically embraced, parting company with those that no longer adequately address current challenges.[84]

Honneth argues that as much as they promoted the development of social freedom as the immanent realization of the insufficiently fulfilled promises of the French Revolution, thinkers such as Saint-Simon, Owen, Blanc, and Proudhon, as well as Marx, were too deeply influenced by the Industrial Revolution and the emerging institutions of industrial capitalism. As a result, they attended almost exclusively to material production, an emphasis that was carried forward by subsequent generations of socialists and socialist thinkers. While understandable, this emphasis has led to an excessively restrictive and no longer tenable focus on the economy, the sphere of social labour, as the sole and necessary forum for the realization of social freedom. Socialists have traditionally believed that overthrowing capitalist relations of production would automatically usher in a new society of freedom, equality, and solidarity because all other spheres were structurally dependent on the economy.

As Honneth sees it, this approach fails to successfully address the reality that in the modern era, ongoing social differentiation has undergirded those relations of recognition he sees as decisive for individual agency. As we have seen, along with the capitalist market economy there have emerged distinctive spheres of, respectively, personal relations of intimacy and political relations of prospectively democratic and discursive will-formation. Social freedom must therefore now be identified and realized not only in the economy but also in personal and political life. Individuals must be seen not just as workers but also as intimate partners and friends, and as citizens. Put otherwise, the sphere of social labour can no longer, if indeed it ever could, be the driving force, the collective directing centre, of a modern, differentiated social order.

Along with a now indefensible exclusive focus on the economy as the forum for the achievement of social freedom, Honneth argues that socialists have adhered to two additional dubious propositions: that socialist theory was the expression of the real interests and actions of a putatively revolutionary social force, the proletariat; and that history was inherently progressive and was thus moving inexorably towards the realization of socialism and social freedom. Honneth claims that both assumptions must be jettisoned. The "agent(s)" of change must now be seen and identified as those who in their outlook and actions challenge social dependencies and exclusions in all areas of social life, and not just the sphere of social labour. In addition, the idea(l) of inevitable progress, which has tended to discount incremental reforms in the present as insufficient for the task of fundamental transformation, must give way to a willingness to build on potentials for change within the existing social order by means of social and historical experimentation. There is not, nor can there be, one "true" path, such as central economic planning, to a socialist transformation. Reflecting the long-standing influence of John Dewey and pragmatism on his thought, Honneth defines his position as "socialism as historical experimentalism."[85]

Nonetheless, if the classic model of proletarian revolution is no longer viable, nor progress guaranteed, and if we must now instead pursue socialism by means of historical experimentalism – and if the exercise of communicative reason and freedom forms the core of this process – the economic sphere must continue to hold a central place in any consideration of what socialism can mean today. Although the realm of production can no longer be viewed as the directing centre of society, realizing social freedom in the economy remains a fundamental aim, as it did for classical socialism. The question of how social freedom in the economy is to be realized under contemporary conditions can, however, only be addressed "by means of experimentation, by exploring different ideas whose sole commonality consists in pointing up possibilities for economic value-creation beyond capitalism as a cooperative process aided by various institutional mechanisms ... The guideline for any experimentation with different economic combinations must lie in strengthening 'the social' in the economic sphere as much as possible, enabling all those involved to satisfy their needs through complementary activity without compulsion or restricted influence."[86] Relevant experiments might include pursuing different ways in which markets could function without being tied to the compulsive requirements of capital accumulation (market socialism); establishing different forms of productive and workplace organization (cooperative work relations); and expanding the range of social rights to include a guaranteed minimum income and greater democratic control of existing market forces (socialized markets in a property-owning democracy). All such experiments, including previous efforts at nationalization or collectivization, should be included in "an internal archive of past attempts at economic collectivization as a kind of memory bank detailing the advantages and disadvantages of specific measures," whereby all such measures must fulfil the principle that experiments "resulting in the violation of established practices for will-formation in line with the rule of law must be viewed as having failed."[87]

For the economic sphere, then, "[w]hen it comes to experimenting with institutional models, we must welcome all proposals that are somehow committed to freeing producers from constraints and dependencies, thus enabling them to view themselves as free contributors to the task of equally satisfying the needs of all members of society, a task that can only be fulfilled in reciprocity."[88]

Hence social freedom, understood in terms of recognitive individualism such that there is cooperation and solidarity whereby the freedom of one is dependent upon and defined by the freedom of the other, is the key and must be achieved in all spheres according to the inner logic of each. Socialism, then, entails a process by which the proper relations between and among differentiated social spheres are identified and established. Honneth ultimately hopes that this revised conception of the socialist project offers at least the prospect of realizing what socialism, with its roots in the French Revolution, has always pursued: the reconciliation of liberty and fraternity, in the process putting society on the path to becoming truly "social."

This is a challenging and thought-provoking reinterpretation of socialism and what a plausible contemporary socialist project would have to include. Honneth is aware that this revision of the socialist idea threatens to turn socialist theory into a narrowly abstract and purely normative account along the lines of liberal theories of justice, theories with which he has taken issue in previous work.[89] His analysis suggests there is nonetheless still a difference. As we read him, he believes that his reconstructed version of socialism can still claim, in a way liberal accounts cannot, to represent genuinely progressive historical possibilities, and that his conception and the project to which it would give rise is rooted in real social relations and thus in the processes of individual identity formation. In short, there is a social dynamic whereby responses to contradictions people encounter in their life experiences could become the basis for a new social order, given the normative "grammar" by means of which they understand their wants, needs, and purposes. Such responses would include the emergence of demands not only for economic justice, or justice for workers, but also for the elimination of relations of domination along the lines of race, gender, and sexuality, as well as demands for radically new ways to relate to our natural world in the face of potential environmental catastrophe. From Honneth's perspective, this approach is not available to standard liberal theories.

Thus, in contrast to such theories he argues that "the natural enemy of socialism – today just as in Marx's day – is the predominant school of economic theory, which has sought for over 200 years to justify the capitalist market as the only efficient means for coordinating economic action under the conditions of an expanding population and its growing needs." Taking on economic theory must involve, as it did for Marx, "viewing the capitalist economy as being already mediated or co-produced by the theoretical terminology of dominant economic theory, meaning that we can only call reality into question by criticizing the theory." (Critics of elite or "realist" democratic theory and its behaviouralist underpinnings in the 1960s held a comparable view.) And in line with his overall reconstruction of the socialist project and its emphasis on realizing social freedom in the personal and political, as well as economic, realms of society, he further claims that

> socialism must always also offer a critique of those dominant theories that also contribute to producing social reality in the spheres of personal relationships and political will-formation, e.g. standard liberal models of the family or the dominant theory of democracy, which is firmly anchored in the concept of negative freedom. If we accept the moral fact of functional differentiation in the sense presented here in a strongly Hegelian manner, then it is not enough to present a critique of political economy. Instead, we must also offer a critique of hegemonial branches of knowledge that deal with the other constitutive subsystems and whose concepts have always contributed to creating the reality within these subsystems.[90]

The close association Honneth enjoys with the Frankfurt School and critical theory, and his attempt to develop conceptions of socialism and social freedom broadly within this framework, are clearly visible in these passages.

However, the adequacy of Honneth's position is not *per se* our primary concern.[91] What is important for our purposes is that he views the realization of socialism as the achievement of what he calls a democratic form of life. His analysis here raises issues that are central to participatory democracy.

Honneth starts from the position that identifying the potential for freedom in the spheres of personal relationships, the economy, and formal institutions of democratic will-formation is insufficient without some conception of how the interdependence of these spheres can be established and maintained: "Their relationship should enable them to follow their own, independent norms while at the same time freely cooperating in order to ensure the continuous reproduction of the society as a whole. Such purposeful cooperation between independent spheres of freedom represents the quintessence of a democratic way of life." Once again acknowledging his debt to John Dewey, Honneth goes on to argue that democracy "does not merely signify free and equal participation in political will-formation; understood as an entire way of life, it means that individuals can participate equally at every central point in the mediation between the individual and society, such that each functionally differentiated sphere reflects the general structure of democratic participation."[92]

The democratic way of life is how socialism should be understood as an emancipated society. This society at one and the same time should provide for the independence of the respective spheres of recognitive social relations and at the same time for a rational, harmonious order – without, however, requiring a central directing core, such as the system of production, to ensure this harmony. The image instead is of "an organic whole of independent and yet purposefully cooperating functions in which the members act for each other in social freedom."[93] The "democratic" element here rests on the willingness of the members of each sphere to cooperate as equals in pursuit of social knowledge that can help determine and develop potentials for enhanced social freedom. Social knowledge so acquired would foster the deepening of communicative and cooperative ties that are essential if the freedom of each is to be constitutive of the freedom of all. The open-ended quest to expand the capacity for social freedom, which cannot be considered apart from ties both within and between spheres, expresses and sustains communicative and developmental possibilities for individual agency. As these capacities grow and develop they would ideally promote the enrichment of norms of interaction consistent with the demands of each sphere, and at the same time and as a consequence enhance the potential for each to become an organ of social cooperation and democratic life. Although Honneth does not explicitly put it this way, we think he touches base here with what has always been a key theme of the Frankfurt School and critical theory: the necessary, dynamic, and dialectical relation between social character and social structure.[94]

A society that is democratic and socialist, without either a single fixed agent of transformation or a directing centre established by an *a priori* logic of social reproduction and progress, would still nonetheless require an authority for managing the relations among the independent spheres, or risk becoming what would essentially be an anonymous and apolitical form of structural-functional coordination. To once again stress that socialism as a democratic form of life must be a continuous accomplishment of social actors whose social freedom is secured through the very exercise of it, Honneth argues that the institution that should be responsible for "the task of integrative steering," the "social organ in a complex society … capable of reflexively steering the desired development of a complex society," is a vibrant public sphere. This is so because "the subsystem of action best suited to the task of reflexively steering overall social reproduction is that which provides the institutional framework for democratic will-formation."[95]

As Honneth spells it out,

> The sphere of democratic action stands out among the other functionally complementary spheres of freedom; it is *prima inter pares*, because it is the only place in which problems from every corner of social life can be articulated for all ears and be presented as a task to be solved in cooperation. In addition to the epistemic leading role of the political public sphere, and owing to its legitimizing influence on the legislature, this is the only social sphere with the power to turn seemingly plausible solutions into law. There can be no doubt that the democratic public sphere, occupied by deliberating citizens, must take over the role of supervising the functioning of the entire organic structure and of making the requisite adjustments. Functional differentiation, which thus far seemed to take place automatically, now becomes an object of democratic politics. In the democratic way of life, that which unfolds automatically in a living organism as the result of its internal structure ... is brought about by the subjects of the democratic process. They are the ones who correct and adjust the outcome of the entirety of their own activity by means of public deliberation.[96]

As with the account of socialism generally, this conception of a democratic way of life poses challenging issues. Key among them: the aspiration for engagement "at every central point in the mediation between the individual and society" notwithstanding, does this admittedly general formulation risk losing sight of a robust politics and citizenship for their own sake, as humanizing qualities crucial to social freedom itself? Is there here the danger of an ironic reiteration of the very "sublimation" of politics against which Sheldon Wolin warned and that Honneth himself associates with the limits of traditional socialism?

Nonetheless, the links between socialism, social freedom, and a democratic way of life, and the theories of participatory democracy we have considered in this chapter, are considerable and significant. Social freedom is an essential contribution to and component of a critical theory of democracy. Both, together, draw from the basic Hegelian formula of being with oneself in the other.

Indeed, the notion of social freedom might be said to incorporate the insights of both participatory and deliberative democracy. Deliberation forms a component of a fully participatory order, but according to Carole Pateman and Jeffrey Hilmer, deliberative theory tends to be indifferent to existing patterns of institutional structure and power, which it largely takes for granted. However, as we suggested in the introduction to this chapter, it is important to distinguish between weak and strong versions of deliberation and democratic theory. Strong versions of deliberative democracy are more critically inclined. They present the formation of individual preferences, norms, commitments, and so forth as itself a legitimate and indeed essential object of the very process of deliberation. This focus at least implies a concern for considering those requirements essential for Gould's equal positive freedom or Macpherson's developmental liberty. That is, strong versions of deliberative democracy can take on board the essential insight and commitment of participatory democracy: the creation of conditions under which individuals can come to view the freedom of the other as constitutive of their own, and where their own needs are not only served by but *defined* by the needs of others.

Theories of participatory democracy such as those of Pateman, Macpherson, and Gould more fully open up the possibilities for developing the conditions for social freedom because they target institutional structures and make the transformation, and not simply the preservation, of key sectors of social life potential objects of participatory initiative. In other words, they represent a form of democracy as a way of life that incorporates social freedom as an essential foundation. However, these theories too face challenges around the question not only of the location of participation and the kind of participation available, but also of whether this participation allows for and in turn builds upon the intertwining as opposed to overlapping of individual aims and purposes.

And for both participatory and deliberative democrats, the threats posed to democratic possibilities by global forces further complicate the challenges a critical theory of democracy must confront. Axel Honneth writes of the "tension between internationalism and an anchoring in local traditions," with the consequence that socialism, and thus democratic forms of life, "can only represent social freedom globally by means of a political doctrine, whereas it can only mobilize concrete and local publics by means of an ethically compact theory adapted to the cultural features of a certain region."[97] Whether considered from the perspective of participatory or deliberative democracy, the challenges posed by globalization, as well as those raised by participation, involve both the range of issues, institutions, and practices accessible to democratic publics, wherever they might be, and the real impact that citizen engagement might generate.

One final point stands out for us here. Social freedom as, so to speak, the essence of radical democracy opens up fundamental questions about individual agency and social structure. Its key elements are surely recognizable as real potentials, and even as actual dimensions, of existing political arrangements, at least as long as and insofar as the heritage of liberty, equality, and fraternity still resonates and can be drawn upon to make sense of this world and guide action towards a better one.[98] But can this heritage emerge unscathed from the impact of a neoliberalism that remains dominant, even in the face of the evident pathologies it has produced and continues to feed?

That a state of affairs may be desirable and even necessary, but may not ultimately be possible, is the sober insight upon which critical theory and the Frankfurt School has built. It is an insight that poses demanding challenges to a critical theory of democracy dedicated to realizing the goals of autonomy and self-development.

Critical Theory and Radical Reform

Throughout this book we have attempted to show that, however remote the possibilities might appear in the current era, there is still nonetheless the need for, and basis for, social transformation in the direction of a more richly democratic and egalitarian social order; and that a critical theory of radical democracy can inform such a project. In this conclusion we briefly revisit our key themes and address questions to which our analysis might give rise.

We have sought in this work to develop a version of critical theory that addresses the problems and challenges raised by neoliberalism. To this end we have considered both the methodological-diagnostic and political-theoretic foundations of critical theory to re-establish it as a radical democratic alternative. This theory can only have a socio-critical force when it offers a diagnosis of the pathologies of the times and points to a radically democratic solution.

Our approach contrasts with much of the dominant political theory today. Since 1989 the alternatives to today's capitalism have been limited. Not only has socialism been off the table, but even a significantly reformed capitalism has seemed unattainable. What remains is a slightly more humane version of liberal democracy. Even where theorists purport to be radical, their critique of liberal consensus and conceptions of conflict are built on dubious philosophical premises that provide little guidance for a democratic social order based on both self-determination and solidarity.

Similar problems plague current approaches to critical theory. Firmly ensconced in secure academic departments in which specialized scholarship is undertaken, many critical theorists have done interesting work but without the broader framework and oppositional stance of an earlier generation. While Jürgen Habermas carried the torch for an integrated interdisciplinary critical theory up to and including *The Theory of Communicative Action*, more recently he seems to have lost touch with larger social trends. The fact that he was surprised by the rise of reactionary populism speaks volumes about the ability, or inability, of contemporary critical theory to diagnose and address neoliberal social formations in an integrated interdisciplinary way. The work of Axel Honneth, Habermas's successor at Frankfurt and perhaps the most influential of the next generation of critical theorists, has also proved limited in important respects, although, as we argued in the previous chapter, in his recent work Honneth has sought to demonstrate that his formulation of democracy and reconsideration of socialism harbour considerable potential for informing the quest for radical social and political change.

We still think, however, that Habermas's account of discursive democracy in *Between Facts and Norms*, and Honneth's notion of social freedom, can contribute significantly to a critical theory adequate to the challenges of neoliberalism. These positions must be placed, however, in a broader context of radical and participatory democracy. More attention must be paid to democratizing the economy and the state and putting them under moral regulation.

The founders of critical theory staked their claim on a position that was politically radical, if no longer revolutionary, at least as revolution had come to be understood in the Marxist tradition. In their view, what was needed was the creation of a society qualitatively different from capitalism. When they were confronted with the reality of the political attitudes of the working classes under advanced capitalism they retreated into cultural pessimism and, in the case of Horkheimer and Adorno, a curious defence of the post–Second World War order. Even then, however, Horkheimer and Adorno did not entirely abandon their original position. In their 1956 discussion, "Towards a New Manifesto," they tried to recover a radical reading of Marxism based on a radical conception of labour.[1]

Still, Adorno and Horkheimer seemed to be left with an either/or. This was especially true of Horkheimer, who in his most Schopenhauerian moments thought that "we can expect no more of mankind than a more or less watered-down version of the American system." Adorno, the more optimistic of the two, thought that if the veil of reification were lifted progress would be possible. Yet both rejected any kind of reformism. The overcoming of what Adorno called the totally administered society could not be achieved peacefully. Both Horkheimer and Adorno were concerned with the question of planning that was central to the administrative state, as well as to the revolutionary reconstruction of society. Somehow planning had to be severed from its ties to bureaucratic domination.

In this respect Marcuse's later theory seemed to have the better of it. He identified a libidinal revolt against capitalist labour relations that rejected the surplus repression of advanced industrial societies. He found the basis for this revolt primarily in the youth and social movements of the 1960s. However useful this analysis of the cultural roots of political change and its location in an immanent dynamic that had emerged within capitalist society, it did not really address the weaknesses of the Frankfurt School's account of late capitalism; nor did it provide insight into a theory of democracy.

Writing in the 1930s to the 1960s (the 70s in the case of Marcuse) the first generation of the Frankfurt School could not have fully anticipated the character of neoliberalism. They were concerned primarily with the dynamics of late capitalism. Specifically, they were interested in the closure of political conflict, or at least class conflict, that the administered order had brought about. While the Frankfurt School theorists identified one important set of tendencies in late capitalist and even state socialist societies, they posited too much closure to the system. Whereas they thought that the administrative state foreclosed the possibility of fundamental change and immunized the social system against the cyclical crises that Marx analysed and that had plagued capitalist societies, a later generation of Frankfurt theorists have argued that late capitalist societies are not so totally immune to change and have generated their own crisis tendencies. Once the burdens of justification had been transferred from the economic to the political a new set of crises had become possible. Habermas, who drew on the work of Claus Offe and others, called these legitimation crises.

Late capitalist societies, as the first generation noted, relies on the depoliticization of much of everyday life and on a privatized familial or vocational ethic. Nonetheless, advanced capitalism still raises questions about justice and fairness. It is not simply the case that capitalism must deliver the goods. To the extent that governments engage in redistribution, or recognize welfare rights, issues around just distribution and of the social rights of individuals come to the fore, at least to the extent that their claims are based not merely on administrative performance but on social democratic and liberal democratic foundations.

As we noted above, the early Frankfurt School theorists especially were not sympathetic to many of the claims of the welfare state and social rights. They saw these as examples of the deformalization of law that typified authoritarian states or the authoritarian tendencies of democracies. (Habermas has advanced a similar view about the problems and limits of the welfare state.) They did not see immanent possibilities for change in these societies. However, developmental theories that took up Marx's ideal of the fullest expression of human potentials and possibilities to criticize the limits of unfettered markets did seem to pinpoint some capacities for critical reflection and action that could not be fully contained within the dominant structures of social life.

Once we get beyond the implicit either/or in some of the work of the first generation, the nature of radical democratic critique is called into question: can radical democracy find an immanent basis within capitalist societies, or must it reject all elements as capitalist machinations? Habermas and Honneth opt for the first alterative, as do other radical democrats. Habermas's early work on a public sphere that was independent of the state and provided the basis of a communicatively structured but institutionally unbounded public world in which participants expressed their political and social autonomy suggested at least the possibility of a radical democracy in which theoretically all could participate. It defended ideals of reflexive freedom and equality, trust, care and solidarity, self-determination and self-realization, even if in a limited form.

As one commentator summarizes it

> ... in the eighteenth and nineteenth centuries, a distinct forum for rational public debate emerged in most Western European countries. It constitutes an area of social life, separate from the state apparatus, within which citizens gather to converse about issues of the day in a free and unrestricted fashion, either literally as in the town square, or in diverse journals and periodicals. Debate proceeded according to universal standards of critical reason and argumentative structure that all could recognize and assent to; appeals to traditional dogmas, or to arbitrary subjective prejudices, were ruled inadmissible. Thus, it was in the public sphere that "discursive will formation" was actualized in the manner that represented the general social interest, as opposed to a class or sectional one.[2]

Of course, in practice the bourgeois public sphere was hardly universal. Still, despite the many criticisms this notion of the public serves as an ideal type that can be used to assess and criticize the (limited) extent of participation in public life. It provides the basis of a conception of popular sovereignty able to counter the neoliberal foreclosure of such sovereignty and active political engagement. It also defines discourse as requiring the mutual accountability, recognition and responsibility necessary for a democratic society. Habermas's earlier work, at least up until *The Theory of Communicative Action*, was clear that free public discourse could be conceived as possible, although not necessarily realized, within a capitalist social order.

To be sure, the rise of neoliberalism has brought back into focus economic issues that have been neglected in recent years, including the effects of social stratification, exploitation and inequality. We cannot, however, return to an unreconstructed accounts of class struggle or revolution that do not fit the conditions of advanced industrial societies. On the other hand, critical theory does not and cannot embrace the sterile alternatives of the third way or post-1989 liberalism. We think that the best way forward is to pursue in combination with a diagnosis of the times radical democratic reforms within society, reforms that could hold transformative possibilities. It is in this context that we considered Axel Honneth's reformulation of socialism as one potentially valuable approach to a radical democratic politics.

Habermas returned to a consideration of publics in *Between Facts and Norms* and expanded it in some respects. He employed there the idea of an institutionally unbounded sphere of communicative action within which public opinion could be formulated. Incorporating some of the insightful feminist critiques of the idealized bourgeois public sphere, Habermas considered publics in the first instance to be anarchic or wild. This idea is also linked to the notion of weak publics, which are constituted by informal discursive practices out of which opinions can be generated but which themselves lack formal decision-making power. Such publics are open and permeable, characteristics often lacking with more formalized practices.

The formation of opinions uncoupled from decision-making would ideally take place in an open and inclusive network of overlapping subcultural publics with fluid temporal, social and substantive boundaries. Within a framework guaranteed by constitutional rights, the structures of such a pluralistic public sphere could develop spontaneously. The currents of public communication would be channeled by mass media and would flow through different publics that develop informally inside associations; taken together these would form a "wild" complex that resists organization. Ideally, in other words, there is an "unsubverted public sphere" of unrestricted communication.[3]

Although this formulation is not immune to excessive idealization, it does provide an open-ended conception of a deeply democratized public life, one that could serve as a social basis for a radical democracy. The anarchic public is not, however, a highly structured discursive forum which is procedurally regulated but involves more informal processes of mutual understanding. We appeal to a variety of sources and influences in order to foster challenges and create new ideas. This can include dramatic and expressive or aesthetic elements. Practices and commitments associated with the structures of anarchic publics would involve the entirety of our relations to ourselves, others, and the world.

In this study we have tried using somewhat different vocabularies to emphasize the importance of these more informal notions of discourse incorporating solidarity and concern, without losing focus on the life-world basis of accountability and mutual recognition. In our view, notions of mutual understanding can incorporate a very wide range of possible forms of intersubjective communication, as well as inclusion of others. The quest for mutual understanding can be dramatic or emotional because it can involve our concern for the welfare of others and/or identification with them because of our common humanity. These are potentially significant ways of expressing equality and responsibility.

We think, however, that the model of interpretive capacities that we employ, while certainly compatible with Habermas's position, is one that permits us to move beyond it and thus at least potentially offer greater explanatory insight. Instead of viewing individuals as engaged in the spontaneous generation of opinions, it might be better to see them as members of a lifeworld who very roughly share a common situation. Lifeworld participants reproduce this world thorough processes of mutual accountability. This might have different dimensions. For example, taken for granted processes and structures could become problematic; that is, we could find our normal expectations are not fulfilled and we have dissonant experiences which cannot fit into our interpretive frames. Or, we might endure disappointments or encounter obstacles to the realization of our aims and purposes. On the other hand, because of our actions we may face informal disapproval and sanctions, including exclusion from opportunities or even from group membership; this could create feelings of guilt or shame. Whatever the nature of such breakdowns of everyday expectations within the context of the requirements of mutual accountability, these may not always be viewed as formal "problems."

Such situations call for reinterpretation, reimagination and renegotiation of our forms of understanding and of acting in concert. It is through these processes of ordinary understanding, which are pre-structured but open to criticism and change, that private troubles can become public issues.

Habermas and feminist theorists recognize that such informal processes are open to the influences of power and systematic inequalities. Communicative interaction can be distorted, elements and topics of discussion excluded, and interests suppressed. Dissonant experiences can be invalidated and denied as pathological by dominant powers and social groups. We outlined some of these possibilities in chapter 2. For

Habermas, this means that the democratic operation of public opinion requires support. The so-called spontaneous generation of weak public opinion relies upon a system of rights that guarantees that individuals have basic forms of equality and freedom. They can in theory appeal to such rights against mechanisms of oppression and domination and make legitimate demands that these be eliminated.

Habermas's conception of constitutional democracy is an attempt to combine what he views as the liberal emphasis on individual rights with the republican discourse of popular sovereignty. He does not see these as opposed principles in which rights trump popular sovereignty, or vice versa, but instead as co-originary. To paraphrase, citizens cannot be free and autonomous in the public sphere that republicans emphasize without private autonomy. Individuals who enjoy only public status would not have sufficient freedom to choose autonomously. But without public freedom there is no constitutional guarantee of private rights. Private rights are not purely natural rights but are secured through the agreement of all. The basic ideas behind both private and public rights are self-legislation and self-determination. We can only assent to those laws that we freely agree to in a process of deliberation.

Habermas's notion of the co-originary character of rights and popular sovereignty distinguishes his conception of radical democracy from, for example, Benjamin Barber's notion of strong democracy.[4] While Barber, like Habermas, rejects unitary democracy – that is, the republican ideal of a single social ethos – and accepts the central significance of rights, he accords rights a lesser role in relation to self-legislation.

Legal (emerging from parliaments and congresses), administrative and judicial decisions among others must be based on a more formal model of deliberation than anarchic publics. These deliberative processes entail the conditions of equality, equal freedom and responsibility on the part of those who deliberate, where all are in principle included. To be sure, legislative and other formal political and legal bodies cannot include every participant, but Habermas believes that in a fully democratic society the discursive impulses of wild publics would be transmitted to deliberative bodies. The constitutional project, however, is not a one-time phenomenon. It is an ongoing project of deliberation in which we try to realize and even reinterpret the basic ideals of a constitution. Habermas terms his approach constitutional patriotism. Rather than viewing patriotism as attachment to tradition and a national culture, he instead conceives it both as solidarity with all those who are subjects of rights and responsibilities and as commitment to the constitution as form of life compatible with a nation of plural cultures.

We agree that a modern society cannot be grasped from the vantage point of a pure popular will but must include a system of rights. There cannot be a single social ethos because division and disagreement are unavoidable. This may disconcert those who think that an emphasis on rights entails an embrace of, at best, a formalist, purely proceduralist liberalism. But as the work of Carol Gould makes clear, when we understand rights as tied to a socially embedded conception of self-determination, and not simply to an isolated or atomized individual, rights discourse can hold considerable potential for a radical theory of freedom. Habermas's position here bears some relation to that of Gould, as well as that of C.B. Macpherson, whose connection to Gould we explored in chapter 6. Gould, Macpherson, and Habermas all defend the radical potential of bourgeois right and protections for a socialist theory. Of course, rights claims here are taken broadly to mean more than just civil or personal, legal rights. The radical potential of these claims lies in the fact that they cannot be realized within capitalism itself. Such claims must include political, economic, and social rights, or what Macpherson called developmental rights.

Critics, however, are not sure that this account of rights goes far enough. They contend that liberal rights and protections, individual or social, are insufficient. The best one can achieve with an emphasis on rights is to provide a basis for a form of social democracy that would ideally tame the excesses of capitalism, but not point to its overcoming.

A second criticism has been voiced by Kenneth Baynes who questions whether informal processes of public opinion associated with a vibrant public sphere will in the long run lead to the kind of productive changes that Habermas assumes. Referring more broadly to Habermas's faith in procedural rationality, he asks, "whether Habermas's confidence in the rationality effect of procedure is sufficiently well founded."[5] Another way of looking at this concern is to ask, as Baynes does, if Habermas's conception of an anarchic civil society can generate solidarity and civic virtue. These questions cannot really be answered in the more theoretical conception of free opinion formation, as we have noted. To properly address them requires not just an emphasis on rights, even social rights, taken in isolation, but also reflection on our embeddedness in a social lifeworld. Conflicts emerge within the lifeworld wherever or whenever problems and troubles arise. Everyday action has a structure based on mutual accountability, a structure that is conducive to deliberation. But the extent to which the lifeworld can be rationalized in this manner depends on social forces. We must place this question within a diagnostic social theory that identifies the crisis tendencies of neoliberal capitalism; this is at the core of our distinction between weak and strong forms of deliberative democracy. If democratic institutions are strong, then there could certainly be a basis for a more democratic social order. But there would also have to be socialization processes of education and the establishment of norms. In a society with wide ranging participation and discussion, and proper institutional support, it seems likely that such issues would be discussed, and more egalitarians and democratic practices would emerge. Of course, there are no final guarantees. But the search for a theory that can provide ultimate guarantees is fruitless.

There are some respects in which Habermas's hope that his theory will tame capitalism seems limited. History shows that the establishment of social democracies in advanced capitalist societies was met by opposition and indeed over the course of the last three decades social democratic reforms have been rolled back in Europe and North America. Under what conditions would these reforms be more permanently anchored in these societies? Habermas's own theory of legitimation crisis indicates that welfare states are subject to multiple dilemmas and contradictions. These include not just political crises, which Habermas emphasizes, but also economic ones. Owners of capital have economic means to disrupt welfare states and certainly social democratic ones. They can engage in capital strikes, that is, they can refuse to invest if they think profitable opportunities are absent or limited, or when they think government policies are unfriendly to investment. They can exert political pressure to enact policies that favour their interests, resulting in greater inequality. These factors would seem to challenge the idea of a radical democratized lifeworld that Habermas desires, but they would also affect those transmission lines between the lifeworld and formal legal institutions that Habermas holds are necessary for a constitutional democracy.

In this regard we believe that an informal democratic public, as well as a formal procedural one, would require a strong component of public property to counter the power of capitalist private property. We do not think Habermas's recent writings on transnational justice and post-national political and economic structures contain a sufficient notion of social crisis that would allow him to analyse the problems neoliberalism generates in national and international economies. These have worked to undermine the protections of the welfare state and have produced greater inequalities. Moreover, in many neoliberal societies a reactionary populist backlash has occurred which threatens both social rights and popular sovereignty. In contrast to Habermas's account, we have tried to indicate some of the major outlines of these pathologies. However, Habermas's conceptions of rights and popular sovereignty can provide an important alternative to neoliberalism.

To realize these principles, however, we think that a critical theory has to more explicitly formulate notions of participatory democracy, social rights and social freedom. The ethical ideals of self-realization that found a new modern form in the developmental theories of the nineteenth century do not simply reflect demands for personal happiness, or an ancient ideal of wisdom, but are elements of the modernist notion of autonomy. They represent ethical ideals of a self-conscious and reflective form of life in which individuals robustly develop their own identities and a conscious reflexive understanding of their life histories within a framework of solidarity with others. Our conception of radical democracy would also include a strong emphasis on self-realization. This seems consistent with Marx's own remarks on self-realization in a post-capitalist society – although we see these developments as immanent in advanced capitalism.

The structures of personality and culture that support these developments are fragile and require, as we have noted above, legal support and protection. Here we think the idea of social rights that we discussed at length in chapter 6 can help identify what such supports and protections might entail.

Habermas often looks at the economy and bureaucracy as non-communicative systems that allow for the greater development of political and social freedoms because they relieve individuals of many of the costly and time-consuming burdens associated with social and material reproduction. For example, he speaks of administration as a command structure in which authority serves the realization of collective goals: "the authority to issue binding commands means that the superior does not have to convince subordinates of the advisability of each task assigned to them, thus reducing the need for explicit consensus."[6] Similarly, markets serve in theory as means to coordinate economic activity without explicit consensus. The strategic actions of individuals pursuing interests in the market are supposed to ensure the most efficient distribution of goods and services.

While such arguments no doubt have a certain plausibility, they overstate the benefits of non-consensual coordination, and indeed to a considerable extent offer only a limited and indeed misleading conception of what such coordination entails. As is well known, these ideal models of strategic coordination have run into serious problems internal to their assumptions. This has led many rational choice theorists to supplement their models with the introduction of conceptions of prior normative constraints. Nor are markets or bureaucracies established through independent logics of strategic action. As we discussed in chapter 3, even ordo-liberals argue that the market is established only under legal constraints – something Habermas and Max Weber would also agree upon – but that it is not truly autonomous and must be constantly maintained by extra-economic forces – something they may not have accepted. Other critics from the left have pointed out that the border between non-consensual and normative bases of the economy are porous. Thus, while we still agree with Weber and Habermas that the differentiation of society into separate spheres is necessary and desirable we think that Habermas's conception of the dominance of non-consensual coordination in some areas must be modified.

It is in this context that we contend that a more participatory democratic approach to all aspects of social life is warranted. Analysts such as Carmen Siriani and Lew Friedlander have illustrated some of the ways in which participation can improve political bureaucracies and not just economic institutions.[7] Forms of collaborative learning and institutional problem solving can make bureaucracies more democratic and less a matter of command and control. Moreover, public administrators can cooperate with citizen groups to accomplish social goals. Here, again, consensual action within the framework of communicative reason with its commitments to mutual accountability and justification can define and facilitate self-development and self-realization, individual and social freedom, public and private autonomy.

Some contemporary theories of radical democracy tie their radicalism to a rejection of consensus. According to these accounts, consensual action is no more than a liberal tool which enforces closure and erases difference. This is a common charge levelled by post-structuralists against communicative and interpretive social theories. The close reader, however, will see that claims of closure and finality advanced against critical theory are unfounded. There is no need for a notion of difference or essential conflict utterly beyond the reach of consensual social action because consensual action provides the medium though which we articulate both conflict and agreement, alienation and solidarity. The intersubjective framework includes both the "otherness" of the stranger and the community we build with those others. The lifeworld is reproduced through acts of mutual understanding in an open-ended and open-textured process in which we engage others through interaction that includes both agreement and disagreement. To exercise communicative power, then, is to act in concert with others to authorize action.

Although it is in the first instance anchored in a theoretical account of practical action, communicative power could easily serve as a crucial element of a radical democracy. The generative quality of communicative power is captured in Hannah Arendt's idea that through collective action we can always begin anew, where new beginnings include radical change or even revolution. Communicative power and the communicative action with which it is necessarily tied also suggests those "moments" of democratic change central to Sheldon Wolin's conception of fugitive democracy, although without his particular neo-Weberian assumptions which limit these occurrences to fleeting moments of freedom in the face of the bureaucratic domination that characterizes modern society.[8] We think this conception of democracy entails a notion of communicative freedom that is too restrictive, even for our society. To develop forms of democratic life is to enhance the communicative power of subjects and their ability to create new practices, new social and political relations. Of course, all this depends upon a more fully developed social theory. But without a notion such as communicative power, or some equivalent, radical democratic theories are not very radical.

In the end, however, we are not concerned about our fidelity to the work of Habermas, or indeed to any other position. We hope the ideas we have sought to develop in this work stand on their own and can contribute to what we believe to be a much-needed reconsideration of the demands of democracy in the neoliberal era.

Notes

Notes to Chapter 1

1 Charles Taylor, "What's Wrong with Negative Liberty?," in *Philosophy and the Human Sciences*, ed. Charles Taylor (Cambridge: Cambridge University Press, 1985), 213.

2 For earlier work that treats the themes and concerns discussed here, see Brian Caterino and Phillip Hansen, "Macpherson, Habermas, and the Demands of Democratic Theory," *Studies in Political Economy* 83 (Spring 2009): 85–110; and Phillip Hansen, *Reconsidering C.B. Macpherson: From Possessive Individualism to Democratic Theory and Beyond* (Toronto: University of Toronto Press, 2015). Parts of this chapter are drawn from this earlier work.

3 C.B. Macpherson, "Humanist Democracy and Elusive Marxism: A Response to Minogue and Svacek," *Canadian Journal of Political Science* 9, no. 3 (September 1976): 423.

4 For a thoughtful analysis of the relation between Macpherson and Laski, see Peter Lamb and David Morrice, "Ideological Reconciliation in the Thought of C.B. Macpherson and Harold Laski," *Canadian Journal of Political Science* 35, no. 4 (December 2002): 795–810.

5 For an account of the move away from a Keynesian "welfare" to a Schumpeterian "workfare" state in the face of changes in capitalism, see Bob Jessop, "Towards a Schumpeterian Workfare State? Preliminary Remarks on Post-Fordist Political Economy," *Studies in Political Economy* 40 (Spring 1993). The form of democracy that accompanied the KWS was labelled by C.B. Macpherson as the "pluralist, elitist, equilibrium" model. See Macpherson, *The Life and Times of Liberal Democracy* (Oxford: Oxford University Press, 1977), 77.

6 See Christopher Pierson, *Beyond the Welfare State? The New Political Economy of Welfare*, 3rd ed. (University Park: Pennsylvania State University Press, 2007).

7 Naomi Klein, *The Shock Doctrine: The Rise of Disaster Capitalism* (Toronto: Alfred A. Knopf Canada, 2007); and David Harvey, *Spaces of Global Capitalism* (London and New York: Verso, 2006); and *Limits to Capital* (London and New York: Verso, 2006).

8 See, for example, Benjamin Barber, *Fear's Empire: War, Terrorism, and Democracy* (New York: W.W. Norton, 2004); and Henry Giroux, *Terror of Neoliberalism: Authoritarianism and the Eclipse of Democracy* (Boulder: Paradigm Publishers, 2004).

9 On this issue see Claus Offe, *Contradictions of the Welfare State*, ed. John Keane (Cambridge, MA: MIT Press, 1984).

10 There has been more extensive discussion of the negative effects of neoliberalism outside of the political theory literature on democracy. Examples include Ulrich Beck, *World Risk Society* (Cambridge: Polity Press, 1999); Ulrich Beck, Anthony Giddens, and Scott Lash, *Reflexive Modernization: Politics, Tradition, and Aesthetics in the Modern Social Order* (Stanford: Stanford University Press, 1994) (on the transfer of risk and vulnerability); Kevin Phillips, *Wealth and Democracy: A Political History of the American Rich* (New York: Random House, 2004); Lawrence R. Jacobs and Theda Skocpol, *Inequality and American Democracy: What We Know and What We Need to Know* (New York: Russell Sage Foundation, 2007); Dean Baker, *The United States since 1980* (New York: Cambridge University Press, 2007); Steve Kerstetter, *Rags and Riches: Wealth Inequality in Canada* (Ottawa: Canadian Centre for Policy Alternatives, 2002); and Armine Yalnizyan, *The Rich and the Rest of Us: The changing Face of Canada's Growing Gap* (Ottawa: Canadian Centre for Policy Alternatives, 2007) (on growing inequality of wealth). Of course Thomas Piketty's *Capital in the Twenty-First Century*, trans. Arthur Goldhammer (Cambridge, MA: Belknap Press of Harvard University Press, 2014), which emerged as a surprise international bestseller despite its daunting size and detailed historical and policy focus, has played a critical role in highlighting the challenge of global inequality.

11 However, it does fit well with a powerful neoliberal conception of democracy that David Held labels "legal democracy": a minimal and constitutional state in which the power of governments to intervene in the workings of the "free" market, particularly in the interests of social justice, is severely constrained. Held identifies Robert Nozick and, especially, Friedrich von Hayek as key contributors to this model. See David Held, *Models of Democracy*, 3rd ed. (Stanford: Stanford University Press, 2006), 201ff.

12 For good summaries of contemporary theoretical perspectives, see Held, *Models of Democracy*; and Frank Cunningham, *Theories of Democracy: A Critical Introduction* (London and New York: Routledge, 2002).

13 Ian Shapiro, *Democratic Justice* (New Haven: Yale University Press, 1999), 144–5.

14 Ian Shapiro, *The State of Democratic Theory* (Princeton: Princeton University Press, 2003), 146.

15 Joseph Heath, *The Efficient Society: Why Canada Is as Close to Utopia as It Gets* (Toronto: Penguin Books, 2001), 36. See also Heath, *Communicative Action and Rational Choice* (Cambridge, MA: MIT Press, 2001). Heath's argument here raises the old problem of who makes the rules to constrain those who make the rules. This problem is unavoidable if one operates from the assumptions of self-regarding self-interest and the primacy of strategic rationality.

16 See, for example, John S. Dryzek, *Democracy in Capitalist Times: Ideals, Limits, and Struggles* (Oxford: Oxford University Press, 1996). To be sure, Dryzek provides here suggestive and useful criteria – franchise, scope, and authenticity – for appraising democratic institutions. We discuss these criteria and their value for democratic thinking in chapter 6.

17 Nancy Fraser and Axel Honneth, *Redistribution or Recognition? A Political-Philosophical Exchange*, trans. Joel Golb, James Ingram, and Christiane Wilke (London and New York: Verso, 2003), esp. 90–2. This issue is at the heart of the debate between Fraser and Honneth, with Honneth's position more closely aligned with the positions of Macpherson and Habermas.

   To be sure, in the wake of the global financial crisis of 2008–9 and subsequent economic turbulence, Fraser has more explicitly sought to address the nature of contemporary capitalism and its consequences for democracy and social justice. Her analysis, which seeks to extend the account of the relation of redistribution to recognition and of the injustices and harms generated by distorted forms of each, relies extensively on the work of Karl Polanyi and his well-known critique of capitalism's propensity to commodify dimensions of human experience that ought to be shielded from commodification because efforts at commodification invariably have a destructive impact. Polanyi famously identified land, labour, and money as the most significant phenomena that ought to be immune to commodification because they are not produced in order to be exchanged. As "fictitious" commodities, they represent social pathologies in terms of their presence and impact. For her analysis of the current situation, and of the value, but also the limits, of Polanyi's approach and ideas for a critical account of the present, see, for example, Nancy Fraser, "Can Society Be Commodities All the Way Down? Post-Polanyian Reflections on Capitalist Crisis," *Economy and Society* 43, no. 4 (November 2014): 541–58.

18 C.B. Macpherson, "On Friedman's Freedom" [1968, in *Democratic Theory: Essays in Retrieval*] (Oxford: Oxford University Press, 1973), 144–5. Hereafter cited as DT.

19 Ibid., 146.

20 Ibid., 151ff.

21 Isaiah Berlin, "Two Concepts of Liberty," in *Four Essays on Liberty* (Oxford: Oxford University Press, 1969), 131.

22 Taylor, "What's Wrong with Negative Liberty?," 211–29.

23 Ibid., 171.

24 Ibid., 130–1.

25 Cf. Jürgen Habermas, "Three Normative Models of Democracy," in *The Inclusion of the Other: Studies in Political Theory*, ed. Ciaran Cronin and Pablo De Greiff (Cambridge, MA: MIT Press, 1998), 239–52.

26 Macpherson, "Berlin's Division of Liberty," in DT, 109.

27 On this distinction, see Alisdair MacIntyre, "On *Democratic Theory: Essays in Retrieval* by C.B. Macpherson," *Canadian Journal of Philosophy* 6, no. 2 (June 1976), 177–81. See also Phillip Hansen, "T.H. Green and the Moralization of the Market," *Canadian Journal of Political and Social Theory* 1, no. 1 (Winter 1977), 80–104.

28 Macpherson, "Berlin's Division of Liberty," 115.

29 Ibid., 114.

30 See, for example, Shapiro, *The State of Democratic Theory*, ch. 5; and Dryzek, *Democracy in Capitalist Times*.

31 Berlin, "Two Concepts of Liberty," 154.

32 Macpherson, "Berlin's Division of Liberty," 113–14.

33 Macpherson, "Problems of a Non-Market Theory of Democracy," in *Democratic Theory: Essays in Retrieval*, 55.

34 Ibid. (emphasis in original). For a comparable account of rights see Carol Gould, *Globalizing Democracy and Human Rights* (Cambridge: Cambridge University Press, 2004). We discuss Gould's analysis more fully in chapter 6.

35 Macpherson, "Berlin's Division of Liberty," 117ff.

36 Ibid., 103.

37 An example of how one way of conceiving Macpherson's argument plays out in the contemporary world is provided by Jonathan Wolff in his treatment of affirmative action, a public policy clearly informed by considerations of developmental liberty. He claims that "a world which includes affirmative action is not an ideal one. As a long-term policy, affirmative action is undesirable, and in certain respects unjust. People should be treated on their individual merits, as critics of affirmative action claim. But without a temporary policy of affirmative action it will be much harder to create a world in which affirmative action is unnecessary: in which people *are* treated on their individual merits. So we should see affirmative action as a transitional policy in a step towards a more just world." Wolff, *An Introduction to Political Philosophy*, rev. ed. (Oxford: Oxford University Press, 2006), 189.

38 Macpherson, "Problems of a Non-Market Theory of Democracy," 74.

39 Macpherson, "Berlin's Division of Liberty," 117–18.

40 For an assessment of Habermas's position, see Rene Von Schomberg and Kenneth Baynes, eds., *Discourse and Democracy: Essays on Habermas's Between Facts and Norms* (Albany: SUNY Press, 2002), hereafter cited as BFN; and Michael Rosenfeld and Andrew Arato, eds., *Habermas on Law and Democracy: Critical Exchanges* (Berkeley: University of California Press, 1998). For a more general treatment of deliberative democracy, see, for example, James Bohman, *Public Deliberation: Pluralism, Complexity, and Democracy* (Cambridge, MA: MIT Press, 2000).

41 This is particularly true of "Three Normative Models of Democracy," although his terminology there is slightly different from the one we've used here.

42 Ibid., 107.

43 Ibid., 110.

44 Jürgen Habermas, "Constitutional Democracy: A Paradoxical Union of Contradictory Principles?" (trans. William Rehg), *Political Theory* 29, no. 6 (December 2001): 767.

45 Ibid., 768.

46 For an excellent review and summary of the ideas and historical significance of the Frankfurt School, see Peter M.R. Stirk, *Critical Theory, Politics, and Society: An Introduction* (London and New York: Pinter, 2000).

47 See Jürgen Habermas, *Postmetaphysical Thinking*, trans. W.M. Hohengarten (Cambridge, MA: MIT Press, 1992).

48 Habermas, BFN, 32.

49 Ibid., 176.

50 This Hegelian element has been laid out explicitly and systematically in the work of Axel Honneth, notably in *Freedom's Right* and *The Idea of Socialism*. We will discuss this aspect of Honneth's work in chapter 6.

51 Habermas, BFN, chs. 7–8.

52 Ibid., ch. 9.

53 Ibid., 438.

54 Ibid., 442.

55 See Jürgen Habermas, *Europe: The Faltering Project*, trans. Ciaran Cronin (Cambridge: Polity Press, 2009); *The Crisis of the European Union: A Response*, trans. Ciaran Cronin (Cambridge: Polity Press, 2012); and, especially, *The Lure of Technocracy*, trans. Ciaran Cronin (Cambridge: Polity Press, 2015), where, commenting on the work of Wolfgang Streeck, who explores the contradictions between capitalism and democracy, and their relation to the crisis in Europe, Habermas explicitly addresses this issue from his cosmopolitan perspective, which suffers from an excess of normativity that seems limited in the face of the challenges involved.

56 For an examination of this issue, see Martin Beck Matustik, *Jürgen Habermas: A Philosophical-Political Profile* (Lanham: Rowman and Littlefield, 2001).

57 There are partial exceptions to this admittedly sweeping claim. See, for example, Jürgen Habermas, "What Does Socialism Mean Today? The Revolutions of Recuperation and the Need for New Thinking," in *After the Fall: The Failure of Communism and the Future of Socialism*, ed. Robin Blackburn (London and New York: Verso, 1991), 25–46. For a thorough account and critical analysis of Habermas's position, see John Sitton, *Habermas and Contemporary Society* (New York: Palgrave Macmillan, 2003).

58 Scheuerman suggests that in *Between Facts and Norms*, Habermas seems simultaneously and inconsistently to offer both an account of "an *ambitious* radical democratic polity, based on far-reaching social equality, and outfitted with far-reaching capacities for overseeing bureaucratic and market mechanisms" and "a *defensive* model of deliberative democracy in which democratic institutions offer at best an attenuated check on market and administrative processes, and where deliberative publics most of the time tend to remain, as Habermas himself describes it, at rest." William Scheuerman, "Between Radicalism and Resignation: Democratic Theory in Habermas's *Between Facts and Norms*," in Baynes and Von Schonberg, eds., *Discourse and Democracy*, 63–4.

59 Macpherson, "The Maximization of Democracy," in DT, 11.

60 For an exception to this neglect or misunderstanding, see Jules Townshend, *C.B. Macpherson and the Problem of Liberal Democracy* (Edinburgh: Edinburgh University Press, 2000), esp. ch. 4. For a discussion that explicitly relates the net transfer of powers to the theory of surplus value, see Victor Svacek, "The Elusive Marxism of C.B. Macpherson," *Canadian Journal of Political Science* 9, no. 3 (September 1976): 395–422. For a fuller treatment of the net transfer of powers and its central place in Macpherson's thought, see Hansen, *Reconsidering C.B. Macpherson*, ch. 2.

61 Macpherson, "Problems of a Non-Market Theory of Democracy," 65–6.

62 Ibid., 66.

63 Macpherson does spell out what he considers distinctively human attributes; these include (but are not necessarily restricted to) "the capacity for rational understanding, for moral judgement and action, for aesthetic creation or contemplation, for the emotional activities of friendship and love, and, sometimes, for religious experience" (Macpherson, "The Maximization of Democracy," 4). It would be difficult to disagree with any of these.

64 For some fascinating and even brilliant comments on these meta-methodological issues, issues he is not normally seen as concerned to address, see C.B. Macpherson, "Humanist Marxism and Elusive Marxism: A Response to Minogue and Svacek," *Canadian Journal of Political Science* 9,

no. 3 (September 1976): 423–30. See also his "The Economic Penetration of Political Theory: Some Hypotheses," *Journal of the History of Ideas* 39, no. 1 (January–March 1978): 101–18. For a fuller discussion of Macpherson's approach to questions of theory and methodology, see Hansen, *Reconsidering C.B. Macpherson*, ch. 6.

65 Macpherson, "Problems of a Non-market Theory of Democracy," 39.

Notes to Chapter 2

1 Max Horkheimer, "The Latest Attack on Metaphysics," in *Critical Theory: Selected Essays* (New York: Continuum, 1999), 132–87.

2 See Anthony Giddens, "Positivism and Its Critics," in *Studies in Social and Political Theory* (London: Hutchinson, 1979), ch. 1, for a good overview of positivism.

3 Horkheimer, "The Latest Attack on Metaphysics," 138.

4 Max Horkheimer, "Materialism and Metaphysics," in *Critical Theory*, 43. This point, as well as Horkheimer's critique of positivism, is discussed in Peter M.R. *Stirk, Max Horkheimer A New Interpretation* (Latham: Harvester/Barnes and Noble, 1992). John Abromeit discusses the early Horkheimer's views on positivism in *Max Horkheimer and the Foundations of the Frankfurt School* (Cambridge: Cambridge University Press, 2011).

5 "Horkheimer, "Latest Attack on Metaphysics," 156.

6 Ibid., 158.

7 See Max Horkheimer, "The Problem of Truth," in *Between Philosophy and Social Science: Selected Early Writings* (Cambridge, MA: MIT Press, 1993), 177–215. See also Thomas McCarthy, "The Idea of a Critical Theory and Its Relation to Philosophy," in *On Max Horkheimer: New Perspectives*, ed. Seyla Benhabib, Wolfgang Bonss, and John McCole (Cambridge, MA: MIT Press, 1993), 127–52.

8 Horkheimer, "The Problem of Truth," 204.

9 Ibid.

10 Horkheimer, "Traditional and Critical Theory," in *Critical Theory*, 209.

11 Ibid.

12 Horkheimer, "Postscript" (to Traditional and Critical Theory), 245–6.

13 *The Encyclopedia Logic: Part I of the Encyclopedia of the Philosophical Sciences*, trans. with introduction and notes by T.F. Geraets, W.H. Suchting, and H.S. Harris (Indianapolis: Hackett, 1991), 286.

14 Horkheimer, "On the Problem of Truth," in *Between Philosophy and Social Science*, 204.

15 T.W. Adorno, "Why Still Philosophy?" [1962], in *Critical Models: Interventions and Catchwords*, ed. T.W. Adorno (New York: Columbia University Press, 1998), 7.

16 Albrecht Wellmer, "Adorno and the Difficulties of a Critical Reconstruction of the Historical Present," *Theodor-W.-Adorno-Prize Lecture*, City of Frankfurt, Germany, 11 September 2006, 11.

17 Axel Honneth, *The Critique of Power: Reflective Stages in a Critical Social Theory*, trans. K. Baynes (Cambridge, MA: MIT Press, 1991); and *The Fragmented World of the Social: Essays in Social and Political Philosophy*, ed. C.W. Wright (Albany: SUNY Press, 1995).

18 Axel Honneth, *Reification: A New Look at an Old Idea*, ed. and intro. M. Jay (New York: Oxford University Press, 2008).

19 Ronald Beiner, *What's the Matter with Liberalism?* (Berkeley: University of California Press, 1992).

20 Seyla Benhabib, "Autonomy, Modernity and Community: Communitarianism and Critical Social Theory in Dialogue," in *Cultural Political Interventions in the Unfinished Project of Enlightenment*, ed. Albrecht Wellmer, Thomas McCarthy, Claus Offe, and Albrecht Wellmer (Cambridge, MA: MIT Press, 1992), 39–61.

21 T.H. Green, *Lectures on the Principles of Political Obligation* [1885] (Kitchener: Batoche Books, 1999).

22 Notably, Dewey linked communication to his idea of the Great Community in *The Public and Its Problems*. The centrality of communication is also emphasized in *Philosophy of Education*. For Mead see *Mind, Self, and Society*.

23 Jürgen Habermas, *The Philosophical Discourse of Modernity*, trans. Frederick Lawrence (Cambridge, MA: MIT Press, 1987), 322.

24 Charles Taylor, "Self-Interpreting Animals," in *Human Agency and Language: Philosophical Papers*, vol. 1 (Cambridge: Cambridge University Press, 1985), 45–76. See as well Taylor's recent major study that further develops and expands upon his long-standing interest in language, *The Language Animal: The Full Shape of the Human Linguistic Capacity* (Cambridge, MA, and London: The Belknap Press of Harvard University Press, 2016).

25 Horkheimer, "Traditional and Critical Theory," 245–6.

26 Thomas McCarthy, *Ideals and Illusions: On Reconstruction and Deconstruction in Contemporary Critical Theory* (Cambridge, MA: MIT Press, 1992), 45.

27 Jürgen Habermas, "Morality and Ethical Life: Does Hegel's Critique of Kant Apply to Discourse Ethics?," in *Moral Consciousness and Communicative Action* (Cambridge, MA: MIT Press, 1990), 195–215.

28 Jürgen Habermas, "From Kant to Hegel and Back Again: The Move Toward Detranscendentalization," in *Truth and Justification* (Cambridge, MA: MIT Press, 2003), 175–212.

29 Habermas, "Morality and Ethical Life." For an account and a qualified defence of Habermas's argument, see David Martinez, "Habermas's Discourse Ethics and Hegel's Critique of Kant: Agent Neutrality, Ideal Role

Taking, and Rational Discourse," *Philosophy and Socialism* (Web, 17 April 2018), 1–18.

30 Anthony Giddens, *New Rules of the Sociological Method*, 2nd ed. (Stanford: Stanford University Press, 1993).

31 Amy Gutman and Dennis Thompson, "What Deliberative Democracy Means," in *Why Deliberative Democracy*, ed. Gutman and Thompson (Princeton: Princeton University Press, 2004), esp. 3–7.

32 Ibid., 7.

33 James Johnson and Jack Knight, "The Priority of Democracy," in *Political Consequences of Pragmatism* (Princeton: Princeton University Press, 2011); David Ingram discusses external and internal approaches to democratic theory in *Habermas: Introduction and Analysis* (Ithaca: Cornell University Press, 2010), 155–60.

34 This argument is made most influentially by Isaiah Berlin in his classic essay "Two Concepts of Liberty," which we discussed in chapter 1.

35 See Charles Taylor, *Philosophical Arguments* (Cambridge, MA: Harvard University Press, 1995), 129. See our discussion in chapter 1. For additional treatment of these points, see Phillip Hansen, *Reconsidering C.B. Macpherson: From Possessive Individualism to Democratic Theory and Beyond* (Toronto: University of Toronto Press, 2015), 204ff.

36 Max Weber, *The Theory of Social and Economic Organization*, ed. and trans. A.M. Henderson and Talcott Parsons (Glencoe: Free Press, 1947), 152.

37 Robert Dahl, "The Concept of Power," *Behavioral Science* 2 (1957): 202–10. The object of Dahl's critique is C. Wright Mills, *The Power Elite* (New York and Oxford: Oxford University Press, 1956), and the work of community power theorists such as Floyd Hunter. See Hunter, *Community Power Structures: A Study of Decision-Makers* (Chapel Hill: University of North Carolina Press, 1969).

38 Terrance Ball, "New Faces of Power," in *Rethinking Power*, ed. Thomas Wartenberg (Albany: SUNY Press, 1992), 16.

39 In response, Dahl and others have conceded that business had an inordinate influence on decisions, but this only goes a short distance in explaining the workings of power. However, see Dahl, *Who Governs: Democracy and Power in an American City*, 2nd ed. (New Haven: Yale University Pres, 2005), which contains important concessions to the power theorists. And Dahl's contemporary, Charles Lindblom, in *Politics and Markets: The World's Political-Economic Systems* (New York: Basic Books, 1977), adopts a neopluralist approach in which he still accepts the centrality of competing interests yet concedes that business interests have a privileged position within elites to gain power and control.

40 William Domhoff, *Who Rules America? The Triumph of the Corporate Rich*, 7th ed. (New York: McGraw-Hill, 2013) This is an updated edition of his classic work.

41 Peter Bachrach and Morton Baratz, "Two Faces of Power," *American Political Science Review* 56, no. 4 (December 1962): 947–52.

42 Ibid., 948.

43 Ibid., 949.

44 Ibid., 948.

45 Matthew A. Crenson, *The Un-Politics of Air Pollution: A Study of Non-Decision-Making in the Cities* (Baltimore: Johns Hopkins University Press, 1972).

46 John Gaventa, *Power and Powerlessness: Quiescence and Rebellion in an Appalachian Valley* (Champaign, IL: University of Illinois Press, 1982).

47 Steven Lukes, *Power: A Radical View*, 2nd ed. (Basingstoke: Palgrave Macmillan, 2004).

48 Pierre Bourdieu, "Social Space and Symbolic Power," *Sociological Theory* 7, no. 1 (1989): 23.

49 Pierre Bourdieu, *The Logic of Practice* (Stanford: Stanford University Press, 1990), 53.

50 Bourdieu, "Social Space and Symbolic Power," 23.

51 Nancy Fraser, *Unruly Practices: Power, Discourse, and Gender in Contemporary Social Theory*, 2nd ed. (Minneapolis: University of Minnesota Press, 2008), 152.

52 Phillip Pettit, *Republicanism: A Theory of Freedom and Government* (New York: Oxford University Press, 1999).

53 Axel Honneth, *The Struggle for Recognition: The Moral Grammar of Social Conflicts* (Cambridge, MA: MIT Press, 1996).

54 Michel Foucault, *Power/Knowledge: Selected Interviews and Other Writings 1972–1977* (New York: Vintage, 1980), 38.

55 Gayatri Chakravorty Spivak, "Can the Subaltern Speak?" in *Marxism and the Interpretation of Culture*, ed. Cary Nelson and Lawrence Grossberg (Chicago: University of Chicago Press, 1988), 271–316.

56 Homi K. Bhabha, "Signs Taken for Wonders: Questions of Ambivalence and Authority under a Tree outside Delhi, May 1817," in *The Post-Colonial Studies Reader*, ed. Bill Ashcroft, Gareth Griffiths, and Helen Tiffin (New York: Routledge, 1995), 33.

57 Judith Butler, *Gender Trouble: Feminism and the Subversion of Identity* (London and New York: Routledge, 1999). See also Judith Butler, Ernesto Laclau, and Slavoj Žižek, *Contingency, Hegemony, Universality: Contemporary Dialogues on the Left* (London and New York: Verso, 2000). In this work Butler in conversation with the other two thinkers relates her position to a broad range of issues in contemporary critical theory.

Notes to Chapter 3

1 The most widely read was Francis Fukuyama, *The End of History and the Last Man* (reissue) (New York: Free Press, 2006).

2 Charles Lindblom, *The Market System: What It Is, How It Works, and What to Make of It* (New Haven: Yale University Press, 2001), 4.

3 Joseph Heath, *The Efficient Society: Why Canada Is as Close to Utopia as It Gets* (Toronto: Viking, 2001).

4 Anthony Giddens, *The Third Way: The Renewal of Social Democracy* (Cambridge: Polity Press, 1998).

5 Jürgen Habermas, "Afterword: Lessons of the Financial Crisis," in *Europe: The Faltering Project* (Cambridge: Polity Press, 2009), 187.

6 Jürgen Habermas, *The Theory of Communicative Action*, vol. 1, trans. Thomas McCarthy (Boston: Beacon Press, 1981).

7 Jürgen Habermas, "The Postnational Constellation and the Future of Democracy," in *The Postnational Constellation: Political Essays* (Cambridge, MA: MIT Press, 2001), 58–112.

8 Ibid., 64.

9 Ibid., 67.

10 Thomas Piketty, *Capital in the Twenty-First Century* (Cambridge, MA: Harvard University Press, 2014).

11 Sanford Schram, *The Return of Ordinary Capitalism: Neoliberalism, Precarity, Occupy* (New York: Oxford University Press, 2015).

12 David Harvey, *A Brief History of Neoliberalism* (Oxford: Oxford University Press, 2005).

13 See David Cieple, "The Corporate Contradictions of Neoliberalism," *Atlantic Affairs* 1, no. 2 (Summer 2017), https://americanaffairsjournal. org/2017/05/corporate-contradictions-neoliberalism.

14 Ibid.

15 Nancy Fraser, "The End of Progressive Neoliberalism," *Dissent*, 2 January 2017, https://www.dissentmagazine.org/online_articles/progressive-neoliberalism-reactionary-populism-nancy-fraser.

16 Ibid.

17 Fred Block and Margaret Somers, *The Power of Market Fundamentalism: Karl Polanyi's Critique* (Cambridge, MA: Harvard University Press, 2014); Nancy Fraser, "Can Society Be Commodities All the Way Down? Post-Polanyian Reflections on Capitalist Crisis," *Economy and Society* 43, no. 4 (November 2014): 541–5.

18 Karl Polanyi, *The Great Transformation: The Political and Economic Origins of Our Time*, 2nd ed. (Boston: Beacon Press, 2001).

19 Wendy Brown, *Undoing the Demos: Neoliberalism's Stealth Revolution* (New York: Zone Books, 2017).

20 Schram, *The Return of Ordinary Capitalism*.

21 Wolfgang Streeck, *Buying Time: The Delayed Crisis of Democratic Capitalism*, 2nd ed. (New York: Verso, 2017).

22 Harvey, *A Brief History of Neoliberalism*, 10–13.

23 Alejandro Reuss, "That '70's Crisis: What Can the Crisis of U.S. Capitalism in the 1970s Teach Us about the Current Crisis and Its Possible Outcomes?," *Dollars and Sense* (2009), http://wwwy.dollarsandsense.org/archives/2009/1109reuss.html.

24 Jürgen Habermas, *Legitimation Crisis*, trans. Thomas McCarthy (Boston: Beacon Press, 1975).

25 Habermas and Offe differ from the earlier Frankfurt School in one important way: whereas the Frankfurt theorists held that the welfare state had solved problems of classical capitalism, Habermas and Offe see a persistent tension that has led to the dissolution of the welfare state compromise.

26 See, for example, Murray Edelman, *The Symbolic Uses of Politics*, 2nd ed. (Champaign: University of Illinois Press, 1985).

27 Claus Offe, *Contradictions of the Welfare State*, ed. John Keane (Cambridge, MA: MIT Press, 1984).

28 Ibid.

29 Michel Crozier, Samuel Huntington, and Joji Watanuki, *The Crisis of Democracy* (New York: NYU Press, 1975).

30 See Daniel Geary, *Beyond Civil Rights: The Moynihan Report and Its Legacy* (Philadelphia: University of Pennsylvania Press, 2015).

31 On the question of austerity and its political function more generally, see Mark Blyth, *Austerity: The History of a Dangerous Idea* (Oxford: Oxford University Press, 2013).

32 Streeck, *Buying Time*. For a more compact summary of his argument, see Wolfgang Streeck, "Crises of Democratic Capitalism," *New Left Review* 71 (September–October 2011), 5–29.

33 Werner Bonefeld, *The Strong State and the Free Economy* (London: Rowan and Littlefield, 2017); Jamie Peck, *Constructions of Neoliberal Reason* (New York: Oxford, 2010).

34 Bonefeld, *The Strong State*, esp. ch. 3, "Democracy and Freedom: On Authoritarian Liberalism."

35 A useful precis of this process, which we follow here, is found in Claus Offe, *Europe Entrapped* (Medford: Polity Press, 2016), 6–10.

36 See, for example, Jennifer Washburn, *University Inc.: The Corporate Corruption of Higher Education* (New York: Basic Books, 2006).

37 See Colin Crouch, *Post Democracy* (Malden: Polity Press, 2004); Jacques Rancière, *Dissensus: On Aesthetics and Politics* (New York: Bloomsbury, 2013).

38 Crouch, *Post Democracy*, 4.

39 Martin Gilens and Benjamin I. Page, "Testing Theories of American Politics: Elites, Interest Groups, and Average Citizens," *Perspectives on Politics* 12, no. 3 (September 2014): 564–81; Sheldon Wolin, *Democracy*

Incorporated: Managed Democracy and the Specter of Inverted Totalitarianism
(Princeton: Princeton University Press, 2008).

40 Hayek's major works are *The Road to Serfdom* (Chicago: University of
    Chicago Press, 2007); and *The Constitution of Liberty* (Chicago: University
    of Chicago Press, 2011). For Karl Popper, see his *The Open Society and Its
    Enemies*, 2 vols. (Princeton: Princeton University Press, 1971).
41 Daniel Stedman Jones, *Masters of the Universe* (Princeton: Princeton
    University Press, 2012), 3ff.
42 Hayek, *The Road to Serfdom*, 28.
43 Stedman Jones, *Masters of the Universe*, 132 ff.
44 Milton Friedman, "Neo-Liberalism and Its Prospects," *Farmand*, 17
    February 1951, 89–93, http://0055d26.netsolhost.com/friedman/pdfs/
    other_commentary/Farmand.02.17.1951.pdf.
45 Ibid., 4. For C.B. Macpherson's criticisms of Friedman's position here,
    see his "Elegant Tombstones: A Note on Friedman's Freedom" and our
    discussion of it in chapter 1.
46 Milton Friedman, *Capitalism and Freedom* (Chicago: University of Chicago
    Press, 1962), 10.
47 For an overview, see S.M. Amadae, *Rationalizing Capitalist Democracy:
    The Cold War Origins of Rational Choice Liberalism* (Chicago: University
    of Chicago Press, 2003). For a sweeping critique of James Buchanan and
    public choice that links them to efforts to fundamentally limit democracy,
    see Nancy McLean, *Democracy in Chains: The Deep History of the Radical
    Right's Stealth Plan for America* (New York: Viking, 2017).
48 This account calls to mind what C.B. Macpherson called protective
    democracy, whose roots he traces back to the work in particular of James
    Mill. See Macpherson, *The Life and Times of Liberal Democracy* [1977]
    (Toronto: Oxford University Press, 2012).
49 James Buchannan, "Politics without Romance: A Sketch of Positive Public
    Choice Theory and Its Normative Implications," in *The Collected Works
    of James Buchanan*, vol. 1: *The Logical Foundations of Constitutional Liberty*
    (Indianapolis: Liberty Fund, 1999), 45–59.
50 Wolfgang Streeck, "Heller, Schmidt and the Euro," *European Law Journal* 21,
    no. 3 (May 2015): 361–2.
51 Ibid., 364.
52 Ibid., 365.
53 Guy Standing, *The Precariat: The New Dangerous Class* (London:
    Bloomsbury Academic, 2016).
54 However, in something of a counter-argument, the American political
    economist and social commentator Doug Henwood notes that recent data
    provided by the US Bureau of Labor Statistics indicate that, at least in the
    United States, less than 4 per cent of the labour force is contingently or

precariously employed, and furthermore, this is a *lower* percentage than was the case two decades ago. Henwood's point in raising this issue is not to deny the extent of economic misery suffered by many workers under neoliberalism but rather to shift the focus of progressive debate or discussion: "our critique should be about wages, benefits, working conditions, and our savage lack of a basic welfare state, not about 'precarity.'" For his treatment of these and other issues, see his blog, https://lbo-news.com, in particular the entries for 7, 13, and 14 June 2018.

55 Pew Research Centre, "Political Polarization in the American Public," http://www.people-press.org/2014/06/12/political-polarization-in-the-american-public.

56 Morris Fiorina, "America's Missing Moderates: Hiding in Plain Sight," *The American Interest* (March–April 2013), https://www.the-american-interest.com/2013/02/12/americas-missing-moderates-hiding-in-plain-sight.

57 Christopher Lasch, *The Revolt of the Elites* (New York: W.W. Norton, 1996).

58 Marc J. Hetherington and Jonathan D. Weiler, *Authoritarianism and Polarization in American Politics* (New York: Cambridge University Press, 2009).

59 Richard Hofstadter, *The Paranoid Style in American Politics and Other Essays* (New York: Alfred A. Knopf, 1965).

60 See T.W. Adorno et al., *The Authoritarian Personality* (New York: Harper, 1950); C. Wright Mills, *The Power Elite* (New York and Oxford: Oxford University Press, 1956).

61 Leo Lowenthal and Norbert Guterman, *Prophets of Deceit: A Study of the Techniques of the American Agitator* [1949], reprinted in *False Prophets: Studies on Authoritarianism* (New York: Routledge, 1986). Recent discussions of its applicability to the present can be found in the contributions of Doug Kellner, John Abromeit, and Samir Gandesha to the special section of *Logos* on the Frankfurt School and the New Right. *Logos* 16, nos. 1–2 (Spring 2016): http://logosjournal.com.

62 An overview of these positions can be found in Andrew Arato and Jean Cohen, *Civil Society and Political Theory* (Cambridge, MA: MIT Press, 1992).

63 Robert Putnam, *Bowling Alone: The Collapse and Revival of American Community* (New York: Simon and Schuster, 2000).

64 Robert N. Bellah et al., *Habits of the Heart: Individualism and Commitment in American Life*, 3rd ed. (Berkeley: University of California Press, 2007).

65 Robert N. Bellah, "Civil Religion in America," *Dædalus: Journal of the American Academy of Arts and Sciences* 96, no. 1 (Winter 1967): 1–21.

66 Jürgen Habermas, *The Structural Transformation of the Public Sphere: An Inquiry into a Category of Bourgeois Society*, trans. Thomas Burger with the assistance of Frederick Lawrence (Cambridge, MA: MIT Press, 1991), 51–7.

67 Arlie Hochschild, *Strangers in Their Own Land: Anger and Mourning on the American Right* (New York: New Press, 2016). For the view that Middle

Americans are duped into voting against their own interests, see Thomas Frank, *What's the Matter with Kansas: How Conservatives Won the Heart of America* (New York: Henry Holt, 2005).

68 J.D. Vance, *Hillbilly Elegy: A Memoir of a Family and Culture in Crisis* (New York: Harper, 2016).

69 Gaventa, *Power and Powerlessness: Quiescence and Rebellion in an Appalachian Valley* (Chicago: University of Chicago Press, 1982).

70 This is discussed in Raymond Plant, *The Neo-liberal State* (New York: Oxford University Press, 2010).

71 On the risks of late modernity, see Ulrich Beck, *The Risk Society: Toward a New Modernity* (Thousand Oaks: Sage, 1992).

72 Richard Sennett, *The Culture of the New Capitalism* (New Haven: Yale University Press, 2007); Zygmunt Baumann, *Liquid Modernity* (Cambridge: Polity Press, 2000).

73 Luc Boltanski and Eve Chiapello, *The New Spirit of Capitalism* (New York: Verso, 2007).

74 Charles Taylor, "What Is Human Agency?" *Philosophical Papers* 1 (Cambridge: Cambridge University Press, 1985), 15–45.

75 Brown, *Undoing the Demos*, 80.

76 Foucault's analysis of neoliberalism is contained in his lectures, *The Birth of Biopolitics: Lectures at the College de France 1978–79* (New York: Palgrave Macmillan, 2008). Discussions of Foucault's relation to neoliberalism can be found in Daniel Zamora and Michael C. Behrent, eds., *Foucault and Neoliberalism* (Malden: Polity Press, 2015); and Mitchell Dean and Kaspar Villadsen, *State Phobia and Civil Society: The Political Legacy of Michel Foucault* (Stanford: Stanford University Press, 2016).

77 An extensive discussion of precariousness is found in Schram, *The Return of Ordinary Capitalism*, ch. 3.

78 This is discussed in Plant, *The Neo-liberal State*, ch. 6.

79 Lawrence Mead, *Beyond Entitlement: The Social Obligation of Citizenship* (New York: Free Press, 1986).

80 Charles Murray, *Losing Ground: American Social Policy 1950–1980* (New York: Basic Books, 1984).

81 Mead, *Beyond Entitlement*, 22.

82 Georg Lukács, *History and Class Consciousness: Studies in Marxist Dialectics*, trans. Rodney Livingstone (Cambridge, MA: MIT Press, 1971).

83 Max Weber, *The Protestant Ethic and the Spirit of Capitalism*. Lukács's classic treatment of reification is "Reification and the Consciousness of the Proletariat," in *History and Class Consciousness*, 83–222.

84 Max Horkheimer and Theodor Adorno, *Dialectic of Enlightenment* (New York: Seabury Press, 1972); Horkheimer, *Eclipse of Reason* (New York: Continuum, 1974).

85 Habermas, *Theory of Communicative Action*, vol. 1, 339–401.

86 The idea of the independent character of economic and administrative systems is developed most fully in *Theory of Communicative Action*, vol. 2: *Lifeworld and System: A Critique of Functionalist Reason*, trans. Thomas McCarthy (Boston: Beacon Press, 1985).

87 Once again, developments in post-secondary education offer clear examples of this process. See Gaye Tuchman, *Wannabe U: Inside the Corporate University* (Chicago: University of Chicago Press, 2011); and Washburn, *University Inc.*

88 Sarah Armstrong, "Bureaucracy, Private Prisons, and the Future of Penal Reform," *Buffalo Criminal Law Review* 7, no. 1 (April 2003): 275–306.

89 David Ingram, "Individual Freedom and Social Equality: Habermas' Democratic Revolution in the Social Contractarian Justification of Law," in *Perspectives on Habermas*, ed. Lewis Hahn (Peru: Open Court, 2000), 289. See also William Scheuerman, "Between Radicalism and Resignation: Democratic Theory in Habermas's Between Facts and Norms," in *Discourse and Democracy: Essays on Habermas's* Between Facts and Norms, ed. Kenneth Baynes and Rene Von Schonberg (Albany: SUNY Press, 2002), 61–85. Also see Timo Jutten, "Habermas and Markets," *Constellations* 20, no. 4 (2013): 587–603.

90 C.B. Macpherson, ed., *Property: Mainstream and Critical Views*, 2nd rev. ed. (Toronto: University of Toronto Press, 1999).

91 This point was developed in Morris Cohen's essay "Property and Sovereignty," in Macpherson, ed., *Property*. See as well the interesting analysis offered in Samuel Bowles and Herbert Gintis, "Contested Exchange: New Microfoundations for the Political Economy of Capitalism," *Politics and Society* 18, no. 2 (June 1990): 165–222.

92 C.B. Macpherson, *Democratic Theory: Essays in Retrieval* (Oxford: Oxford University Press, 1973), 117.

93 Phillip Hansen, *Reconsidering C.B. Macpherson: From Possessive Individualism to Democratic Theory and Beyond* (Toronto: University of Toronto Press, 2015), 93.

94 Michael Foessel and Jürgen Habermas, "Critique and Communication: Philosophy's Mission. An Interview with Jürgen Habermas," *Eurozine*, 16 October 2015. An attempt to use Habermas's categories for an analysis of financialized capitalism that he does not provide is Nancy Fraser, "Legitimation Crisis? On the Political Contradictions of Financialized Capitalism," *Critical Historical Studies* 2, no. 2 (Fall 2015): 157–89.

Notes to Chapter 4

 1 George Herbert Mead, *Mind, Self, and Society: The Definitive Edition* (Chicago: University of Chicago Press, 2015). See also Hans Joas, *G.H.*

Mead: A Contemporary Re-examination of His Thought (Cambridge, MA: MIT Press, 1997); and Mitchell Aboulafia, *The Cosmopolitan Self: George Herbert Mead and Continental Philosophy* (Chicago: University of Illinois Press, 2001).

2 Michael J. Thompson, "The Wrath of Thrasymachus: Value Irrationality and the Failures of Deliberative Democracy," *Theoria* 62, no. 2 (June 2015): 33–58. According to Thompson, prominent theories of deliberative democracy tend to view deliberative mechanisms in isolation from conditioning socio-economic and cultural forces. These forces shape the taken-for-granted assumptions, presuppositions, and even world views that lead people to hold value commitments that block the development and exercise of the kind of critical rationality decisive for achieving deliberative aims.

3 Jürgen Habermas, "A Genealogical Analysis of the Cognitive Content of Morality," in *The Inclusion of the Other: Studies in Political Theory*, ed. Ciaran Cronin and Pablo De Greiff (Cambridge, MA: MIT Press, 1999), 3–47.

3 Ibid.

4 Habermas, *The Inclusion of the Other*, 29.

5 Axel Honneth, *The Struggle for Recognition: The Grammar of Social Conflicts* (Cambridge: Polity Press, 1995).

6 For example, see Seyla Benhabib's early criticism of the Generalized Other in Habermas in her *Critique, Norm, and Utopia: A Study of the Foundations of Critical Theory* (New York: Columbia University Press, 1986).

7 See Emile Durkheim, *The Division of Labor in Society* (New York: Free Press, 2014), 159–60, in relation to Rousseau.

8 Benjamin Nelson, *The Idea of Usury: From Tribal Brotherhood to Universal Otherhood* (Princeton: Princeton University Press, 1949); 2nd ed. (Chicago: University of Chicago Press, 1969).

9 Habermas, *The Inclusion of the Other*, xxxv–xxxvi; italics in the original.

10 Jane Mansbridge, with James Bohman, Simone Chambers, David Estlund, Andreas Follesdal, Archon Fung, Christina Lafont, Bernard Manin, and Jose Luis Marti, "The Place of Self-Interest and the Role of Power in Deliberative Democracy," *Journal of Political Philosophy* 18, no. 1 (2010): 64–100. In what follows, for economy of expression we will use Mansbridge as shorthand for the collective product.

11 See, for example, Habermas's essay, "On the Pragmatic, the Ethical, and the Moral Employments of Practical Reason," in *Justification and Application: Remarks on Discourse Ethics* (Cambridge, MA: MIT Press, 1994), 1–18.

12 Randall Calvert, "The Rational Choice Theory of Social Institutions: Cooperation, Coordination, and Communication," in *Modern Political Economy: Old Topics, New Directions*, ed. J. Banks and E. Hanushek

(Cambridge: Cambridge University Press, 1995), 222f. See also Brian Caterino, *Interpretation and Institution in Perestroika: The Raucous Rebellion in Political Science* (New Haven: Yale University Press, 2005).

13 Jack Knight and Itai Sened, "Introduction," in *Explaining Social Institutions,* ed. Knight and Sened (Ann Arbor: University of Michigan Press, 1998), 10.

14 James Johnson and Jack Knight, *The Priority of Democracy: Political Consequences of Pragmatism* (Princeton: Princeton University Press, 2011).

15 These paragraphs are adapted with slight changes from Brian Caterino's review of Johnson and Knight, "The Priority of Democracy," *New Political Science* 35, no. 2 (2013): 313–16.

16 See, for example, Charles Allen McCoy and John Playford, *Apolitical Politics: A Critique of Behaviouralism* (reprint) (New York: Forgotten Books, 2012); and Christian Bay, *Strategies of Emancipation* (South Bend: University of Notre Dame Press, 1981). On the history of the Caucus for New Political Science, see Clyde Barrow, "History of the Caucus for a New Political Science," *New Political Science* 21, no. 2 (1999): 417–20.

17 Bonnie Honig, *Political Theory and the Displacement of Politics* (Ithaca: Cornell University Press, 1993).

18 William Connolly, *Identity/Difference: Democratic Negotiations of Political Paradox* (Minneapolis: University of Minnesota Press, 2002).

19 Chantal Mouffe, *The Return of the Political* (New York: Verso, 1993); see also her *Agonistics: Thinking the World Politically* (New York: Verso, 2013). Among her many works with Ernesto Laclau, see *Hegemony and Socialist Strategy towards a Radical Democratic Politics* (New York: Verso, 1985).

20 Jacques Rancière, *Dissensus: On Politics and Aesthetics*, trans. Steven Corcoran (New York: Continuum, 2010).

21 For an overview of radical and participatory approaches, see Jason Vick, "Participatory Versus Radical Democracy in the 21st Century: Carole Pateman, Jacques Rancière, and Sheldon Wolin," *New Political Science* 37, no. 2 (2015): 214–23; and Jeffrey D. Hilmer, "The State of Participatory Democratic Theory," *New Political Science* 32, no. 1 (2010): 43–63. We discuss this material more fully in chapter 6.

22 Sheldon Wolin, "Fugitive Democracy," *Constellations* 1, no. 1 (December 1994): 11–25; see also his "Political Theory as a Vocation," *American Political Science Review* 63, no. 4 (December 1969): 1062–82.

23 Wendy Brown, "Democracy and Bad Dreams," *Theory and Event* 10, no. 1 (2007).

24 Chantal Mouffe, "Deliberative Democracy or Agonistic Pluralism," in *Deliberative Democracy or Agonistic Pluralism*, ed. Institut für Höhere Studien (IHS), Wien (Wien, 2000) (Reihe Politikwissenschaft / Institut für Höhere Studien, Abt. Politikwissenschaft 72), http://nbnresolving.de/urn:nbn:de:0168-ssoar-246548.

25 Nico Carpenter and Bart Cammaerts, "Hegemony, Democracy, Agonism and Journalism: An Interview With Chantal Mouffe," *Journalism Studies* 7, no. 6 (2006): 964–75, doi:10.1080/14616700600980728.

26 Axel Honneth, "Democracy as Reflexive Cooperation: John Dewey and the Theory of Democracy Today," in *Disrespect: The Normative Foundations of Critical Theory* (Cambridge: Polity Press, 2007), 229. For a critical appraisal, see David Owen, "Self-government and 'Democracy as Reflexive Co-operation': Reflections on Honneth's Social and Political Ideal," in *Recognition and Power: Axel Honneth and the Tradition of Critical Social Theory*, ed. Bert van den Brink and David Owen (Cambridge: Cambridge University Press, 2007), 290–320.

27 Axel Honneth, *Freedom's Right: The Social Foundation of Democratic Life* (New York: Columbia University Press, 2014), ch. 5.

28 Habermas, "A Genealogical Analysis of the Cognitive Content of Morality."

29 Axel Honneth, *Suffering from Indeterminacy: An Attempt at a Reactualization of Hegel's Philosophy of Right: Two Lectures*, 22, 23 (Amsterdam: Van Gorcum, 2000).

30 Hegel, *The Philosophy of Right*, rev ed. (Cambridge: Cambridge University Press, 1991), 7A.

31 Phillip Hansen, "Hannah Arendt and Bearing with Strangers," *Contemporary Political Theory* 3, no. 1 (March 2004): 3–22. See also Hansen, "Individual Responsibility and Political Authority: Hannah Arendt at the Intersection of Moral and Political Philosophy," in *Action and Appearance: Ethics and the Politics of Writing in Hannah Arendt*, ed. Anna Yeatman et al. (New York and London: Continuum, 2011), 134–49.

32 Nadia Urbinati and Maria Paula Saffon, "Procedural Democracy, the Bulwark of Equal Liberty," *Political Theory* 41, no. 3 (2013).

33 Andrew Feenberg challenges this reading; see his *The Philosophy of Praxis: Marx, Lukács, and the Frankfurt School*, rev. ed. (New York: Verso, 2014).

34 Mark E. Warren, "What Can Democratic Participation Mean Today?" *Political Theory* 30, no. 5 (October 2002): 677–701; Warren, "Citizen Participation and Democratic Deficits: Considerations from the Perspective of Democratic Theory," in *Activating the Citizen: Dilemmas of Participation in Europe and Canada*, ed. Joan DeBardeleben and Jon H. Pammett (New York: Palgrave Macmillan, 2009), 17–40.

35 On Strong Democracy, see Benjamin Barber, *Strong Democracy* (Berkeley: University of California Press, 1985).

36 Miriam Ronzoni, "How Social Democrats May Become Reluctant Radicals: Thomas Piketty's *Capital* and Wolfgang Streeck's *Buying Time*," *European Journal of Political Theory* 17, no. 1 (January 2018): 118–27.

37 Wolfgang Streeck, *The Crisis in Context: Democratic Capitalism and Its Contradictions*, Discussion Paper, Max Planck Institute for the Study of Societies, Cologne, October 2011, 2.

38 E.P. Thompson, *The Making of the English Working Class* (New York: Vintage, 1966); James Scott, *Domination and the Arts of Resistance* (New Haven: Yale University Press, 1976).

39 Claus Offe, "Europe Entrapped: Does the EU Have the Political Capacity to Overcome Its Current Crisis?," *European Law Journal* 19, no. 5 (September 2013), 595–611.

40 Wolfgang Streeck, *How Will Capitalism End? Essays on a Failing System* (New York: Verso, 2016).

41 Ibid.

42 See C.B. Macpherson, *The Life and Times of Liberal Democracy* (Oxford: Oxford University Press, 1977).

43 On this and related issues, see Thompson, "The Wrath of Thrasymachus."

Notes to Chapter 5

1 Albrecht Wellmer, "On Critical Theory," *Social Research* 81, no. 3 (Fall 2014): 712.

2 For a discussion of criticisms that the "normative" turn in critical theory has resulted in excessive academic specialization and a narrow moralism and legalism, see William E. Scheuerman, "Recent Frankfurt Critical Theory: Down on Law?" *Constellations* 24, no. 1 (March 2017): 113–25.

3 Hannah Pitkin, *The Concept of Representation* (Berkeley: University of California Press, 1967), 43.

4 A good account of the early stages of rational choice in political theory is S.M. Amadae, *Rationalizing Capitalist Democracy: The Cold War Origins of Rational Choice Liberalism* (Chicago: University of Chicago Press, 2003).

5 Iris Young, *Inclusion and Democracy* (New York: Oxford, 2002).

6 William Scheuerman, *Between the Norm and the Exception: The Frankfurt School and the Rule of Law* (Cambridge, MA: MIT Press, 1994). John Abromeit and Mark Cobb argue that Marcuse's work suffers from a similar problem in their introduction to *Herbert Marcuse: A Critical Reader*, 24. Richard Wolin holds a similar thesis.

7 Herbert Marcuse, "The Struggle against Liberalism in the Totalitarian View of the State," in *Negations: Essays in Critical Theory* (Boston: Beacon Press, 1969), 3–42.

8 Ibid., 5.

9 Max Horkheimer, "Authority and the Family," in *Critical Theory: Selected Essays* (New York: Continuum, 1999), 55.

10 Max Horkheimer, *Eclipse of Reason* (New York: Continuum, 1974).

11 Friedrich Pollock, "State Capitalism: Its Limits and Possibilities," in *The Essential Frankfurt School Reader*, ed. Andrew Arato and Eike Gephardt (New York: Continuum, 1985), 71–94. See also Max Horkheimer, "The End of Reason," in ibid., 26–48.

12 Horkheimer, *Eclipse of Reason*.

13 See Scheuerman, *Between the Norm and the Exception*, ch. 1.

14 Ibid., ch. 7.

15 For example, see Otto Kirchheimer, "The Rechtsstaat as Magic Wall," in *The Rule of Law under Siege: Selected Essays of Franz L. Neumann and Otto Kirchheimer*, ed. William Scheuerman (Berkeley: University of California Press, 1996), 243–61; and Franz Neumann, "The Concept of Political Freedom," in Scheuerman, *Between the Norm and the Exception*, 195–230.

16 To be sure, Neumann had some reservations in later years about the viability of social rights, but he still accepted them in a limited way. Macpherson's theory seems a better alternative.

 It is interesting that Macpherson and Neumann were for a time in the 1930s housemates in London, where Macpherson was a graduate student from Canada while Neumann was a political refugee from Nazi Germany. For a discussion of Macpherson's experience in England and the impact that the decline of democracy and the rise of fascism had on his thought at the time, and particularly his views on the prospects of and need for socialism and revolution, see Karl Dahlquist, "The Young Macpherson on the Transition into Socialism and the Rise of Fascism," *Canadian Journal of Political Science* 51, no. 2 (June 2018), 405–24. Dahlquist suggests that Neumann's own views at the time significantly influenced Macpherson's.

17 Jürgen Habermas, *The Structural Transformation of the Public Sphere: An Inquiry into a Category of Bourgeois Society*, trans. Thomas Burger and Frederick Lawrence (Cambridge, MA: MIT Press, 1993).

18 Jean Cohen, "Why More Political Theory?," *Telos* 12, no. 2 (Summer 1979): 70–94.

19 Douglas Kellner, "Habermas, the Public Sphere, and Democracy: A Critical Intervention," in Lewis Edward Hahn, ed., *Perspective on Habermas* (Peru: Open Court Press, 2000), 259–87.

20 Ibid.

21 Jürgen Habermas, "The Classical Doctrine of Politics in Relation to Social Philosophy," in *Theory and Practice* (Boston: Beacon Press, 1974), 41–81.

22 Jürgen Habermas, "Technology and Science as Ideology," in *Toward a Rational Society: Student Protest, Science, and Politics* (Boston: Beacon Press, 1970), 81–121.

23 Max Horkheimer and Theodor Adorno, *Dialectic of Enlightenment* (New York: Seabury Press, 1972). See also Martin Jay, *Reason after Its Eclipse: On Late Critical Theory* (Madison: University of Wisconsin Press, 2016).

24 Jürgen Habermas, "Natural Law and Revolution," in *Theory and Practice*, 82–119. See also James Miller, *Rousseau: Dreamer of Democracy* (New Haven: Yale University Press, 1984).

25 In addition to his remarks in the Natural Law essay, see his discussion of Rousseau in *The Structural Transformation of the Public Sphere: An Inquiry into a Category of Bourgeois Society*, trans. Thomas Burger with the assistance of Frederick Lawrence (Cambridge, MA: MIT Press, 1991), 92–9; and in Craig Calhoun, ed., *Habermas and the Public Sphere* (Cambridge, MA: MIT Press, 1992), 445–7.

26 Habermas, "Natural Law and Revolution."

27 Jürgen Habermas, *The Theory of Communicative Action*, vol. 1, trans. Thomas McCarthy (Boston: Beacon Press, 1981), 345.

28 Jürgen Habermas, "Three Normative Models of Democracy," in *The Inclusion of the Other: Studies in Political Theory*, ed. Ciaran Cronin and Pablo De Greiff (Cambridge, MA: MIT Press, 1998), 248–9; emphasis in the original.

29 Jürgen Habermas, *Between Facts and Norms*, trans. William Rehg (Cambridge: Polity Press, 1996), 442.

30 Andrew Feenberg, *The Philosophy of Praxis: Marx, Lukács, and the Frankfurt School* (London and New York: Verso, 2014), 201.

31 See Markus Perkmann, "Social Integration and System Integration: Reconsidering the Classical Distinction," *Sociology* 32, no. 3 (August 1998): 491–507. The relations between David Lockwood's, Jürgen Habermas's and Anthony Giddens's usage of these distinctions is explored in Nicos Mouzelis, "Social and System Integration: Lockwood, Habermas, Giddens," *Sociology* 31, no. 1 (February 1997), 111–19.

32 Habermas, *Between Facts and Norms*, xli; emphasis in the original.

33 Ibid., 478.

34 Interview with Hans Peter Kruger (1988) cited in Matthew G. Specter, *Habermas: An Intellectual Biography* (Cambridge: Cambridge University Press, 2010), 177.

35 Habermas, *Between Facts and Norms*. See also Habermas, "The New Obscurity: The Crisis of the Welfare State and the Exhaustion of Utopian Energies," in *The New Conservatism: Cultural Criticism and the Historians' Debate* (Cambridge, MA: MIT Press, 1991), 48–70.

36 Another perspective is given by Rainer Forst in *The Right to Justification: Elements of a Constructivist Theory of Justice* (New York: Columbia University Press, 2014).

37 On Neumann's view of deformalized law, see Scheuerman, *Between the Norm and the Exception*, esp. chapter 3. For the later views of Otto Kirchheimer and Franz Neumann, see chapter 7.

38 Habermas, *Between Facts and Norms*, 300.

39 See, for example, Robert McChesney, *The Political Economy of Media: Enduring Issues, Emerging Dilemmas* (New York: Monthly Review Press, 2008); and *The Problem of the Media: U.S. Communications Politics in the Twenty-First Century* (New York: Monthly Review Press, 2004).

40 Specter, *Habermas: An Intellectual Biography*, 103.

41 One problem with Habermas's conception of basic rights concerns the freedom of individuals from government regulation, or what are generally called negative rights. Here Habermas argues that individuals not subject to government authority in particular cases are thereby exempted from obligations of mutual accountability. He notes that in such instances the individual is no longer called upon to exercise communicative freedom and is thus not required to give reasons for his or her actions. However, while the individual may not incur legal obligations, that person is still subject to ethical and moral demands and, potentially, opprobrium. A person who makes a poor choice, or an evil one, may not be legally sanctioned but could nonetheless forfeit the respect of others, and even the expectation of their active cooperation in pursuit of their purposes. Such people are not fully relieved of the burdens of mutual accountability.

42 Habermas, "Three Normative Models of Democracy."

43 Here Habermas's concerns intersect with those of Hannah Arendt. See Arendt, *The Human Condition* (Chicago: University of Chicago Press, 1959); see also Habermas, "Arendt's Communications Concept of Power," *Social Research* 44, no. 1 (Spring 1977): 3–24.

44 Habermas, "On the Internal Relation between the Rule of Law and Democracy," in *The Inclusion of the Other*, 258.

45 Habermas, *Between Facts and Norms*, 438; emphasis in the original.

46 Ibid., 442.

47 See, for example, Jürgen Habermas, *The Crisis of the European Union: A Response*, trans. Ciaran Cronin (Cambridge: Polity Press, 2012); and *The Lure of Technocracy*, trans. Ciaran Cronin (Cambridge: Polity Press, 2015).

Notes to Chapter 6

1 See, for example, Robert Goodin, *Innovating Democracy: Democratic Theory and Practice after the Deliberative Turn* (Oxford: Oxford University Press, 2008).

2 John S. Dryzek, *Democracy in Capitalist Times: Ideals, Limits, and Struggles* (Oxford: Oxford University Press, 1996), 5.

3 Jeffrey D. Hilmer, "The State of Participatory Democratic Theory," *New Political Science* 32, no. 1 (March 2010): 46.

4 Frank Cunningham, *Theories of Democracy: A Critical Introduction* (London and New York: Routledge, 2002), 144.

5 Ibid., 143.

6 Lane Davis, "The Cost of Realism: Contemporary Restatements of
   Democracy," in *Apolitical Politics: A Critique of Behavioralism*, ed. Charles
   A. McCoy and John Playford (New York: Thomas Y. Crowell, 1967), 188,
   193–4, 195. This collection is perhaps the most identifiably representative
   example of the critique of behavioural social science and the elite theory
   of democracy. Other critical sources, widely acknowledged at the time,
   include William E. Connolly, ed., *The Bias of Pluralism* (New York: Atherton
   Press, 1969); and Henry S. Kariel, ed., *Frontiers of Democratic Theory* (New
   York: Random House, 1970). In her account of participatory democracy,
   Carol Pateman establishes her analysis on the basis of a critique of
   alternative democratic theories, in which elite theory and its architects
   play a significant role. See Pateman, *Participation and Democratic Theory*
   (Cambridge: Cambridge University Press, 1970).

   Davis further argues that from the perspective laid out by the pluralist
   model, "politics is only a method of managing public affairs. The goal of
   full human development must be sought in many ways, and a democratic
   society provides for responsible activity in many non-political spheres of
   human life. Political activity can only be directly important for a few. For
   the rest, government can best serve as an expert and beneficent steward
   who clears away obstacles, manages the vital necessities, and submits his
   accounts – simplified to his master's level of understanding – for periodic
   review" (194).

7 Tony Blair, "Against Populism, the Center Must Hold," *New York Times*,
   3 March 2017 (emphasis added). To be fair, Blair does argue that the
   "progressive" centre must propose policies that as fully as possible
   ameliorate the unequal impact of globalization on communities
   experiencing social dislocation through job and income loss and the
   cultural disorientation that frequently accompanies these. Still, the tenor
   of his argument about what constitutes acceptable "normal" politics is
   telling. Wolfgang Streeck has recently noted that "the fissure between
   those who describe others as 'populists' and the objects of their description
   is the dominant political fault line in the crisis-ridden societies of
   financial capitalism. The issue at stake is none other than the relationship
   between global capitalism and the state system." "Populism" is used by
   defenders of neoliberalism and globalization to denote "left-wing and
   right-wing tendencies and organizations alike that reject the TINA [there
   is no alternative] logic of 'responsible' politics in the world of neoliberal
   globalization." Wolfgang Streeck, "The Return of the Repressed," *New Left
   Review* 104 (March–April 2017): 11.

8 Wolfgang Streeck has noted a published comment from November 2016 by
   the director of a German digital research centre that explores digital issues

on behalf of German companies: "We need a 'gnosocracy.' Whoever wants to vote must demonstrate political competence ... To this end, every poll booth must be provided with a variable multiple-choice test, with simple questions from every sphere: external, internal, the environment, the economy, etc. Whoever passes the test may vote." In ibid., 9.

9 A notable exception was Otto Kirchheimer. See his classic study of the emergence of the "catch-all" political party, "The Transformation of Western European Party Systems," in *Political Parties and Political Development*, ed. Joseph LaPolombara and Myron Weiner (Princeton: Princeton University Press, 1966), 177–200. For an analysis of Kirchheimer's argument and its contemporary relevance, see Andre Krouwel, "Otto Kirchheimer and the Catch-all Party," *West European Politics* 26, no. 2 (April 2003): 23–40. Krouwel notes that Kirchheimer perceptively drew attention to vanishing principled opposition in both parliamentary bodies and society, along with the cartelization and professionalization of political parties as they increasingly assumed a narrowly managerial role in the state. The result was apathy and cynicism on the part of citizens, who were denied any significant influence on the exercise of political power – in other words, the erosion of democracy. For Krouwel these ideas continue to offer important insights into the dynamics of contemporary political and party systems.

In a more contemporary context, the work of the late Peter Mair addressed comparable issues around the erosion of competitive party systems and consequences for democracy today. See Peter Mair, *Ruling the Void: The Hollowing Out of Western Democracy* (London: Verso, 2013).

10 Lane Davis essentially concedes the point: "In considering the indictment against classical democratic theory, the charge that it fails as a descriptive and explanatory tool can only be met by a plea of *nolo contendere*." He goes on to claim that classical theory "was not created to describe any existing democratic polity of any considerable size employing representative institutions. It grew from many sources as an essay in prescription. As such, it contains a prescription for a worthwhile polity which should be sought after." Davis, "The Cost of Realism," 188–9.

11 On the renewed interest in participatory democracy, see, for example, Jeffrey D. Hilmer, "The State of Participatory Democratic Theory," *New Political Science* 32, no. 1 (2010): 43–63; Carole Pateman, "Participatory Democracy Revisited," *Perspectives on Politics* 10, no. 1 (March 2012): 7–21; and Jason Vick, "Participatory Versus Radical Democracy in the 21st Century: Carole Pateman, Jacques Rancière, and Sheldon Wolin," *New Political Science* 37, no. 2 (June 2015): 204–23.

12 Antonio Florida, "Participatory Democracy *versus* Deliberative Democracy: Elements for a Possible Theoretical Genealogy. Two Histories,

Some Intersections," 7th ECPR General Conference, Sciences Po, Bordeaux, 4–7 September 2013.

13 "The Port Huron Statement," in James Miller, *Democracy Is in the Streets: From Port Huron to the Siege of Chicago* (New York: Simon and Schuster, 1987), 332–3.

14 Ibid. The work of Mills that is especially significant in this context is *The Sociological Imagination* (New York: Oxford University Press, 1959), which argued for the need to transform ostensibly private troubles into public issues. Hayden himself specifically emphasized the impact on his own thinking of Mills's best-known book, *The Power Elite*.

15 David Held, *Models of Democracy*, 3rd ed. (Stanford: Stanford University Press, 2006), 215.

16 Pateman, *Participation and Democratic Theory*; and "Participatory Democracy Revisited."

17 See Pateman, *The Sexual Contract* (Stanford: Stanford University Press, 1988); and *The Problem of Political Obligation: A Critique of Liberal Theory* (Berkeley: University of California Press, 1985).

18 Pateman, *The Problem of Political Obligation*, 169. In her critique of obedience masquerading as obligation, Pateman shares common ground with Hannah Arendt, who herself is often seen as a proponent of at least a certain sort of participatory democracy through her generally positive view of popular revolutionary councils. Arendt challenged as pernicious the link between consent and obedience that she identified with dominant forms of modern political thinking. See Arendt, "Personal Responsibility under Dictatorship" (1964), in her *Responsibility and Judgment*, ed. and with an introduction by Jerome Kohn (New York: Schocken Books, 2003), 17–48. For a treatment of this issue in the context of a discussion of the relation between political and moral philosophy in Arendt's work, see Phillip Hansen, "Individual Responsibility and Political Authority: Hannah Arendt at the Intersection of Moral and Political Philosophy," in *Action and Appearance: Ethics and the Politics of Writing in Hannah Arendt*, ed. Anna Yeatman, Phillip Hansen, Magdalena Zolkos, and Charles Barbour (New York: Continuum Books, 2011), 134–49.

19 This is a core claim of the now classic study by Hanna Pitkin, *The Concept of Representation* (Berkeley: University of California Press, 1967).

20 For an analysis which holds that the political and administrative structure of the European Union represents this process of insulating core economic decision-making bodies from democratic direction and control, see Wolfgang Streeck, "Heller, Schmitt and the Euro," *European Law Journal* 21, no. 3 (May 2015): 361–70, which we discussed in chapter 3 in the context of our analysis of neoliberalism and its relation to both the authoritarian liberalism of Carl Schmitt and postwar German ordo-liberalism. Of course,

the work of Otto Kirchheimer and Peter Mair, cited earlier, is highly
relevant here as well (see note 9).

21 Sheldon S. Wolin, *Politics and Vision*, expanded ed. (Princeton: Princeton
    University Press, 1960, 2004), 316.

22 Ibid., xv, xx.

23 Carole Pateman, "Sublimation and Reification: Locke, Wolin, and the
    Liberal Democratic Conception of the Political," *Politics and Society* 5, no. 4
    (December 1975): 452.

24 Ibid., 454.

25 Ibid., 459.

26 See Karl Marx, "On the Jewish Question" [1843], in *Writings of the Young
    Marx on Philosophy and Society* (1967), ed. Loyd D. Easton and Kurt H.
    Guddat (Indianapolis: Hackett, 1997), 225–6.

27 Pateman, "Sublimation and Reification," 454–5.

28 To be sure, Pateman does write of the increased presence of the state in
    the economy with the growth of state-managed capitalism in the post–
    Second World War era (460ff). It is worth noting, though, that when the
    article was published in 1975, world capitalism was entering a new, more
    unstable era that saw the decline of the so-called Keynesian welfare state
    consensus and the emergence of the much more aggressively free market
    outlook associated with neoliberalism. As we have noted throughout this
    study, neoliberalism has entailed a retreat from democratic regulation of
    the economy and, along with this, the limitation of social rights. There
    have also been restrictions on democratic will formation – to borrow from
    Pateman, an increasing fictionalization of citizenship.

29 Pateman, "Sublimation and Reification," 456.

30 Ibid., 456–7.

31 Ibid., 462.

32 Ibid., 465.

33 Hannah Arendt, "Thoughts on Politics and Revolution: A Commentary,"
    in *Crises of the Republic* (New York: Harcourt Brace Jovanovich, 1972), 230.

34 Jean-Jacques Rousseau, "The Social Contract," in *The Social Contract and the
    Discourses* (New York: Alfred A. Knopf, 1993), 192–3. Rousseau goes on to
    argue that "the maxim of civil right, that no one is bound by undertakings
    made to himself, does not apply in this case; for there is a great difference
    between incurring an obligation to yourself and incurring one to a whole
    of which you form a part" (193). This is a crucial passage for a full grasp
    of Rousseau's position because it complicates the received (liberal)
    understanding of individualism, whereby to be fully an individual is to
    stand apart from the social whole. Pateman does not discuss this passage,
    although it would seem to be vital to her argument.

35 Ibid., 228.

36 Pateman, "Sublimation and Reification," 465–6.
37 Ibid., 464–5.
38 Ibid., 466.
39 See Pateman, *Participation and Democratic Theory*, esp. chs. 4–7. Pateman devotes considerable attention to appraising evidence drawn from forms of worker self-management in the former Yugoslavia, as well as evidence demonstrating that workers in Western democracies, including the United Kingdom, both desired a greater role in the workplace and enjoyed a significant increase in the level of political efficacy when their role was enhanced.
40 Pateman, "Sublimation and Reification," 466. Although obviously unintended, there seem clear parallels here with Habermas's claim that a radically democratic system must establish and protect the private as well as the public autonomy of citizens.
41 Pateman, *Participation and Democratic Theory*, 42–3.
42 Pateman, "Participatory Democracy Revisited," 10.
43 Ibid., 8, 10. We would note here again the distinction we drew previously in this chapter between weak and strong versions of deliberative democracy. Pateman's target here is clearly a weak version; but as we have argued, this does not exhaust the range of deliberative perspectives.
44 Ibid., 10.
45 Ibid., 10, 11, 12.
46 Ibid., 11–12.
47 Celina Su, "From Porto Alegre to New York City: Participatory Budgeting and Democracy," *New Political Science* 39, no. 1 (March 2017): 67. Other analysts have offered different totals of cities and municipalities that have adopted participatory budgeting practices, likely an indication of the flexibility, if not ambiguity, of the meaning of participatory budgeting.
48 Ibid., 14.
49 Ibid., 15, 14.
50 Michael J. Thompson, "The Wrath of Thrasymachus," *Theoria* 62, no. 2 (June 2015): 33–58.
51 Pateman notes that, however significant deliberative democratic theory has become, both in the academy and to some extent in the larger society, the fact that it largely takes as given the existing institutions "presents a sharp contrast to the democratic theory of the 1960s where the meaning of democracy itself – 'realistic' or participatory? – was at the heart of the debate." "Participatory Democracy Revisited," 10.
52 John Locke, *Second Treatise of Government*, ed. C.B. Macpherson (Indianapolis: Hackett, 1980), S171.
53 To be fair, Pateman's critique of the limits of liberalism was extended to include dominant accounts of participatory democracy, including her own

treatment of it in *Participation and Democratic Theory* and in "Sublimation and Reification," as her work came to incorporate the insights of feminist theory. Radical criticism, she writes, "has stopped short because political theorists ignore both the construction of the individual within the patriarchal separation between public and private, and the fact that, although the two spheres are separated, they are also the two, interrelated sides of the one coin of liberal democratic social and political life." She concludes that "a distinctively feminist perspective in political theory provides as searching and as fundamental a critique of radical democratic theory as it does of liberalism, precisely because both theories are sexually particular, predicated upon the patriarchal separation of public and private, woman and men ... The enormous task facing anyone wishing to develop a genuinely democratic theory of political obligation is to formulate a universal theory, including civil equality, that also embodies a social conception of individuality as feminine and masculine, that gives due weight to the unity and differentiation of humankind." Pateman, *The Problem of Political Obligation*, 192, 193.

Pateman subsequently developed her analysis in her now classic study *The Sexual Contract*, in which she demonstrated that the social contract as understood in liberal democratic theory and as a cornerstone of actual political relations represented the formula for patriarchal domination. This was because it was undergirded by a sexual contract, from which indeed it could not be separated. The sexual contract secured and indeed defined the rights and freedom of men through the subjugation of women: male political right presupposed and incorporated conjugal right, the right of men to the bodies and lives of women. For this reason, formally expanding the contract to include the formerly excluded – for example, extending the franchise to women – fails to touch the core of the matter, which is that the freedom of some not only comes at the expense of, but is also constituted by and through, the unfreedom of others. (Charles Mills advances a comparable argument about race in *The Racial Contract*.)

Given the intimate association of the social contract with liberalism and liberal democracy, it is understandable why Pateman would argue for a radical democratic theory that was non-liberal. However, we still believe that the seeds of a radical and critical theory of democracy must be sought out within the existing social order if it is to be possible to identify potentials for change, even while acknowledging the distorting effects of reification.

54 Pateman, *The Problem of Political Obligation*, 171.
55 Held, *Models of Democracy*, 211.
56 C.B. Macpherson, *The Life and Times of Liberal Democracy* [1977], with a New Introduction by Frank Cunningham (Toronto: Oxford University Press, 2012), ch. 5.

57 Ibid., 91–2. Macpherson went on to note that the problem of implementing participatory democracy on a mass scale is intractable "if we simply try to draw mechanical blue-prints of the proposed political system without paying attention to the changes in society, and in people's consciousness of themselves, which a little thought will show must precede or accompany the attainment of anything like participatory democracy" (98).

58 Joshua Cohen and Joel Rogers, *On Democracy: Toward a Transformation of American Society* (New York: Penguin Books, 1983), 50–67.

59 Wolfgang Streeck argues that a key source of legitimacy for contemporary neoliberal capitalism, within which insecurity of employment has dramatically increased, has been "the conversion of *insecure workers* – kept insecure to make them obedient workers – into *confident consumers* happily discharging their consumerist social obligations even in the face of fundamental uncertainty of labour markets and employment." Wolfgang Streeck, *How Will Capitalism End? Essays on a Failing System* (London and New York: Verso, 2016), 2–3. For Streeck, the current era of what he calls an "entropic" or dying capitalism, with no real successor in sight, poses even more ominous threats to democracy and developmental individualism than Macpherson identified.

60 Carol C. Gould, *Globalizing Democracy and Human Rights* (Cambridge: Cambridge University Press, 2004), 2, 4; emphasis in the original.

61 For Gould's criticisms of Pateman, see ibid., 85; for those of Macpherson, see ibid., 48–9.

62 Ibid., 41. As was the case for Macpherson, Gould bases her conception of social ontology to a considerable extent upon key elements in the work of Marx. See her significant and insightful study, *Marx's Social Ontology: Individuality and Community in Marx's Theory of Social Reality* (Cambridge, MA: MIT Press, 1980).

63 James D. Ingram, *Radical Cosmopolitics: The Ethics and Politics of Democratic Universalism* (New York: Columbia University Press, 2013), 229, 251. For a discussion of the relation of Ingram's position to Macpherson's treatment of human rights, see Phillip Hansen, *Reconsidering C.B. Macpherson: From Possessive Individualism to Democratic Theory and Beyond* (Toronto: University of Toronto Press, 2015). 219–22. We do not suggest that Gould and Ingram hold identical views. Indeed, it is likely that Gould would see Ingram as assimilating human rights to (democratic) politics, a criticism she also levels at Macpherson. We would take issue with such an interpretation inasmuch as for Ingram, human rights are not defined by a democratic politics whereby such a politics would involve an institutional procedure structured along deliberative lines for establishing such rights. Rather, rights are generated through political action and the creation of a public sphere or space within which claims are articulated.

This conception owes more to Hannah Arendt and Etienne Balibar than to John Rawls and Jürgen Habermas. Rights are dependent upon but not reducible to democratic practices. Rights do not and cannot exist as real features of individual and social identities independently of such practices. If both human rights and democracy are to be properly understood and appreciated in their interconnection, each has to be reconceived. It cannot be the case either that human rights understood as moral imperatives trumps democracy; or that actually existing liberal democracy is *inter alia* the precondition for and/or the realization of human rights claims.

In any event our linking of Gould and Ingram is intended primarily to make the case that from the point of view of a critical theory of democracy, human rights, or justice, and democracy are best understood and realized in and through participatory democratic practices and institutions. And both Gould and Ingram hold what might be called a social interactionist account of rights, in Gould's case rooted in her social ontology.

64 Gould, *Globalizing Democracy and Human Rights*, 27.
65 Ibid., 34–5, 175–6. In a more recent piece devoted to questions of global democracy, Gould offers this lucid summary of her position: "The democratic principle requires equal rights of participation in decisions concerning the *common activities* in which people engage, where such common or joint activities are understood to be defined by shared goals and practices. To put the argument very briefly, justice is interpreted as a principle of equal positive freedom, or prima facie equal rights to the conditions of freedom as self-transformative activity, whether individual or collective. Since engaging in common activities is one of the main conditions for freedom, it follows that individuals must be self-determining in such activity. But since these activities are collective in character and no participant has more of a right than the others to make the decision for the collectivity (if domination is to be avoided), then decisions about such common activities necessarily take the form of codetermination of the course of this activity, hence of equal rights to participate in decisions about it. On this view, then, democratic participation is seen as widely required in a range of economic and social institutions, as well as in the recognized political ones … [I]ndividuals operating in these institutions and in communities of various sorts have equal rights to participate in shaping them, because this participation is a condition for the self-transformation of each of them." Carol C. Gould, "Structuring Global Democracy: Political Communities, Universal Human Rights, and Transnational Representation," *Metaphilosophy* 40, no. 1 (January 2009), 28.
66 Ibid., 31. See also Gould, *Globalizing Democracy and Human Rights*, ch. 9, where she discusses what she calls the global justice deficit, that is,

deepening global income and wealth inequality that fosters the denial of basic economic rights essential for free individual agency and self-development.

67 For an approach that implicitly connects Pateman's and Macpherson's respective positions, see Frank Cunningham, "Democratic Theory and Racist Ontology," *Social Identities* 6, no. 4 (2000), 463–82. While conceding that Enlightenment abstractions about universal rights *can* lead to and *have* led to racist distortions, Cunningham argues that "Macpherson's neo-Aristotelian value perspective is less easily turned to racist purposes and provides a good basis from which to articulate and defend egalitarian developmentalism" (475). He goes on to claim that "participatory democracy, beginning if needs be only in local and informal circumstances, was thus seen by Macpherson as a way of nurturing developmental values and habits by showing people in practice that it is possible to develop and exercise their potentials in collective action with others, whetting their appetites for more such opportunities, and by identifying obstacles, encouraging oppositional politics to overcome them. The obstacles Macpherson mainly had in mind were economic and political, but if racist exclusions are added to these obstacles and are recognised as such, then overcoming them, that is, combating racism, becomes an important democratic project" (477).

68 Charles Taylor, "Atomism," in *Powers, Possessions, and Freedom: Essays in Honour of C.B. Macpherson*, ed. Alkis Kontos (Toronto: University of Toronto Press, 1979), 39–61.

69 Gould, *Globalizing Democracy and Human Rights*, 33.

70 The most extensive exercise in reconstructing the *Philosophy of Right* is Axel Honneth, *Freedom's Right: The Social Foundations of Democratic Life*, trans. Joseph Ganahl (New York: Columbia University Press, 2014). Briefer treatments of the key themes of this reconstruction are Honneth, *Suffering from Indeterminacy: An Attempt at a Reactualization of Hegel's Philosophy of Right*, with an introduction by Beate Rossler, translated by Jack Ben-Levi (Amsterdam: Van Gorcum, 2000); and *The Pathologies of Individual Freedom: Hegel's Social Theory*, translated from the German by Ladislaus Lob (Princeton: Princeton University Press, 2010).

71 Honneth, *The Pathologies of Individual Freedom*, 7. Honneth's approach to Hegel, which explicitly severs the connection between Hegel's theoretical and practical philosophy, his metaphysics as articulated in his *Logic*, and his social and political theory, raises important questions about how to read Hegel and establish his contemporary significance. For an account that challenges this separation, see Robert Pippen, "Reconstructivism: On Honneth's Hegelianism," *Philosophy and Social Criticism* 40, no. 8 (October 2014): 725–41.

72 Ibid., 8.
73 G.W.F. Hegel, *Elements of the Philosophy of Right*, 7A. In Hegel's words, where we relate in this way to one another, particularly in relations of friendship and love, "we are not one-sidedly within ourselves, but willingly limit ourselves with reference to an other, even while knowing ourselves in this limitation as ourselves" (42).
74 Honneth, *Freedom's Right*, 43, 58, 60.
75 Ibid., 60–1.
76 Axel Honneth, *The Idea of Socialism: Towards a Renewal*, trans. Joseph Ganahl (Cambridge: Polity Press, 2017), 12, 13.
77 Ibid., 14.
78 Ibid., 19. Charles Taylor offers a comparable contrast in his treatment of public goods provided through state action. Taylor distinguishes between, on the one hand, convergent public goods, and on the other, mediate and immediate public goods. The difference is roughly between goods that are wholly individual in meaning but are provided publicly because individuals are unable to procure them by themselves, and goods whose very public character is essential to their constitution. The first suggests market exchange; the second implies solidarity. See Taylor, "Cross-Purposes: The Liberal-Communitarian Debate," in *Liberalism and the Moral Life*, ed. Nancy Rosenblum (Cambridge, MA: Harvard University Press, 1989), 159–82.
79 Allen Wood nicely captures the meaning for Marx of solidarity in production, which he lays out and defends in contrast to capitalism's denial of this possibility: "Marx explicitly contrasts the 'reciprocal plundering' depicted by political economy with a possible way in which people might 'produce things as human beings,' where their own self-fulfillment (Marx even says their 'egoism') is combined inseparably with the concern for the needs of others. In true human production, the producers look upon the needs of others not as vulnerabilities to be exploited but as opportunities to affirm the producer's own species being and the being of those whose needs are satisfied by the production." Allen Wood, *Karl Marx*, 2nd ed. (New York: Routledge, 2004), 249.
80 Honneth, *The Idea of Socialism*, 24.
81 Ibid., 78.
82 It seems no coincidence that on the two hundredth anniversary of the French Revolution Margaret Thatcher, the ultra-conservative/neoliberal prime minister of the United Kingdom, questioned the very legitimacy of the Revolution itself and denounced what she saw as its destructive legacy – including the ideals of socialism and radical democracy. This was in effect an attempt to marginalize if not jettison the ideas of equality and fraternity or solidarity, leaving only a restrictive notion of (primarily

economic) freedom to ground modern bourgeois society. Hence we
have Thatcher's famous claim that there is no such thing as society, only
individuals and families. Needless to say, there can be no social freedom,
either.

83 On these and related developments that threaten to doom capitalism,
without necessarily as a result ushering in a better, more humane society,
see Streeck, *How Will Capitalism End?*

84 Honneth, *The Idea of Socialism*, chs. II and III.

85 Ibid., esp. 59ff.

86 Ibid., 67.

87 Ibid., 70, 127.

88 Ibid., 69.

89 See, for example, Axel Honneth, "The Fabric of Justice: On the Limits
of Contemporary Proceduralism," in Honneth, *The I in We: Studies in
the Theory of Recognition*, trans. Joseph Ganahl (Cambridge: Polity Press,
2012), 35–55. For a detailed account of, and criticism of, Honneth's reliance
on normative reconstruction with a critical intent, see Jorg Schaub,
"Misdevelopments, Pathologies, and Normative Revolutions: Normative
Reconstruction as Method of Critical Theory," *Critical Horizons* 16, no. 2
(May 2015), 107–30.

90 Honneth, *The Idea of Socialism*, 67, 125, 133.

91 See, however, *Critical Horizons* 16, no. 2 (May 2015), which devotes
the entire issue to a critical appraisal of *Freedom's Right* and includes a
rejoinder from Honneth. Aside from the article by Jorg Schaub, cited
previously, see also in particular Timo Jutten, "Is the Market a Sphere of
Social Freedom?" *Critical Horizons* 16, no. 2 (May 2015), 187–203, which
argues that the capitalist market cannot realize social freedom in the sense
that Honneth defends. Another entire journal issue devoted to *Freedom's
Right* is *Philosophy and Social Criticism* 40, no. 8 (October 2014); especially
noteworthy from the point of view of this chapter and our study overall
are Pippin, "Reconstructivism: On Honneth's Hegelianism," and Michael
J. Thompson, "Axel Honneth and the Neo-Idealist Turn in Critical
Theory," 779–97.

Were we to offer a fuller, more critical exploration of Honneth's
position, it might proceed along the following lines: Honneth seeks to
distinguish capitalism from markets and thus clearly favours a form of
market socialism as a way of realizing social freedom in the economy.
Yet as we see it, he seems to miss the extent to which contemporary
globalized capitalism "colonizes" other social domains, thereby rendering
problematic the successful pursuit of social freedom in these domains.
This process has expanded in recent times, something that in the past
Honneth seemed to have more fully recognized. It strikes us that it is

insufficient to claim that socialism is about securing the appropriate relations among differentiated social spheres, in a way that ostensibly recognizes and preserves their distinctiveness, when all have been invaded by the (commodity) "spirit" of the age. In this respect, Honneth's position demonstrates comparable limitations to Jürgen Habermas's *Between Facts and Norms*, which we discussed in the previous chapter.

In other words, the market, which for Honneth is a sphere of ethical life and thus a locus of social freedom, can be vulnerable to what he calls social pathologies. Social pathologies involve the inability of individuals to realize existing rational potentials, primarily where they mistakenly believe that negative and reflexive freedoms constitute the fullest and most complete realization of freedom. Honneth had assumed that, in Hegelian terms, social pathologies were restricted to the spheres of abstract right (law) and morality; whereas the spheres of ethical life were prone to what he called misdevelopments, that is, the undermining of already achieved social freedom. Capitalist markets structured by the commodity form, whose spread has aggressively intensified under neoliberal globalization, always already fail to achieve social freedom because commodity relations sustain the illusion of individual isolation – that is, they present themselves as the embodiment of negative freedom as the only "real" form of freedom. Honneth has more recently come to recognize this as an issue. (See Honneth, "Rejoinder," *Critical Horizons*, 215–16.)

In a sense the debate over the critical possibilities of Honneth's position recalls the distinction the early Habermas, with his focus on knowledge-constitutive interests, drew between a hermeneutic interest in mutual understanding and an emancipatory interest in overturning the structures of domination. (Of course Habermas subsequently abandoned this framework, and his influence on Honneth reflected his later communicative turn.) The difference between hermeneutic and emancipatory interests required that hermeneutic understanding pass over into the critique of ideology. The claim that Honneth's theory is insufficiently critical is in effect based on his perceived failure or inability to make this move. For his part, in response to this criticism Honneth now argues that his gradualism or reformism relates to the normative frameworks underlying social spheres, but not necessarily to institutional forms, which in principle could be radically transformed. As he puts it: "This consists in the possibility that the underlying norm of a particular sphere of action can only be realized in a more appropriate and comprehensive way, through a fundamental change to the institution that had previously been served to realize it." Honneth, "Rejoinder," 208.

92 Honneth, *The Idea of Socialism*, 92.
93 Ibid., 93.

94 Hans Gerth and C. Wright Mills, *Character and Social Structure: The Psychology of Social Institutions* (New York: Harcourt, Brace, 1953). The work of Erich Fromm on social character is also relevant here. See Rainer Funk, "Erich Fromm's Concept of Social Character," *Social Thought and Research* 21, nos. 1–2 (1998), 215–29; and Roger Foster, "Social Character: Erich Fromm and the Ideological Glue of Neoliberalism," *Critical Horizons* 18, no. 1 (2017), 1–18.

95 Honneth, *The Idea of Socialism*, 96.

96 Ibid., 96–7. There is a clear parallel here to the work of Habermas, and in particular *Between Facts and Norms*.

97 Ibid., 103–4. Honneth borrows the distinction between the political and the ethical from John Rawls's well-known defence of justice as fairness as a political and not a metaphysical account.

    For a comparable and insightful analysis along the lines sketched by Honneth here, see Frank Cunningham, "Globalization and Developmental Democracy," *Ethical Perspectives* 15, no. 4 (2008), 487–505. Cunningham argues that the challenges facing democracy today are twofold: extending democracy to inter-country problems and relations; and protecting democracy within countries from the destructive forces of globalization. He further notes what he sees as three approaches to these problems. One is political-institutional, the preferred response of defenders of cosmopolitan democratic initiatives. The second is economic, the option favoured by proponents of unfettered global free markets and free trade. The third, which Cunningham takes up, is political-cultural. Suggesting certain themes in common with the ethical focus of Honneth, and also the analyses of Carole Pateman and especially Carol Gould, the political-cultural approach stresses the central place that core values hold in defining the type and scope of democracy that is possible in specific circumstances.

    Cunningham takes as his model here the developmental democratic theory of C.B. Macpherson and the critique of possessive individualist ontology underlying it. The backdrop for his analysis is his attempt to revisit, revise, and update Macpherson's account from the 1960s of the "real world" of democracy, in which Macpherson compared liberal democratic, communist, and non-communist Third World conceptions from the vantage point of the need for democracy to address and incorporate the demands and requirements of developmental individualism. Cunningham argues that developmental and hence participatory democracy, which as we have seen depends upon individuals coming to see themselves as doers and exerters of their distinctively human capacities, provides the potential for a robust citizenship that more fully enables people to withstand the global forces currently undermining democratic norms and practices. On this view, democratization at the national or country level is primary and essential for global or inter-country democratic development: "a citizenry motivated by developmental-democratic values is best equipped to resist challenges from outside its country's borders to democracy within it, and ... such a citizenry is also prone to cooperate with the citizens of other countries to promote and sustain trans-country democratic institutions and procedures" (494).

In working up this argument and basing it on Macpherson's account, Cunningham's analysis suggests the importance of solidarity, an underdeveloped element in Macpherson's writings. A commitment to solidarity, forged locally, that would allow citizens to care for the well-being of their fellow citizens in the face of the destabilizing and threatening qualities of contemporary global capitalism, can ground solidarity with those equally threatened elsewhere – with "strangers." As we have seen, like Macpherson, Cunningham believes that developmental democracy requires and sustains egalitarian and socialist policies. Such policies would be essential to tame untrammelled market forces.

Cunningham's position here is thus comparable to Honneth's and to his claim that "when it comes to a 'global public,' we can say that socialism can only be a 'political,' ethically neutralized doctrine. In relation to its respective addressees, it can only take the shape of a theory that generates meaning for a certain life-world." Honneth, *The Idea of Socialism*, 104. Developmental democracy at the country level is an "ethicized" form of democracy; in fact, in an early version of his account of human capabilities, Macpherson used the term ethical power for what he would ultimately call developmental power.

98 Honneth argues that it "might seem surprising that 'fraternity' or 'solidarity' should also belong to the principles of legitimation established in our modern democratic societies. But we can easily get a sense of this fact if we consider the idea of distributional justice, deeply anchored in democratic culture and demanding redistribution in favor of those who are worse off, thus appealing to a feeling of solidarity among all member of society." *The Idea of Socialism*, 115.

Notes to Conclusion

1 Theodor Adorno and Max Horkheimer, *Towards a New Manifesto* (New York and London: Verso, 2011).
2 Michael E. Gardiner, "Wild Publics and Grotesque Symposiums: Habermas and Bahktin on Dialogue, Everyday Life, and the Public Sphere," *Sociological Review* 52, no. 1 (June 2004), 28.

3 Jürgen Habermas, *Between Facts and Norms*, trans. William Rehg (Cambridge: Polity Press, 1996), 307–8.

4 Benjamin Barber, *Strong Democracy: Participatory Politics for a New Age* (Berkeley: University of California Press, 1984), esp. 151ff.

5 Kenneth Baynes, *Habermas* (New York: Routledge, 2016), 147.

6 Habermas, *Between Facts and Norms* (translator's introduction), xviii.

7 Carmen Siriani and Lewis Friedman, *Civic Innovation in America: Community Empowerment, Public Policy, and the Movement for Civic Renewal* (Berkeley: University of California Press, 2001).

8 Sheldon S. Wolin, "Fugitive Democracy," *Constellations* 1, no. 1 (April 1994): 11–25.

Index

Coughlin, Charles, 135
Crenson, Matthew: *Unpolitics of Air Pollution*, 85
critical theory: aim of, 232; central dimension of, 239; challenges of, 13; current approaches to, 18, 52–3, 282–3; democratic deficit of, 198; diagnostic element of, 105; economic critique within, 111; evolution of, 63, 196; Horkheimer's idea of, 55–62; justice in, 14; knowledge in, 70; on liberalism, 14; limitation of, 14; methodological requirements for, 52; neoliberalism and, 104, 105, 283; normative assumptions of, 61; participant's perspective of, 70; on political economy, 104; *vs.* positivism, 61; as radical democratic alternative, 282; radical theory of democracy and, 54; rational choice and, 106; social subjects and objects in, 70; solidarity in, 14
critical theory of democracy: analysis of, 11, 195–6; challenges of, 280–1; communicative turn in, 54; components of, 10–11; development of, 11, 201; key elements of, 16, 53, 194; neoliberalism and, 155; post-Marxist, 12, 45; requirements of, 10, 11, 26–7
Crouch, Colin, 123
Cunningham, Frank, 17, 235, 236, 268, 326n67, 330–1n97

Dahl, Robert, 82, 83, 303n39
Davis, Lane, 237, 238, 318n6, 319n10
deliberation: in communicative action, 90; concept of, 80, 233; conditions of, 7, 77, 184; emergence of, 225; as form of social action,

71–2; human capacities for, 225; legislative, 223; moral discourse of, 168–9; rationality and, 185; self-interest and, 167–70; strategic, 172; weak and strong versions of, 279–80
deliberative democracy: advocacy of, 184; communicative action and, 156–62; *defensive* model of, 300n58; definition of, 79–80; *vs.* developmental democracy, 19; emergence of, 253; important factors in, 79; participant's perspective and, 80, 157; *vs.* participatory democracy, 232–3; positive liberty and, 19; potential of, 20; theories of, 79, 80, 174, 311n2; weak and strong versions of, 233, 279–80, 289–90
deliberative mechanisms, 7, 164, 311n2
deliberative processes, 77, 185, 214, 220, 288
democracy: in Ancient Greece, 197–8; authoritarian potential of mass, 134; autonomous theory of, 195; capitalism and, 14, 107, 156, 209–10; citizens and, 254–5; civil life and, 136–9; of Cold War era, theories of, 8; communicative freedom and, 293; conception of "classical," 8, 237; criticism of parliamentary, 200; decline of idea of, 4, 319n9; definition of, 156, 196–8, 235; descriptive and normative dimensions of, 9; developmental theory, 7, 10, 31, 66, 200, 284–5; direct *vs.* representative, 243–4; extractive power and, 37; as form of politics, 176; formulation of theories of, 8–9, 18; globalization and, 280,

Lightning Source UK Ltd.
Milton Keynes UK
UKHW041420080919
349363UK00002B/300/P

9 781487 505462